# Courting Conflict

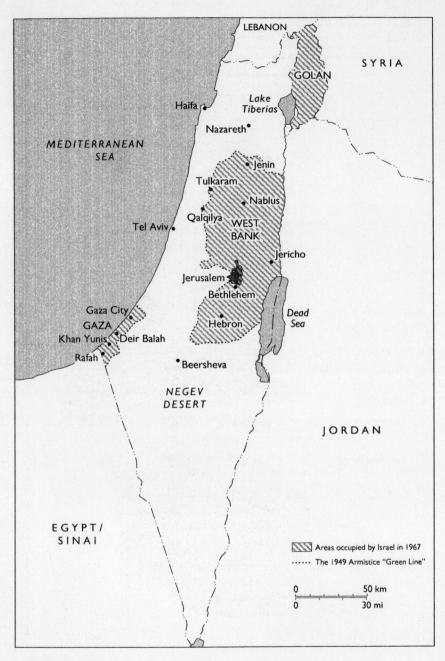

LEBANON

SYRIA

GOLAN

MEDITERRANEAN
SEA

Haifa

Lake
Tiberias

Nazareth

Jenin

Tulkaram

Nablus

Qalqilya

WEST
BANK

Tel Aviv

Jericho

Jerusalem

Bethlehem

Dead
Sea

Gaza City

GAZA

Hebron

Khan Yunis

Deir Balah

Rafah

Beersheva

NEGEV
DESERT

JORDAN

EGYPT/
SINAI

Areas occupied by Israel in 1967

The 1949 Armistice "Green Line"

| 0 | 50 km |
| 0 | 30 mi |

Israel/Palestine and surrounding countries.

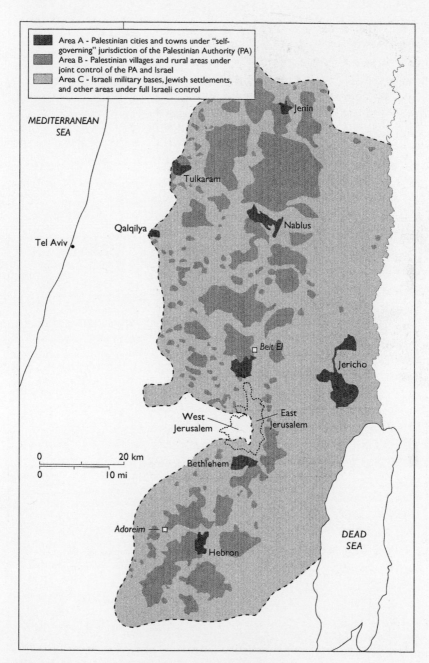

MEDITERRANEAN
SEA

Jenin

Tulkaram

Qalqilya

Nablus

Tel Aviv

Beit El

Jericho

West
Jerusalem

East
Jerusalem

0          20 km

0          10 mi

Bethlehem

Adoreim

DEAD
SEA

Hebron

West Bank under Oslo II Interim Agreements (1995).

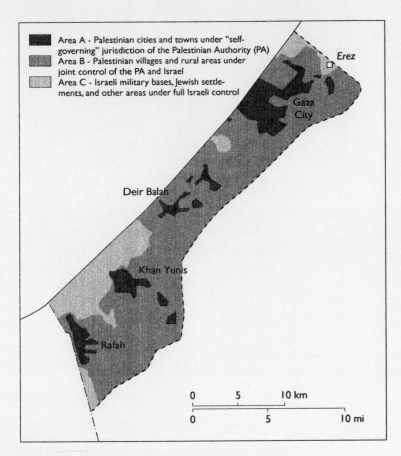

Area A - Palestinian cities and towns under "self-governing" jurisdiction of the Palestinian Authority (PA)
Area B - Palestinian villages and rural areas under joint control of the PA and Israel
Area C - Israeli military bases, Jewish settlements, and other areas under full Israeli control

Erez

Gaza City

Deir Balah

Khan Yunis

Rafah

0    5    10 km

0    5    10 mi

Gaza Strip under Oslo II Interim Agreements (1995).

# Courting Conflict

The Israeli Military Court System
in the West Bank and Gaza

Lisa Hajjar

UNIVERSITY OF CALIFORNIA PRESS
Berkeley / Los Angeles / London

University of California Press, Ltd.
London, England

© 2005 by the Regents of the University of California

Library of Congress Cataloging-in-Publication Data

Hajjar, Lisa, 1961–.
   Courting conflict : the Israeli military court system in the West Bank and
Gaza / Lisa Hajjar.
       p.   cm.
   Includes bibliographical references and index.
   ISBN 0–520–24193–2 (cloth : alk. paper). — ISBN 0–520–24194–0
(pbk. : alk. paper)
   1. Military courts — West Bank.   2. Military courts — Gaza Strip.
3. War and emergency powers — Israel.   4. Rule of law — Israel.
5. Palestinian Arabs — Civil rights.   6. Israel-Arab War, 1967 —
Occupied territories.   I. Title.

KMM876.7.H35   2005
343.5695'30143 — dc22                                          2004005278

Manufactured in the United States of America
13   12   11   10   09   08   07   06   05
10   9   8   7   6   5   4   3   2   1

The paper used in this publication meets the minimum requirements of
ANSI/NISO Z39.48–1992 (R 1997) *(Permanence of Paper)*.

*For my parents, Maija and Victor*

# Contents

# Acknowledgments

Many individuals and organizations supported me over the years of researching and writing this book. Foremost are the people who permitted me to interview and spend time with them. Although relatively few are mentioned by name in this text, I am grateful to all of them.

Research and travel were funded by grants from the American Association of University Women, the Joint Committee on the Near and Middle East of the American Council of Learned Societies and the Social Science Research Council, The American University, the Institute for Intercultural Studies, the Harry Frank Guggenheim Foundation, the John D. and Catherine T. MacArthur Foundation, the National Science Foundation's Law and Social Science Program, Swarthmore College, Morehouse College, and the University of California–Santa Barbara.

This study began as a doctoral dissertation. I would like to thank Samih K. Farsoun, a most supportive advisor, as well as Gay Young and Julie Peteet, who helped me hone my research agenda and analytical skills. Talal Asad pointed me toward the Israeli military court system, and taking his suggestion has shaped the course of my life.

Conducting research in Israel/Palestine, I was greatly aided by the advice, insights, and connections provided by many friends and colleagues. I am deeply indebted to Salim Tamari, Stanley Cohen, Rema Hammami, Lee O'Brien, Joost Hiltermann, Mouin Rabbani, Geoff Hartman, Elia Zureik, Graham Usher, Alex Pollack, Mark Taylor, Franco La Torre, Hassan Jabarin, and Rina Rosenberg for their wisdom and generosity. Nadia Abu El-Haj, with whom I shared an apartment and the joys and travails of field research from 1991 to 1993, provided intellectual inspiration, social release, and access to really good food: the Abu El-Haj family helped make Jerusalem my home away from home. Every time I returned to Israel/Palestine, Lee, Rema, Alex, Salim, Graham, Hassan, and Rina generously shared their homes and their thoughts about the latest developments. I treasure the time I spent with all of them.

Many people in Israel/Palestine were helpful and supportive of my research. I especially thank Lea Tsemel, Usama Halaby, Tamar Peleg, Raji Sourani, Raja Shehadeh, Penny Johnson, Andre Rosenthal, Allegra Pacheco, Jamal Susi, Iyad Alami, Rabiʿ Halaby, the late Makram Qupty, Oren Yiftachel, Tikva Parnass, Michel Warshawsky, Rachel Jones, and all the people associated with the Alternative Information Center. I also express deep gratitude to many people in the Golan Heights, which became my other home away from home, especially Taiseer Maray, Ataf Safadi, the late Ali Safadi, Munir Fakradin, and all those associated with the Arab Association for Development.

Joel Beinin, Zachary Lockman, and James Ron, whose own works on Israel/Palestine have been an inspiration, read my work in various incarnations and assisted me with their critical insights. In the dissertation-to-book conversion process, Bruce Grant was a reader extraordinaire, and in the draft-to-final-text process, my colleagues in the Law and Society Program at the University of California–Santa Barbara were unstintingly generous with their time and thoughts. Thanks to Eve Darian-Smith, Juliet Williams, Kathleen Moore, Elvin Hatch, Stuart Streichler, Jeanne Umana, Hillary Berk, and Tom Hillbink.

I discovered the field of law and society, which I now claim as my academic home, thanks to Ronen Shamir and George Bisharat. Both also taught me a great deal about law and conflict in Israel/Palestine. I have benefited greatly from relationships with many people in the Law and Society Association, especially those associated with the cause lawyering project.

When I was a young graduate student, I cut my political teeth working at the Middle East Research and Information Project (MERIP) and honed my writing skills from the example provided by Joe Stork, then the editor of *Middle East Report*. My ongoing association with MERIP is one of my greatest professional pleasures, and I thank all the comrades for doing their part to keep the progressive fires burning (metaphorically speaking, of course) in these damp times.

My friends Dru Burtz and Ana Maria "Ia" Carbonell have provided an endless supply of moral support. Dru's home in Rome often served as a decompression chamber when I left Israel/Palestine, and Ia's creative mind conjured the title for this book.

I owe the most gratitude of all to the wise and wonderful Bashar Tarabieh and to my family, especially my parents, to whom I dedicate this book.

# Prologue

The weather was bitter cold and rainy on February 3, 1992, when I made my first visit to the Israeli military court in the West Bank town of Hebron. Over the previous six months, I had been to the military courts in Ramallah, Gaza City, and Nablus. That day, I went to Hebron with Lea Tsemel, a Jewish Israeli lawyer who has been representing Palestinian clients in this system since the early 1970s.

Two weeks earlier, the Israeli military had launched a large-scale arrest campaign, part of an ongoing effort to stamp out the Palestinian *intifada* (uprising), which had been going on since December 1987. This round of arrests had netted hundreds of Palestinians suspected of membership in the Popular Front for the Liberation of Palestine (PFLP). The roundup was in retaliation for that group's role in organizing opposition to the Palestinian-Israeli negotiations launched at Madrid the previous November and for some recent attacks on Jewish Israeli settlers in the West Bank and Gaza.

That day in Hebron, Tsemel and her colleague Na'ila Attiyeh, an Arab Israeli lawyer, had eight clients scheduled for extension-of-detention hearings. In this procedure, which usually takes place on the eighteenth day of detention, a prisoner is taken out of interrogation and brought before a military judge. If the detainee has not yet confessed, the military prosecutor typically uses the hearing to request an extension of the detention order so that the interrogation can continue. Extension hearings generally take place in prisons, frequently in the absence of a defense lawyer. On this occasion, however, the hearings were being conducted in the judge's office of the Hebron court.

When we arrived at the court, Tsemel, Attiyeh, and I went into the office of the judge, Shmuel Knobler. The small room quickly filled up. In addition to Knobler and the three of us, there was a court secretary, a military translator, a military prosecutor, an agent of the General Security Services (GSS), and two soldiers serving as guards.

When the first prisoner was brought in, a gaunt man shackled hand and foot, Tsemel began asking him questions in Arabic about his interrogation. He did not have the chance to utter more than a few words before the judge and the prosecutor shouted for them to be quiet. Although lawyers are permitted to attend extension-of-detention hearings, they are prohibited from communicating directly with clients who have not yet confessed because these people are still "under interrogation." Following that exchange, the GSS agent insisted that I leave the room, probably out of concern that I would be privy to discussions about the interrogation of the detainees. The judge agreed and I left, frustrated at the lost chance to witness the extension-of-detention process firsthand.

Out in the lobby, I joined the wives of two of Tsemel's clients. They were both young women in their late twenties. One was wearing a *hijab* (head scarf) and traditional dress; the other, bareheaded, wore slacks. We sat in silence for a long time, shivering from the cold in the unheated lobby. Eventually we struck up a conversation. They told me about the arrest of their husbands and how their houses had been torn apart by soldiers. One of the women had brought along a bag of clothes because her husband had been wearing pajamas when he was arrested.

Israeli soldiers passing through the building stopped in the administrative office to chat with the secretaries, get files, drink coffee, and warm themselves near the electric heaters. I took a walk around the building and came upon the courtroom. Looking in, I saw about a dozen Palestinians sitting in silence.

Eventually an old Palestinian man came out of the courtroom to find out when the court session would begin. He asked a couple of Israeli soldiers, who told him to go back and wait. Another hour passed. This time three Palestinians, including the old man, came out to ask again. They went into the secretaries' office, where they were told that the hearings had been canceled. Soldiers were sent to clear the Palestinians out of the courtroom. As they were leaving the building, they tried to get some information from the secretaries about when the hearings would be rescheduled, but no one answered them. After they were gone, soldiers opened a metal door in the hallway between the lobby and the courtroom. Out of the dark room, a holding cell, came five or six handcuffed prisoners. These were the people whose relatives had been waiting. They were taken back to prison.

Each detainee who was brought into the building for his extension-of-detention hearing was escorted by a group of soldiers, who would form a circle around him to prevent him from seeing or speaking with anyone, namely the two wives and me, since we were the only ones in the lobby. The first few detainees didn't even look our way as they were taken into the judge's office and then back out again when the hearing was over.

When the husband of the woman wearing the *hijab* appeared, a very large soldier blocked his line of vision so that he couldn't see his wife and she couldn't see him. Another soldier held the man's jacket over his face. During the twenty minutes that his hearing was going on, his wife sat on the edge of her seat, tears streaming down her face. The other woman tried to comfort her. When her husband was brought out at the end of the hearing, she called out that the children were fine and that everyone was praying for him. As he turned to respond, he was shoved out of the building by the big soldier and taken back to prison. Tsemel came out and told the wife that her husband had no injuries and that his detention had been extended for only eight days, not the thirty that the prosecutor had requested. The woman, desperate for information, asked Tsemel a barrage of questions, but there was little that Tsemel could add because she hadn't been permitted to speak directly to him.

The next prisoner to be brought in was the other woman's husband. In this instance, the soldiers allowed the wife to see her husband, who looked dazed and had difficulty focusing on her. He was obviously in pain, and the soldiers treated him less roughly than the other detainees. When Tsemel came out twenty minutes later, she said that the judge had called a break to give the prosecutor and the GSS agent an opportunity to come up with some satisfactory answers about how this man had been injured and why continuing his detention was necessary. Tsemel explained to his wife that she was trying to use his injuries to demand that the judge release him on bail.

Before the proceeding resumed, the man was allowed to put on the clothes that his wife had brought. Because of his injuries, he couldn't lift his own arm and had to be helped into his clothes by the soldiers. When the hearing was over and he was being taken from the building, the soldiers allowed his wife to give him a kiss. Despite his condition, the judge had extended his detention for eight days.

In the middle of the day there was a break for lunch. Tsemel and Attiyeh joined us in the lobby and expressed their satisfaction that the judge was extending the detentions for less time than the prosecutor was requesting. By the standards that defense lawyers are used to in the military courts, this was a virtual victory for them. This news provided some relief for the wives, and Tsemel and Attiyeh played it up to reassure them. I found the whole situation to be surreal; a man was so badly hurt that he couldn't lift his own arm, yet these lawyers were heralding a victory.

Tsemel went out to the food cart in the military compound and bought several bags of chips and cookies, joking as she returned, "Who says we don't have fun in Hebron?" When the break ended, Tsemel and Attiyeh went back into the judge's office and the hearings resumed.

The last prisoner brought in that day entered the building with a force of energy, unlike the others, who had seemed so passive. In the lobby, he stopped abruptly, clicked his shackled ankles together, and said, "Salaam alaykum" before being pushed into the judge's office. When he came out forty-five minutes later, he nodded in our direction. As he was about to step outside into pouring rain, he insisted that the soldiers put up his hood so that he wouldn't get so wet.

Tsemel and Attiyeh came out a few minutes later and told us that this man had bruises on his upper body and had complained to the judge of chest pains. In his case, the judge clearly had been moved, not enough to release him on bail, but at least enough to order that he be taken to the clinic of the prison for a medical checkup rather than being returned to interrogation. But like the others, his detention had been extended for eight more days. The lawyers were worried about him but had to content themselves with the knowledge that he would see a doctor and that this might ease the conditions of his interrogation.

Two days later, I had arranged to go with Tsemel to the Ramallah military court. When I arrived at her office in East Jerusalem in the early morning, I found a crowd of people gathered around her, engaging in heated discussion. She turned to tell me that one of the prisoners we had seen in Hebron had died in interrogation. Which one? The last one. Mustafa Akawi was dead.

. . .

Akawi's death in detention made him a public figure. The details of his arrest and death were widely reported in the media.

On the night of January 22, Akawi was at home with his wife and two-year-old son in the Jerusalem suburb of Dahiyat al-Barid. Soldiers broke into the house around 1 A.M., crashing simultaneously through the front and back doors. At the same time, other soldiers broke into his parents' home in another part of Jerusalem and, once in, coordinated their activities by phone. Before locking his wife and child in the bedroom, they told her to say a "good" goodbye to her husband because when she came out he would be gone.

Akawi was taken to the Hebron prison and held in the interrogation wing. What occurred after Akawi's extension-of-detention hearing was made public as part of the official report about his death. He was fed and then placed in an unheated hallway, seated on a small chair with his hands cuffed behind his back and a cloth sack over his head. At 9:30 P.M., prior to being taken into interrogation, he was examined by a paramedic, who recommended that he see a doctor in the morning. He was interrogated for approximately two hours, then put back in the hallway. At 3:30 A.M. he told a guard that he felt sick and wanted to see a doctor. Instead, he was taken back to the paramedic, who determined that because his blood pressure and pulse were normal, he should be returned to the interrogation wing. He was placed in a freezing *zinzana,* a closetlike structure used to hold detainees between rounds of questioning. A guard removed Akawi's hood and handcuffs and went to fetch him some hot tea. When the guard returned, he found Akawi unconscious. The paramedic and a doctor on duty at the prison were called. They tried to revive him, but he was pronounced dead at about 5:20 A.M. According to the official report, an ambulance was never called.

• • •

Three days after Akawi died, a press conference was held at the National Palace Hotel in East Jerusalem to report the findings of his autopsy. Dr. Michael Baden, an American forensic pathologist, had been sent to Israel by Physicians for Human Rights to participate in the autopsy. This was not the first Palestinian death in detention that Baden had been brought to investigate.

An official statement issued the day after Akawi died tentatively explained it as a heart attack, relieving the authorities of responsibility if the autopsy confirmed "natural causes." Under these circumstances, the press conference was tense. A hundred people, including myself, were crowded in the room to hear how Akawi had died.

In his statement at the press conference, Dr. Baden said that the "exertion" Akawi had been subjected to during interrogation — physical and emotional stress and severe cold — had precipitated his death but that ultimately, in accordance with a clinical interpretation of what constituted "natural," the death had to be described as one of natural causes linked to Akawi's preexisting physical condition. Akawi had been suffering from a severe hardening of the arteries, very unusual for a man his age and unknown to him, his family, or the prison authorities. As soon as it became clear that the autopsy had confirmed the official Israeli explanation, the Israel TV crew people, dominating the center of the room, packed up and left. They had their sound bite.

But the press conference continued. Most people in the room couldn't accept that a thirty-five-year-old man's death in detention could be deemed natural and that the Israeli authorities were being exonerated. Anger was mounting. Dr. Baden explained Akawi's physical condition in more detail: the traumas found on his body during the autopsy included bruises on his chest caused by the interrogation method known as "shaking," which involves grasping the detainee around the chest and shaking him to produce a whiplash effect with the head and neck. Dr. Baden used a man from the audience to demonstrate how this method could cause such bruises. He also said that Akawi had rib fractures, which were sustained as a result of the hour of cardiopulmonary resuscitation that had been administered after he collapsed. When asked directly by someone in the audience if Akawi had been tortured, Baden said, "Torture is hard to define. There was evidence of marks on his body due to poking him and shaking him. But . . . there was no evidence of subtle forms of physical torture."

Throughout the press conference, Dr. Baden was very careful not to imply a direct connection between the interrogation methods applied to Akawi and his death, beyond a reiteration that exertion had precipitated his demise. Clearly discomfited by the anger of people in the audience, he pointed out that brutality goes on in prisons in many countries, including the United States. However, in a statement he gave in New York several days later, he offered a more direct link between Akawi's interrogation and death.

At the press conference, Tsemel, who was sitting on the dais along with Dr. Baden and Akawi's wife and father, interjected to point out that an Israeli judge had ordered that he undergo an immediate medical examination. But this never happened. Akawi was returned to interrogation and was seen by a paramedic, not a doctor. If the medical evidence relieved the authorities of responsibility for Akawi's death, they were at least guilty of negligence in ignoring the order of a military judge.

Several thousand people attended Akawi's funeral. While the Israeli authorities generally prohibited large funerals for Palestinians, they made an exception in Akawi's case because of the publicity surrounding his death in detention. As throngs gathered in the East Jerusalem neighborhood near the home of Akawi's parents, hundreds of soldiers remained at a distance, allowing the crowd to chant and wave Palestinian flags. Photographers were positioned alongside the soldiers, using telephoto lenses to shoot pictures of the crowd that would go into GSS files.

The intensity of the funeral heightened as the moving crowd squeezed through the narrow alleys of the Old City, the chants echoing. When the crowd arrived at the Haram al-Sharif, several young men with their heads covered by *kuffiyahs* (checkered scarves) defied gravity and armed soldiers positioned all around to scale al-Aqsa mosque and hang a huge Palestinian flag. The crowd erupted with cheering and applause for their feat.

At the funeral, posters with a picture of Mustafa Akawi's face were distributed. I took one and hung it over my desk as a visceral reminder of the suffering and violence at stake in the subject that I was researching.

. . .

Several months later, I interviewed Amin Amin, a Palestinian student from Birzeit University. He talked about Akawi's death because it had a personal significance. Amin, who suffers from a chronic liver condition, was arrested in February 1992, several days after Akawi had died. When he got sick, his interrogators warned that if he did not confess, he would "die like Akawi." It was only when they mentioned Akawi's name that he realized that he was being held in Hebron. Until then, he had thought that he was in the Moscobiyye interrogation center in Jerusalem.

Amin said that the realization that he might die in Hebron like Akawi bolstered his resolve, or perhaps resigned him to a seemingly unavoidable fate. The interrogators were using Akawi's name to threaten him, saying that if he helped them by confessing, they would help him by giving him the medical care he needed. But when Amin was on the verge of death, the interrogators became concerned about the consequences if he should die and took him to a prison doctor.

Amin was so sick on the day of his extension-of-detention hearing that his lawyer, Jawad Boulos, demanded that he be either immediately released or immediately hospitalized. The judge refused both options and remanded Amin for an additional ninety-six hours under medical supervision in the Hebron prison. When I interviewed Boulos, he said that after the hearing, the prosecutor had told him there was no guarantee that Amin would get proper medical treatment. Boulos recounted that he was so upset by the judge's decision and the prosecutor's comment that when he got to his car in the parking lot of the Hebron military compound, he cried in frustration and anger. He drove directly to the Israeli High Court of Justice and submitted a petition for Amin's immediate release, which was granted the next day. But according to both Amin and Boulos, the court granted the release not because of the gravity of his condition, as evidenced by the fact that other sick prisoners died without being released, but because of the international attention the Akawi case had attracted. Amin told me, "Akawi saved my life."

. . .

A year and a half after Akawi's death, on June 13, 1993, a conference about torture was held in Tel Aviv, organized by several Israeli and Palestinian human rights organization. There were a number of subjects on the agenda. Foremost was the continuing furor surrounding the 1987 report by an official Israeli commission of inquiry into the interrogation methods of the GSS. The report had confirmed the routine use of physical and psychological violence but had argued that such tactics were legitimate and necessary to combat "hostile terrorist activity." The report's authors had recommended official sanctioning of "moderate physical pressure," and the government had adopted this as policy. Other topics of discussion included numerous deaths in detention over the last few years and a campaign by Israeli human rights lawyers petitioning the High Court to prohibit violent interrogation methods. Finally, there was a fresh scandal surrounding a standardized medical form with questions for prison doctors about how much "moderate physical pressure" a detainee could withstand. A copy of the form mistakenly had been left in a defendant's file and found by Tamar Peleg, a Jewish Israeli lawyer, who had released it to the press.

Akawi's name was raised several times during the conference. One of the speakers, Mamduh Akar, a Palestinian medical doctor who, at the time, was head of the Palestinian human rights delegation in the Israeli-Palestinian negotiations, pointed out that the Israeli medical community shared in the responsibility for torture in Israeli prisons, since hundreds of doctors were assigned to military reserve duty that placed them in contact with prisoners during interrogation. Akar asked, rhetorically, why the doctor on duty at the Hebron prison when Akawi died hadn't come forward to protest the way this particular kind of service to the state forces a violation of the Hippocratic oath.

. . .

During the first two years I spent conducting research on the Israeli military court system, I spoke with dozens of Israelis and Palestinians about their experiences and opinions. But Mustafa Akawi's case remained a deeply personal issue for me. Several weeks before I was scheduled to leave the country, I contacted the Akawi family and arranged a meeting.

When I stepped into the living room of Akawi's parents' home, I saw that it contained huge pictures of Mustafa Akawi hanging on every wall. His parents and brother Sami started telling me about his arrest and death, having told the same thing to dozens of reporters and others inquiring into the case. I interrupted to say that I had been with Lea Tsemel in Hebron and had seen Mustafa the evening before he died. Suddenly everything changed. Now they were asking me questions. How did he seem? What was he wearing? Did he look sick? I told them what I remembered, including the way he had clicked his heels and said, "Salaam alaykum."

After taking so much from people who had willingly shared their stories with me, I felt like I was able to give something back. I was giving Mustafa Akawi's family one more image of him as brave and endearing. His family's memories of the violence that ended his life and their memories of him as a gentle and loving man are interwoven, a contradiction integral to peoples' experiences of the occupation and the conflict. As I was leaving, his father turned to me and said, "Why Mustafa?"

Had Mustafa Akawi not died, his experience would have been indistinguishable from that of the hundreds of thousands of other Palestinians who have passed through the Israeli court and prison systems. But in death, he became a public symbol of Palestinians' plight, their vulnerability, their mortality. In life, he had been a salesman for a local company. He also was involved in a collective project to establish health committees in the West Bank. Perhaps this work was the reason he was arrested, although no reason was ever provided in the public statements following his death.

These memories have haunted me and prodded me.

# Introduction

The Israeli military court system is the central subject of this book, as well as the main setting for a sociological inquiry into law and conflict in Israel, the West Bank, and Gaza, an area I refer to collectively as "Israel/ Palestine" (see Chapter 1). This duality, subject and setting, reflects the fact that the military court system is both a product and a site of the Israeli-Palestinian conflict. To describe a court system — or any institution — as a product points toward one set of questions that this book addresses: Why and how was this institution created? What purposes does it serve? How does it work? Describing it as a site points toward another set of questions: What happens in this setting, and why? How does this site, and the activities that occur within it, connect to the broader context? Relating these questions to the Israeli-Palestinian conflict presents a third line of inquiry: What can be learned about the conflict by studying the military court system? How has the court system affected and reflected the history and politics of the conflict?

The Israeli military court system was created in 1967, when Israel captured and occupied the West Bank and Gaza during the war with the surrounding Arab states of Jordan, Egypt, and Syria. The court system is part of the Israeli military administration that was established to govern the Palestinian residents of the West Bank and Gaza.[1] It has been in operation since 1967 and, presumably, will continue to operate as long as the conflict continues.

The legal status and the political fate of the West Bank and Gaza and of the Palestinians who reside there are hotly contested and subject to a

I

multitude of interpretations. One of the aims of this book is to describe and explain the contents and contours of these debates and to connect these debates both to the workings of the military court system and to the politics of the conflict. However, by way of introduction, a few general points are worth noting. First, Palestinians living in these regions are an "occupied" population. Israel is not their state, they have no sovereign state of their own, and their status vis-à-vis Israel is that of "foreign civilians" residing in areas under Israeli control. A second and related point is that although the West Bank and Gaza are not sovereign Israeli territory, since 1967, Israel has been the de facto sovereign because it is the only *state* exercising control over these areas. Although there have been changes in the administration of the West Bank and Gaza since the early 1990s, including the establishment of a Palestinian Authority (PA) in 1994, Palestinians remain occupied and stateless, the PA is not a sovereign state, and Israel remains the de facto sovereign.

Third, a military occupation that results from war is tantamount to a cease-fire and is, at least in principle, temporary. Moreover, a military occupation, by its very nature, perpetuates conflict because it negates the occupied population's right to self-determination. Indeed, the Israeli state has never claimed or sought the right to represent Palestinians in the West Bank and Gaza, only the right to rule them. Therefore, although Israel's occupation of the West Bank and Gaza is the longest in modern history and has taken on many permanent-looking features, the principle of temporariness obtains because military rule over a "foreign" population is legally unacceptable and politically unstable as a permanent arrangement. However, there is no consensus on what kind of permanent arrangement should supplant the occupation. Over the last two decades, the fate of the West Bank and Gaza has emerged as the crux of the Israeli-Palestinian conflict, and deciding their final/future status has been the primary focus of diplomatic efforts to resolve it.

The military court system is an institutional centerpiece of the Israeli state's apparatus of rule over Palestinians in the West Bank and Gaza. As such, it has its own history as an institution, but one that is integrally tied to and affected by the conflict in Israel/Palestine and throughout the Middle East. The military court system lies, literally and figuratively, at the center of the conflict and therefore constitutes a crucial consideration of what elevates this conflict as a source of inspiration and agitation for people, groups, and governments beyond the geographical domain of Israel/Palestine. The military court system also has been a setting for the deployment of legal strategies and the cultivation of legal discourses to contend with the conflict (notably, those connected to national security and human rights), thereby illuminating contestations (practical and theoretical) about what is legal in the context of conflict more generally.

The primary purpose of the military court system is to prosecute Palestinians who are arrested by the Israeli military and charged with security violations and other crimes. The military and emergency laws enforced through the military courts criminalize Palestinian violence, as well as a wide array of other types of activities, including certain forms of political and cultural expression, association, movement, and nonviolent protest — anything deemed to threaten Israeli security or to adversely affect the maintenance of order and control of the territories. The scope of these laws is expansive, penetrating virtually all aspects of Palestinian life, and their enforcement by the military has affected all Palestinians, albeit in varying ways.

Since 1967, hundreds of thousands of Palestinians have been arrested by the Israeli military. Although not all Palestinians who are arrested are prosecuted in the military court system (some are released, others are administratively detained without trial), of those who are charged, approximately 90 to 95 percent are convicted. Of the convictions, approximately 97 percent are the result of plea bargains.

While every state uses strategies of arrest, prosecution, and imprisonment to enforce its laws and maintain its power and control, the incarceration rate of Palestinian residents of the West Bank and Gaza is extremely high by any standards. Between 1987 and 1993, during the first *intifada* (uprising), when Palestinians mounted a mass resistance to protest the enduring Israeli occupation, Israel/Palestine had the highest per capita incarceration rate in the world.

Of course, incarceration rates do not in themselves explain crime and punishment. Rather, they provide an illustration of how law is used in a given context to define the permissible by establishing what is punishable, and they demonstrate the will and capacity of the state to punish those charged with breaking the law.[2] High incarceration rates have a disputed political currency; they can be cited to back up arguments that criminality is pervasive or as evidence of legal repression by the state. Disputes about what incarceration rates illustrate turn on (also disputed) interpretations of the legitimacy of the laws and the legitimacy of the state that enforces them.

The issue of legitimacy provides a salient analytical hook for the study of any type of legal system, including the present study. In contexts where — or to the extent that — a state is popularly regarded as representative of its subjects (a characteristic or ideal of liberal governance), the state's exercise of its legal powers to arrest, prosecute, and imprison law-breakers is legitimized — even idealized — as serving the public interest. Conversely, where a state does not represent its subjects (variations of illiberalism include colonial, authoritarian, and military regimes, as well as states that discriminate along lines of religion, race, ethnicity, nationality, or class), law enforcement is exercised to serve narrow (i.e., particularistic) interests. But even illiberal regimes command and cultivate a degree of legitimacy, at least among the constituencies they do represent. Only for an extremely narrow dictatorship or a state that ruled by force rather than law would the concept of legitimacy be utterly irrelevant.

Military occupation is a distinctively illiberal type of political arrangement, combining elements of colonialism (foreign rule) and a state of emergency (martial law). In this context, the "emergency" is the conflict. Consequently, Israeli control strategies are driven by the imperatives of national security and tend to be treated as tantamount to counterinsurgency.

If the military court system were a purely political instrument of the Israeli state to control and punish Palestinians, frankly, it would not be very interesting. But it is not purely political; it is also legal and as such opens up to questions, debates, and controversies about law, legality, and legitimacy. This study looks inside the military court system to see how law is enforced and what is done or not done in the name of the law. Exploring what happens there reveals the veracity of the adage that law is a "double-edged sword": it can be deployed to serve the interests of the state, including the maintenance of order and control, and legitimization of state power, but it also can serve as a resource to protect from and to contest, criticize, and resist that power. In these regards, the military court system is a site of competing discourses of legal legitimacy and wide variations of legal agency and legal consciousness.

One of the most interesting aspects of the military court system is its unique sociological function as an intersection where a diverse cross section of Israeli citizens and Palestinian residents of the occupied territories have had regular and sustained contact with one another. No other institutional setting in Israel/Palestine compares to the military courts in this regard.

As in any legal system, the people who "come together" in the military court system participate in its functioning as an institution, albeit with substantially different degrees of freedom, choice, and opportunity. Participation is constituted through the specific legal roles that people fulfill, the kinds of legal and extralegal practices in which they engage, and

the ways in which they relate to one another within legalistically orchestrated parameters.

There are five main categories of participants: judges, prosecutors,
defense lawyers, translators, and defendants. To briefly introduce the variations: all of the judges, prosecutors, and translators are Israeli citizens
and soldiers. All of the judges are Jewish Israelis, as are most of the prosecutors, although a few prosecutors are Druze Israelis. Most of the translators are Druze Israelis. Defense lawyers, all civilians, include Palestinian
residents of the occupied territories, Jewish Israeli citizens, and Palestinian
citizens of Israel. For the sake of clarity to distinguish between Palestinian
residents of the occupied territories and Palestinian citizens of Israel, I
refer to the latter by the (admittedly problematic) term *Arab Israelis*.[3]
Finally, the defendants are Palestinian residents of the occupied territories.

In terms of its function as a legal system authorized to mete out punishments to those found guilty of breaking the law, the military court system is rife with problems. Indeed, anyone with substantial knowledge
about the court system and certainly those involved directly in it discuss
it in terms of problems, from the problem of the conflict that underlies
its very existence to the host of problems that characterize its day-to-day
operations. Commonly cited problems include the inherent blurring
and contradictions between military and legal dimensions of control, the
use of soldiers in a policing capacity, administrative and legal provisions
that permit the holding of detainees incommunicado for prolonged periods and impede lawyer-client meetings, the prevalent and routine use of
coercive interrogation tactics to obtain confessions, the use of "secret evidence" to detain and convict people, the complexities and vagaries of the
laws enforced through the courts, and the disputable competence of the
various categories of legal professionals. But to note that these issues often
are cited as problems is not to suggest that there is any concurrence on
how or why they are regarded as problematic. On the contrary, debates
about these issues are part of what makes the military court system a subject of controversy.

Controversy about the military court system extends to a broader
range of issues, including disputed interpretations of the rights of the
Israeli state in the West Bank and Gaza; the rights of the Palestinian people who reside there; the legality of the military and emergency laws
enforced in the court system; and, perhaps most contentious of all, the
availability of legal justice. These controversies are informed and compounded by disagreements about the applicability of international
humanitarian and human rights laws to Israeli rule in the West Bank and

Gaza. Indeed, issues of law, legality, and legitimacy in Israel/Palestine are so complicated and contentious because of the combined effects of the enduring conflict, Palestinian statelessness, Israeli aspirations to retain permanent control over all or part of the West Bank and Gaza, and the fact that international humanitarian laws were not formulated to address a situation of decades of military rule.

Hence, a book about the Israeli military court system would be — must be — a study of problems and controversies. However, the aim of this book is not merely to highlight and explain the array of problems that characterize the functioning of the system and inform debates about its legitimacy, although these concerns feature prominently. Rather, as a sociological study of a legal institution, the central problem that this book addresses is the role of law in the context of conflict.

Methodologically, much of the research on which this study is based is ethnographic. By going inside the system to observe its operations, interview participants, and engage them in discussion about their perspectives and experiences, I seek to describe and explain how the system functions and why. However, this subject resists conventional ethnography because the court system is not itself a social world but a set of sites where a variety of worlds intersect. Relatively little can be understood about how this system works or how participants perceive it by concentrating on the courts. The context in which this system is located and from which participants are drawn encompasses all of Israel/Palestine, and so, too, does the ethnographic scope of this study.

Of the ideas I hope to convey in this book, two bear mention at the outset. One is that the military court system resists and confounds "Israeli versus Palestinian" explanations. People who come together in this institutional setting are not simply enemies, nor can their participation or their perspectives be understood or represented in rigid national terms. While an Israeli-Palestinian national dichotomy is by no means irrelevant — since it serves to ground the grand narratives of national struggle and conflicting claims to the West Bank and Gaza — its explanatory power is partial and often inaccurate (see Chapter 1). By delving into the nature and dynamics of participation, I found that what happens in this system and the relations among participants are complex, fluid, and far from "nationalistically" predictable. On this point, my own assumptions were challenged through the process of conducting research, and I hope that this book challenges the assumptions of its readers.

The second idea I hope to convey, which emanates from my political and intellectual interests in this subject, is a challenge to the exceptionalism often accorded to the study of topics related to the Israeli-Palestinian conflict. While this conflict is indisputably destructive and exceptionally difficult to resolve, it is not incomparable to other conflicts, which is what exceptionalism would suggest. Many aspects of the military court system lend themselves to or evoke comparison with other legal systems, and much about the uses of law in Israel/Palestine resembles other contexts in which people are embroiled in conflict. To the extent that narratives of exceptionalism are cultivated and deployed to authorize and justify various sorts of violence, challenging those narratives through critical and comparative analysis of law and legalism has political as well as analytical import. "Justice" is a deeply politicized and complicated issue in Israel/Palestine, but it is neither beside the point nor impossible to imagine and invoke in evaluating "what happens."

## Reading and Writing about the Military Court System

For people who have no direct dealings with the Israeli military courts, the only way into the system is through the literature. Literature dealing explicitly with the military court system constitutes a specialized subfield of the literature on the Israeli-Palestinian conflict, mainly books, articles, and reports authored by legal scholars, Israeli officials, and human rights organizations.

Like literature on other aspects of the Israeli-Palestinian conflict, texts about the military court system reveal sharp differences in perspective and opinion. Someone who delved into this literature unaware of the prevailing polemics characterizing discourse on Israeli-Palestinian relations might be confused to find not one Israeli military court system but two. One system is characterized, to varying degrees, by chaos, a flagrant disregard for the principles of the rule of law, insufferable conditions, and endemic injustice. The other is characterized, again to varying degrees, by order, adherence to legal principles, and fairness.

Writing on a subject as highly politicized and controversial as the military court system is itself a form of political practice. The nature of this practice relates — or, I should say, is related by authors and readers alike — to the politics of the conflict. Debates over "the facts" become weapons in a war of words, claims to objectivity become a line of defense, and accusations of a lack of objectivity are used to attack or undermine the credibility of those who produce conflicting accounts or draw contradictory conclusions. For those authors who present a positive or defensive view of the military court system, their political standpoint coincides or concurs (often in self-conscious and overt ways) with the "Israeli side." Since the military court system itself is Israeli, portraying it in positive terms is undertaken as a defense of the state against those who would criticize it. Authors who present a negative or critical view of the military court system (or some aspect thereof) are more varied in terms of political standpoint (i.e., whether articulating a commitment to Palestinian national rights, international human rights, or some combination). Since critical texts occupy, by authorial design or default, the "other side" of the polemic, they tend to be read by Israeli officials and supporters of the state as "pro-Palestinian" and, consequently, unobjective and unreliable. Such discrepant representations of the system derive from different views about the causes of the conflict, the legal status of the West Bank and Gaza and their Palestinian residents, and differently prioritized sets of concerns, whether these be security and terrorism or the right of self-determination and the enforcement of international human rights standards.

This study overlaps with and shares some of the same concerns as critical legal and human rights literature. But my approach is sociological and thus involves certain fundamental differences in terms of perspective, methodology, and objectives. First, I treat debates over law, legality, and legitimacy as subjects of inquiry rather than merely a backdrop against which I would position my own views, and I explore these debates at length to explain how different people, especially those involved directly in the system in some capacity, embrace or accept certain arguments or policies and reject others. Second, I neither conceptualize the system as an autonomous institution, as legal scholars tend to do, nor limit my attention to specific features or problems, as is characteristic of reports by human rights organizations. Rather, I strive to illuminate and analyze how the military court system — as an institution and an institutional setting — connects inextricably and in manifold ways to the history and the politics of law and conflict in Israel/Palestine.

To date, this is the only study of the Israeli military court system involving protracted research among the five main categories of participants. Part One provides a general overview of the empirical context and the theoretical issues that inform this study. Chapter 1 details the history, politics, and contours of law and conflict, including a general discussion of the identities and ideologies of populations in Israel/Palestine. Chapter 2 addresses the development of legal doctrines and debates about the legality of Israeli rule in the West Bank and Gaza, including a discussion of the development of human rights activism in this area. Part Two is a sociolegal ethnography of the military court system. Chapter 3 describes the courts as institutional settings and the kinds of interactive dynamics that happen there. Chapters 4 through 7 each focus on specific categories of participants and, together, present a tapestry of the legal roles, practices, and perspectives of those directly involved in the system. Chapter 4 focuses on judges and prosecutors, Chapter 5 on translators, Chapter 6 on defense lawyers, and Chapter 7 on defendants. Chapter 8 focuses on the legal process, which is dominated by plea bargaining. The conclusion reflects on the ramifications of the second *intifada* (which began in 2000) on law and conflict in Israel/Palestine and the influence of this conflict on the global "war on terror." The appendix, for readers with a specialized interest, details the institutional structure and administrative features of this court system.

## An Ethnography of Law and Conflict

When I began doing field research in Israel/Palestine in August 1991, the first *intifada* had been going on for almost four years. During that period, scores of Palestinians had been killed or wounded, and tens of thousands had been arrested and imprisoned. Israeli soldier and civilian casualty rates, while substantially lower than those of Palestinians, were significantly higher than in any period since 1967.

Within the Palestinian community, the initial optimistic view that sustained collective resistance could force an end to the Israeli occupation had given way to an embattled determination that things would not return to the status quo ante. While strikes, boycotts, stone throwing, demonstrating, graffiti writing, and barricade building remained popular and pervasive, violent attacks on Israeli targets and on Palestinians suspected of collaborating with the Israeli authorities were on the rise.

One of the unforeseen consequences of the first *intifada* was an escalation of Palestinian factional tensions and conflicts. Since the late 1980s, Islamist activists affiliated with Hamas and Islamic Jihad had come to rival their secular counterparts affiliated with the various factions composing the Palestine Liberation Organization (PLO), and struggles for leadership of the Palestinian community had become increasingly internecine and bloody. The factional divisions and infighting would only worsen after November 1991 when a "peace process" was launched at an international meeting in Madrid, Spain.

The Palestinian community had paid a high toll for resistance to the occupation in terms of the number of dead, injured, deported, homeless, and those physically and psychically wounded by the experiences of arrest, interrogation, and imprisonment.[4] While social networks were crucial in helping people contend with the arrest or death of relatives or the destruction of property, the losses had exacerbated the social suffering of life under military occupation. Clinical depression, post-traumatic stress syndrome, domestic violence, and other afflictions and disorders had reached staggering proportions, to the degree that one Palestinian mental health professional described the Gaza Strip as "a huge asylum."

Within Israel, the *intifada* had taken a heavy toll as well. Only months before it started, Dan Horowitz, a prominent Israeli sociologist, had written, "The impact of the occupation of territories captured in 1967 on Israeli society has barely been studied."[5] But in the intervening years, Israelis had been made to feel and face the implications of the occupation more directly than ever before. The costs had been raised for maintaining control of the West Bank and Gaza and protecting the large population of Jewish Israeli settlers who resided there. The increased military presence meant stepped-up reserve duty for soldiers, which was enormously costly and disruptive.

The Israeli military's rules of engagement for use of deadly force had been loosened, and undercover units, sometimes disguised as Arabs, had taken to hunting and executing "wanted" Palestinians who had evaded capture and arrest by regular troops. These kinds of measures, coupled with skyrocketing arrest rates, had become the subject of intensive scrutiny and often scathing criticism by foreign governments, political commentators, and local and international human rights organizations. This negative attention had spurred increasingly sharp disagreements within Jewish Israeli society over the future of the territories and the standards of military behavior that should apply to deal with the *intifada*. Some were concerned that the military was incapable of crushing Palestinian resistance and thwarting violence against Israelis, while others were concerned about the means being used to try.

Tens of thousands of Palestinians had been arrested and prosecuted in the military courts since December 1987, and thousands more had been administratively detained (imprisoned without trial). Every day, courtrooms were packed to capacity with legal professionals, soldiers, defendants, and their family members. There were often crowds of people in the streets outside the military compounds where the courts were located, denied permission to enter because of the space constraints. Every day dozens of defense lawyers were appearing in court with piles of client files, and it was not uncommon for the busier lawyers to shuttle between sev-

eral courts on a single day. The number of Israeli military judges, prosecutors, and translators working in the courts was higher than at any time
prior to 1987. To meet the demands, some retired career soldiers had
returned to full-time service, and some civilian Israeli lawyers with no previous military court experience were fulfilling reserve military duty as
prosecutors.

On any given day in any of the military courts in the West Bank and
Gaza, I was sure to see unsettling scenes of crying, shouting, slapping,
children in handcuffs, women pleading with soldiers, anxious people
thronging lawyers for information. The courts were, in short, sites of
untold frustrations, animosities, and indignities. I soon became accus-
tomed to the atmosphere, although I never lost that feeling of trepidation
whenever I entered a military compound, wondering what harrowing
sights or stories the day would yield.

Many judges, prosecutors, and defense lawyers whose experiences in
the military courts predated the *intifada* expressed an almost nostalgic
longing for the past, when the number of cases was lower and more attention could be devoted to each one. Some spoke frankly of the legal compromises they were being forced to make in order to contend with the deluge of arrests. While some of the judges and prosecutors welcomed the
increased incarceration and the institution of higher sentences as crucial to
deterring resistance, others were ambivalent about the facility of imprisoning such large numbers of people and found their own views increasingly at odds with official policies. One young prosecutor, who had immigrated to Israel from the United States in 1984, said, "I signed onto this life
to support Israel, but I don't think what I'm doing helps the cause."

Defense lawyers, especially those whose motivations for doing such
work derived from a sense of political solidarity with the Palestinian struggle against the occupation, were increasingly concerned that their services
were merely legitimizing a legal order that many of them abhorred.
Lawyers' inability to provide *legal* relief for most clients, always an aspect
of their work in this court system, had become a more obvious problem
in the last few years. But the pressures manifested in other ways as well:
some lawyers made sharp negative comparisons between their *intifada*
clients and the types of people they had represented in the past, who were
more politically seasoned and were willing to pay the price for their resistance. One Arab Israeli lawyer described his pre-*intifada* clients as the
"lions and tigers of Palestinian society." Now, he noted, those people were
all in jail, deported, or dead, and his current clients were "children and
political novices."

The professional crisis facing defense lawyers was compounded by the emotionally exhausting and dispiriting task of having to educate inexperienced clients and their families about the military court system as a necessary first step in disabusing them of the notion that a conviction could be avoided. Lawyer-client tensions were exacerbated by conflicting expectations: lawyers expected people to understand the difficulties in fighting charges, while many defendants and their families expected lawyers to provide them a legal out and felt cheated if none was forthcoming. A prominent theme in lawyers' criticisms of their clients was a lack of preparation for the rigors of interrogation and ignorance about the legal implications of confessions; both self-incrimination and information about third parties carry sufficient weight to ensure convictions in most cases. According to one Jewish Israeli defense lawyer, "With the first slap, some people will name their whole village. Then we're really lost."

There were other tensions and conflicts among the various categories of legal professionals working in the system, beyond those deriving from the adversarial legal relationship pitting the prosecution against the defense. Veteran judges, prosecutors, and defense lawyers alike disparaged some of the lawyers who had taken up military court work when the *intifada* began, arguing that their weak grasp of the workings of the system resulted in avoidable mistakes and sometimes appalling performances of their duties on behalf of their clients. Many *intifada* lawyers were criticized by their more experienced colleagues for being as green as *intifada* clients, and more than a few had earned reputations as mercenaries aiming to capitalize on a flourishing legal market.

There was rarely any love lost between Israeli military judges and prosecutors and the Palestinian and Israeli civilian defense lawyers. Nevertheless, especially among those with a longer tenure in the courts, the shared work environment had created, to use Liisa Malkki's term, "accidental communities of memory."[6] People who might never have met outside the courts and who held profoundly different worldviews had spent years working together under harsh and difficult conditions.

People who have experienced such things together carry something in common — something that deposits in them *traces* that can have a peculiar resistance to appropriation by others who were not there. These . . . periods of shared history can produce (more or less silent) communities of memory that neither correspond to any ethnologically recognizable community, nor form with any inevitability. They might not even be articulated as communities, not even by those who were "there." For those "who were there" usually get drawn back into other, more publicly consecrated collectivities like families and nations. They get normalized "back where they belong." In the face of these other, recognized, nameable communities, the communities of memory that form through accidents of life and hazards of history can be fragile and easily disembodied.[7]

The day-to-day interactions in the courts were characterized by a commingling of biases and hatreds with an edgy collegiality born of familiarity and the common purpose of handling cases. Even people who openly regarded one another as political foes would interact like colleagues, sometimes joking, teasing, or inquiring about each other's health. Conversely, many erstwhile allies, whether Israeli soldiers or lawyers and their clients, were prone to criticize one another and to try to distinguish themselves from their associates and peers.

The initiation of direct Israeli-Palestinian negotiations in November 1991 added new fissures to the lines of alliance and animosity in Israel/Palestine, which were reflected in relations in the military court system. Some sectors of Israeli and Palestinian societies strongly opposed the negotiations from the outset because they would necessarily entail compromises and concessions. Trenchant opposition from influential constituencies in Israel/Palestine (and beyond) had an inhibiting effect on diplomacy, and even those who initially supported negotiations soon became frustrated by the process. And the *intifada* continued.

Several days after I left Israel/Palestine in August 1993, it was revealed that secret high-level Israeli-Palestinian negotiations (separate from the regular negotiations between delegations) had been going on for months in Oslo, Norway, and had produced a framework for an agreement. Although I was skeptical that backroom brokering was a viable means of resolving the conflict, my initial thought, upon hearing the news, was that the Israeli military court system would soon become "history."

In September 1993, Israeli Prime Minister Yitzhak Rabin and PLO Chairman Yasir Arafat signed a Declaration of Principles. This led, over the next six months, to the start of an Israeli military redeployment from parts of the occupied territories and the establishment of the PA, which was accorded limited "self-governing" powers. These changes ushered in an era that became known as the "interim," connoting a transition in the making, although the final outcome remained to be decided.

Over the next few years, negotiations produced a set of agreements termed the Oslo Accords. Under the interim arrangements, the West Bank and Gaza were divided into three types of jurisdiction: Area A comprised Palestinian towns administered by the PA, Area B comprised Palestinian villages and rural areas under joint Israeli-Palestinian control, and Area C comprised the rest, including Jewish settlements, under full Israeli control.

The Israeli military court system was "downsized," and the courts were relocated from evacuated bases in Palestinian towns to bases in Area C.

The interim was marked by some noteworthy achievements, such as the Palestinian elections in 1996 for a Legislative Council and other institution-building initiatives. But Palestinian support for Oslo waned in the face of continuing Israeli demolitions of Palestinian homes, confiscation of land and settlement building, and stringent closures that had an economically strangling effect. The authoritarianism and corruption of the PA also undermined support. In Israel, the Oslo Accords heightened animosities between the Israeli left and center, who tended to support the negotiations, and the right, who staunchly opposed territorial concessions and the prospect of a future independent Palestinian state.

While violence had never abated, its continuation during the interim heightened political tensions and enlarged the camps of opponents of Oslo.[8] In 1996, Benjamin Netanyahu was elected prime minister of Israel on a platform that sought to recast and roll back the underlying premise that the negotiations would lead to a "two-state solution."

In 1997, I made two short trips back to Israel/Palestine to assess how the Oslo Accords had affected the military court system. Because of the relocation of the courts and the division of the West Bank and Gaza into separate areas, enforced through hard-to-get permits and closures barring Palestinians' movement, it had become nearly impossible for Palestinian lawyers or family members to gain access. The courts continued to conduct their business, but the crowds of people were gone. Most of the casework during the interim was handled by Israeli lawyers and Palestinian residents of East Jerusalem, who were unaffected by permit restrictions.

During the interim, the number of arrests by the Israeli military was lower than in the past because the PA had been vested, by negotiated agreement, with the responsibility to maintain order and provide for Israeli security. The Israeli military courts were handling mainly two kinds of cases: permit violations and attacks on Israeli targets, the latter waged primarily by members of factions opposed to the negotiations. The PA had instituted its own security courts, which replicated many of the problems of the Israeli military court system and in a few ways — such as the introduction of the death penalty — were actually worse. A Palestinian lawyer from Gaza offered an assessment of the interim that was, in retrospect, eerily prescient: "This is not an era of peace; it is an era of uncertainty. All options are open, but it is likely that the future will be violent. In Gaza, the mood is more violent than it has ever been. Forget demonstrations and stone throwing. If you want a suicide bomber, you can get one hundred volunteers. There is a political vacuum. The PA doesn't express people's political ambitions. It wants power for itself, and it does Israel's dirty work. Opposition is growing stronger, and it will probably get much more violent if things get any worse."

Political strife within Israeli and Palestinian societies over the objectives of the negotiating process, recriminations between leaderships about failures to fulfill negotiated responsibilities, and difficulties in reaching mutual agreement about the "final status" issues led, ultimately, to a collapse of the negotiations in July 2000. This became the focus of intense debate because the breakdown signaled the demise of the Oslo Accords and the end of the interim.[9] In September 2000, a second *intifada* started, which was far more violent than the first because of the political and geographic changes that had been instituted under Oslo. The violence — including Israeli assassinations, Palestinian suicide bombings, and full-scale Israeli military assaults on Palestinian population centers — caused spiraling tolls of death and injury. The conflict in Israel/Palestine was compounded and complicated by the September 11, 2001, terrorist attacks on the United States and by the U.S. government's launching of a global "war on terror." By the spring of 2002, when the Israeli military reoccupied previously evacuated areas, the infrastructure of the PA had been all but eviscerated.

I returned to Israel/Palestine again in September 2002 to investigate the effects of the second *intifada* on the military court system. Although dozens of "wanted" Palestinians were assassinated (and dozens of bystanders killed in these assaults), thousands were arrested to face trial. The Israeli military court system was back to full-time business to handle the new deluge. I found that the situation everywhere — including in the military courts — was far worse than it had ever been. It was sobering to see how far this subject was from becoming "history."

As an author, I harbor no pretensions nor offer readers any hope that a solution to the Israeli-Palestinian conflict can be found in the pages of this book. What I do hope to contribute is a richer understanding of how the conflict has affected the lives of people in Israel/Palestine and of the role — and limits — of law.

## Research

My research entailed participant observations in all of the military courts. Until 1994, the courts were located in the Palestinian towns of Ramallah,

Hebron, Nablus, Jenin, Tulkaram, and Gaza. (The courts in Jenin and Tulkaram were set up during the first *intifada*.) With the Israeli redeployment, the courts were relocated to Beit El, Adoreim, and Erez.[10]

My research also entailed unstructured interviews with more than 150 people, including members of all the categories of participants (20 judges and prosecutors, 55 defense lawyers, 15 translators, and 34 defendants). This diversity falls short, however, among people with brief tenure or limited experiences in the military courts. Overrepresentation of the "big (or long-term) players" relates to the process of obtaining contacts (i.e., snowball sampling), as these were the names most easily, readily, and frequently provided. Most of the judges and prosecutors I interviewed were reservists, including some who had been career officers in the legal branch of the Israel Defense Forces (IDF). More than half of the lawyers I interviewed worked exclusively in the military courts, and many had been doing such work for years. Many of the translators I interviewed had become the head translators of the courts to which they were assigned. And many of the defendants I interviewed were prominent activists in the Palestinian community who had been arrested numerous times. I also interviewed many people not directly involved in the system but knowledgeable about some aspect(s) of it, including representatives of human rights organizations, Israeli and Palestinian academics and legal professionals, and family members of defendants.

Considering that the military court system is a central site of the Israeli-Palestinian conflict, the problems and obstacles I encountered in conducting research were relatively — and surprisingly — minor. For the most part, I could move around without difficulty, although movement into and through the West Bank and Gaza was more difficult in 2002. I rarely had problems getting into the courts, although on a few occasions lawyers had to intervene with soldiers on guard duty who were trying to turn me away. I had relatively easy access to most of the people I wanted to interview, with some notable exceptions. For example, it was impossible to interview people during any stage of incarceration; the only defendants I could interview were those who had already been released, aside from a few brief conversations in the courtrooms. Judges, prosecutors, and translators on active duty technically are prohibited from giving interviews without prior permission from the military, and therefore, most of those whom I interviewed were, at the time of the interviews, not on duty. Several, however, did agree to be interviewed in the courts. When I first arrived in 1991, I applied to the IDF for permission to interview high-ranking officials, but it took almost two years for this permission to be granted, and when it was, I was required to do the interviews in the presence of a person from the IDF Public Relations office.

Whenever the territories were closed (meaning that Palestinians were barred from traveling to East Jerusalem or Israel) or when tensions were running particularly high (e.g., in the aftermath of episodes of intense violence of some sort), I would concentrate on meeting with people inside Israel. At other times, I traveled about the West Bank and Gaza, either alone when conducting interviews in people's homes or offices or with lawyers when visiting the courts. During the first *intifada,* Israel and the occupied territories were flush with foreign researchers and journalists. I found that I had little to do in the way of explaining or justifying my project, although occasionally I had to emphasize that I was neither a journalist nor a representative of a human rights organization. On subsequent trips, I reconnected with some of the people I had interviewed during my first research stint and interviewed some new people.

In Israel/Palestine, issues of identity are enormously important politically, and I frequently was asked probing and detailed personal questions about my own identity by interviewees. "Who I am" certainly affected my research: I was born and raised in the United States and have U.S. citizenship. Given the close relationship between the U.S. and Israeli governments, being an American proved advantageous in my interactions with Israeli officials and members of the military. Conversely, many Palestinians were enthusiastic that an American was interested in this subject, since they regarded most Americans (correctly) as uninterested or ignorant about the circumstances of their lives under Israeli occupation. Some interviewees questioned me about my funding and institutional affiliations. One Israeli official, surprised at the detailed and probing nature of my questions, asked (in jest, I assume) if I was a "secret CIA spy."

Interviewees often asked about my ethnic and religious background. My ethnic origins are Syrian (on my father's side) and Finnish (on my mother's). Most people could easily identify my family name as Arabic, and many came to regard me as such once they heard my name or questioned me about my heritage. Several Jewish Israeli interviewees expressed their gladness that "an Arab" was interested in hearing "their side," including one representative of the Israel Bar Association who advised me to publish this study in Arabic in order to "let the Arabs know how fair we treat them." Among some Palestinians, my Arab heritage distinguished me from "foreign" researchers, and I enjoyed greater receptivity than some other American and European researchers working in the area, as I learned by comparing research experiences. When interviewees asked directly about my religion, "atheist" was never accepted as a satisfying answer, since what people wanted to know had nothing to do with my self-selecting beliefs. I was pushed to identify as Christian since this is my family's religion.

To the extent that appearances matter, as they often do in people's processes of cognitively "placing" strangers in some category, Palestinians and Israelis alike frequently assumed on first encounter that I was Jewish American. To give one example of this, about twenty minutes into an interview with an elderly Palestinian lawyer in his office in Ramallah, he started lecturing me on what "people like you" should know. I asked him what he meant, and it became clear that, because he was hard of hearing, he had not heard my giveaway name. He had assumed, on the basis of my appearance, that I was a Jewish American and was using the interview to give me a basic lesson in Palestinian history. When I pointed out his mistake, he got so flustered that he had to excuse himself on the pretext of making coffee. When he returned, he started the interview all over again, this time being much more forthcoming.

My interactions with interviewees were affected by their perceptions of me, and I negotiated my relations to accommodate the way they wanted to treat me. I was, after all, the one who wanted something from them (information), not the other way around. Overall, the significance and combination of my particular characteristics (nationality, ethnic and religious heritage, and gender) enabled me to evade the problem of being pigeonholed in ways that would have been counterproductive to my research. Some Israeli and Palestinian researchers commented that it would be difficult or impossible for them to interview the variety of people or to travel as widely and freely as I did (e.g., from military headquarters in Tel Aviv to refugee camps in Gaza). Falling "between the lines" as I did in this context, I was able to move with relative ease across boundaries (social, political, and spatial) that often obstruct or impede other researchers working in Israel/Palestine.

## Fruits of Method

Conducting qualitative research is a building process, and whatever progress I was able to make at any stage informed the next step of the way. The most obvious example was the process of tapping into various social and professional networks. I met people and acquired names of potential

interviewees through my interactions with other people. I frequently concluded interviews by asking for suggestions of additional names. Some
interviewees questioned me about whom I had already interviewed, and
I found that the more names I could drop, especially when the initial
contact was by telephone, the more readily people agreed to be interviewed. People sometimes picked up on the names I mentioned to provide their own views or stories about those others.

During interviews, I usually began by gathering various kinds of
background information. For judges, prosecutors, and defense lawyers,
this included educational and employment histories and tenure in the military courts. For translators, this included information about their military postings and the processes of selection and training. And for defendants, this included information about their political (i.e., factional)
affiliations (if any), history of arrests, and questions about relations with
their lawyers. Beyond these generalities, however, each interview differed
depending on the circumstances of the meeting, the kinds of information
I had about the person going into the interview, and what I was interested
in learning from him or her. This latter point related to the phase of
research as my understandings and interests changed over time.

While participant observation was an important means of obtaining
a firsthand perspective on the interactional dynamics in the courts,
interviews provided the most significant and substantial primary data
contained in this study. As Kristin Bumiller notes: "Intensive interviewing . . . is a particularly obtrusive form of interaction between the
researcher and the subject. The interviewer is aggressive, challenging the
person's responses in order to bring out the full extent of her or his
understanding and to make obvious the internal contradictions in the
subject's positions. Even the researcher who approaches the situation
with neutrality (to the extent of not offering personal opinions) is
involved in a discussion that calls into question the researcher's legitimacy and purpose when intervening in the lives of the respondents."[11] I
would acknowledge that my own interviewing was, indeed, obtrusive.
Most interviews lasted two hours or longer, and I interviewed some people more than once. I spent entire days, even many days, with some
interviewees (notably lawyers).

When I started this research, I used interviews to gather basic information about the military court system (e.g., legislative and institutional
history) and the roles and practices of participants. As I became more
familiar with the issues, I began using interviews to broach a wider range
of topics, including interviewees' political identifications, views, and

aspirations. Eventually, many interviews could be described more aptly as interactive discussions in which I engaged people in debates about various aspects of the system and about political developments in the broader context.

This certainly throws into relief the issue of researcher objectivity and neutrality. In general, objectivity is complicated by the fact that qualitative, ethnographic research is a process that hinges on opportunities and choices about how to proceed. Speaking to the issue of neutrality, in such a politically charged environment, where even the most basic issues pertaining to the military courts are subjects of contention, maintaining an entirely neutral position would be not just difficult but impossible. Indeed, I neither could nor would claim to have functioned as a neutral observer. But to foreswear neutrality does not leave as the only alternative a partisan approach to research. Rather, by engaging actively and on occasion aggressively with interviewees, I have tried to bring out the issues that inform people's understandings, including internal contradictions in their positions and views. Much of my analysis derives from participants' own views and comparative assessments of contradictory perspectives. I hope that the readers of this book will hear not only my voice but those of the numerous people who gave so generously of their time and allowed my intrusion into their lives.

# PART ONE

# Law and Conflict
in Israel/Palestine

# CHAPTER I

# A Political Geography of Law and Conflict

---

*[L]aw constitutes or participates in the constitution of a terrain or field within which social relations are generated, reproduced, disputed and struggled over, the most important implication being that within such a field . . . the legal discourses in play both place limits of possibility on social action and impose specific forms of discursive possibility.*

Alan Hunt, "Foucault's Expulsion of Law: Toward a Retrieval"[1]

Law inspires, commands, and narrates social life. It creates or identifies categories of social being and meaning, marking boundaries to connect and differentiate its subjects. It authorizes, prohibits, and in other ways regulates desires and relations and the activities to pursue them. It constitutes a terrain of social action and interaction where individuals and groups operate to define, promote, and protect their interests and their rights. It provides a form of ideological reasoning that influences the ways in which people understand their own place in the world, their relations with others, and their ideas about justice and fairness, order and change. In short, law provides an incomparable lens through which to view any social landscape because it permeates every level of society, from the most intimate and personal relations between individuals to the most bureaucratized and formal associations among institutions.

This chapter, as the title suggests, maps law onto a landscape of social and political structures, relations, and ideologies. Like any project of mapping, mine accentuates certain elements and not others. I am particularly interested in law's paradoxical capacity to serve and secure the authority of the state while also enabling means of resisting that authority. I emphasize the terms *authority* and *resistance* because they are capable of denoting subtleties, complexities, and, in combination, the transactional nature of power. Their meanings are more expansive than, for example, *repression* and *revolt*, or *domination* and *rebellion,* because they express ideas of competing rationalities rather than simply forceful struggles. Together they suggest an asymmetrically ordered arrangement constantly reinforcing itself against challenges. *Authority* and *resistance* are particularly appropriate for conceptualizing and studying the impacts and uses of law.

The central subject and setting of this book is the Israeli military court system in the West Bank and Gaza. In the political geography of Israel/Palestine, this system lies at the center of the conflict. Mapping this system involves a consideration of the various identity categories, ideological orientations, and relational networks among people involved in the system and the various discourses drawn upon to explain or represent it (e.g., nationalism, security, terrorism, rule of law, human rights). Law is a constitutive factor in the conflict because of the ways it is used to mark and reinforce — as well as contest — differences in people's legal statuses and rights and struggles that derive from them.

In this chapter, I lay out the analytical framework that I use to assess law and conflict in Israel/Palestine. Although military occupation is exceptionally problematic as a political arrangement, the military court system is not so *legally* anomalous that it defies comparison. The issues that lend themselves to comparative sociolegal analysis include the ways in which law figures in institutionalizing and legitimizing state authority and in inspiring and affording resistances of various kinds.

## Beyond Nationalism

In the scholarly literature on the Israeli-Palestinian conflict, there is a prevailing tendency to rely on a national dichotomy as the analytical framework. The underlying assumption is that the conflict is, at root, a struggle over land — specifically a problem of "two peoples, one land." The explanatory power accorded to nationalism and national difference hinges on notions of separateness, including an assumed a priori distinction between "Jews" and "Arabs," which has manifested in the contemporary era as "Israelis versus Palestinians." The result is a vast body of scholarship that reinforces an Israeli-Palestinian nationalist polemic by treating history as mutually exclusive and competing narratives and interpreting politics largely in terms of the gains, losses, and goals of national political establishments. According to Zachary Lockman, "[M]any, if not most, of the historians, sociologists, and others who have contributed to this literature have worked from within (and implicitly accepted the premises of) either Zionist or Arab/Palestinian nationalist historical narratives."[2]

This book presents an alternative to the national dichotomy and the assumptions of separateness that underlie it. To anticipate several points I develop below, first, what becomes obvious when mapping law onto the political geography of Israel/Palestine is a *lack of separation* between peoples. Second, while the conceptualization of the conflict as a problem of "two peoples, one land" has some irrefutable merit, this conflict is more appropriately conceived as a *struggle over rights,* of which the right to land is but a part. I emphasize the rights of sovereignty and self-determination and the relations between them. The politico-legal architecture of sovereignty constitutes the basis and the archetype of states' rights; it vests the state with the right to rule the territory and population within its domain (i.e., domestic autonomy and independence) and informs international relations among states by promoting (a degree of) respect for boundaries (i.e., noninterference). Self-determination constitutes the politico-legal principle upholding — or promising — people's right to rule themselves. While the "self" is a collectivity, usually configured and imagined as a nation, the right of self-determination is not simply a national matter of having a sovereign territorial state of one's "own," although sovereignty is a common aspiration and expression of this right. Rather, self-determination affects the availability of all sorts of rights because it hinges on the willingness and capacity of the state to represent the political, social, and economic interests of the people it rules.

Granted, in the main the struggle over rights in Israel/Palestine is polarized along national lines and is highly unequal, given the vast differences in institutional power and international status between collective adversaries. With the creation of Israel in 1948, the Zionist project changed from a Jewish national movement seeking the right of self-determination to a sovereign Jewish state — from the right *to* a state to the rights *of* a state. For Palestinians, in contrast, the right of self-determination remains unrealized. Even those Palestinians who have acquired citizenship in one country or another are affected by the problem of Palestinian statelessness, since states are the primary arbiters of national rights.

Palestinians' lack of national self-determination is central to the perpetuation of the Arab-Israeli conflict, which has engulfed the entire region of the Middle East for over fifty years. Throughout, struggles for the rights of Palestinians have been integrally linked to the political and legal processes of denying those rights and have involved, to some degree, all of the states in the region. These processes have varied across place and time, as have the means and goals of struggle. For Palestinian residents of the West Bank and Gaza, since 1967 their struggles for rights have been waged primarily against the Israeli occupation. In turn, Israeli authorities, acting on their rights as the de facto sovereign in these regions, have treated all manifestations of resistance against Israeli rule as prosecutable security violations. The military courts have been a locus of this struggle over rights.

Nationalism and national differences are undeniably important for understanding the conflict between Jews and Palestinians in terms of their respective political institutions and the differing interests to which they lay claim as "peoples." And nationalism is certainly significant for understanding the politics of the Israeli occupation of the West Bank and Gaza and resistance against it. However, relying on the national dichotomy to frame and explain relations among people in Israel/Palestine is problematic politically and conceptually. First, it reifies Israeli-Palestinian relations by conflating them with or reducing them to the conflict. The kinds of relations that contradict or confound a nationalist interpretation tend to be either ignored or treated as exceptional. Second, the dichotomy subsumes people's interests to their national identity. People's activities, motivations, and commitments are read as expressions or transgressions of the collective (national) good, making nationalist ideology a basis for judging the content and character of social action and interaction. Third, the dichotomy encourages "state as actor" explanations for events and processes associated with the conflict, thus promoting a conceptual symmetry (as distinct from a political symmetry) between the Israeli state and Palestinians' national representative, the Palestine Liberation Organization (PLO) and, since 1994, the Palestinian Authority (PA). Fourth, the dichotomy projects a zero-sum interpretation of interests, where one "side's" gain is perceived as the other side's loss — especially when those interests are territorialized. And fifth, the dichotomy tends to underplay the fact that conflict itself is a relationship that richly — and adversely — infuses relationships of all sorts, not only those between self-declared enemies. In the context of Israel, the West Bank, and Gaza, conflict is not a discrete event or series of events but an ongoing feature and force of life.

The national dichotomy is limiting as an analytical framework because it contributes to the polarization of the subjects it purports to explain, as I became aware through the process of conducting research for this book. In fact, my original plan was to study how nationalism and national difference affected the operation of the military court system. However, I soon realized that the assumption of a rigid distinction between "Israelis" and "Palestinians" was thoroughly inadequate for understanding and representing the roles and activities of the Israeli citizens and Palestinian residents of the West Bank and Gaza who come together in the courts and the kinds of practices and relations that make up the functioning of the system. Specifically, I came to realize that my ability to apprehend the court system required an understanding of 1) the diversity (i.e., not dichotomy) of legal and political identities among the various population groups in Israel/Palestine; 2) the territorially contiguous but politically and legally differentiated power of the Israeli state throughout this area; and 3) the structure of sociopolitical relations in which people (and land) are integrated through relations of rule (and economics).

I also assumed, when I began, that law in the military court system was a monopoly of the Israeli state. But I came to appreciate that law — as a realm of practices, relationships, and ideologies — subverts the relevance of the national dichotomy because of the ways in which legality works simultaneously to advance and curb national agendas and to cut across national lines (geographic and demographic).

Law and legality have distinct effects on the dynamics of Israeli-Palestinian relations that cannot simply be conflated with or subsumed under the rubric of nationalisms.[3] For example, while the Israeli state has the political leverage and military strength to advance its own national and strategic agendas in the West Bank and Gaza, the state's commitment to law has provided some constraints and deterred the untrammeled use of force. Although force and violence have been integral components of the state's strategies to maintain order and control and to thwart and punish resistance, the main mode or model of rule has been "law enforcement" rather than "war" (at least until the second *intifada*). Israeli military rule has entailed arresting and imprisoning rather than expelling or massacring Palestinians en masse, and resorting to closures, curfews, and permits rather than aerial bombing to achieve order and subdue resistance. While the legality of these policies is contestable, the state has relied on law to undertake and justify them.

Israel's preference for a law enforcement model to govern Palestinians in the West Bank and Gaza derives from the status of the state in these areas. The military victory in 1967 enabled Israel to take control of the

West Bank and Gaza, transforming those areas into an "internal" domain and installing itself as the de facto sovereign. (In south Lebanon, in contrast, which Israel also occupied, the state never assumed de facto sovereignty and therefore could and did opt to use a war model.)[4] The use of law and legally regulated force has been necessary to legitimize this arrangement and to sustain support from important constituencies, both domestic and international.

Although by its very nature military occupation deprives the occupied Palestinian population of any control or input over the laws and institutions used to rule them, it does provide a legal basis for rule. Being ruled by law certainly can be oppressive and restrictive, but it differs from rule by brute force and provides certain opportunities for maneuver and resistance. Moreover, because the Israeli state has committed itself to legality (i.e., ruling by law), it has opened itself to being judged and criticized by standards of law.

One potent example of law's capacity to inspire and enable resistance to Israeli authority has been the adoption of human rights discourse and strategies. Starting in the late 1970s, human rights activism and organizing emerged as legalistic means to criticize and challenge Israeli policies and practices that violate Palestinians' rights, as well as to articulate and focus appeals to the international community to support Palestinian rights claims. It is noteworthy that human rights activism in Israel/Palestine was started by people directly involved in the military court system. By the mid-1980s, human rights activism had developed into a movement spanning "national boundaries." Although the impact of human rights activism in Israel/Palestine has been limited, it undoubtedly has affected the course and the discourse of the conflict. Not only is the national dichotomy unhelpful, but it actually impedes an understanding of the contours and dynamics of human rights activism as a form of legalistic resistance.

In Israel/Palestine, the struggles over rights that constitute the conflict manifest themselves not as the pitting of two "peoples" with diametrical interests against one another but as a far more complex contest over the powers and practices of the state that affect the rights of all people. Struggles for the rights of Palestinians living under occupation have involved not only people acting on their own behalf (and certainly not all people living under occupation have struggled against it) but also Israeli citizens who have contributed to this effort in various ways. In a nationalistic account, the latter would be construed as traitors to their "side," and indeed such accusations are not uncommon. Yet such an understanding, which exemplifies attempts to read the activities of people as expressions or transgressions of collective national interests, is simplistic if not patently incorrect. For example, the defense lawyers who represent Palestinian defendants in the military courts include citizens of Israel. Some have done this work as an expression of solidarity or identification with the collective Palestinian struggle for the right of self-determination — and against the occupation — while others have been motivated by concerns about the rule of law and the need to protect the legal rights of Palestinians under the prevailing circumstances. On the other hand, even some Israeli state representatives, namely, military judges and prosecutors, have been critical of the occupation and deeply conflicted about their own roles in mediating between Israeli security policies and Palestinian rights. In other words, the various categories of participants in the military court system are neither divided along clear national lines nor lined up on opposing sides to act out some grand clash of nations.

## Government in Israel/Palestine

To find an analytical framework that could accommodate the complexities and contradictions of political and legal identities and relations and sociopolitical structures in Israel/Palestine, I came to rely on the concept of *government*. In the Foucauldian sense, government is relational, emphasizing institutional practices and processes of rule over populations and territories. Conceiving of government as relational allows for an appreciation of people as participants in governing relations, not (simply) as the instruments or objects of state control or the vehicles of a collective countervailing movement to resist and subvert that control. In such a way, people are endowed conceptually with the power they exercise empirically, namely the power to act. Yet such power is not idealized or fetishized as it is in the rhetorics of national liberation and national security; rather, it continually questions how people's options and motivations to act and interact are informed by their relations to the institutional structures of politics and law. A focus on government does not ignore the ideological content and political importance of nationalism or the relevance of national differences; instead, it makes nations, nationalisms, and national institutions subjects of inquiry rather than explanatory devices. As Colin Gordon explains, "A rationality of government will thus mean a way or system of thinking about the nature of the practice of government (who can govern; what governing is; what or who is governed), capable of making some form of that activity thinkable and practicable both to its practitioners and to those upon whom it is practiced."[5]

However, studying government in Israel/Palestine presents some distinct challenges because the parameters of analysis do not correspond to the sovereign boundaries of a state or to a society that is legally and politically unified. Since 1967, Israel has been the governing state — and the only state governing this area — so Israel/Palestine must be regarded as governmentally integrated. But because the boundaries of "nation," "state," and "society" do not coincide in any meaningful way, Israel/Palestine is also governmentally transnationalized. It is territorially transnationalized through various processes of jurisdictional mapping and administration that divide the area into several politico-legal formations with different statuses: sovereign Israeli territory (i.e., inside the 1949 armistice or "Green Line"), military administration in territories occupied in war, and de facto annexation through the extension of Israeli domestic law to some areas conquered in 1967 (including East Jerusalem, Jewish Israeli civilian settlements, and other confiscated or appropriated properties in the West Bank and Gaza). Government is also demographically transnationalized through the processes and consequences of administratively and legally distinguishing among population groups whose national identities and identifications span geographic boundaries. Although government changed in the 1990s as a result of the Oslo Accords, and again as a consequence of the second *intifada,* Israel/Palestine has remained a governmentally integrated entity because there is only one state here.

Mapping the military court system as an institutional setting demands a panoramic perspective of Israel/Palestine in its entirety because participants are drawn from every corner. This mapping also requires a rethinking of the meaning and significance of boundaries (social, political, and spatial). In fact, my use of the term *Israel/Palestine* speaks directly to this effort to capture the integrated and transnationalized nature of government in this area.

The boundaries of identity among population groups in Israel/Palestine are complex and overlapping. People's legal statuses and rights, their political interests, and their relations to the state are consolidated through myriad formal and informal categories that demarcate and reinforce an array of relevant differences (e.g., Israeli citizens and noncitizen residents of occupied territories; Jews, Arabs, Druze; West Bankers, Gazans, East Jerusalemites; urbanites, villagers, refugees, settlers, and so on). Likewise, the significance of spatial boundaries demarcating "sovereign" and "occupied" (or, in official Israeli parlance, "administered") areas confounds dichotomization in terms of both the practices of state rule and the territorial claims and aspirations of populations. While the territoriality of Israeli state power is coordinated, there is neither a single legal order nor a shared set of rights available to all people living in this area. The structure of sociopolitical relations in Israel/Palestine, which reflects the articulation of identity categories and territorial boundaries, is hierarchical, as evident in the differentiation of people's rights (collective and individual), as well as their access to resources, political options to act, and so on.

In terms of the character of its domestic institutions, Israel is a parliamentary democracy. But it is also a Jewish state governing non-Jewish citizens and noncitizen residents of militarily occupied areas. As *the* Jewish state, Israel's national mandate extends to noncitizen Jews around the world. Thus, the Israeli state can be characterized as an "ethnocracy." Oren Yiftachel defines ethnocracy as "a regime built on two key principles: First, ethnicity, and not citizenship, is the main logic around which state resources are allocated; and second, the interests of a dominant ethnic group shape most public policies. The combination of these two principles typically creates an ethno-class type of stratification and segregation."[6]

The Israeli state exercises its sovereign prerogative of domestic autonomy over the content and character of law to privilege Jewish individuals over non-Jews and to prioritize Jewish national/collective interests. The two most important laws affirming and consolidating the Jewish nature of the state are the Law of Return (1950), which guarantees automatic and immediate citizenship to any Jew upon immigration to Israel, and the Nationality Law (1951), which establishes the basis upon which people have a right to claim citizenship. Israel's Basic Law: the Knesset (1985), makes it illegal for any political party to participate in the parliamentary process if it rejects the definition of Israel as the state of the Jewish people.[7]

In Israel, Jewishness is, among other things, a legal categorization with benefits, privileges, and protections unavailable (or unequally available) to people who are not Jews. The state represents and prioritizes the interests of the Jewish national collectivity, and this serves to configure the rights of all population groups in Israel/Palestine in relation to those interests. The interests most relevant to a study of the military court system (and, by extension, the conflict) relate to national security, which Israeli officials tend to conceive broadly to encompass anything that might menace or infringe on the survival, maintenance, viability, and character of the state or might negatively affect the safety and well-being of Jews. Israeli national security is interpreted by the state as Jewish security.

Israel has been in a state of war since it was established in 1948, and this has fostered a powerful "national security consensus" among Jewish Israelis.[8] A majority of Jewish Israelis accepts — even demands — legal discrimination and political repression against Arabs living under the rule of the state as necessary and therefore legitimate. As Itzhak Zamir explains: "It is particularly difficult in Israel to reach a suitable balance between the interest of national security and that of human rights. The special conditions [that] prevail here foster an extreme approach, which tends to assign absolute priority to national security above all other interests and to disregard the need to strike a balance between them. This approach finds adherence both among the general public as well as in ruling circles."[9]

The state openly, actively, and pervasively discriminates against — and between — Arabs in order to protect and enhance Israeli national security. The "Arab threat" against which Israeli national security is invoked obviously includes violence and subversion. But it also includes the threatening impact of rights claims and resistance against discrimination and repression, including, for example, challenges to the characterization of Israel as a Jewish state rather than a state of its citizens.

The discourse and politics of Israeli national security emphasize the Jewish/Arab distinction, and law is deployed by the state to promote and protect national security in ways that reinforce this "national boundary." This is evident in the ways security laws are written, interpreted, and applied and in the ways (potential and actual) "victims" and "perpetrators" are construed. For example, intercommunal violence tends to be treated as a threat to security if it involves Arab-on-Jewish attacks, but if the protagonists are reversed, rarely is it treated as a security violation except in instances when the violence is so extreme *and* unauthorized that it can menace state control (e.g., bombing attacks by Jewish vigilante groups).

But to accept this Jewish/Arab dichotomy uncritically assumes or concedes that security is the monopoly of the state and that only Jews have a right to security. Israel/Palestine is a decidedly insecure place, and this affects everyone, albeit in markedly different ways. The point is that security — like conflict — is relational: no group or constituency can "have it" alone. National differences factor heavily in security and insecurity in Israel/Palestine, but the Jewish/Arab national divide is not the only difference that matters, nor is it adequate to frame the benefits or costs of the security policies and practices of the state.

The "Arab" side of the national divide has in common a historic residence in Palestine (which geographically encompasses what is now Israel/Palestine). This includes Palestinians who fled or were expelled in 1948 and those who have remained in this area. Among the latter, the designation *Arab* or *Palestinian* does not begin to capture, let alone suffice to explain, their identities, nor do these national designations express with any accuracy their relations to the Israeli state.

At the end of the 1948–49 war, the 130,000 Palestinian Arabs who remained inside the borders of Israel became Israeli citizens. (Their numbers have grown to more than one million.) Israeli officials responded to the problem of governing a sizable Arab population by instituting a military administration within Israel, which remained in effect until 1966,[10] and deploying a divide-and-rule approach, separating this population into several politico-legal categories: Arabs (i.e., Muslims and Christians), Druze (members of a sect of Shi'i Islam; originally designated Arabs, in 1961 they were recategorized as a distinct "national/religious" group), Bedouin (Muslim Arabs identified as having or having had a pastoral/nomadic lifestyle), and Circassians (non-Arab Muslims). Hence, inside Israel, *Arab* became a descriptive term to refer collectively to Israel's Palestinian citizens (who are also referred to officially as a "national minority"), but it has no coherence as a legal category except in marking people as non-Jews.

As non-Jews in a Jewish state, Arab Israelis are not afforded and cannot claim the same rights as Jewish citizens.[11] As citizens, they have rights as individuals, including the right to participate in elections and the right to due process protections in the domestic legal order. As non-Jews, they are collectively subordinated within the hierarchical identity-based structure of the Israeli polity. Their status as citizens but not "nationals" of the state raises questions (and stimulates debates) about Israel's claims to democracy. At minimum, it defies the principle of popular sovereignty, since Arab citizens cannot claim the state as "theirs." Consequently, their relations to the Israeli state are problematic and contradictory because of the ways in which domestic law and politics discriminate against and marginalize them, limit their access to national resources, and restrict — without entirely denying — their options to protest and resist their second-class status. However, because the Arabs in Israel have status as citizens, their relations to Palestinians in the occupied territories are also contradictory. Some have been inclined to envisage their own struggles for rights in terms of collective Palestinian national interests, while others have aspired to rights associated with democracy, namely full equality with Jews in Israel. Even their collective status as "non-Jewish Israelis" is contradictory because of their categorization and separation into distinct subnational groups; Arab, Druze, Bedouin, and Circassian Israeli citizens do not have identical rights (or lack of rights) or a common/collective relationship to the state.

Palestinians residing in the West Bank and Gaza are not citizens of the Israeli state, and their rights are lesser than those of all categories of Israeli citizens by virtue of their being an occupied population. They are subject to the military and emergency laws in force in the territories, which carry over even when they are inside Israel or in Jewish settlements. The legal boundary demographically demarcating "occupied Palestinians" from "Israeli citizens" is further complicated by the Israeli state's unilateral annexation of East Jerusalem in 1967 (reaffirmed in 1981) and the expansion of the municipal boundaries of the city. Consequently, Palestinian residents of East Jerusalem became "noncitizen residents of Israel," with a legal status and rights somewhat different from those of Palestinians in other parts of the occupied territories. Moreover, the administrative/juridical separation of East Jerusalem from the rest of the West Bank has affected the rights and relations among all Palestinians. In the early 1990s, the changes resulting from the Oslo Accords affected these geographic and demographic divisions among Palestinians, adding a new layer in the form of separate jurisdictions for Area A (population centers) and Area B (villages and rural areas).

This governmental complexity is a legal and political construct: the differences noted above and elaborated below and throughout this book are manifestations of the state's legal authority to organize and regulate the lives and relations of those subject to its rule. But law is a double-edged sword that also can serve to resist and contest these arrangements and to constrain the power and discretion of the state. The other side of law can be seen in the ways it inspires and empowers people to act in their own interests and even to imagine what those interests are. The sociological study of law seeks to apprehend and analyze the rich and varied ways in which law affects life.

## Sociology of Law

Two general observations can be made about the sociological study of law. First, law confounds heuristic distinctions between "the discursive" and "the material": it is always and explicitly both. As Terrence Halliday explains: "Law has two components: a rule-making, conceptual, textual, discursive side, including both substantive and procedural law; and an institutional side — that is, a set of organizational arrangements that, internally, structure law's behavior and, externally, structure law's relations with other elements of the state and the institutions of civil society."[12] Sociology of law engages the articulation of text ("law in the books") and context ("law in action"), combining analysis of the lawful relations and legal categories with the processual interplays that operationalize law in any given context. It is, therefore, a comparative enterprise.

Second, law is semi- or relatively autonomous. Although the force of law (legislation, enforcement, and adjudication) derives from political authority, political analysis is inadequate to understand legal discourses or processes, and legalistic action is not a simple reflection of political power. Politics affects but does not predictably determine the nature and uses of law. The semiautonomy of law is reinforced by the specialized knowledge and rarified logics that shape legal reasoning and guide legal practices.

In general, sociology of law attends to the mutually constitutive relationship among law, society, and the state. States make and use laws to exercise and rationalize their authority over society, to respond to the specter of conflict, and to contend practically with the inevitable conflicts that arise, from the deadly and dangerous to the mundane.[13] For example, administrative and regulatory laws are enacted to divide and control space (public and private properties, jurisdictions), to manage time (waged labor, age-specified categories like children and the elderly), to enable or restrict movement (immigration, travel), and to provide for collective well-being (health, education, commerce, resource management). Criminal law is the grimmest of spheres, making explicit law's capacity to do violence through a claimed or imagined necessity to maintain order through "legitimate force."[14] The common equation of law and order both implies violence and sanctions its legality when used by state agents or institutions. If maintaining order is the responsibility of the state, legal violence is in its repertoire of means.

Law serves the state by contributing to an aura of legitimacy. The legitimacy of any state is evaluated in large part through the legal instruments and processes of governmental authority (e.g., constitutions; participatory, inclusive, and competitive electoral systems; independent judiciaries; representative legislatures). *Rule of law* refers to governance according to laws and the employment of legal means to transform laws. Thus, the rule of law fosters a form of legal consciousness that concedes legitimacy to the state.

The concept of hegemony is useful for framing and analyzing the relationship among law, society, and the state.[15] Hegemony suggests consent, and consent distinguishes hegemony from brute domination; states that rely exclusively on force and violence to maintain control may be powerful, but they are not hegemonic. Law plays a vital role in securing the hegemony of the state through its perceived efficacy in benefiting and protecting, at least to some degree, all sectors of society. As Sally Engle Merry states, "Political authority always relies to a greater or lesser extent on the consent of the governed, and any form of domination requires some level of consent by the dominated group, some willingness to accept its own subordination."[16] Any state's hegemony is contingent on its capacity to legitimize its authority, to rationalize its use of force, and to produce and maintain social, political, and legal arrangements that are popularly apprehended and accepted as "normal."

Yet there are always limits to a state's capacity to rationalize, legitimize, and normalize itself in the hearts and minds of the governed. For example, when a state engages in or tolerates discrimination against certain sectors of society, its claims to legitimacy are open to challenge. People and groups who suffer discriminatory disadvantages may struggle to remake the social order and/or revise their relations to the state. Short of civil war, resistance can manifest itself as militancy or civil disobedience. It can be expressed through mobilizing calls for separatism for the disaffected group (e.g., autonomy or independence) or through reforms to enhance the availability of rights, benefits, and protections. The legal terrain often provides a site of counterhegemonic resistance.[17] As Martha Minow explains: "Centralized, governmental authority may govern people whose own normative commitments rest on incommensurate premises: people may comply, people may resist, people may live quietly with conflicts, and people may bring conflicts into spheres of public attention and debate. We must not pretend that the law provides one comprehensive scheme that orchestrates all the legal relationships among subgroups and between the central government and each group; instead, law provides multiple languages and institutions within which to play out struggles."[18]

## Hegemony and Its Discontents

Even in Israel/Palestine, where conflict is rampant, the concept of hegemony is crucial to understand the reasons and ways in which people consent. However, a Weberian conception of hegemony is inadequate because the politico-legal distinctions among population groups and the categorically unrepresentative character of Israeli rule over Palestinians in the occupied territories produce no common normative order and no basis for consensus. Nor does this context lend itself to a Gramscian conception of hegemony, which sees state power as reflecting, enforcing, and promoting the interests of the dominant class(es); although there is a class dimension to the stratified sociopolitical structure in Israel/Palestine, neither hegemony nor counterhegemony is rooted in or reducible to class interests and differences.

Because of the transnational nature of government in Israel/Palestine, I have found it useful (and necessary) to distinguish between the political and ideological dimensions of hegemony.[19] Political hegemony reflects the fact that the Israeli state is the governing authority throughout the area and bears upon the ways people consent to and/or contend with this. Ideological hegemony reflects the interests represented, protected, and advanced by the Israeli state. For all its success in maintaining political hegemony, the Israeli state has had no corresponding success in terms of ideological hegemony, nor has it tried. The enduring conflict is a principal factor. But it can also be said that the ideology of the Israeli state (i.e., Zionism) offers little that would legitimize or "normalize" it in the hearts and minds of its non-Jewish citizens or foreign subjects.

Even inside the Green Line, there is a disjuncture between political and ideological hegemony. For Jewish Israelis who identify as Zionists (a description befitting the vast majority), legitimacy derives from the mutually reflecting relationship between the state, which they can claim as their "own," and the state's ideology, which prioritizes their (Jewish national) interests.[20] The small number of Jewish Israelis who identify themselves as non- or anti-Zionists do not accept the Jewish character of the state as legitimate or condone the privileging of Jews at the expense of non-Jews, even though they benefit as Jews.

When it comes to Israeli rule of the West Bank and Gaza, a majority of Jewish Israelis has tended to accept that the ways in which the state exercises its power have been legitimate under the circumstances of an ongoing conflict and the shared perceptions of security threats posed by Palestinians. This legitimation hinges on the idea that the state governs legally and that the kinds of policies that the state has used to govern and control Palestinians are within its purview as the de facto sovereign. This consensus narrows over the state's policies to allow or encourage the settlement of Jewish citizens in areas heavily populated by Palestinians and the forms of violence used by the state to maintain control of the territories.

However, when it comes to the political future of the West Bank and

Gaza and their relationship to Israel, the consensus breaks apart, and differing ideological perspectives among Jewish Israelis are brought into sharp relief. Those whose ideological commitments could be described as right-wing religious and/or nationalist advocate permanent Israeli control of all or most of these areas on the grounds that they constitute an inseparable part of *Eretz Israel* (literally, "the land of Israel") and thus are the rightful and exclusive possession of Jews. The extreme right couples this ideology of possessive right with aspirations to "transfer" Palestinians out of those areas. Jewish Israelis whose commitments are more centrist and secular advocate a continuing and possibly permanent possession of areas deemed crucial to the security of the state but would accept territorial concessions as a means of bringing the conflict — and the occupation — to an end. Liberals, whose views could be located left of center in the Jewish Israeli politico-ideological spectrum, tend to favor a substantial territorial withdrawal and the creation of a demilitarized Palestinian state alongside Israel as necessary to reconcile the national interests of "two peoples" in this "one land." Ultraleftists, a tiny minority among Jewish Israelis, advocate Israeli withdrawal to the Green Line and the creation of an independent, fully sovereign Palestinian state in the West Bank and Gaza. An even smaller minority advocates the de-Judaization of the Israeli state and the transformation of all of Israel/Palestine into a single democratic entity affording full and equal rights for all inhabitants. If there is any consensus among Jewish Israelis about the future of the West Bank and Gaza, it is that perpetual conflict is untenable.

Most Arab citizens of Israel concede the political hegemony of the state, but many are critically conscious that the state's Zionist ideology (and the policies that derive from it) perpetuate their ongoing social and political marginalization and limit their rights. This critical consciousness is reinforced by the fact that many Jewish Israelis perceive Arab citizens as a potential "fifth column" because their identity links them nationally to other Arabs and ethnonationally to other Palestinians, including those residing in the occupied territories. Thus, they are identified with the state's enemies. Furthermore, their very presence is perceived as an impediment to the maximization of Jewish control over and in the land of Israel.[21]

But the issue of legitimation is more complicated than a Jewish/Arab national dichotomy would suggest; notwithstanding their second-class status, Arabs' rights as citizens provide some compensations and protections, enabling people to concede a functional legitimacy to the hegemonic order inside the Green Line.[22] Most Arab Israelis who have protested and contested their disadvantages seek to change the state and their relations to it, not destroy it.[23] While many Arab Israelis have been extremely critical of Israel's occupation of the West Bank and Gaza and supportive of aspirations and demands for an independent Palestinian state, the vast majority regard their place as "in Israel" and would not opt or concede to leave if a Palestinian state came into being in the West Bank and Gaza. As Nadim Rouhana explains, "For the Arabs in Israel, the issues of national consensus differ. They focus on the establishment of a Palestinian state in the West Bank and Gaza, achievement of equality within Israel, and the operational proviso that political actions such as protests be made within the framework of Israeli law."[24]

For Palestinian residents of the West Bank and Gaza, there is little basis upon which to accord Israeli rule any kind of political or ideological legitimacy because it amounts to a colonial — albeit changing — arrangement in which their collective/national rights are denied and their individual rights are minimal and sorely restricted.[25] While resistance against the occupation has been a defining and enduring aspect of Palestinian politics, living with the occupation has been a necessity born of a lack of alternatives, which has forced grudging concessions and accommodations. The legalistic nature of Israeli rule has shaped the ways in which Palestinians have tried to make sense of the choices they are forced to make and to justify the options they choose. Even though Palestinians' status as an occupied population is politically and legally constricting, they are subjects (i.e., not merely objects) of the state, and some have sought opportunities and means to mobilize law counterhegemonically to advance and protect their interests.[26]

## Law and the Politics of Rights

Law's ideological currency as semiautonomous suggests that "law" can be distinguished from "politics." Indeed, law's interests often are framed in terms of rights, and rights tend to be accorded transcendental values.[27] Laying claim to rights and/or appealing to the idea of rights are means of investing social agency with moral authority. According to Austin Sarat and Thomas Kearns, "Rights authorize action and yet undermine authority's claims. They are, by definition, mandatory claims, yet they are fecund with interpretive possibilities. They both constitute us as subjects and provide a language through which we can resist that constitution and forge new identities."[28]

To "have" rights means to have legal rights — those entitlements, protections, and freedoms that are established through law and enforced by legal institutions. In practice, the rights that people actually can claim, exercise, and enjoy are determined by the nature and enforceability of law in any given context. But the "semi" in law's semiautonomy serves to remind that rights are inherently political and social — created, contested, understood, and sought by people. Aspirations and demands for rights are shaped and saturated by the ideological appeal of socially generated norms and values: who deserves (or does not deserve) what rights and why.

There is a common tendency to (mis)perceive rights as things (which can be "owned," "given," or "lost"). Such reification might derive from the ways in which law tends to categorize, define, and analogize its concerns. But rights are not actually things; *rights are practices that are required, prohibited, or otherwise regulated within the context of relationships governed by law.*

During the imperial age, when vast portions of the world were ruled by European states, the rights privileged and advanced through colonial legal orders were those benefiting the metropolitan centers of power and colonizing populations. Of course, colonialism was not simply a unidirectional exercise of power of "centers" over "peripheries" but a relationship involving rulers and ruled in institutionalized political arrangements through which rights were both internationalized (i.e., extraterritorialized) and hierarchized (e.g., racially, nationally, ethnically, religiously). Anticolonial struggles were forms of resistance to the illiberal rationalities that maintained colonial authority (e.g., civilizing missions, balance-of-power politics). In many contexts, nationalist resistance was fueled by a desire for rights, foremost the right of self-determination. Peoples of Asia, Africa, and Latin America wanted, expected, and acted to see *themselves* in the government that ruled them.

The successes of anticolonial/nationalist struggles around the world refashioned global geography and the basis of governmental legitimation on principles that earlier had prevailed in Europe: people's right to self-determination and states' right to sovereignty. Louis Henkin aptly described the twentieth century as "the age of rights."[29] His point is twofold: that the idea of rights and associated practices to obtain, guarantee, and protect them are premised on the diffusion and expansion of "modern" politico-legal cultures and that rights (individual and collective) are institutionalized through the powers and authority of modern states.

The modern state, despite the manifold forms it takes, claims legitimacy (domestic authority and international recognition) in no small part on its representative status. Representativeness of society through the state, although historically contingent, has become a globalized norm for "good government," regardless of — or despite — the different ways in which representativeness is conceived (e.g., liberal democracy, one-party state, ethnonational state). A representative state is a necessary condition for self-determination, and self-determination is enshrined in international law as a basic, inalienable, and universal right. However, the universality of the right to self-determination is paradoxical because this right is inherently particularistic. Self-determination simultaneously universalizes nationalist particularism (although the nature of the national "self" varies significantly) and reinforces the role and power of the sovereign state as the national representative. While international law recognizes self-determination as a universal right, it also recognizes states' rights to rule, including the right to counter and punish those who challenge or rebel against their authority. Thus, international law not only lacks a clear capacity to reconcile the contradictions between self-determination and sovereignty where the boundaries of state and nation do not harmonize but also makes the interpretation of law part of the conflict in contexts where there is a contradiction. In Israel/Palestine, the rights of sovereignty and self-determination are at the heart of the conflict, so this context illuminates the paradox.

## States and Conflicts

States' rights have changed substantially as a result of developments in international law since World War II. But the sovereignty principle continues to dominate international relations and often discourages or impedes outside (i.e., "foreign" or "international") intervention in the defense of people whose rights are being violated, especially when those violations can be framed as "necessary" for national security and/or other state interests (e.g., preserving territorial integrity, maintaining or restoring law and order, sustaining or protecting the national economy). Even the most politically stable states find occasions to restrict and violate people's rights, authorizing and rationalizing such practices as necessary for the "greater good" of the society they represent.

In countries rent by violence, rights often are the very stakes of the conflict, and conflict increases the likelihood of rights violations. States facing or fearing challenges to their authority and control from opposition movements or resistance groups often use discrimination, repression, and violence to restore order or protect national security, as those in power perceive it. Such practices commonly are justified by demonizing individuals and groups engaged in resistance as dangerous enemies, and one of the most common idioms of demonization is the charge of "terrorism." Terrorism smacks of danger and thus provides an ideal rationale for the suspension or derogation of rights and, possibly, state violence. Portraying adversaries and enemies as terrorists (or the slightly less controversial term *subversives*) enables a state to legitimize and gain public (domestic and/or international) acceptance or tolerance for whatever kinds of policies it mounts to combat and control them.[30]

Terrorism is a broad and flexible concept, and there is no clear, internationally accepted definition.[31] It is used, variously, to describe certain kinds of actions (e.g., attacks on civilians, hijackings, organized resistance or repression) and/or to identify certain types of actors. In national security discourse, the latter tends to prevail: terrorism typically is used to refer to nonstate actors or organizations engaging in struggles against the state (emphasizing but not necessarily limited to violence), to which the state responds with "counterterrorism." Moreover, in this state-centric discourse, the political motivations and goals of groups branded as terrorist are castigated as inherently illegitimate and threatening, lacking any cognizable (or at least credible) logic beyond a will to terrorize and destroy. In national security discourse, support for those goals often is equated with support for terrorism.

Terrorism is not a figment of the politically paranoid imagination. Deliberately targeting civilians or civilian infrastructures as a tactic in the furtherance of some cause, whatever the political or ideological motivation and whoever the targeting agents, is terroristic. By this definition, states can be as culpable as nonstate groups. However, the power to name and to blame that accrues to states and manifests itself in the language and politics of national security tends to focus *not* indiscriminately on effects (i.e., deliberately harming civilians) but rather discriminately on the organizations and motivations of those who act against and menace the interests of the state. The interpretation and practice of national security as "state security" militates against a critical evaluation of state violence. As Richard Falk explains, "With the help of the influential media, the state over time has waged and largely won the battle of definitions by exempting its own violence against civilians from being treated and perceived as 'terrorism.' Instead, such violence was generally discussed as 'uses of force,' 'retaliation,' 'self-defense,' and 'security measures.'"[32]

Hence, national security discourse tends to analytically obfuscate the relational nature of conflict and violence. It also tends to delegitimize whatever grievances stimulate or motivate antistate activism (e.g., repression, discrimination, denial of the right to self-determination), thereby contributing to the delineation between "legitimate" and "illegitimate" communities, leaving the latter vulnerable to state violence, and enabling the state to justify that violence as a necessary reaction to terror.

These issues bear directly on the politics and discourse of conflict in Israel/Palestine. In Israeli national security discourse, Palestinians have been depicted, broadly and collectively, as terrorists or terrorist sympathizers. This depiction is not contingent on the idea that all Palestinians have engaged in or are supportive of activities like bombings, hijackings, and kidnappings or on the waxing and waning uses and popularity of "armed struggle" as a tactic of "national liberation." Rather, Israeli national security discourse has conflated Palestinian nationalism writ large with terrorism because it articulates demands and mobilizes aspirations that are incompatible with — and therefore threatening to — the Israeli state. Aspirations for a Palestinian state, if ever politically requited, would necessarily "carve into" or "roll back" the geographical space over which Israel exercises sovereignty. Even Palestinians' presence is construable as threatening (i.e., the "demographic threat") because, to accommodate their right to self-determination under Israeli rule, the character of the state would have to change.

Since 1948 and more so after 1967, Israeli national security discourse and policy making have dealt with this threat by criminalizing Palestinian nationalism. As Dana Briskman notes, "Generally speaking, everything connected to Palestinian Nationalist [sic] activities and especially to the PLO was considered prima facie a threat to security which could justify limitations and restrictions of rights."[33] Criminalization includes the obvious threats of violence and sabotage, but it also encompasses nonviolent activities, such as expressions of national identity (e.g., wearing the Palestinian national colors) and membership in or support for nationalist organizations.[34]

In the West Bank and Gaza, Israeli counterterrorist policies and practices have included arresting or killing individuals suspected of engaging in or planning violent actions against Israeli civilians or other Israeli targets; using violent interrogation tactics against tens of thousands of prisoners; clamping down on national organizations; and imposing collective punishments such as house demolitions, deportations, curfews, and closures. While these state practices differ and are instituted for different types of purposes (e.g., deterrence, reprisal, intelligence gathering), together they emanate from a state-centered view of Palestinians as threatening and thus punishable individually and collectively.

But the authority of the state to punish and constrain that which is deemed threatening is neither static nor a unidirectional exercise of power. Nor would it be accurate to say that Palestinians living under Israeli military occupation have no rights (as is sometimes argued by critics of the occupation as well as by some right-wing Jewish Israelis). Since 1967, there have been expansions and contractions of Palestinians' rights to education, assembly, and speech and opportunities afforded them to work, to travel, and to practice their religion.

In the early years of the occupation, punishment was directed mainly at those Palestinians engaging in militant resistance, thereby promoting an interest among the majority to be quiescent and cooperative in order to avoid punishment. As the occupation endured and the punishing powers of the state came to be seen as targeting all Palestinians, not only those who adopted a militant stance, a popular consciousness was fostered about the necessity and legitimacy of resistance. Resistance included initiatives to build national institutions (e.g., trade unions, schools, health and agricultural cooperatives) and struggles against routinized repression. By the mid-1980s, tens of thousands of Palestinians had been arrested and imprisoned, and an average of 4,500 people were in custody at any given time. The occupation had become a thoroughly carceral enterprise, and resisting it involved broad sectors of Palestinian society. For example, in early 1987, Ehud Barak, then head of the Central Command (the division responsible for the West Bank), was quoted as saying: "No longer is the [Israel Defense Forces (IDF)] pitted in battle in the territories mainly against terrorism, but against indigenous ideologies and ideas that flourish, not die when countered with force. The 'enemy' has been transformed from well-trained infiltrators and saboteurs, whom the IDF and security services were well-equipped to deal with, to students and school children; the weapons from bombs and grenades to stones, placards and slogans."[35]

The military court system is an exemplary setting for assessing the history and the dynamics of state security, resistance, and rights. Exercising its right to prosecute Palestinians has provided the state with a legalistic means of dealing with the political problem of resistance to the occupation (and the rights claims that animate that resistance). The state has used military and emergency laws and restricted or denied the application of international humanitarian and human rights laws to enhance Israeli security by putting a high cost on resistance. But the deleterious consequences of these laws and policies for growing numbers of Palestinians over the years have made the military court system a setting where law (specifically, international law) has been deployed to criticize and constrain the power and discretion of the state.

## Human Rights

In principle, human rights are "universal" because they extend to all human beings. Human rights, like other kinds of rights, are legal constructs, established and defined by international laws and conventions. Although the genealogy of human rights can be traced back to the eighteenth century, as a distinct category of legal entitlements they were "created" in the aftermath of World War II in a process triggered by the devastations and horrors of that war.

International lawmaking and legal reforms to establish and define human rights asserted a heretofore nonexistent recognition that people have rights *as humans* and not merely as protected classes of subjects in relations between states. As a consequence, people became "international subjects" with certain basic and common rights. Human rights laws established new international norms and rules of government, thereby circumscribing states' rights to do what they willed to people within their domain.[36] But this did not undermine the centrality and authority of states; rather, human rights obtain their "universalizing" character from the fact that people are subjects of states, and states are subjects of international law. In crucial ways, human rights law accommodates and even reinforces state sovereignty because it relies on individual states to behave and conform[37] and depends on the system of states to act against those that do not.

The processes associated with the establishment, development, and enforcement of human rights are manifestations of globalization — particularly the globalization of law. The term *human rights regime* refers to the global(ized) array of governmental and nongovernmental institutions and agents with mandates to make, monitor, and try to ensure adherence to a growing body of international laws and conventions. Its function could be compared to a legal order that operates on an international scale, although it lacks both a centralized power base (other than the amorphous "international community") and the kind of semiautonomy that would provide independent means of enforcement.

Because of the institutional weaknesses of law enforcement mechanisms at the interstate level, human rights activism emerged as an organized response to promote adherence and enforceability of international laws. Nongovernmental organizations (NGOs) with human rights mandates were established to operate in the breach, beginning in the early 1960s with the founding of Amnesty International and escalating in the 1970s and 1980s as human rights NGOs mushroomed around the world.[38]

Human rights activism comprises a variety of strategies, notably monitoring and reporting on violations to foster awareness, advocacy work to encourage actions or interventions to curb or stop violations, and litigation to adjudicate the applicability and enforceability of international laws. Over the last thirty years, human rights activism and networking developed to fulfill a panoptic function of international surveillance by investigating, documenting, protesting, and sometimes prosecuting violations.[39]

These developments, and the social, legal, and political forces behind them, indicate the ways in which international law affects and influences people's consciousness about themselves and the world and stimulates politically significant action and interaction. Even enduring and divisive debates over human rights (e.g., the legitimacy or biases of "universal" standards, appropriate means of enforcement) exemplify the globalization of law by encouraging people around the world to appropriate — or forcing them to contend with — the language and principles of international human rights in relation to local needs, expectations, and circumstances.[40]

Although human rights are, by definition, "international," they are available as legal entitlements only when they gain "local" recognition and enforceability. In many countries, even the most modest provisions (e.g., the right to freedom of movement) or widely recognized prohibitions (e.g., torture and slavery) have been stymied, ignored, or violated by local authorities.

When people's rights are denied or violated by the state that rules them, international law serves as a last resort, a countervailing source of authority to challenge prevailing arrangements of power and opportunity. Forms of resistance that draw upon international human rights laws are strategic uses of legalism to legitimize and wage local struggles for rights. While resistance clearly can provoke crises and retributive responses on the part of those whose interests are being assailed, the utility of framing resistance as demands for human rights (as compared, for example, to more expressly militant or particularistic demands) is that it serves to internationalize local conflicts: it subjects local authority to international scrutiny and sometimes stimulates responses, solidarity, and pressures to bring human rights standards to bear.

## Sociology of Human Rights

Since human rights are legal rights, a sociology of human rights shares many of the concerns relevant to sociology of law. One obvious commonality is the importance and centrality of the state to any analysis of rights. Yet given that human rights are international, sociology of human rights "liberates" inquiries from the confines of the domestic/national arena.

This study is, in some regards and by necessity, a sociology of human rights. First, the complexity of social, political, and legal categories and boundaries in Israel/Palestine and the transnational nature of government defy any attempt to frame analysis in terms of a nation/state/society relationship. Second, because of the origins (war) and nature (foreign occupation) of Israeli rule in the West Bank and Gaza, international laws have provided particularly salient points of reference; in fact, debates over the Israeli state's rights and responsibilities in the West Bank and Gaza have constituted some of the most elaborate efforts to interpret the Fourth Geneva Convention, the main body of international humanitarian law governing military administration of occupied territories, and the circumstances under which it might be superseded or ignored by other considerations (e.g., security, "historic rights").

Third, because military occupation in general, and Israeli military rule over Palestinians as a particular manifestation, is "foreign," there is no domestic/national politico-legal order to which Palestinians can orient their claims and demands for rights. Thus, international law serves not as a "last resort" but as the only *legal* resort available to Palestinians to articulate their demands and aspirations for rights. But perhaps most importantly, a sociology of human rights allows for an engagement with the range of issues implicated in the struggles over rights — of individuals, nations, and states — that shape and sustain the Israeli-Palestinian conflict.

The military court system provides an important institutional setting for mapping the history and development of human rights in Israel/Palestine. Starting in the late 1970s, human rights discourse and strategies were adopted and deployed not only to explain the problems and rights violations inherent in prolonged occupation but also to provide a frame of reference for arguments about how things should be. This constituted an explicit challenge to the discourse and politics of Israeli national security that anything could be justified in the fight against "terrorism." But it also challenged the discourse of Palestinian nationalist militancy that anything could be justified in the fight for "liberation."

What is explored in detail in the following chapter is the ways in which human rights discourse emerged as a counternarrative to official Israeli legal discourse, providing language and criteria to evaluate and criticize the policies and practices of the state. In this regard, the military courts have served as a setting that is both vital and central to understanding how local politics in Israel/Palestine link up with — affect and are affected by — the globalized discourse and politics of human rights.

# CHAPTER 2

# Legal Discourses
# and the Conflict in Israel/Palestine

*Law works in the world not just by the imposition of rules and
punishments but also by its capacity to construct authoritative
images of social relationships and actions, images [that] are
symbolically powerful.*
Sally Engle Merry, *Getting Justice and Getting Even*[1]

The Israeli state has made prodigious use of law to maintain and legitimize its rule over Palestinians in the West Bank and Gaza and to punish
and thwart resistance. Three bodies of law have been particularly important: international humanitarian law (especially the Fourth Geneva
Convention), the British Defense (Emergency) Regulations of 1945, and
original Israeli military laws. Israeli domestic law also figures into an
analysis of Israeli rule in the West Bank and Gaza because it was extended
to annexed and appropriated areas and to citizens who have settled
there.

Opponents and critics of Israel's occupation also have used law to contest and resist Israeli policies deleterious to Palestinians and to frame
Palestinian aspirations and interests as rights claims. Indeed, it was Israel's
enthusiasm for law and the ornate legalism of official discourse that cat-
alyzed and propelled the development of a local human rights movement,
which served as the harbinger of legalistic resistance. Because of the
importance the Israeli state attaches to law and to its own image as law
abiding, legal challenges and critiques could not be ignored; rather, they

provoked or necessitated refinements, reforms, and defensive justifications for the state's positions and policies.

In this chapter, I present a social history of legal discourses and conflict in Israel/Palestine. I begin with the history of the military administration instituted by Israel in the West Bank and Gaza and the legal doctrines formulated to support state policies in these areas. I situate these developments within the broader context of the conflict to show how Jewish historical claims and Israeli political ambitions and national interests, as well as security contingencies, have informed official legal discourse — what Israeli officials and supporters of the state could claim as "legal" and why. I then track the subsequent development of a counterdiscourse that criticizes and challenges the state's interpretations and uses of law and the claims of legality of state policies and practices that harm the interests or infringe on the rights of Palestinians. The final section focuses on the legal debates, policy developments, and litigation relating specifically to interrogation and torture.

## War, Conquest, and Control

The 1967 war massively transformed the territorial and demographic maps of the Middle East and the political agendas of the various parties to the Arab-Israeli conflict. While there is no debate that the Israeli military launched the first strikes in 1967, there is disagreement as to whether this was a "defensive" war to preempt an impending attack by Arab states[2] or an "offensive" war waged for the purpose of conquering additional territories. The official Israeli position holds that the neighboring Arab regimes incited hostilities through incessant warmongering and preparations to attack[3] and that Israel preempted the risk of a multifront assault by striking first.

A consideration of the history of the military administration in the West Bank and Gaza provides an interesting perspective on events and developments leading up to the 1967 war. The Israeli military court system was established on the third day of the Six Day War as one of the first official acts of the military administration.[4] This timing is significant because it suggests not only the primacy that Israel attaches to law but also a high degree of preparedness for war and occupation. Israeli preparations for military occupation began in the early 1960s, spurred by political instability in Jordan in 1963. These plans were informed by Israel's brief experience of occupying Gaza during the 1956 invasion of Egypt by Israel, Britain, and France.[5]

The most extensive planning for occupation occurred under the direction of the Military Advocate General (MAG). Meir Shamgar, who served as the MAG from 1961 to 1968, provides an account of his unit's activities in the years preceding the war.[6] According to Shamgar, in the early 1960s he developed courses for officers of his unit through which they "carried out skeleton exercises in military government problems."[7] He also prepared a comprehensive *Manual for the Military Advocate in Military Government,* which consisted of "moveable emergency kits including basic legal textbooks and other material necessary for the performance of their duties, and *inter alia* a large set of precedents of military government proclamations and orders, vital at the initial stages of military government, as well as detailed legal and organizational instructions and guide-lines. These facilitated, from the outset, the legal and administrative activity of the sections, according to a *previously planned scheme.*"[8]

Shamgar explains that in developing the MAG unit's legal manual he incorporated "a concise resume of the municipal law in force in the different enemy countries neighboring Israel, [although the manual] did not refer specifically to the modalities of applying [them because it] was prepared a long time before hostilities began."[9] The preface to the manual states: "[T]raining and exercise [in peacetime] cannot reflect precisely either the reality of an administered area or the specific circumstances of time and place. . . . The main obvious limitation which this Manual is unable to remove is inherent in the fact that it was prepared *before* the development of the actual circumstances in which it will have to be applied in practice. Not all problems and their solutions could be foreseen."[10]

In the immediate aftermath of the 1967 war, most Israeli military and political decision makers assumed that the defeated Arab regimes would be forced to recognize Israel and pursue a diplomatic resolution to the conflict in order to regain their own lost territory. However, the prospect of a land-for-peace exchange among states would apply only to the Syrian Golan Heights and the Egyptian Sinai Peninsula. The conquest of the West Bank and Gaza — the remainders of historic Palestine — raised entirely different issues for Israel. Of particular importance was the fact that the West Bank and Gaza were not sovereign territories of the states ruling them at the time of the 1967 war (Jordan and Egypt, respectively), that their Palestinian inhabitants had no state of their own to enter into negotiation on their behalf, and that these areas constituted part of the ancient Jewish kingdom.

Israel's conquest of the West Bank and Gaza with their 1.5 million Palestinian inhabitants (a population now numbering almost three million) was, in the words of Shabtai Teveth, a "cursed blessing." It transformed the "Palestinian problem" from a largely external matter of defending borders into an internal matter of government. After 1967, one-third of the population living under Israeli rule was Palestinian Arabs. Territorially, the conquest provided Israel with new strategic depth, which was capitalized upon immediately through the confiscation of sparsely populated areas along the Jordan valley for military settlements. But politically, the problems of governing such a sizable population of "enemy civilians" were considerable, more so in Gaza than the West Bank; the Gaza Strip is one of the most densely populated areas in the world, and over 60 percent of the population are refugees from the 1948 war and their descendants, living in squalid, crowded camps.

Palestinians, who found themselves literally overnight living under Israeli military rule, were shocked by the Arab defeat and unprepared for the new arrangements. For the first several years, manifestations of open resistance were limited, for the most part, to armed attacks by *feda'yin* (guerrillas; literally meaning those who sacrifice themselves), including some people residing in the occupied territories and others sneaking across the new boundaries of Israeli control. Palestinian *feda'yin* in Gaza were aided by Egypt as part of a war of attrition (1969–71), waged to offset the humiliating Arab defeat. Those based in Jordan had the benefit of a long, difficult-to-monitor border to enter into the West Bank.

Some *feda'yin* who were captured by the Israeli military were tried and convicted in the new military courts. But at that early stage, the court system was functioning in a rather limited capacity because the Israeli authorities were making broad use of administrative measures such as detention and deportation to punish and deter armed resistance. Because *feda'yin* generally regarded themselves as soldiers in a war of liberation, those who were captured and tried tended to regard themselves as prisoners of war.[11]

In 1970–71, the Israeli military undertook a "pacification" campaign in Gaza to crush the armed resistance. Thousands of Palestinians (including entire families) were transferred to camps in the Sinai to undercut local assistance for fighters, and wide avenues were bulldozed through crowded camps and towns to facilitate Israeli surveillance and the movement of troops and military vehicles. The imposed quiescence provided the authorities with the latitude to institute more legalistic means of control, including expansion of the military court system.

## The Changing Conflict

The larger, long-term consequences of the 1967 war were dramatic, notably an escalation of the Israeli-Palestinian dimension of the Arab-

Israeli conflict. The defeat of the Arab regimes emboldened the Palestinian resistance movement, composed of a number of militant political factions based in the surrounding Arab states, to assume leadership of the national struggle.[12] The Palestine Liberation Organization (PLO), created in 1964 by the Arab regimes, was taken over and transformed into an umbrella organization by these factions after the war. Ahmed Shuqueiry, the appointed PLO leader, was replaced by Yasir Arafat, head of the largest faction, Fatah. Despite the further fragmentation of the Palestinian people as a result of the war, the "new" PLO provided an increasingly popular symbol of national solidarity and a vehicle of national liberation.[13]

The political agenda of the PLO conformed to prevailing tendencies across the region to interpret the stakes of the conflict in zero-sum terms; Palestinian victory was envisioned as a thorough defeat of Israel and the creation of a Palestinian state in all of historic Palestine. Israeli political discourse also propounded zero-sum visions; there was a national consensus opposing an independent Palestinian state, and Israeli officials sought to offset the growing popularity and influence of the PLO by promoting a states-only framework for conflict resolution. While most of the international community came to recognize the PLO as the legitimate national representative of the Palestinian people by the mid-1970s, the Israeli state was at the forefront of efforts to disqualify the PLO from playing a role in regional and international relations on the grounds that it was nothing but a terrorist organization. As far as most Jewish Israelis were concerned, Palestinians had no independent, legitimate representative, and those who supported the PLO were in effect proponents of terrorism.[14] However, Israel did recognize the PLO in one regard: as a party to the conflict.

## The Construction of a Legal Doctrine for Governing the Territories

In the early years, the idea of retaining permanent control of the West Bank and Gaza, especially the large Palestinian population centers, was not seriously entertained within Israeli decision-making circles.[15] However, from the outset, Meir Shamgar constructed a legal doctrine to legitimize permanent Israeli retention of at least part of the conquered areas. Prior to 1967, Shamgar had conceived that that the extension of Israeli rule over any additional part of *Eretz Israel* (i.e., the West Bank and Gaza) would not constitute a "foreign occupation" because Jews had historic rights in these areas and because no other state had sovereign claim to them. After 1967, he used his position as a high-ranking policy maker to institute his views as the cornerstone of official Israeli doctrine on the legal status of the territories.

This doctrine incorporated a number of interrelated components and premises, which together reflected selective use and "original" interpretations of international humanitarian law (i.e., laws of war). First, Shamgar reasoned that Israeli control of the West Bank and Gaza did not constitute an "occupation" because the displaced rulers, Jordan and Egypt, were themselves occupants who had seized control during the first Arab-Israeli war in 1948. This was premised on the assertion that territory is "occupied" in war only if it has been part of the sovereign domain of the defeated and expelled state. According to Shamgar's formulation, Israel was not "occupying" but "administrating" these "disputed" areas, whose legal status was sui generis.[16]

A second component, building on the first, held that the Fourth Geneva Convention, the most important humanitarian law pertaining to occupation of conquered territories and their civilian population, was not applicable to Israeli rule on a de jure basis. Shamgar reasoned that if Israel were to regard the Fourth Geneva Convention as applicable, this would constitute an acknowledgment of Israel's own status as an "occupant," which, in turn, would both give Jordan and Egypt an ex post facto status as displaced sovereigns that they had not enjoyed prior to their defeat, and would compromise or jeopardize Israeli prospects to claim permanent control over (all or some of) the territories in the future.[17] The history and language of the Geneva Conventions bear upon this interpretation; they were promulgated in the aftermath of World War II to prohibit the grotesque "liberties" that the Axis powers had exercised in the areas they occupied during the war. The Fourth Geneva Convention delineates the rights and duties of "High Contracting Parties" (i.e., signatory states) vis-à-vis territories and populations of other High Contracting Parties. Since Jordan and Egypt had been occupants rather than sovereigns in the West Bank and Gaza, according to Shamgar's reasoning, they did not have the status as High Contracting Parties *in these areas*. And while Israel was a High Contracting Party to the Geneva Conventions, this would have no bearing on territories that were not "occupied."

A third and somewhat contradictory component of Shamgar's doctrine was that Israel would abide by the Fourth Geneva Convention on a de facto basis, namely to respect its "humanitarian provisions." However, Israeli officials have never specified which provisions of the convention they do — or do not — regard as "humanitarian,"[18] whereas the International Committee of the Red Cross (ICRC), official guardian of the Geneva Conventions, regards them as humanitarian in their entirety and rejects any attempts to interpret this legislation selectively.[19] Shamgar noted but dismissed the relevance of the ICRC's views: "From the very outset of the military government, Israel and the International Committee of the Red Cross arrived at diametrically opposed conclusions concerning the applicability of the Fourth Geneva Convention to the administered areas. This difference of views was mainly and primarily of a legal and theoretical nature, because the Israeli Governmental [sic] authorities stated several times that Israel had decided to distinguish *a priori* between the formal legal conclusions arising from its approach and the actual observance of the humanitarian provisions of the Convention."[20]

A fourth component of the doctrine held that the Fourth Geneva Convention could not be binding on Israel even if there were no dispute over the status of the West Bank and Gaza because at least part of the convention constituted "conventional" rather than "customary" international law.[21] Therefore, even if the convention were deemed applicable on a de jure basis, it would not supersede "local" laws unless the Israeli Knesset enacted the convention as domestic legislation or until the state recognized that it had ripened into customary international law. However, the international community overwhelmingly regards the Geneva Conventions as customary international law.[22]

A crucial aspect of this doctrine is the way in which Palestinian statelessness was made legally significant. Interpreting international humanitarian laws as pertaining exclusively to the rights and duties of sovereign states ("High Contracting Parties") made it possible to argue that stateless people in militarily conquered areas were not their intended beneficiaries. This assumed that because there never had been an independent state of "Palestine," the Palestinian people could not be the rightful sovereigns of the West Bank and Gaza because nothing in international law prescribed the recognition of sovereignty to a "nonstate" and nothing demanded the creation of a heretofore nonexistent state in territories seized in war. Nodding to the de facto applicability of undefined "humanitarian provisions" in the Fourth Geneva Convention was a means of acknowledging that Palestinians had rights as individuals but not as a national entity.[23] According to this doctrine, Israel was under no *legal obligation* to withdraw from any part of the West Bank and Gaza to allow them to revert back to their pre-1967 status[24] or to concede to the creation of a Palestinian state.

Shamgar's focus on the status of land (holding that it was sui generis) rather than the population (with national rights to self-determination) was a strategic legal maneuver to separate the land from the people residing there. The doctrine and the interpretations of international law on which it was based came to define official Israeli legal discourse and policy making regarding the state's rights and duties in the West Bank and Gaza and was reinforced by rulings of the Israeli High Court of Justice (HCJ).[25] Within a domestic Israeli context, HCJ support was crucial to legitimizing these interpretations and gaining public sanction for activities and policies that violated the letter and/or spirit of the Fourth Geneva Convention, such as the settlement of Israeli citizens in the territories, the deportation of Palestinians, house demolitions, and other forms of collective punishment. However, the international community never accepted the official Israeli interpretation that the West Bank and Gaza were not occupied or that Israeli rule was not governed by the Fourth Geneva Convention and other international laws.

This contradiction between international opinion and the official Israeli position suggests a larger tension between the rights of sovereign states and the trend in international legal discourse since World War II, which seeks to curb the excesses of state autonomy. In charting such an original course for itself, the Israeli state has reinforced its own sovereign authority locally and internationally by resisting or ignoring the authority of the international community in the interpretation of humanitarian laws governing states in war and conflict. However, Israel has not rejected the importance of legality to assessments of its rule in the West Bank and Gaza. Rather, officials and state supporters have maintained that Israeli policies and practices are legally viable, if different from international opinion; that Israel has the right, as a sovereign state, to interpret its obligations independently because these interpretations arise out of actual conditions on the ground (including claims of historic Jewish rights and the imperatives of national security); and that the state cannot be forced to accept alternative interpretations because these are advanced in an attempt to constrain Israel politically (and perhaps to benefit its enemies).[26] Moreover, international criticism of Israel has been countered with criticism of the international community, whose historic hostility and/or indifference to the rights and the fate of Jews culminated in the Nazi Holocaust. Criticisms have been taken as evidence of an enduring global anti-Semitism, a perception reinforced by Israel's treatment as a pariah by the General Assembly of the United Nations[27] and by international recognition and support for the PLO.

## The (Limited) Role of the High Court of Justice

Meir Shamgar's other crucial contribution to the administration of the West Bank and Gaza was instituted after 1968 when he became attorney general. He established Palestinians' right to submit petitions to the HCJ to challenge the administrative policies and practices of any state institution, including the military. He did this by never raising "the plea of a lack of *locus standi* of alien enemies who were inhabitants of territory not under Israeli sovereignty."[28] This contributed significantly to Israeli claims and pronouncements that the administration of the territories was "enlightened," "benign," and unique in the history of war: Israel was under no legal obligation to subject the military administration to domestic judicial oversight. To do so, Shamgar argued, demonstrated the state's commitment to the rule of law: "Military government did not succumb to the dangers inherent in the exercise of absolute power. . . . Furthermore, the individuals manning the diverse positions in military government, were inevitably the products of their culture and carried with them the impact of the legal and moral concepts of their society. . . . It seems that the institutional pluralism and the dispersion of power in the Israeli political system and to a very large extent the supervisory powers of the Supreme Court of Justice, imposed additional constraints and ensured the prevention or correction of transgressions."[29]

Although the role of the HCJ is parenthetical to the subject of the military court system,[30] it does pertain to questions and debates about the legality of Israeli rule in the West Bank and Gaza. Using legal concepts of "reasonableness," "justicability," and "necessity," the HCJ has reviewed the activities of the military administration when petitioned to do so. In practice, however, the HCJ rarely has rendered decisions that provide substantive relief to Palestinian petitioners, tending either to find in favor of the state or to dismiss the petitions on the grounds that they raise issues that are not justiciable.[31] For example, in a 1972 case *(Abu Hilu et al. v. Government of Israel)*, the HCJ decision states: "The court is not the proper place to decide whether a military-security operation . . . — if grounded in law and undertaken for reasons of security — was indeed warranted by the security situation or whether the security problem could have been resolved by different means. . . . [I]ssues related to the army and defense, similar to issues of foreign affairs, are not among the subjects fit for judicial review."[32]

The HCJ has played an important role in supporting and sanctioning military and administrative policies that have negatively affected Palestinians. The availability of judicial review maintains a perception among the majority of Jewish Israelis, who hold the court in the highest regard, that such oversight guarantees that Palestinians' rights are adequately safeguarded under the prevailing circumstances and that the ways the state interprets its own rights and duties in the territories are legal. This perception has been fortified by the fact that over the decades Palestinians have brought thousands of petitions before the HCJ.[33]

The actual record of the HCJ, however, has not restrained the state in its policies toward Palestinians in the West Bank and Gaza. According to David Kretzmer, who published a detailed study of cases from the occupied territories, "The Court has not seen itself as a body that should question the legality under international law of policies or actions of the authorities, or should interpret the law in a rights-minded fashion. On the contrary, it has accepted and legitimized policies and actions the legality of which is highly dubious and has interpreted law in favor of the authorities."[34]

## Dual Legal System

Israel's official legal doctrine maintaining that the conquered territories were separable from the Palestinians residing there made it possible to legalistically justify the extension and entrenchment of Jewish control over this land. This "ethnonational" specification is crucial to understanding the reasoning and the policies that ensued.[35] Israel's claims to the land are grounded in the idea that the Jewish nation has historic rights to these areas because they were the site of the ancient Jewish kingdom. Indeed, the official term for the West Bank became *Judea and Samaria* to mark this history and claim. As this has translated into policy, among Israeli citizens, only Jews are allowed the "right" to settle in the territories.

The process of extending domestic Israeli jurisdiction into the West Bank and Gaza began immediately. On July 2, 1967, only weeks after the war, the Knesset enacted a law giving domestic Israeli courts concurrent jurisdiction with courts in the territories.[36] This law ensured that Israeli citizens would not be subject to military and emergency laws used to govern Palestinians and provided an alternative venue to try those accused of committing offenses in the territories.[37] An explanatory note stated that this law was not intended to apply to "a person who is a resident of the territories," meaning a Palestinian. A decade later, when tens of thousands of Israelis had become "residents" of the territories (i.e., settlers), a further clarification was made, stating that the law applied exclusively to people "registered in the [Israeli] Population Register."

The dual legal system in the West Bank and Gaza is constituted through separate jurisdictions, laws, and legal institutions for Israeli citizens and Palestinians.[38] The system that applies to citizens is, for all intents and purposes, an extension of Israeli sovereignty into the territories and amounts to a de facto annexation. The extension of domestic laws and access to domestic legal institutions to citizens who have taken up residency in the West Bank or Gaza as settlers has profoundly reduced — if not altogether erased — the legal significance of the Green Line as far as the rights of Jewish Israeli citizens are concerned.

Palestinians in the West Bank and Gaza have been governed by the Israeli military, and virtually all aspects of their lives have been related to Israeli security and regulated by military and emergency laws. Israeli military officials have made abundant use of their lawmaking powers to generate a vast body of original military legislation and have justified this as their right according to international law. The Fourth Geneva Convention establishes the right of an occupying force to legislate original military orders as well as to amend existing legislation (i.e., local laws) to allow for the contingencies of security and public order. However, when faced with criticism that the content and enforcement of some military orders violate the Fourth Geneva Convention, the official response has tended to emphasize that the convention is not binding on Israel in these areas on a de jure basis.[39] In other words, the Fourth Geneva Convention has been drawn upon to justify the making of law but has been rejected as a framework for the content of law.

By the early 1990s, the Israeli military had legislated over 1,300 orders for the West Bank and over 1,000 for Gaza. Although Israeli authorities have claimed that military orders were properly promulgated and distributed in Hebrew and Arabic, IDF has never published a comprehensive compendium of orders in force in the territories.[40] Furthermore, assessing the enforcement of this legislation has been difficult because of the scarcity of publicly available information about rulings of the military courts.[41]

In addition to military orders, Israel also has used the British Defense (Emergency) Regulations (1945), which date from the British Mandate over Palestine, to govern Palestinians. Ironically, when these laws were applied to the Jewish community prior to 1948, Jewish leaders condemned them as outrageous and reprehensible. At a 1946 meeting of the

(Jewish) Lawyers Association, Dr. Dunkelbaum (who later became a High Court justice) said, "The laws contradict the most fundamental principles of law, justice and jurisprudence. They give the military and administrative authorities the power to impose penalties which, even had they been ratified by a legislative body, could only be regarded as anarchical and irregular."[42]

However, after independence, Israeli officials decided to preserve the British Defense Regulations in order to use their emergency powers, while deflecting responsibility for their draconian character to the British, who had imposed them in the first place. In the early years of statehood, right-wing Jews feared that the British Defense Regulations would be used by the Labor government against them, but Jewish opposition dissipated in 1951 when it became unwritten policy that they would not apply to Jews, only to Arabs, who had no influence over the state's legislative policies.

Although the British Defense Regulations were used against Arab citizens of Israel for several decades,[43] the first challenges to their legality were mounted in the HCJ on behalf of petitioners from the West Bank and Gaza after 1967.[44] One type of challenge contested the state's right to use these laws at all because the British had revoked the Defense Regulations on May 12, 1948,[45] several days before the mandate ended. Thus, they were no longer in effect on May 15 when Israel declared independence. According to this argument, the regulations could not be "maintained"; rather, they would have to be reissued as original Israeli legislation. The official Israeli response countered that the regulations remained in force because the British had not published the revocation order in the *Palestine Gazette,* thus characterizing the order as a "hidden law." This position was upheld and confirmed by the HCJ in 1979.[46]

A second type of challenge related to the legality of the British Defense Regulations on the grounds that they have become anachronistic in the post–World War II era because many of their provisions have been outlawed by developments in international law. The official response was that Israel was *bound by international law* — including the Fourth Geneva Convention — to maintain the regulations in the West Bank and Gaza as part of the "local laws" in force at the time of the conquest.[47] This was based on the assertion that the regulations remained in effect because the Jordanian and Egyptian governments had never canceled them (thus implying that these states also rejected the validity of the British revocation), even though they were never used in either region between 1948 and 1967. Thus, the Fourth Geneva Convention was drawn upon for the purpose of justifying the maintenance of the regulations as local laws, while at the same time being disregarded because it explicitly prohibited certain provisions of the regulations. The rationale for this contradiction was premised on the principle that local laws have precedence over "conventional" international laws.[48]

## Forging a Legal Critique of Israeli Rule

From the beginning of the occupation through the end of the 1970s, some scholars wrote critically about Israeli policies in the West Bank and Gaza and the legal premises underlying them.[49] But these works did not constitute a comprehensive critique of the official legal doctrine or the legality of the military and emergency laws. Nor was much attention focused on law or legalism in scholarly writing about the Palestinian national struggle.

This general inattention to law extended to the Israeli military court system, about which very little was written in the first decade of occupation. One possible explanation is that the military courts tended to be regarded by everyone as a space where resistance "ended." Viewed in this light, resistance was seen as — and limited to — militancy and public protests, and arrest was deemed a foreclosure of political agency and opportunity.

Looking more closely at the operations of the military court system, one can see early signs of resistance within this setting, including the decision of politicized lawyers to take up military court work (see Chapter 6). Yet until the end of the 1970s, lawyers who aspired to challenge the military administration by engaging larger questions and debates about the legality of Israeli law and policies found few opportunities to do so through their legal practice. Part of the problem was the lack of any already formulated critique of official Israeli legal discourse. The first efforts to redress this lacuna were undertaken by a few military court lawyers.

The process of forging a legal critique of Israeli military rule began in 1979 with the creation of Law in the Service of Man (LSM, later renamed Al-Haq). LSM, the first Palestinian human rights organization, was established as a West Bank affiliate of the International Commission of Jurists (ICJ). By adopting an explicit rule-of-law mandate (in keeping with that of the ICJ), the lawyers who founded LSM eschewed nationalist militancy and promoted the organization as nonpolitical and legal. Framing their criticisms of the occupation in terms of international law was a significant innovation: it represented the first organized effort to engage law as a form of resistance.

LSM's monitoring and reporting strategies challenged the official Israeli narrative that the state was governing legally by documenting how (and how pervasively) the military administration failed to adhere to rule-of-law standards and to abide by relevant international laws. LSM produced two types of publications, one geared mainly to an international audience that presented legal rebuttals of Israeli positions based on international law, the other geared to a local constituency to inform them of their rights and offer ways of challenging specific actions of the military administration.[50]

From the outset, LSM faced three major problems: being a Palestinian organization under Israeli occupation; seeking to address grievances in a context in which Palestinians "were generally held to be incapable of dispassionate investigation of anything concerning Israel"; and documenting violations by the Israeli state at a time when Israel had an international reputation as "not a serious offender" of human rights compared to other Middle Eastern regimes.[51] LSM responded to this predicament by denying the relevance of politics to human rights and referring exclusively to international law in its appraisal of Israeli conduct. While such a position earned the organization credibility among international human rights organizations,[52] Israeli officials consistently tried to discredit its work by charging that that the organization was a front for the PLO, and some Palestinians disparaged LSM's avowedly nonpolitical stance.

The people affiliated with LSM were pioneers in the development of a critical legal discourse on the Israeli military administration. In 1980, two of the organization's founders, Raja Shehadeh and Jonathan Kuttab, published *The West Bank and the Rule of Law*.[53] This book, describing changes in the West Bank legal system since the onset of occupation, was the first effort to compile a comprehensive account of Israel's uses of emergency laws and military orders. It was, in part, a response to their own and their colleagues' needs as practicing lawyers to understand and evaluate the environment in which they were working (and living). The publication of this book was groundbreaking in that it translated the problems of the occupation into a human rights framework and set in motion what would come to characterize the production of knowledge about the legality of Israeli rule: a cycle of criticism and rejoinder.

A rejoinder to Shehadeh and Kuttab's book was published in 1981 under the title *The Rule of Law in the Territories Administered by Israel*.[54] Although not an official publication, it was authored by Israeli govern-

ment lawyers and quickly acquired the status as one of the most important public articulations of the government's position on the legal basis
for its policies. In the foreword, Haim Cohen, a justice on the HCJ,
describes Shehadeh and Kuttab's book as a *tracatus politicus,* contrasting
it with the book he is introducing, which he refers to as "a sober statement
of law and fact."[55] He asserts that "[w]hile the study of Messrs. Shehadeh
and Kuttab can in no way be accepted as a correct statement either of the
facts or the law, it is a welcome challenge to state both fact and law as they
really are — not unlike a legal pleading whose *ratio vivendi* is to stand until
authoritatively corrected."[56]

In 1985, Shehadeh published a second book, *Occupier's Law: Israel and
the West Bank,* which includes a rejoinder to *The Rule of Law in the
Territories Administered by Israel.* In the introduction, he writes:

Lawyers in the military administration of the West Bank . . . attempted to justify Israel's activities by referring to international law to prove the consistency of
these actions with the law of occupation. It is clear, therefore, that Israel takes
the position that its activities in the West Bank are governed by international law
and are consistent with it. . . . This declared policy is irreconcilable with the facts
which seem to indicate that the Israeli goal is gradually to drive out the local
Palestinian population and to annex the territory. Israel has been astute in the
way it has tried and still tries to present all it is doing in terms of the international
law of occupation.[57]

By the mid-1980s, a modest but mounting body of scholarship was
formulating increasingly elaborate critiques of Israel's violations of international law in the occupied territories.[58] As a result, issues that previously
had been ignored or treated as political problems were coming to be
couched in a legal language, and this helped foster a local human rights
movement through the establishment of new organizations.

The Gaza Center for Rights and Law, a Gaza affiliate of the ICJ, was
established in 1981. It pursued strategies similar to those of LSM/Al-Haq,
although with fewer resources and a smaller staff. The Palestine Human
Rights Information Center, a branch of the Jerusalem-based Arab Studies
Society, put more emphasis on political activism and networking with
other local institutions and less on legal research and argumentation than
LSM/Al-Haq.[59]

On the other side of the Green Line, through the mid-1980s the main
Israeli organization engaged in work relating to the rights of Palestinians
was the Association for Civil Rights in Israel (ACRI). Modeled on the
American Civil Liberties Union, ACRI's mandate pertained to civil and

political rights. Its work in the territories concentrated on cases in which individuals' right to due process was being violated or compromised (especially administrative detention and forms of collective punishment). Although ACRI was critical of some of the Israeli state's practices, it did not criticize the occupation, champion Palestinians' national/collective rights, or assert a position independent of the state's official legal doctrine.[60]

## The Palestine Problem
## and the International Human Rights Movement

By the mid-1980s, the international human rights movement was becoming increasingly attentive to the situation in the West Bank and Gaza. This attention was spurred by escalating tensions in the region, including Israel's invasion of Lebanon in 1982, the expulsion of the PLO from Lebanon to Tunisia, and the massacre of hundreds of civilians in the Sabra and Shatila refugee camps outside Beirut.

In 1985, to crush growing resistance and capitalize on the weakness of the PLO, the IDF instituted harsher governing policies, referred to officially as the "Iron Fist." This entailed more vigorous and violent efforts to prohibit political demonstrations in support of the PLO and solidarity with other Palestinian communities, as well as heightened restrictions (including closures) of Palestinian institutions. The Iron Fist also entailed an expanding use of administrative measures such as detention, deportation, and house demolitions. In such an atmosphere, local human rights organizations were appealing to international human rights organizations for support to bring international pressure to bear on Israel.

One of the most difficult issues facing the international human rights movement in the 1970s and 1980s, not only in Israel/Palestine but in other trouble spots around the world, was disagreement and uncertainty over how international laws could or should apply in conflicts pitting nonstate movements against states. These questions were further complicated by the fact that many such movements included militarized wings and that armed struggle was supported by large sectors of the populations. Such questions applied not only to the conflict in Israel/Palestine but also to conflicts raging in South Africa, Northern Ireland, and elsewhere.

Amnesty International (AI), the most prominent international human rights organization at that time, pursued a narrow mandate focusing on political prisoners, fair trials, and an end to torture and executions. In charting its position on the relationship between human rights and conflicts, AI made the use or advocacy of violence the crucial point of distinction. In its work on Israel/Palestine, AI "refused to accept Israel's argument that membership in the [PLO] by itself constitutes the advocacy or use of violence and is therefore a punishable offense."[61] However, in comparison to its coverage of the situation in apartheid South Africa, AI was more cautious in its support for Palestinian prisoners and more circumspect in its criticisms of the Israeli state.[62]

International human rights organizations' criticisms of state agents, institutions, and activities in turn elicited countercriticisms that they were politically and/or ideologically biased, since they were not offering up comparable critiques of the activities of nonstate organizations (e.g., the PLO, the African National Congress, the Irish Republican Army). In their defense, human rights organizations often pointed out that international law did not provide the kinds of obligations or evaluative measures for nonstates as it did for states. At the heart of these debates were discrepant views over how to interpret the conflicts themselves, namely whether resistance activities against states constituted terrorism or legitimate struggles for self-determination. Such debates reflected, more generally, the stakes and opportunities during an era when international politics were dominated by Cold War rivalries. Human rights monitoring, reporting, and advocacy about the situation in Israel/Palestine were affected by the enduring Arab-Israeli conflict, as well as Israel's "special relationship" to the United States and the strategic alignment between some "frontline" Arab states and the USSR.

## The First *Intifada*

The outbreak of the Palestinian *intifada* in December 1987 had dramatic effects on all aspects of Israeli-Palestinian relations. Extensive media coverage of the popular resistance and the military's responses made local events into international news and increased international awareness and concern about Israel's policies in the West Bank and Gaza. International demands for information about what was happening in Israel/Palestine elevated the profile and expanded the role of local human rights organizations. Holly Burkhalter, the former advocacy director of Human Rights Watch, expressed particular praise for Al-Haq's work during the *intifada*: "There weren't at that time many groups in the [global] South that were doing such highly sophisticated human rights investigations. To have *that* kind of quality of documentation, especially from Palestinians, was very important in dispelling the prejudice that existed. In the United States, 'Palestinian' was an adjective modifying the noun 'terrorist.' Al-Haq's work was essential in getting out the truth not only about human rights violations in the occupied territories, but about Palestinians themselves."[63]

The *intifada* focused unprecedented attention on the military court system because arrest and prosecution were key strategies used by the Israeli military to try to crush resistance and restore order. Most local human rights organizations and many international organizations issued reports on some aspect(s) of the military court system.[64] In keeping with the prior pattern of criticism and rejoinder, there was a concurrent out-pouring of texts aiming to defend the system and refute the criticisms. Consequently, the modalities of Israeli military rule in the territories were subjected to greater scrutiny, analysis, and explanation than ever before, and debates became much sharper.[65]

A few examples can illustrate the polemical tone of this discourse. In 1991, AI published *The Military Justice System in the Occupied Territories*. In the summary, the report's purpose was explained as an effort to address the concerns and criticisms by local and international observers about the operation of the military courts.

The report describes the prolonged incommunicado detention of Palestinians after arrest, which facilitates arbitrary arrest as well as torture or ill-treatment. Confessions . . . are often the primary evidence against defendants. . . . Improper pressures are exacted on defendants to plead guilty and enter into a plea bargain with the prosecutors. Many defendants do so because confessions cannot be effectively challenged in court, or because those who ask for a full trial risk spending more time in detention than they would if they plead guilty. They also risk much heavier sentences. Their fundamental right to a fair trial is prejudiced in these circumstances.[66]

In the Israeli government's response to this AI report, the introduction began by stating that the military court system was vital to Israeli efforts to combat Palestinian terrorist organizations committed to destroying Israel.

The [AI] Report, rather than making a systematic, statistical survey of legal practices in the administered areas, attempts to present a number of isolated examples as representative of the whole. Due to the high rate of intifada crime, the military justice system . . . has had to cope with a caseload of 19,435 trials during 1991 alone. The total of 11 isolated examples presented in the Report . . . cannot, in any way, be an indication of the functioning of the system as a whole. . . .

In its allegations of torture and maltreatment, AI disregards the reality that individuals arrested, tried or convicted often have both personal and political motives for exaggerating or fabricating tales to justify their own actions or to embarrass the government. . . . Simply put, for a terrorist who would firebomb a civilian bus or kidnap and torture an Arab on the rumor that he has contacts with Israeli authorities, lying to a delegate of a human rights organization comes easily.[67]

A 1992 report by the Lawyers Committee for Human Rights, *Lawyers and the Military Justice System,* examined "the functioning of the system from the point of view of practicing lawyers"[68] in light of international standards. The official Israeli response, authored by the MAG's office, criticized the report on the ground that key informants were "politically motivated" defense lawyers who were not reliable sources.[69] The Lawyers Committee responded to the criticism in a follow-up report, *A Continuing Cause for Concern:*

In its Reply, the Israeli authorities [sic] state that our findings were based "mostly on conversations with politically motivated defense attorneys." We find this statement to be an unfortunate expression of the authorities' contempt for the adversarial system. . . . If the primary motivation of these lawyers was "political," they would not subject themselves to the daily drudgery, privations and physical discomfort which life as a lawyer in the Territories entails. There are easier ways to make a political statement. This tendency to disregard the often legitimate concerns of lawyers as being "politically motivated," and therefore not worthy of consideration, is an example of precisely the complacency in the face of manifest problems in the functioning of the justice system of which we accused some Israeli officials.[70]

In 1993, the MAG's office published an edited book, *Israel, the "Intifada" and the Rule of Law,*[71] to provide a comprehensive official response to the deluge of criticism against Israel since the beginning of the *intifada.* Chapter 16, "Monitering [sic] of IDF [Israel Defense Forces] Conduct in the Areas by Independent Human Rights Organizations and the Press," provides a telling picture of the government's assessment of its critics. The two local human rights organizations most active in publishing reports critical of the military administration, Al-Haq and B'Tselem, are discussed:

[B'Tselem] is an Israeli formed organization established in February 1989, associated with Israeli politicians of the left, to monitor human rights in the Territories. "*Al Haq, Law in the Service of Man*" is a Ramallah based Palestinian Human Rights Organization. The latter group is considered by Israeli government officials to be distinctly hostile and unobjective in its operations and its posi-

tions. The former group's political connections, on the other hand, would tend
to deny it the aura of objective neutrality enjoyed by, say, ACRI. B'Tselem's various reports . . . have met with sharp criticism by Israeli government officials, cit-
ing inaccuracy or lack of objectivity. Nonetheless, the reports published by both
these groups have been studied by the Israeli government.[72]

In 1994, former MAG Amnon Straschnov published a semiautobio-
graphical book, *Justice under Fire,* discussing the changing legal measures
in the territories instituted under his authority, such as making stone
throwing a felony offense and holding parents legally accountable for the
resistance activities of their children.[73] He offered a candid assessment of
the tensions between the military security and legal aspects of Israeli rule.

Unfortunately, the legal system in the territories was an "easy target" for continuing attacks by different sides. [The critics] were not without a predetermined and
hostile attitude toward Israeli rule in the territories in general, and found the military courts something easy to be exploited and to use for political and ideological purposes in the area of civil rights. . . .
    It seems that criticism of the legal system in the territories was not only the
concern of lawyers, international organizations, and civil rights organizations. The
criticism came more than once from the security system as well, addressing the
legal system from the opposite angle [i.e., arguing that it was too easy on
terrorists].[74]

As these examples illustrate, the *intifada*-era literature not only
reflected but reinforced the deeply contested nature of all issues relating
to the military court system, from narrowly construed matters such as
procedural rules to the larger political problems associated with the
conflict.[75] But the most contentious issue of all has been interrogation.

## Interrogation, Torture, and the Law

In any criminal justice system, interrogation of suspects is a central
aspect of law enforcement, since confessions are sought to confirm the
validity of other evidence or to compensate for a lack of evidence.
Interrogation is vitally important to understand the Israeli military court
system because confessions represent the most common source of evidence (sometimes the only source) to charge and prosecute Palestinians.
    The IDF and the police conduct some interrogations, but the main
agency responsible for interrogation of Palestinians is the General Security
Services (GSS, also known by its Hebrew acronym Shin Bet). GSS inter-

rogations feed the legal process by procuring confessions that are then turned over to police and prosecutors.

A history of Israeli interrogation of Palestinians has never been written, and the conditions do not exist for such an undertaking because of the GSS's institutional insularity (it is accountable directly and exclusively to the office of the Israeli prime minister) and the classified and clandestine nature of its activities. But because of the heavy reliance on confessions, a partial account of this history can be deduced from the public record relating to the functioning of the military court system since 1967 and from litigation in the HCJ to contest the use of torture.

After the "pacification" campaign in 1970, the capabilities of the military court system expanded, increasing the demand for forms of evidence that would hold up in court. Consequently, interrogation was increasingly aimed at producing confessions to be used for conviction. By 1970, the complete isolation — and thus effectiveness — of interrogation as a component of the legal process had been achieved.[76] Some lawyers representing Palestinians began reporting claims by their clients of beatings, electric shock, death threats, position abuse, cold showers, sexual abuse, and denial of access to toilets. In 1970, the Israeli publication *Zu Ha-Derech* reported a new policy to discourage military courts from investigating the conduct of interrogators: "Noting the importance and vitality of [the GSS's] security responsibilities in this area, it is the duty of the court to avoid disturbing them in their tasks."[77]

Reports about Israeli interrogation methods that claimed the routine use of torture and ill-treatment were officially challenged as anti-Israel lies and smears and were refuted by arguments that such claims were based on pernicious fabrications by Palestinians and other "enemies of the state." Since interrogation occurs in inaccessible sites and is conducted by secret agents, the only sources of information are people who have been interrogated. But because of this need to rely on Palestinians for information about Israeli interrogation, and the impossibility of independently confirming allegations of torture, many international observers were skeptical or reluctant to label Israel a torturing state. For example, AI did not use the word *torture* in reports on Israel until 1990.[78] Certainly another factor was the zeal with which claims of torture were challenged by officials and supporters of the state.

Both the discourse and practices of interrogation underwent a qualitative change following the 1977 publication of a detailed inquiry by the *Sunday Times* (London) into "Arab allegations and official Israeli denials of the use of torture." The *Times* reported, "Torture of Arab prisoners is so widespread and systematic that it cannot be dismissed as 'rogue cops' exceeding orders. It appears to be sanctioned as deliberate policy. Some of the ill-treatment is merely primitive: prolonged beatings, for example. But more refined techniques are also used, including electric-shock torture and confinement in specially-constructed cells. This sort of apparatus, allied to the degree of organisation evident in its application, removes Israel's practice from the lesser realms of brutality and places it firmly in the category of torture."[79]

The Israeli government, through its embassy in London, ridiculed the findings and conclusions of the article as "fantastic horror stories" in a published response in the Letters section.[80] But Prime Minister Menachem Begin ordered a curtailment of violent interrogation tactics in Israeli prisons and detention centers. As a result, for the next several years, allegations of torture declined.[81] However, by the end of the 1970s, local and regional events (including intensified Jewish settlement activity and the signing of an Egyptian-Israeli peace treaty) led to an escalation of Palestinian protests and resistance, which in turn led to an escalating number of arrests and interrogations. By the early 1980s, the hiatus on torture had ended.[82]

The most significant affirmation that violent interrogation tactics were standard practice was provided, ironically enough, by an official Israeli source. In 1987, a government-appointed commission of inquiry headed by Moshe Landau, a retired justice of the HCJ, issued a groundbreaking report on the activities of the GSS.[83] The events that precipitated the establishment of the Landau Commission were not related directly to the interrogation of Palestinians. Rather, two scandals implicating GSS agents had come to the Israeli public's attention, one involving torture of a Circassian Israeli officer in the army (who had been convicted of treason) and the other involving the murder of two Palestinians already in custody (who had hijacked a bus) and a subsequent cover-up.[84] The Landau Commission's mandate was to bring to light any illegal actions perpetrated by the GSS and, in doing so, to begin the process of restoring public (Jewish Israeli) confidence in the security establishment, which had been damaged by the scandals.

The Landau Commission report confirmed what had long been alleged by Palestinian detainees, their Palestinian and Israeli lawyers, and local human rights organizations: that GSS agents had used violent interrogation methods routinely on Palestinian detainees since at least 1971 and that they had routinely lied about such practices when confessions were challenged in court on the grounds that they had been coerced.[85] The Landau Commission was harsh in its criticism of GSS perjury but adopted the GSS's own position that coercive interrogation tactics were necessary in the struggle against "hostile terrorist activity." The Landau Commission accepted the broad definition of terrorism used by the GSS, which encompassed not only acts or threats of violence but virtually all activities related to Palestinian nationalism. The Landau Commission described GSS interrogators as "ideological criminals" who had erred while doing their "national duty."[86] According to the report:

The investigation staff of the GSS is characterized by professionalism, devotion to duty, readiness to undergo exhausting working conditions at all hours of the day and night and to confront physical danger, but above all by high inner motivation to serve the nation and the State in secret activity, with "duty being its own reward," without the public glory which comes with publicity. It is all the more painful and tragic that a group of persons like this failed severely in its behavior as individuals and as a group. In saying this we are not referring to the methods of interrogation they employed — which are largely to be defended, both morally and legally . . . — but to the method of giving false testimony in court, a method which now has been exposed for all to see and which deserves utter condemnation.[87]

The most contentious aspect of the report was not what it revealed about the past but its conclusions and recommendations. The report's authors argued that national security imperatives required coercion (physical and psychological) in the interrogation of Palestinians and that the state should sanction such tactics in order to eliminate GSS agents' need to resort to perjury. The Landau Commission's justification for this recommendation was based on a three-part contention: that Palestinians had no right to legal protections given their predisposition toward terrorism,[88] that the GSS operated morally and responsibly in discharging its duties to preserve Israeli national security, and that GSS interrogation methods did not constitute "torture."

The Landau Commission argued that Israeli penal law could be interpreted to give interrogators license to use "moderate amounts of physical pressure" (as well as various forms of psychological pressure) as part of the fight against terrorism.[89] According to this argument, the "necessity defense" permits people to use violence in "self-defense,"[90] thereby mitigating criminal liability on the grounds that they acted to prevent grievous harm.[91] However, if this argument is applied to interrogation, the "self" is the Jewish nation, and "defense" is exercised by state agents acting in an official capacity against people already in custody. This is a striking contravention of international law, in which the prohibition against torture is universal and customary (i.e., applicable to all people everywhere) and nonderogable under any circumstances. The Landau Commission used the "ticking bomb" scenario as part of its justification for "pressure".[92]

The Israeli government adopted the Landau Commission's recommendation to authorize the use of "moderate physical pressure," making Israel the first state in the world to publicly sanction interrogation methods that constituted torture according to international law. In doing so, Israel challenged the core principle underlying the international legal prohibition against torture: that the individual's right not to be tortured is nonderogable.

The coincidental timing of the Landau Commission report's publication (October 30, 1987), its endorsement by the Israeli cabinet (November 8), and the outbreak of the first *intifada* (December 9) bore directly on the handling of security suspects at a time when the number of people being arrested was skyrocketing. Thus, it could be said that the Landau Commission report decisively transformed official discourse of Israeli interrogation while preserving the practices. Whereas prior to Landau the Israeli government had denied torture categorically, afterwards it adopted the position that permissible "moderate physical pressure" did not constitute "torture."[93]

The Landau Commission report provoked a firestorm of protest by local and international human rights organizations, as well as some prominent members of the Israeli legal community.[94] At minimum, critics observed, giving interrogators a license to use "pressure" denied Palestinian detainees even a pro forma presumption of innocence. But the report did serve a positive — if unintended — function by providing a now-public focus for efforts to criticize — with the aim of ending — coercive and illegal interrogation practices. In 1990, a group of Israeli lawyers and human rights activists formed the Public Committee against Torture in Israel (PCATI) to spearhead this campaign.[95]

The specific interrogation methods that the Landau Commission recommended and the state accepted were contained in a classified appendix to the report. In 1991, PCATI petitioned the HCJ to void the Landau Commission report and publicize the secret interrogation guidelines. The court rejected the petition, stating that the guidelines had the status of an "internal directive" and therefore were not subject to judicial intervention. Although the justices handling the petition were privy to the guidelines, they did not render an opinion regarding their legality vis-à-vis Israeli or international laws. But the contents of the secret guidelines could be deduced through investigations by human rights organizations and through petitions brought before the HCJ that forced the state to admit or acknowledge that permissible methods included the routine use of threats and insults, sleep deprivation, hooding and blindfolding, position abuse, physical violence (including "shaking" to produce a whiplash effect while leaving no physical marks),[96] solitary confinement (including in refrigerated or overheated closetlike cells), and subjection to excessively filthy conditions.[97]

The policy of permitting "moderate physical pressure" became more legally problematic in 1991 when the Knesset ratified the UN Convention against Torture and Other Cruel, Degrading or Inhuman Punishment. However, the government exempted itself from adhering to this convention in its conduct vis-à-vis Palestinian residents of the West Bank and Gaza on the grounds that the political status of these areas remained to be determined,[98] a line of legal reasoning that drew on the Israeli distinction between "administration" and "occupation."[99]

In September 1991, for the first time in Israeli history, two GSS interrogators were sentenced to prison (for six months) on charges connected with their work; they had been found guilty of causing the death of Khalid Sheikh 'Ali, a Palestinian from Gaza, who had died of internal bleeding as a result of being kicked in the stomach. After their appeal hearing in the HCJ, which upheld the conviction, Justice Aharon Barak said, "The interrogators acted, indeed, for the sake of state security . . . but acted unlawfully."[100] But since 1994 (significantly, the year ushering in the Oslo Accords), "not a single GSS interrogator has been tried in a criminal court, not even when detainees left interrogation wings with permanent physical or mental disabilities, and not even when a GSS agent tortured a Palestinian detainee ('Abd a-Samad Harizat) to death with his own hands."[101]

In 1993, in response to litigation challenging the legality of the Landau guidelines, the Israeli government reported that the GSS had modified its interrogation procedures. The "new procedures" were the product of deliberations of a ministerial committee and were disseminated to interrogators in a classified booklet titled *The Procedure for Extraordinary Authorizations during Interrogation*. Ostensibly, the new procedures set out a tighter framework for use of "exceptional means," to be used in stages, under supervision of members of particular echelons of the GSS, and in consideration of the detainee's health.[102] However, in an investigation to assess the ramifications of these new procedures, B'Tselem found that the only notable change was the elimination of forced physical exercise.[103]

In 1994, PCATI brought a petition that called again on the HCJ to order the state to publish the new secret guidelines and challenged the GSS's activities as "extralegal." The petition charged that the GSS operated a shadow regime unregulated by law and that it usurped jurisdiction from institutions with public authority and accountability (i.e., the IDF, police, and prison services), which functioned as subcontractors, providing services and facilities over which they had relinquished control. According to Avigdor Feldman, the Israeli lawyer representing PCATI in this petition, "[T]he GSS maintains parasitical relations with the competent authorities. . . . The GSS is located in the internal organs of the competent body, hidden away from all public and judiciary criticism. From its hiding place it operates the authority, sucking from it both power and its invasive means, while preventing these authorities from exercising any independent opinion."[104]

The PCATI petition also asserted that GSS interrogation methods were "aberrant" and illegal because the prohibition against torture was universal, customary, and absolute. Part of the legal grounding for the petition was a new Israeli Basic Law: Human Dignity and Liberty (1994). According to the petition, "[T]he fact that the government authorizes the [GSS] interrogators to harm the bodies and dignity of persons is a constitutional disgrace which undermines the integrity of the legal system and challenges its right to exist."[105] The HCJ issued an order nisi impelling the state to respond but left the case pending.

In the meantime, Israeli lawyers continued to submit hundreds of petitions on behalf of individual Palestinian clients in interrogation. The HCJ was not entirely immune to granting relief in certain cases. For example, in a 1996 decision *(Mubarak et al v. GSS)*, the HCJ ruled that "painful handcuffing" was prohibited (although it refused to prohibit other practices raised in the petition).[106] But its general pattern of decisions and delays served to preserve the secrecy of GSS interrogation practices and, in effect, to support the state's refusal to adhere to international law in its treatment of Palestinian detainees. Thus, the HCJ effectively added its stamp to the "legalization" of torture in Israel/Palestine, rationalizing that any harm perpetrated by interrogators was lesser or even was mitigated by the possible harm that detainees posed to national security and the safety of civilians who might be victims of terrorism. In 1998, Eitan Felner of B'Tselem wrote: "In Israel, torture is institutionalized, with its own routine and systematic bureaucracy. Torture is governed by detailed regulations and written procedures. A whole contingent of public officials participate in the practice of torture: in addition to the GSS interrogators who directly perpetrate torture, doctors determine whether a detainee is medically fit to withstand the torture, a ministerial committee headed by the Prime Minister oversees the procedures, state attorneys defend the practices in courts and finally the High Court of Justice has effectively legalized torture by approving its use in individual cases without ruling on its legality in principle."[107]

Despite criticism and negative international publicity surrounding Israeli interrogation tactics, a majority of the Jewish public and even some leading Israeli legal liberals refused to condemn the use of torture or to accept that the international prohibition applied to Palestinians. For example, Ruth Gavison, a law professor at Hebrew University, was president of ACRI when she was quoted as saying, "I don't know of any state which confronts terror attacks of the sort we deal with here, and which doesn't strike against the body or welfare of detained persons suspected of being connected to terrorist activity."[108] Such attitudes served to marginalize and even demonize human rights lawyers and activists as "sympathizers" or "defenders of terrorism" for their efforts to expose and prohibit torture.[109]

In January 1998, the HCJ combined a number of petitions pertaining to interrogation and convened an unprecedented panel of nine justices to consider the matter.[110] While the case dragged on, the HCJ issued a statement calling on the Knesset to take responsibility by promulgating legislation, rather than leaving it up to the court to decide about the legality of specific methods. Finally, in September 1999, the HCJ rendered a decision prohibiting GSS agents from routinely using physical "pressure," although the decision neither called these tactics "torture" nor completely closed the window of opportunity for their continued use under exceptional circumstances.[111] After the ruling, some methods all but disappeared (e.g., violent shaking, covering a detainee's head with a thick cloth sack, exposure to extremely loud and constant music, and tying to small tilted chairs). But other methods, including sleep deprivation, position abuse and painful shackling, exposure to extremes in temperature, and intense pressure applied to various body parts remained common practice.[112]

In Part Two, I return to the issue of interrogation because of its importance to the functioning of the military court system. Interrogation, as I will explain, influences the perspectives of the various categories of participants about the legality and legitimacy of the military court system.

# An Ethnography of the Military Court System

CHAPTER 3

# Going to Court

---

*It is ugly to be punishable, but there is no glory in punishing.*
Michel Foucault, *Discipline and Punish*[1]

The Israeli military courts and the compounds in which they are located exemplify how architecture can provide for control and surveillance. The space itself operates as a technology of power to facilitate or impede visibility and to regulate movement and interactions. The physical design and management of the courts reinforce the disciplinary potential of the space, as people internalize the possibilities and limits of their own position.

Power relations are visible in the military courts and provide a stark reflection of power relations in the broader context of Israel/Palestine. In the courtroom, although the judges' bench and the prisoners' dock are only feet apart, a wide gulf separates them. Each represents more than a mere location in the room. The bench is on an elevated dais, enabling judges to survey the room over which they preside. It requires little stretch of imagination to read the position of judges as analogous to that of the Israeli state that they represent, or the courtroom as a synecdoche of Israeli surveillance and control over the occupied territories. Defendants see the courtroom through the bars of a fenced enclosure that surrounds the dock. This, too, is analogous to the constraints and punitive dimensions of life under occupation. Palestinians are simultaneously present and excluded in an Israeli-controlled environment. But their large numbers also suggest a pervasive will to resist and the costs of doing so.

The space of the courts can be read as a reflection of the broader context in other ways as well. As I explain in Chapter 1, Israel/Palestine is governmentally integrated, and Israelis and Palestinians reside in rather close geographic proximity. The court system brings together members of the multiple "publics" who inhabit this area. As settings, the courts are spaces shared by Israeli citizens and Palestinian residents of the territories. But being "together" in the courtroom tends to reinforce collective differences and national divisions. No one I spoke with claimed to find the interpersonal proximity in the courts as an occasion to forget differences, as a humanizing experience of identifying with the "other." Rather, for most people, the proximity was experienced as an occasion in which differences became more heightened, obvious, and fraught. In this regard, the courts, like Israel/Palestine, are simultaneously shared and divided. Allen Feldman, whose work on the conflict in Northern Ireland suggests striking similarities with the situation in Israel/Palestine, describes such "bifurcated space" as "a component of a shared material culture that reproduces ideological and ethnic polarities."[2]

Between this chapter and the ones to follow, I want to tease out a contrast between that which is visible in the courtrooms, often unsubtle spectacles of power and powerlessness, and that which confounds such polarities. In this chapter, I focus mainly on the surface, on what is literally visible. In subsequent chapters, I probe into the functioning of the system to reveal fissures in national consensuses and insurgent actions by individuals who resist the prevailing order and/or their positions within in it. The contrast I raise for consideration is not categorical, nor is the surface of the courts "separate" from the system. But the power of law, legalism, and legalistic agency resists the kinds of explanations that do apply to the visual displays of power and subordination that mark the surface of the courts. In this vein, Feldman writes: "The historiographic surface is a place for reenactments, for the simulation of power and for making power tangible as a material force. These surfaces are frequently located at the edge of social order. Yet they fabricate an edifice of centralized and authorized domination."[3]

On the surface, the military courts epitomize an Israeli-Palestinian nationalist dichotomy. Regardless of how one would interpret what is "see-able," there is no ignoring the blatancy of national difference, the imbalances of national power, or the polarizing dimensions of national conflict. The most obvious manifestation of difference is the military-civilian distinction, which translates loosely into an Israeli-Palestinian distinction. Most of the Israelis in the courts, with the notable exception of Israeli defense lawyers, are there as soldiers. All of the Palestinians are civilians. In court, these differences are visibly marked by military uniforms and weapons. But the differences also are visible in sharply distinguished prerogatives of movement, speech, and other behavior. Even the legal process, at least on the surface, confirms this military-civilian Israeli-Palestinian divide; the adversarial system pits the Israeli military administration against the civilian Palestinian population. In short, the courts are places where the exterior signs militate against a critical reevaluation of national dichotomy and nationalist essentialism.

The courts are run by Israeli citizen-soldiers and derive their authority from the Israeli state. But the courts are not "for" Israelis except to the extent that the prosecution of Palestinians serves Israeli national interests. When Israeli soldiers go to court, they leave "Israel" and enter "Israeli administered areas."[4] Although Palestinians are the subjects of the courts' jurisdiction, the courts are not "for" them, either; they are used against them to punish all manifestations of resistance to the occupation and to reinforce Israeli control.

The courts are harsh, alienating places. Their very existence confirms that this is a world embroiled in conflict. As one can easily see on any day in any given court, relations between soldiers and civilians are tense and hostile. Occasionally these relations turn violent. However, *in the courts,* violence is not reciprocal because only soldiers have the license to give expression to their hostilities. What is visible on the surface is often a caricature of the most brutish aspects of military rule over a foreign civilian population.

Outside of activities and practices associated with the legal processes, the rules governing what happens in the courts are normative and political rather than juridical. These rules include how people obtain access to the courtrooms, how the use of space is controlled, how people behave and interact with one another, and how disputes or transgressions are handled. Although there are differences between the various courts, and even within the same court at different times, there are observable patterns and commonalities. Bourdieu's concept of *habitus* is useful for reflecting critically on the dynamics in the courts as a "shared" environment and their relation to (and reflection of) the broader context. As Bourdieu explains: "The *habitus,* a product of history, produces individual and collective practices — more history — in accordance with the schemes generated by history. It ensures the active presence of past experiences, which, deposited in each organism in the form of schemes of perception, thought and action, tend to guarantee the 'correctness' of practices and their constancy over time, more reliably than all formal rules and explicit norms."[5]

Identity differences are of preeminent importance to the schemes of perception, thought, and action. Even a person going to court for the first time could easily and quickly comprehend where to sit, what to do, how to behave. First-timers entering the courtroom would recognize their place, which is among others like them. Likewise, "proper behavior" could be gleaned by watching and emulating the actions of others. The patterns compose logics of practice, where the possibilities for action and interaction are neither finite nor entirely predictable but they are ordered, regulated, and, in those ways, limited.

For example, if an Israeli soldier wanted to "get friendly" with a Palestinian, invite him to step outside the courtroom for a smoke and a chat, this would defy the logic of "normal" practice. Although such a thing might happen, it would not pass unnoticed, nor would it be applauded by other soldiers as a positive gesture of sociability. Most soldiers (especially those not directly involved in the legal process) perceive the courts through a lens of militarism; they are there *as soldiers,* authorized and expected to control, not socialize with, Palestinians.

On one occasion, I encountered a soldier, a recent immigrant from the former Soviet Union, who told me that he could not understand why other soldiers teased and scolded him for spending so much time chatting with Palestinian lawyers. He found them charming and was particularly impressed by their apparent commitment to the well-being of their clients. Yet the negative repercussions from his peers unsettled him, reminding him of his own difference from other Israelis and intensifying his sense of alienation from his newly adopted society. While it was possible for him to cultivate friendly relations with Palestinians, since no one would punish a soldier for doing so, apprehending the breach that such behavior constituted reproduced the very divisions that he was transgressing. The rules governing behavior and interaction in courts, although not formally codified, nevertheless maintain patterns, lines, and limits that become particularly obvious when they are crossed or violated.

My aims in focusing on the "see-able" surfaces of the courts in this chapter are threefold: to describe the courts as spaces in which various kinds of interactive "dramas" take place with a certain patterned regularity; to explain who occupies the space of the courtrooms and how; and to illuminate how the national conflict is tangible as a material culture in this institutional setting. Yet these aims merit some qualification. As I elaborate in other chapters, much of what happens in the court system is never on display in the courtrooms. Interrogation of suspects, plea bargaining over charges and sentences, discussions between lawyers and their clients, and decision making about the uses and interpretations of law all occur, for the most part, elsewhere, out of public view.

If one aim of this book is to critique the explanatory power of the "Israelis versus Palestinians" dichotomy, why devote a chapter to describe dynamics that confirm its validity? As stated above, on the surface this dichotomy obtains and therefore merits discussion. Moreover, it validates how some people — perhaps most people — see the courts. Finally, an accounting of the surface features and dynamics is warranted by the scant coverage of such matters in the literature on the military court system. This lacuna is striking when compared with the wealth of detail in writings about other social settings: streets, prisons, interrogation centers, schools, hospitals, homes, and so on. Since most readers probably have never entered the Israeli military courts to see for themselves, I strive to describe the settings under discussion in this study.

I would not claim that my views or viewpoint could be generalized, nor would I suggest that others see the courts as I did. For example, I did not see Palestinians as inherently dangerous or degraded, as many soldiers did, nor did I feel scared or intimidated by soldiers, as many Palestinians did. People's views and viewpoints are shaped by their experiences. I brought the perspective of a foreigner in this world, with far less personally invested or at stake in the history or the future of Israel/Palestine. But by going to court, I could see *what,* if not *how,* other people saw. I should add that my perspective on the courts was affected by my own position(s). It was never entirely clear where I "belonged."[6] But this afforded flexibility, enabling me to occupy a variety of spaces, to see the court from several angles, and to traverse boundaries that rigidly restricted others.

When I began field research, I expected — or at least hoped — that time spent in the courts would provide a steady stream of legal drama, vivid displays of the adversarial legal process. What I found instead were long delays between sessions. Initially, I was frustrated by the delays, despite the opportunities they afforded to converse with whomever I was sitting beside. Eventually, though, as I gained a better understanding of how the system works — of the centrality of plea bargaining, which typically occurs out of the courtroom — I came to appreciate the waiting, and even the frustration, as integral to people's experiences of and in the courts.

## Going to Court

One of the most obvious things about the military courts is that no one *wants* to be there. Being there, in court, is an experience that exposes individuals to personal stresses, anxieties, humiliations, and deprivations, and it exposes everyone to antagonisms that sustain the conflict.

As one would expect, military compounds in which the courts are located are imposing structures fortified with cement barriers, fences, and barbed wire.[7] Through the main gates roll military vehicles: jeeps of soldiers patrolling the areas, vans carrying soldiers to their postings in the compound, buses with blackened windows transporting prisoners. The only private cars allowed to drive inside are those of Israeli military personnel and security agents. Everyone else enters on foot, after parking cars in the street or descending from taxis and buses.

Lawyers, family members of defendants, witnesses, and other civilians enter by passing through a guard booth or inspection area where soldiers check identification papers and conduct bag-and-body searches. Such security measures are completely routinized in Israel/Palestine, with similar practices typically occurring at many sites, from roadblocks to college campuses to grocery stores. No one is exempted from searches, although Palestinians are subjected to more probing checks and certainly more harassment than Israelis and foreigners.

As an American, or rather as a white middle-class American, I had never experienced such security measures until I moved to Israel/Palestine in 1991. I had to adjust to the expectation that I submit to scrutiny, however perfunctory, at virtually every turn. This adjustment was not entirely smooth. On one occasion, I had gone to a movie in West Jerusalem with a friend. After about twenty minutes we decided to walk out. Emerging from the theater into the lobby we were immediately surrounded by several security guards, who demanded our papers and bags and began questioning us about why we were leaving before the movie ended. At first, we were confused about why we would be checked *going out,* since inspections usually occur when people enter a building. But then we realized that they were suspicious that we might have left a bomb behind. I joked, "The bomb is on screen." To say the guards were not amused would be an understatement. But the experience drove home for me the intensity and ubiquity of Israeli security anxieties, where even the most innocuous activity (leaving a bad movie, for example) could be interpreted as dangerous. It helped me internalize the kind of self-discipline — submission, acceptance, compliance — that was routinely expected. Even before that experience, though, I had never hesitated to submit to inspection at the military courts. The very atmosphere left little room to question the inevitability of such procedures.

In Gaza, where the inspection process is most elaborate, male and female soldiers run their hands over Palestinians' bodies. One Jewish Israeli leftist wrote of his impression of entering the Gaza court:

The dehumanization here is so thorough, that even one [soldier] who comes for a short while, and without necessarily being particularly coarse, immediately adjusts himself to suit a world where on one side there are human beings — in uniform, or in the case of police officers and [security] men, with a pistol, and on the other — the natives, or the "locals" as they are called. An example is the young female soldier whose job it is to search the women before they enter the courthouse: a good girl from a good family, who behaved towards the Palestinian women as if they were a herd of undisciplined monkeys. When I pointed out to her that she would never behave like that in civilian life, she answered in complete seriousness, "You can't imagine how much they stink."[8]

I always entered the compounds with lawyers. Whoever was serving as my "host" for the day would lead me past the Palestinians lined up in the street waiting to enter. The lawyers usually don the requisite black robe before approaching the gate or at least toss it over a shoulder to mark themselves as legal professionals with an incontrovertible right to enter, whereas for other civilians, entry is dependent on the permission of the soldiers on duty, and on space constraints within the courts.

The mark of a lawyer signified by the robe often caused people in the crowd outside the compound to react, perhaps stopping the lawyer for some roadside counsel or pleading for some news about a family member's case. Such solicitations illustrate the competing demands on lawyers who choose such work: to serve "the community" by making time for talk on the streets or to rush past in order to have a few extra moments with their clients inside.

The robes that the civilian lawyers must wear suggest a magisterial aura that is completely lacking in these military courts. Whether intentionally or inadvertently, lawyers subvert their majesty by throwing the robes into greasy car trunks or onto trash-strewn back seats after a day in court. But their crumpled, dirty robes coordinate rather well with their shoes, which are invariably dusty or muddy, depending on conditions of the streets they traverse on their way to court.

Within the courts, the robes serve as a means of governing space. Lawyers have access to areas that are off limits to other civilians, namely the administrative offices of Israeli military personnel. If a soldier were to try to stop a lawyer from heading into the offices, the lawyer could just point at the robe and brush past. Such a gesture would indicate a certain hierarchy within the courts, where legal professionals are "above" the soldiers who function as guards. For Palestinian lawyers in particular, the robes shield them from some of the indignities they are subjected to in any other environment. Nowhere else could they disregard a soldier's behest to stop.

In the courtrooms, the robed lawyers congregate on their designated benches at the front of the room, piling their papers and files on the table in front of them. Across the front of the room are the benches and table for the prosecutors. They, like the judges and other military personnel, wear uniforms bearing the insignia of their rank. Few of the men wear *kippas* (religious skullcaps). Some of the prosecutors are young, recent university graduates who are performing their mandatory military service. Others are older, reservists or career soldiers.

There is a perceptible distance between the prosecutors and other soldiers in the courtroom; the prosecutors are busy legal professionals, whereas the others, whatever they do in civilian life, have no professional duties other than the mundane responsibilities of keeping order in the court. While there is also a distance between prosecutors and defense lawyers, they actively engage with one another, poring over files together as they work out the details of plea bargains. These interactions may be jocular and casual or hostile and tense depending on the circumstances and the nature of relations between individuals. Although most plea bargaining takes place in the prosecutors' offices, when the number of cases passing through the system is large, negotiations often continue in the courtroom while the court is in session.

In the front of the courtroom, between the defense and the prosecution, is the stand where people go to testify. Beside it is the cubicle where the translator sits, usually positioned with his back toward the lawyers' bench. The translators are low-ranking soldiers, usually Druze, who are selected for their role on the basis of a relative proficiency in Hebrew and Arabic. In addition to translating court proceedings, they translate documents in the case files and facilitate plea-bargain negotiations between prosecutors and defense lawyers who do not share a language. When the court is not in session and their duties do not keep them busy in the back, the translators pass their time with soldiers guarding the courtrooms. Within the courts, the translators occupy an ambiguous position: because they have a role in the legal process, they have a higher status than soldiers on guard duty, but their Druze identity, which is constantly on display when they speak Arabic, marks them as "different" from Jewish soldiers and is, at least for some, a source of insecurity and embarrassment.

At the front of the room is the elevated dais where the judges and the court secretary sit. The judges tend to be older than other soldiers in the military courts. The secretaries are all young, always women.

On the wall behind the dais hangs an Israeli flag. Beside it hangs the symbol of the legal branch of the Israel Defense Forces, an image of a sword pointing upward, from which the scale of justice is suspended.

When judges appear through a door behind the dais, everyone in the room rises until they are seated. Any time judges are in the courtroom, the court is in session and they are conducting official business. In the courtroom, judges have limited interactions with anyone not directly involved in the legal process. The public and the soldiers guarding the room are like "extras" or "audience" in the legal dramas over which the judges preside.

From the middle of the courtroom to its back wall are long benches designated for the public. In 1988, partitions were installed to reinforce the governability of space in the courtroom, to confine and separate the Palestinian public from everyone else. These barriers formalized divisions that previously had been tacit. The nature of these barriers varies from court to court. In most courts, the barriers are waist-high, a wood or metal fence with a latched gate. But in the main Gaza court, the barrier was a mesh wall extending to the ceiling. The installation of physical barriers in the courtrooms during the first *intifada* was a response to the intensification of violence in the territories, where all space was becoming harder to control and more intensive and restrictive security measures were adopted.[9] These courtroom barriers function like roadblocks or checkpoints in the larger context, enabling soldiers to monitor and regulate Palestinians' movement. They also encode nationally differentiated rights and prerogatives; the barriers affect everyone's mobility, but they obstruct Palestinians, whereas they merely inconvenience Israelis.

Family members of defendants represent a broad cross section of Palestinian society. Those in court on any given day may include *fellahi* (peasant) and refugee camp women wearing distinctively embroidered *thobe*s (floor-length black or maroon dresses), men in traditional garb and *kuffiya*s (kerchiefs), women in *hijab*s (headscarves), bareheaded men and women in fashionable suits and others in the kinds of simple clothing their challenged budgets allow. Sometimes there are children of all ages, from toddlers to teens, some wearing trendy sneakers and expressive T-shirts, others in ragged hand-me-downs. Some people sit in silence, fearful of the soldiers nearby. Others may chat with those around them, a bold or naive gesture because excessive talk can get them ejected from the building.

Along the walls in the back half of the courtroom are benches or chairs for soldiers assigned to guard the courts. Some take their guard duties seriously, keeping their attention focused intently on the Palestinians and, perhaps, a firm hand on their guns. Some use the occasion to joke or gossip with one another. Some may be dozing, bored by the monotony of sitting in a courtroom day after day. Other soldiers often wander into the courtroom to see what is happening as they pass through the compound between patrols or while waiting for a ride home.

The enclaves of the military compounds — highly controlled environments — are obviously different from other locales in the West Bank and Gaza. But the behavior and interactions among soldiers in the courts provide some indications of the dynamics of Israeli military service. The camaraderie is palpable, evincing a communal cohesion that the Israeli military represents and reinforces.[10] Although guarding a courtroom is mundane and tedious, individuals perform this role as soldiers and therefore are participating in a larger field of military practices that both derive from and solidify these individuals' membership in a national community. As Sara Helman explains: "[I]n the process of production of 'national security,' and while being engaged in military activities there develops the experience of common bonds and solidarity [among] anonymous individuals [i.e., 'strangers']. This experience gives rise to the perception of the [military] field as a community that is interpreted by its participants as embodying and defining who an Israeli is and the very content of Israeliness."[11]

The camaraderie among soldiers in the courts also hints at the shared burdens of national defense in a situation of ongoing conflict, which create common experiences of disrupted careers or education and sacrifices to personal and family life.[12] The behavior and interactions among soldiers involve occasional displays of machismo and sexualized behavior as male soldiers pinch or grab female soldiers, who reciprocate or rebuff their advances.[13]

In the courts, soldiers on guard duty exhibit an almost uniform disdain and hostility toward Palestinians. For them, Palestinians are the problem, the enemy, the reason they have to be there, armed, sitting in a courtroom. Eyal Ben-Ari, an Israeli anthropologist, describes soldiers' practices and attitudes during army service, especially for reservists, as a contradiction of their civilian "selves."[14] Ben-Ari proposes that people deal with the contradictions by donning "masks" and "disguises":

For the duration of their performances, the disguised are in a position to express hostility with impunity because they are "not themselves." . . . On one level these circumstances work toward allowing many reservists to display "irregular" *public* behavior like cursing and swearing, belching and farting, urinating and spit-ting, or talking dirty. This situation also allows many men to freely exhibit the "macho" dimension of their army character. . . .

On another level, however, the disguises donned during reserve duty have had a number of implications for the way in which relations with local Palestinians have taken shape during the uprising. . . . [T]he use of disguises and masks has, to state the obvious, very serious and direct implications[,] . . . [providing] at least some reservists with a legitimate license to behave in ways that they would not normally — that is, within the bounds of their everyday civilian life — associate with them- "selves."[15]

This "legitimate license" infuses the atmosphere in the courts, occa-sionally taking the form of physical violence. But more often the mere suggestion of violence that soldiers embody has a chilling effect that Palestinians internalize, often acting even before soldiers have a chance to hush someone who is talking, in the hope of preventing a scene. They hastily signal where to sit to any newcomer to avert the possibility that someone might inadvertently transgress a boundary and become vulner-able to some rebuke or punishment.

Yet in such an environment, nasty little dramas between soldiers and Palestinians are both inevitable and common. One day, in the smaller courtroom in the Gaza compound, Palestinians were sitting quietly on benches so crammed that they were pressed shoulder to shoulder. A man at the end of the bench, one buttock hanging off the edge, kept looking over at an empty chair beside the wall. Eventually, he decided to move to the chair. A few minutes later a soldier entered the room looking for a place to sit. He grabbed the man by his hair and dragged him back to the bench, shoving him onto it. This caused a chain reaction, and a woman sitting in the middle of the long bench, who had been perched on the edge to minimize the space she was using, fell to the ground. When she stood up, her face was red with embarrassment. I looked over to see the soldier's reaction, but he hadn't noticed; he was busy playing with his gun. Throughout this episode, no one uttered a word.

When the court is not in session, there is no obvious place or activity for people to focus their attention. Palestinians try not to make eye con-tact with soldiers, to avoid some unwanted attention. Men play with prayer beads, women smooth their skirts, people huddle to whisper to one another. Their faces are canvases of anxiety and the hardships of life under occupation. But in the courts, there rarely is any evidence of the spirited, confrontational resistance on open display beyond the com-pound walls.

For Palestinians, going to court is motivated by the desire to see a family member who has been arrested. But doing so — being there — puts them in a position of heightened vulnerability themselves, where they are subject to the will and whim of every soldier in the compound. It also represents personal sacrifices — for example, having to travel from a distant village or refugee camp and submit to checks at military roadblocks along the way, any one of which could become a dead end in their journey. Perhaps they have to give up a day of work, sacrificing income or foregoing other responsibilities to be there. And many know that they will have to do it all again if their family member's case is delayed for a later hearing.

Until the session when their case is called, defendants are kept in a holding cell. Before 1994 (when the courts were relocated), the holding cells were adjacent to the courtrooms, which people passed as they went into the court. The cell's metal door had a small window with bars. Sometimes the door became a scene of activity, as prisoners pressed their faces against the bars to converse with their lawyers or to have a quick glimpse at a passing family member. In the relocated courts, the holding cells are in areas inaccessible to the public.

When defendants are brought into court, several soldiers enter first and take up positions, prepared to react if anyone in the public section should make a move toward that area. The defendants are shackled with handcuffs and often with leg cuffs. Sometimes, if the group is particularly large, they are shackled together, forcing them to move with caution and difficulty, trying not to trip as they slide into place on their benches.

Defendants' entry into the courtroom is always a moment of pathos as the prisoners and those in the public section scan each other's faces and gesture greetings. Some women break down in tears or quietly ululate with relief at the sight of a loved one. The courtroom is often the first occasion for family members to see each other since the arrest.

Defendants generally present a motley picture. Although many Palestinian women and girls have passed through the court system as defendants, the vast majority are men and boys. Although they, like the public, represent a cross section of Palestinian society, it is difficult to tell much about individuals' social identity, political affiliations, or economic status from their appearance. Whether defendants are wearing prison uniforms or regular clothes, they tend to look dirty and tired, with unkempt hair, unshaven faces, bloodshot eyes. Some seem disconcerted, blinking to adjust their eyes to the bright light of the courtroom after hours spent in the holding cell. Some look scared. Others have the swagger of people who are entering familiar territory. Like those in the public section, they tend to regulate their own behavior, speaking to one another in hushed tones, remaining seated unless a lawyer or judge tells them to stand.

Once defendants enter the room, all eyes become focused on them, and their area becomes a center of activity until the judges appear. Bored or distracted soldiers are now fully alert, and the possibilities of a disciplinary scene become all the more likely. Lawyers use the opportunity to speak with their clients, informing them about the state of their case and the kind of deal being negotiated on their behalf. These exchanges can be revealing of the tensions between lawyers and clients. Sometimes defendants argue with their lawyers, protesting the terms of the deal or news of a further delay. Sometimes defendants just moan with resignation at the prospect of months or years in prison or a hefty fine. People in the public section scrutinize the faces of family members in the dock and their lawyers, trying to read what to expect from the hearing.

Sometimes lawyers disrupt the regulated spatial order in the courtrooms by crossing the barrier dividing them from the public. Moving into those areas to sit and talk with family members, they conduct business, perhaps saving those relatives a trip to their office. If soldiers try to order them back behind the barrier, this becomes a battle of wills over whose authority prevails when there is a conflict over use of space and movement. Unlike the scenes between soldiers and members of the public, in which the power to punish is an unequivocal prerogative of soldiers, those between lawyers and soldiers open up greater possibilities for reciprocity because lawyers can use their relations with court officials to demand a reprimand for soldiers who treat them or speak to them disrespectfully.

Lawyers occasionally facilitate communication between prisoners and their family members, passing cigarettes or letters or even surrogate hugs and kisses. On one particularly hectic day in the main Gaza court, a Palestinian lawyer took a pack of cigarettes from someone in the public section, then stood with her back pressed up against the fence surrounding the defendants, spread her robe out to hide her actions, and proceeded to slip the cigarettes one at a time through the fence into the handcuffed hands of her client, who then slid them into his sock. When she finished, everyone who had observed the exchange was grinning, relieved that the soldiers appeared to have missed this small defiance. But then one soldier pushed his way across the crowded room and demanded that the prisoner relinquish the cigarettes. After a few moments of quarreling with the lawyer, the soldier prevailed and the defendant emptied his sock, pushing the cigarettes back through the fence into the hands of the soldier, who threw them to the floor and ground them with his boot. The soldier then recrossed the room and returned to his seat. The lawyer, angry at being overridden by a soldier, grabbed some photographs and made a showy display of holding them up one at a time for her client to see. They were pictures of his children.

When judges enter the courtroom, the atmosphere changes. Judges control the rhythm and course of the main events. But lawyers, prosecutors, and soldiers often continue talking to each other, and there is a continuous movement of people in and out of the room.

When I first started going to the courts, I was surprised by people's failure to pay close attention to the hearings. While soldiers' distraction is understandable because they have no direct stake in the cases, I wondered why people in the public section and even lawyers and defendants often appeared indifferent to the business being conducted in the court. Over time I came to understand what others already knew: what happens in the courtroom is only a fragment of the legal process, and not the most important part at that, although the reasons it lacks importance differ among the various categories of people. Lawyers and prosecutors tend to regard their backroom brokering as the crux of the legal process. For them, what happens in court is often merely a formality, an occasion to confirm their deal before the judges or seek a delay for further negotiation.

Defendants' lack of attention relates to their marginal role in the courtroom. By then, their fate is in the hands of the lawyers and judges. They are the objects of legal transactions rather than subjects vested with a power to act on their own behalf. Many are never even afforded an opportunity to speak other than to identify themselves when their case comes up. In the courtrooms, defendants tend to rely less on their own observations and more on explanations that their lawyers provide before or after the session, especially when the outcome hinges on a plea bargain. Defendants' lack of interest also reflects a pervasive lack of interest about the courts within the Palestinian community. In contrast to other sites (streets, prisons, and national institutions), which are the focus of intense interest, the military courts function in the popular imagination as mere transit points on the way to prison.

For those in the public section, the atmosphere of the courtroom contributes to their lack of interest in the proceedings. Poor acoustics make it hard for them to hear anything going on at the front of the room, and those who understand no Hebrew have to rely on the translators. Since

the verbal translations often are partial, poor renderings of the legal arguments, and since many people have a very rudimentary understanding of
the military legal system, even those who may be paying attention are
likely to be confused by what they hear. But many do not even bother trying to follow the legal proceedings because they know that they will learn
what is going on from the lawyers later, outside the courtroom.

The proceedings rarely unfold smoothly. For example, a judge may call
a case of a defendant who is not in court. Soldiers then have to scramble
to see if the person is in the holding cell. Or a judge may find that the
defendant's lawyer is absent, in which case other lawyers chime in to say
that the lawyer is outside, or in the back offices, or perhaps not there at
all. If, for example, the penalty for a case is a fine, the judge may ask for
a representative of the defendant's family, to see whether the fine will be
paid or the person will be returned to prison. If no one from the family
is in the courtroom, soldiers may be dispatched to the street to see if a relative is out there, perhaps still waiting for permission to enter the
compound.

For cases involving plea bargains, the hearings usually are brief. The
prosecutor summarizes the evidence and presents the charges, and then
the defense lawyer may comment on the charges and provide some personal information about the defendant in an appeal for leniency. Rarely
are substantive matters of law raised for discussion or judicial consideration. If the prosecutor and lawyer have struck a deal on the sentence, they
present this to the judge, who decides whether to accept it, ask them to
renegotiate something more appropriate, or pronounce his own decision.
Often, the lawyer and prosecutor use the session to request a further delay
until they have time to come to an agreement on their own. On such
occasions, the judge consults with the secretary to find a new date on the
court calendar.

Very few cases actually go to trial. But a lawyer may, on occasion, call
for a trial if he or she believes that the judge assigned to the case may find
the evidence inconclusive or insubstantial or if no deal can be reached
with the prosecutor. When there is a trial, witnesses are called, and the
defendant may be asked to testify and undergo cross-examination. The
witnesses may be Israeli soldiers or security agents or Israeli or Palestinian
civilians.

Although court proceedings tend to be perfunctory and formulaic,
tensions often run high. It is not unusual to see legal professionals shouting at one another or exchanging insults. Nor is it unusual to see defendants being roughed up by soldiers on their way in or out of the court-

room. Everyone seems to have exceedingly low expectations for civility within the courtrooms. One day in the Ramallah court, a defendant was very angry with his lawyer, who had just requested another delay, which meant that he was going back to prison. As he was being led away by a soldier, under his breath he muttered "*arse*" (pimp), intending the insult for his lawyer. But the soldier, assuming it was directed at him, turned to the defendant and began shouting, "*Ani arse?*" (I [Hebrew] am a pimp [Arabic]?). He then slapped the defendant and dragged him outside. Everyone in the room could hear him continue hitting the defendant, but no one uttered a word of protest. On the contrary, the judge and the defendant's lawyer pointedly ignored what was happening, while other soldiers laughed about it with one another. By the time the soldier and his charge moved out of earshot, another case was already underway.

The rough atmosphere in the courts encourages some people to express their views in the roughest of terms. One afternoon, I was sitting in the lobby of the Nablus court when several teenaged soldiers on guard duty began haranguing me about my having come with Lea Tsemel, a renowned — and in some circles despised — Jewish Israeli left-ist. They told me that she was a vile "Arab lover" and "Arafat's whore" who had Jewish blood on her hands for defending terrorists. To illustrate his disdain, one of the soldiers hit a passing Palestinian detainee in the back with the butt of his gun, then turned to me and said, "Go tell Lea what I did." Although I was tempted to walk away, I decided to remain to hear what they had to say, which turned out to be a narrative mix of the "clash of civilizations" and a militarized social Darwinism. One soldier remarked that the contrast between the barbarism of Arab society and the civilization of Israeli society should be obvious to anyone who crossed the Green Line. He said, "These people live like animals. Look how poor, dirty and crowded Nablus is. It is nothing like Tel Aviv!" He continued by saying that he could easily and without any regret shoot any Palestinian, even a small child, because they were all uncivilized terrorists whose entire existence was motivated by a desire to kill Jews. Then he compared the military's rule over the territories to man's struggle against nature.[16] What made this whole episode even more disconcerting for me was the way he kept smiling as he spoke.

Sometimes, though, my conversations with people in court revealed more subtle and sophisticated views. Although the predictable animosi-ties inflected these discussions, people were forthcoming with critiques of their own society and leadership as well. For example, some soldiers would use our chats as an opportunity to express disdain or despair at having to serve as an occupying force. Some were sharply critical of the Israeli military and political establishments, condemning those who bore responsibility for creating such degrading conditions that Palestinian resistance was inevitable or who lacked the will and vision to devise a workable political resolution. Similarly, some Palestinians disparaged the ineffectiveness of their political leaders, the discord of political factionalism, and intracommunal violence between Islamists and secularists. But only in conversation could people escape the sticky grip of national polarities. The actions and demeanor of people in the courts tended to reinforce their roles and juxtapositions as enemies and the grinding pattern of hatred and suspicion.

What happens and what can happen in the courts are contingent: that is, neither entirely predictable nor unpredictable. The normative rules, although unwritten, are clear. But this does not diminish the instability wrought by a common knowledge that any interaction could turn violent. On the surface, the courts function like a standoff space in the conflict, a stalled moment of ongoing violence. As Robin Wagner-Pacifici writes, "Participants in standoffs usually spend a good deal of time just waiting, waiting to see what the 'enemy' will do. Everything is placed in high relief— actions and reactions, language, gestures, behaviors. . . . A paradox of the standoff is that while all participants have committed themselves to the situation (with highly variable degrees of freedom), they have . . . committed themselves to *different* situations. They have taken their 'stands,' that is, positioned themselves around some set of issues."[17]

However, unlike conventional types of standoffs (e.g., kidnappings or hostage situations), there is no dramatic resolution and no end.[18] People go to court and leave and are replaced by others who take their positions. Nor is there any affirming conclusion that people can derive, whether on site or retrospectively, about the meaning of going to court. The atmosphere is so unpleasant and tense, yet at the same time so monotonous, that I had a hard time getting people to reflect on their experiences and impressions of the courts when I interviewed them in some other setting. The experience of going to court defies and contradicts what people want to glorify, honor, and remember about themselves and their world. People resisted going back there, even for a moment of remembering.

# CHAPTER 4

# The Face and Arms of Military Justice

*Judges and Prosecutors*

---

*Military justice is to justice what military music is to music.*
A quote attributed to Georges Clemenceau
during the Dreyfus trial

The Israeli occupation of the West Bank and Gaza is the longest military occupation in modern times. According to the official Israeli narrative, the military administration, established in 1967 to govern Palestinians in the occupied territories, has exercised its powers legally and acted reasonably and with relative restraint under the circumstances of enduring conflict (see Chapter 2). Indeed, Israel's use of law, rather than resorting exclusively to force, is a core component of this narrative of legitimacy and restraint.[1]

However, the legality of military and emergency laws, the means by which they are enforced through the military court system, and the availability of legal justice are heavily disputed. Even some Israeli officers who serve in the military administration do not unanimously concur with or uncritically accept the official narrative. This chapter focuses on military court judges and prosecutors. The central aims are to analyze their legal roles and practices and to explore variations in their perspectives on the functioning of the military court system and the legitimacy of Israeli military rule over Palestinians in the West Bank and Gaza.

Few published studies about the military court system analyze the judiciary and the prosecution at all, and those that do tend to discuss them as homologous subsets of actors, conflating them with the state that they represent. To some extent such generalizations are valid because the roles that judges and prosecutors fulfill demand a fairly high level of conformity and because they serve in the same military unit of the Israel Defense Forces (IDF; see Appendix). Moreover, the people who fulfill these roles have much in common. Almost all judges and prosecutors are Jewish Israeli lawyers, most are male, and many are Ashkenazi *sabras* (born in-country of European descent). Most of the judges and prosecutors I interviewed identified themselves as "centrists," "liberals," or "leftists" within the ideologico-political spectrum of Jewish Israeli society.[2] But the commonalities belie differences in the ways individuals understand what they do and why, and their perceptions of the nature and purpose of the military court system. These differences illustrate the parameters of consensus and dissent within Jewish Israeli society regarding Israeli control over the West Bank and Gaza and the national interests being served or compromised by its continuation.[3]

Ethnographic analysis of the roles and practices of state agents provides a means of exploring the gaps between official discourse, what Allen Feldman refers to as "the Archimedean point of the authorizing center," and the views of those who exercise the state's authority "in the sites of instantiation."[4] These gaps are not incidental or anomalous; rather, they serve an important purpose, what organizational sociologists refer to as an "organizational decoupling," which enables institutions (in this case the military court system) "to maintain standardized, legitimating, formal structures while [participants'] activities vary in response to practical considerations."[5] The practical considerations that bear upon the roles and practices of judges and prosecutors encompass changing dynamics of the Israeli-Palestinian conflict and matters specific to the courts' functioning as a legal institution. But judges' and prosecutors' personal experiences and political views also bear upon their participation in the court system, and some hold views that deviate from the "official story."

In principle, the role that judges fulfill distinguishes them from prosecutors, police, members of the security services, and all other state agents. Judges are obliged to act impartially and to ensure the fair enforcement of the law.[6] They represent, in short, the "legal face" of Israeli rule in the West Bank and Gaza.[7] In practice, some judges regard their role as complementary to the role of prosecutors and tend to fill it accordingly; they emphasize the need for close coordination of military and legal measures to maintain Israeli security, order, and control. Others are motivated by the requirements of judicial independence and demonstrate this by maintaining a degree of distance from the prosecution and (judicial) skepticism toward prosecution evidence. As high-ranking military officers, they are no less concerned about security, order, or control than prosecutors, but they see their first duty as judges to be impartial.

For prosecutors, a different set of professional norms and standards applies. Their primary concern is conviction of the accused. As one head prosecutor in the West Bank explained, "We don't look after the [interests of the] accused, but after the principle of punishment [which] must be a deterrent for others." In fulfilling their role, prosecutors have less latitude and discretion than judges; their work is overseen and directed by their superiors in the military hierarchy, and their mandate is defined by directives that emanate from the military establishment (see Appendix). Whereas judges have to reconcile the contradictory aspects of the system as both military and legal, for prosecutors these aspects converge. If judges are the "legal face" of Israeli rule in the territories, prosecutors are the "legal arms."

## Telling Tales

> [P]eople tend to explain their actions to themselves and to others through stories. . . . As a form of social action, stories thus reflect and sustain institutional and cultural arrangements, bridging the gap between daily social interaction and large-scale social structures. . . . [T]he stories describe the world as it is lived and is understood by the storyteller.
>
> Patricia Ewick and Sustan Silbey,
> *The Common Place of Law*[8]

One day, an Israeli military judge was driving to work in Nablus when his car was stoned by Palestinians. When he arrived at the court, he was very angry.

Telling the tale of this event was enormously popular in military court circles, even years after it occurred (1989). I heard the story from a dozen people, including the man who was its central subject. In every version, the basic outline was the same. Beyond that, however, accounts differed, as did the conclusions the tellers drew.

In some accounts, the judge, who was generally regarded as a reasonable man, was so enraged by the stoning that he vented his anger on the defendants whose cases came before him that day by imposing excessively high sentences. In other accounts, the judge did not allow the stoning to affect his work and handled the day's cases just as he would on any other day. And then there were the accounts that highlighted not what the judge did but who he was: this judge was a settler.

What is most interesting about this story is not what "really happened" but why it became a local legend, told by people who were in the Nablus court that day and by others who heard it second- or thirdhand themselves. People told this story to make a point about justice. But the point that tellers wanted to make varied, like the versions of the story. For those who claimed that the judge acted differently on that day, that his anger affected his work by inspiring him to use his power more punitively, the point was to illustrate the tenuousness of judicial impartiality in this system. According to one Palestinian teller of this version, "How can you expect the courts to do justice when you never know from one day to the next if the judge is motivated to act as jurist or enemy?" For those who claimed that the judge acted the same as he would on any other day (including, not surprisingly, the judge himself), the point was to emphasize that Israeli military judges behaved in a professional and objective manner and did not use their position for axe grinding. And for those who emphasized the fact that the judge was a settler, the point was to illustrate Israeli disregard for legality and justice because settlers' very status as such was a violation of international law.

In the various versions of this story, the narrative elements were used to present tellers' (conflicting) views of Israeli authority, Palestinian resistance, and the legitimacy of the military court system. The stones that rained upon the judge's car provided a narrative device to generalize about Palestinian resistance. For some tellers, throwing stones against Israeli targets was a justifiable expression of Palestinian frustration and an inevitable response to the repressive and enduring nature of the occupation. For others, throwing stones was a riotous and violent disruption of public order and a threat to security. None of the tellers suggested that the stone throwers knew the driver of the car was a military judge; all they knew — all they had to know — was that this was an Israeli vehicle, identifiable by its yellow license plates. Telling the story of this particular incident provided a means of dramatizing and moralizing about the commonplace; the event took place during the first *intifada* when Palestinians of all ages were using something available in abundance (stones) to make it dangerous for Israelis to be in the territories. The Israeli military, in turn, had responded to the rise in stone throwing by making it a felony offense. In some cases, when stone throwing resulted in accidents or casualties, the throwers' houses were demolished. This administrative policy was officially justified as a means of deterrence and was sanctioned by the High Court of Justice (HCJ).

The issue of the judge's anger provided another narrative device to reflect on the influence of emotion in individuals' relations with others in the military court system. Interviewees frequently used emotion-laden language to talk about their work and those with whom they interacted, coloring their discussions with references to feelings of anger, hurt, fear, scorn, humiliation, sympathy, and pride. Tellers of this story used the judge's emotional state both to talk about the judge as an individual — whether to say that he acted "reasonably" or "irrationally" on that particular day — and to generalize about judges in the abstract — how emotional proclivities influenced (or did not influence) the exercise of institutional power.

The sentences that the judge meted out that day functioned, for many of the storytellers, as the moral of this tale. If they were higher than normal, the moral was that justice was a myth. If they were not higher, the moral was that justice prevailed — as usual. Interestingly, in none of the versions I heard did any teller argue that those Palestinian defendants who appeared before the judge in court that day might have been "innocent" of resistance activities. Rather, the question was whether resistance was "criminal" or "legitimate." Moreover, while the outcome of their cases was the subject of disagreement, there was no contention — in fact, there was no discussion at all — of the inevitability that defendants would end up in prison; the question was for how long.

In my opinion, this tale became a legend because it provided a succinct — if contested — illustration of the relationship between justice and judging. Although judges are obliged to act as impartial mediators between legal adversaries, such high-minded principles rarely obtain in any criminal court system. In this court system, the issue of judicial impartiality is weighted by the fact that judges are also soldiers serving in a conflict zone. No one involved in this system, including judges, regards it as "normal." On the contrary, everyone discusses the system in terms of problems. How, then, do people perceive and explain the role of judges as arbiters of legal justice?

Some people argue that although judges are soldiers serving a military administration that governs an "enemy" population, in their role as legal professionals they act impartially (at least to the degree that the prevailing circumstances allow) in their handling of cases. In this schematization, the ideal of legal semiautonomy prevails, and the system is represented as a triangular equation:

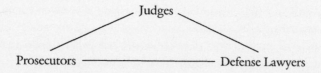

Other people argue that the role of judges is so deeply embedded in the politics of military occupation that they must be placed alongside the prosecutors and in opposition to defense lawyers and the Palestinians they represent. In this schematization, the system conforms to an "Israeli versus Palestinian" nationalist dichotomy, and is represented as an oppositional equation:

| Israeli Military | Palestinian Population |
|---|---|
| Judges and Prosecutors | Defense Lawyers |

Finally, some argue that judges, prosecutors, and defense lawyers are all system "insiders" who act in concert, whether by design or default, against the interests of Palestinian defendants. In this schematization, the oppositional equation takes a different form:

| Judges, Prosecutors, and Defense Lawyers | Defendants |
|---|---|

People I interviewed would argue for one schematization or another as the "correct" one, using tales — stories and anecdotes about their own experiences, observations, recollections, and impressions — along with discussions of legal, political, and even cultural factors to justify and explain their views and to discredit conflicting opinions. For example, one Arab Israeli defense lawyer told a personal story to prove his point that judges regularly violated impartiality by colluding with prosecutors and security agents. The lawyer's brother-in-law, a resident of the West Bank, had been arrested and interrogated for two months without confessing to the allegation that he was a leader of the Popular Front for the Liberation of Palestine (PFLP). One day the lawyer, his wife, and his sister-in-law were at the Ramallah military court to inquire about the case. The president of the court, whom the lawyer knew quite well from years of working in the system, invited them into his office as a courtesy. As they were talking, a prosecutor popped his head into the office and told the judge that a certain prisoner was still refusing to cooperate (i.e., confess). The prisoner he named was the brother-in-law. The judge turned red with embarrassment. The lawyer said, "What's this? A judge getting information about an interrogation?" The following week, the lawyer met the deputy legal advisor and the head prosecutor for the West Bank to discuss the incident. They told the lawyer that the prosecutor was dropping most of the charges out of respect for him, not as an admission of wrongdoing by the judge. But they asked that he refrain from publicizing the incident in the judge's office, which he agreed to in the interest of his brother-in-law.

Like the first story, this story was relayed to me to illustrate a larger point the teller wanted to make about judicial impartiality and, by extension, justice. The lawyer stressed that the incident had not surprised him. Rather, it had merely confirmed what he and many of his colleagues suspected: that judges routinely act in a partisan manner. But, as his own behavior also revealed, the pressure to "go along" is great and the alternatives are few. Whatever people involved in the system think of it — and *why* they think as they do — they tend to cooperate to keep it functioning through their own roles and interactions in the handling of cases. Defense lawyers and defendants are not the only ones who feel pressured to "go along." Some judges and prosecutors, too, have felt constrained and compromised by a lack of alternatives.

## Questioning the Order

In October 1991, Israeli journalist Sara Leibovitz-Dar published an article in an Israeli newspaper, *Hadashot,* that featured the views of Aryeh Cox, an Israeli lawyer who did reserve duty as a military court judge in Gaza. Cox delivered a brutal indictment of the system and the role that judges were expected to fulfill. He said:

It is clear that this is not a natural and ordinary court system, but some solution that the military administration found for the purpose of enforcing the occupation regime. The job that is done there is not purely jurisdictional. In fact, the situation in the military court in Gaza does not look like something of this world. Hundreds of families are outside, dozens of prisoners are inside, most very young. The impression is that they have lost faith in the system and do not even try to defend themselves. They confess to everything. The defense counsels, who are in many cases pathetic characters, also accept the situation and act, in fact, as mediators for the purpose of punishment. I found there a total symbiosis between the prosecution, the judges and the lawyers, while the accused are at the side. And everything is taking place in stoic agreement.[9]

Cox's critique caused quite a stir among those with an interest in the Israeli military court system, and people talked about the article long after it was published. It was one thing for Palestinians, or foreign observers, or Israeli leftists to criticize the system; it was an entirely different matter for such harsh public criticism to come from "inside," from a judge no less.

Aside from its critical view of the court system, the article provided a vivid insight into Jewish Israeli political culture and debates about the occupation that had become downright rancorous since the start of the first *intifada* in 1987. Cox said that his personal slogan, "Live and let live," meant that he regarded Arabs as humans who should be treated as such. The next line of the article read: "He knows that saying such things labels him immediately a leftist." He responded, "In a normal state I would be considered a man of the center. . . . [H]ere . . . I found myself on the left." Cox, who was born and raised in a right-wing (Revisionist Zionist[10]) family, charted his move "leftward" as a result of the negative effects that key political events had on him, notably the 1973 war, the Likud Party victory in 1977, the Israeli invasion of Lebanon in 1982, and the *intifada*.[11] He had come to the conclusion that Israel should take bold steps to end the occupation, and he hoped that his public criticism of the military court system might serve as a push in that direction. Yet the difficulty of translating opposition to the occupation into practice was the subject of the exchange between Cox and Leibovitz-Dar that concluded the article:

"How did it happen that no prosecutor or military judge has refused so far to serve in the territories?"

"It is hard to answer this question. I think this is due to the [military unit in which judges and prosecutors serve], that is a warm unit, like a family."

"If you are called up again, will you refuse?"

"No. I, too, will go if they ask me, and for the same reason. It is simply a matter of companionship. But I do hope they will not ask me."

"Will you judge and cry?"[12]

"The main [issue] is not really crying, but the question why I am involved in such a thing. In the distant future, when the situation will be resolved, I shall certainly ask myself why I have done all this work."

Cox's views were emblematic of a crisis in civil-military relations within Jewish Israeli society that was heightened by the first *intifada*. In those years, the crisis often was compared to yet ultimately distinguished from the domestic crisis that had resulted from Israel's invasion and occupation of Lebanon, which had stimulated the growth of an Israeli peace camp that sought to challenge military policy and discretion.[13] But the domestic crisis over Lebanon was circumscribed by the degree to which Israeli military activities north of the border were popularly perceived as a war because they were waged against armed adversaries in unequivocally "foreign territory." The *intifada* was a crisis of a different nature, since the Israeli military was contending with rampant unrest and resistance by a largely unarmed civilian population.[14] Moreover, the military's options in the West Bank and Gaza were constrained by the status of the Israeli state as the de facto sovereign.

The Israeli citizens called upon to serve as judges and prosecutors were affected by public debates over military and governmental responses to the *intifada*, although few took the kind of public stance that Cox did. One subject of debate was whether the *intifada* constituted a "war."[15] Aryeh Shalev, a retired general and staff member of the Jaffee Center for Strategic Studies, began his book on the *intifada*: "The uprising is a war being waged by the Palestinians against Israel for control and rule in Judea, Samaria [the West Bank,] and Gaza."[16] According to Yoram Peri, a scholar also associated with the Jaffee Center and then managing editor of *Davar,* "[I]t's a war that has gone on between us and the Arabs for more than 40 years now. Thus in one fell swoop the difference between [sic] an Iraqi pilot, an Egyptian commando, and a six-year-old Palestinian child from the Balata refugee camp is wiped out. They're all the same. It's the same old sea, the same old Arabs, and the same old war."[17]

In some ways, the *intifada* looked like war: mass resistance and stone throwing had inspired the military establishment to change the rules of engagement to permit looser open fire regulations. Media coverage captured and disseminated the warlike images of confrontations, clashes, and deaths. But for the Israeli state and many of its Jewish citizens, warring against civilians, even militantly rebellious ones, fueled national angst, as Peri noted: "What meaning can the notion 'purity of arms' possibly have after two years of doing battle with women and children?"[18]

Another prevailing concern was the negative effect of the *intifada* on Israeli society, national security, and the military establishment. According to Emmanual Sivan, a professor at Hebrew University,

What has changed in the military sphere is the high price which the continued rule over the territory entails: in killed and wounded among the security forces and Jewish civilians, the burden of reserve duty and the type of especially harsh service, the tensions between security forces and the judicial authorities, the increase of "aberrations" and the damage to the soldiers' morale, and we have still not mentioned the financial cost of the army's operations in the West Bank and Gaza Strip, estimated at one billion shekels, and the possibilities that the army's preparedness for an overall war has been harmed.[19]

Supporters and defenders of the Israeli military sought to counter media images of stone-throwing Palestinian "Davids" facing a heavily armed Israeli "Goliath." Presenting Palestinians in the West Bank and Gaza as warlike and profoundly dangerous could justify the harsh measures being used to restore "law and order." Sivan opined, "We perhaps like our conduct in the territories less and less, but neither does the conduct of the Palestinians aid empathy (not to mention sympathy) toward them."[20]

There was also an outpouring of Israeli journalistic reporting, first-person accounts, and documentaries that presented individual Israelis' deep antipathy over what they were being made and asked to do to contend with the *intifada* and maintain the occupation.[21] Rela Mezali, an Israeli human rights activist, asked, "When is the very existence of a country endangered?"[22] She related this abstract question to the imperatives of military service. "[M]y society understands the word 'compulsory' in the expression 'compulsory military service' in a sense much stronger than that of legal obligation. . . . [W]e interpret 'compulsory' to mean inevitable, a necessary fate leaving room for no other possibility. . . . This amounts to a fatalistic, quasi-religious, ritualistic attitude."[23] She suggested that the inability to question either the obligation to serve or the nature of service was evidence of larger problems relating to the militarization of Israeli society and the dehumanization of Palestinians.

In a similar vein, Stanley Cohen, a professor of sociology and criminology then teaching at Hebrew University and active in the Israeli human rights movement, criticized Israeli intellectuals' collusion with the military and security establishments through a failure or refusal to question security policies and military practices. "Most of my academic colleagues have no sense of being on the edge of their society, of seeing it from the outside. As a result, they are reluctant to take a stand that might be interpreted as 'disloyal' or 'unpatriotic' or (worst of all) 'anti-Zionist.' So, even [during the *intifada*], they defend an idealized version of Israeli history and culture as if it were reality."[24]

Public debates about the *intifada* forced Jewish Israelis (many for the first time) to be concerned about the military's rule in the West Bank and Gaza. But in the Jewish Israeli mainstream, the *intifada* was perceived as a cause rather than a result of problems. This was evident in the shock and surprise among military and political leaders at the *intifada*'s outbreak, early projections that the situation would be brought under control quickly and order restored, mounting anger at Palestinians, and popular sanction for escalating military violence and punitive reprisals like beatings, house demolitions, deportations, and administrative detentions as the uprising continued. Yet, for all the efforts the government and its supporters made to market the *intifada* in a Manichean discourse of good versus evil, or order versus chaos, such as referring to stones as "weapons that kill" and justifying the massive arrests as a "war on crime," the erosion of a pre-*intifada* security consensus was evident in the growing polarization among Jewish Israelis.

Among secular liberals, the *intifada* raised long-simmering concerns about the negative consequences of protracted military occupation on Israeli society. It became an Israeli liberal preoccupation that the expressly undemocratic and carceral nature of the military administration was diminishing Israelis' commitment to the rule of law and universalistic values "at home." At the other end of the political spectrum, the religious-national right resented the military's self-imposed restrictions on combating the Palestinian resistance and scoffed at the concerns of liberals that state policies should conform to international humanitarian law.

## Views from inside the Court System

For judges, the crisis of the first *intifada* affected them directly, since they were positioned simultaneously as soldiers facing an enemy population engaging in open rebellion and as jurists obliged to deal impartially and fairly with the cases that came before them. Some judges, like Cox, felt increasingly conflicted about their role in the military court system. Others rallied to defend the military establishment from charges of excess and abuse. One reservist judge said that Israel needed to go on a media offensive to combat "the imagery of Palestinian Davids against the Israeli Goliath." He continued: "The stones versus guns imagery has hurt Israel, so to counter this problem Israel should do more public relations to show what Palestinians really do and the results of their attacks with stones and knives. The media should publish more [photos] of wounded and killed Israelis."

Although all of the judges I interviewed acknowledged that the military was in crisis "on the streets," some rejected the idea that the court system had been adversely affected by the *intifada*. According to one full-time judge, "Nothing has changed. The interest of the court has always been to convict a guilty man and acquit an innocent man."

Yet the situation in the military courts had changed profoundly as a result of the *intifada*. At the most basic level, the vast increase in the number of people being arrested put pressure on the system to finish more cases quickly and to use prosecution as a deterrent for continued resistance. One judge with a long tenure in the courts said that judicial impartiality was an ideal but that in reality judges had to be conscious of the relationship between their role and the larger military goal of restoring order by punishing those who resisted. He said, "Judges know that what they do in court — how they decide cases and the kinds of sentences they give — are being watched, and they care about what people think. What they do affects their chances for promotion. Judges who are promotion-minded must do what the MAG [Military Advocate General] wants. It's not really a political line, but there is definitely tension."

While all the judges I interviewed stressed that there was no direct pressure on them to decide cases in any particular way, several mentioned that those with reputations for being "easy" might become the target of complaints. According to one former judge, "This is because the army does hard work capturing those people and then doesn't want to see the court letting them off without sufficient punishment." One reservist judge, formerly the president of the Ramallah court, was widely regarded by other judges, prosecutors, and defense lawyers alike as "lenient." When we spoke about his reputation, he said, "I don't care what others think. I am proud of my record. I tried to do the best job I could, and it wasn't easy. Sometimes people complained about me, but as a judge I had to make hard decisions. I'm not there to make people happy. It was my job to enforce the law fairly."

Some prosecutors also were discomfited by the way the system was operating and by their duties on what was effectively the front line of the military administration's efforts to crush the uprising by using harsh punishment to deter resistance. One young prosecutor, who had started working in the military courts in 1989, said, "I don't let myself think about the fact that practically every Palestinian whose case comes before these courts — thousands of people — is convicted. If I dwelled on this, I wouldn't be able to do my job."

Although the percentage of arrested Palestinians who were convicted in the military courts did not change (it remained approximately 90–95 percent), the numbers increased massively. Between 1988 and July 1993, some 100,000 Palestinians were arrested by Israeli forces, and 83,321 were prosecuted. This increase in prosecution and incarceration focused increasingly critical attention on the court system, raising questions and stimulating debates about *how* such large numbers of people were being convicted.

A number of factors contribute to the facility of convicting Palestinians in the military court system and generally are understood and discussed as prosecution advantages vis-à-vis the defense. These factors include the interrogation methods used to extract confessions and their evidentiary weight; the use of "secret evidence" to detain and convict; and a general tendency on the part of judges to accept prosecution evidence and prefer it to contradictory evidence or testimony from the defense. In the following two sections, I elaborate on these issues as they inform the practices of judges and prosecutors and influence their perspectives about the military court system's legitimacy.

## Confessions and Secret Evidence

As I discuss in Chapter 2, interrogation is the most contentious aspect of the military court system. In 1987, the revelations of an official Israeli commission of inquiry shattered the official narrative denying that Israeli interrogation methods included routine violence.[25] However, the new official policy, based on the Landau Commission's recommendations, sanctioned the use of "moderate amounts of physical pressure." While this sanctioning bolstered the security establishment, it tainted the legal process.

Prosecutors were placed in the position of having to mediate between the now publicly acknowledged use of "pressure" tactics to obtain confessions and the state's declared commitment to the right of people in custody to be free from torture. In principle, the state is obligated to respect the rights of people in custody (i.e., by refraining from coercion and violence), and the only confessions that should be accepted as legally admissible are those "given" rather than taken by force. But the sanctioning of "moderate physical pressure" illuminated the deviations between principle and practice and raised questions about whether confessions were viable means of discerning between "innocence" and "guilt."

Many judges and prosecutors told me that they were shocked by the Landau Commission report. Nevertheless, as participants in the military court system, they were forced to take a position in the controversy it had provoked. Many accepted the official line that the sanctioned interrogation methods did not amount to "torture." According to one former prosecutor, "As we know, sometimes [interrogators] have to use force. But many people automatically say they were tortured even when they weren't. I know what people go through isn't easy, but I wouldn't call it torture. . . . They sit with police or Shabak [General Security Services (GSS) agents] or whoever and are asked specific questions. Then people admit [what they did]. It's not like the movies — it's simple. They know they will sit in prison and don't see this as a terrible thing. Once a person is caught, he knows it's all over."

In principle, a defense lawyer can challenge a confession that a client claims was coerced by calling for a *zuta* (*voir dire;* often called a "mini-trial" or a "trial-within-a-trial"). This entails a hearing in camera in which a judge hears testimony from the defendant, the interrogators, and any others who might have relevant information (e.g., police, prison guards, and doctors). But for such a challenge to succeed, the judge would have to consider the testimony of the defendant more credible than that of the interrogators. According to the Landau Commission report: "From the testimonies we heard it turns out that the percentage of cases in which a confession was rejected due to the court's disbelief or doubt in the inter-rogators' statements on the witness stand was very small. In the vast majority of cases the courts preferred the interrogators' testimonies to the accuseds' allegations concerning the use of illegitimate methods against them."[26]

These tendencies did not change after (or despite) the revelations of the Landau Commission. When questioned about the issue of interro-gation, most of the judges and prosecutors I interviewed said that *zuta* provided an effective legal remedy. But not one judge recalled ever hav-ing excluded a confession. And due to the overwhelming likelihood of failure, most defense lawyers said that they did not consider *zuta* either a meaningful protection or a viable option and were further disinclined to call for one because doing so could actually hurt the defendant by increasing the final punishment as retribution for "wasting the court's time." Ironically, some judges and prosecutors argued that the infre-quency of *zuta* demonstrated that torture was not a significant problem. According to one head prosecutor, the GSS would neither have to nor be tempted to resort to "torture." He said, "The Shabak wants the truth, just like the entire legal system, so the correct person gets convicted."

If prosecutors and judges were inclined to believe that "pressure" tac-tics did not rise to the level of torture and ill-treatment, how did they understand and explain why so many people confessed? One common explanation was that Palestinians confessed — even to things that they did not do — because they wanted to "show off" to the interrogators and appear as heroes in their community. Another common explanation was that Palestinians' allegations of torture were face-saving measures to jus-tify the fact that they confessed or to alleviate the stigma of being per-ceived as cowardly or weak.

During the Landau Commission's investigations, GSS agents claimed that judges were fully aware of the use of violence and the fact that agents were lying about these methods whenever a confession was challenged. The Landau Commission rejected this GSS claim as an insult to judicial integrity but never questioned any military court judges to assess the veracity of the allegation. According to Avigdor Feldman, an Israeli lawyer, even if judges did not actively collude with the GSS, their credulity (as demonstrated by an overwhelming willingness to accept perjured GSS testimony) had been confirmed by the findings of the Landau Commission. Feldman argued,

Then there are two possibilities as far as the courts are concerned. If the Landau Commission determines that the GSS agents lied in almost all of the cases in which they appeared in court, and that this practice had been going on for a long time, then either everything that we know and think we know about the courts being able to assess evidence, uncover the truth, and distinguish between truth and falsehood is total rubbish, and the courts do not know how to tell truth from lies, or there is a real case of cooperation [between judges and security agents]. In both cases, the implications . . . are both shocking and disturbing.[27]

Prosecutors' use of "secret evidence" also came under increasing scrutiny and criticism during the first *intifada*. Secret evidence is always the basis for administrative detention (i.e., incarceration without trial). Within the military court system, prosecutors can use secret evidence at extension-of-detention hearings to support their request that judges remand detainees. Secret evidence also can serve as a basis for charges.

Israeli officials and spokespeople for the military have justified the use of secret evidence as necessary in light of the security situation in the occupied territories, where fighting crime and maintaining order are tantamount to counterinsurgency. Since much of the evidence classified as "secret" comes from Palestinian informants, this raises questions about how their services are procured and how the information they provide is used. The most substantial study of Palestinians who collaborate with the Israeli state was published during the first *intifada* by B'Tselem, an Israeli human rights organization. According to the authors: "Since 1967, the security forces have recruited tens of thousands of Palestinians from the territories to serve as collaborators. This was made possible in part by the great dependence of the Palestinians on the services provided by the Israeli administration. In recruiting collaborators, the security forces used methods that contravene international law, such as providing certain services only on condition that the recipient cooperate with the authorities. They also resorted to extortion and pressure, and offered various inducements."[28]

The relationship between the use of collaborators and the functioning of the military court system is twofold. First, collaborators form an integral part of the state's "resources" to gather incriminating information that can be used to detain, charge, and prosecute suspects. Second, collaborators often are recruited while undergoing interrogation or in detention and, once recruited, provide a window for the authorities both within the prisons and outside.[29] To ensure a continuing source of information and to protect Palestinians who collaborate from reprisals by other Palestinians, it is crucial to maintain a high level of secrecy.

But using secret evidence, which is unavailable to either the defense lawyer or the defendant, taints the legal process; the defense is afforded no opportunity to know the contents or contest the veracity of the evidence directly. Under such circumstances, a defense lawyer's only option is to request that the judge evaluate the merits of the secret evidence. Thus, the judge becomes the de facto representative of the defendant, since the lawyer is barred from playing such a role. Whether judges are capable or inclined to evaluate secret evidence skeptically and impartially is debatable. Indeed, many participants (including some judges and prosecutors) regard secret evidence as a serious derogation of due process protections for defendants. According to one judge, who vigorously condemned the pervasive use of secret evidence, "Justice has to be shown, and not just done."

## Prosecutorial Advantages in the Legal Process

A number of other factors contribute to the facility of convicting Palestinians and compromise the notion of a "level playing field" between legal adversaries. In a "normal" court system, the parity derives (in principle) from the presumption of the defendant's innocence, which puts the burden on the prosecution to prove guilt. While the prosecution has access to state resources (e.g., police power and investigative services), the burden of proof and judicial impartiality compensate the defense.

In the Israeli military court system, there is no basis in law or practice for the presumption of innocence. The three-pronged practice of arrest, interrogation, and detention is premised on a de facto presumption of guilt (see Chapter 7). This is evident in the fact that any soldier can arrest any Palestinian for the slightest suspicion or cause, and once arrested, people can be held for prolonged periods incommunicado. The presumption of guilt is further confirmed by a general pattern of refusing to release detainees on bail, prolonged denials of lawyer-client meetings, and the pattern of judicial concession to prosecutors' requests for extension of detention.

Once the prosecution has enough evidence for a prima facie case to bring charges,[30] another set of prosecutorial advantages kicks into effect, which, for all intents and purposes, place the burden on the defense to *disprove guilt*.[31] A confession, whether first- or third-party, is usually sufficient to ensure a conviction as long as there is an additional scintilla of evidence (*dvar ma* in Hebrew). Whereas in the domestic Israeli criminal justice system a confession must pass certain logical tests to ensure that it was not "invented" by the accused, such as a scintilla that the accused had the opportunity to commit the crime or that the confession does not contradict other types of evidence, in the military court system, the scintilla can be extremely tenuous; it does not have to corroborate the confession or even implicate the accused directly. All it has to show is a *possible* connection between the accused and the crime. Even if a defendant subsequently rescinds a confession on the grounds that it was coerced, or other exculpatory information becomes available, according to the rules of evidence that apply in this system, the court has the option to retain — *and prefer* — the confession over other evidence. Hence, the practice of judges fortifies the weight and value of confessions.

Another advantage prosecutors enjoy is the tendency of judges to favor the testimony of their witnesses over those of the defense. The judges with whom I spoke acknowledged that this was the case, pointing out that most criminal court systems tend to prefer the testimony and evidence provided by those involved in law enforcement. The justifying assumption is that those responsible for the enforcement of law have no interest in lying to the court, whereas other types of witnesses might be motivated or pressured to lie. The president of the military court of appeals, while acknowledging this tendency, said that this was "irrelevant" to the issue of justice. He added, "Judicial impartiality and objectivity correct for any undue influence or errors of soldiers."

But law enforcement in the occupied territories is not disinterested; it is provided primarily by soldiers, most of whom, by all accounts, are deeply hostile to and suspicious of Palestinians. This raises serious questions about soldiers' capacity to function as "neutral" officers of the law, even in a capacity as witnesses. Moreover, soldiers are untrained and ill prepared to do the kind of investigative police work necessary to gather material evidence. But military solidarity and Jewish Israeli national cohesion fortify a tendency for judges and prosecutors to identify with soldiers and to trust or prefer their evidence or testimonies over that provided by Palestinians.

The tendency of judges to prefer prosecution evidence is openly acknowledged. But there are variations and exceptions. Two defense lawyers, one from Gaza and the other from the West Bank, provided personal accounts about this issue that bore a striking similarity but different outcomes. The Gazan lawyer told of a soldier who testified in a case against one of his clients, saying he had witnessed the man throwing stones at 9:15 A.M. in Jabalya refugee camp. The client was found guilty. Several days later, the same soldier testified against another client, reporting that he had seen the man throwing stones at 9:30 A.M. (on the same day as the earlier case) in Rafah refugee camp. The lawyer questioned the soldier about how long it would take to get from Jabalya to Rafah, to which the soldier responded that the trip would take about forty-five minutes if there were no traffic. The lawyer then asked the judge to dismiss this case because the soldier could not possibly have been in both places as he had testified. Rather than acknowledging that the soldier was perjuring himself in at least one of the cases, the judge ordered that the lawyer be thrown out of court because his line of questioning had insulted the soldier.

The West Bank lawyer told of two cases in which the testimony of the same soldier was the cornerstone of the prosecution's evidence. The soldier testified that he had arrested one of the lawyer's clients at 1:00 P.M. Several days later, the soldier testified that he had witnessed the second client throwing stones at 1:30 P.M. The lawyer questioned the soldier about how much time it took to process someone who had been arrested. The soldier responded that it would take about thirty minutes. The lawyer then argued to the judge that the soldier's testimony could not be true, since both incidents occurred on the same day and, according to the soldier's own testimony, he would not have had time to get back into the streets to witness the alleged stone throwing. The judge not only concurred and released the client but berated the prosecutor for introducing specious evidence.

This latter story illustrates another point of contention about the legal system: that prosecutors collude with their witnesses to present false testimony in order to obtain a conviction. I was in the Nablus court one day when an already incarcerated prisoner was being brought up on additional charges that he had beaten another prisoner. Both men were brought to court for the hearing. The defendant said that he had acted in self-defense because the other was a collaborator who had attacked him first. During the hearing, the defense lawyer tried to pursue a line of questioning about whether the other man actually was a collaborator, since collaborators' use of violence in prisons was well documented. The prosecutor denied the allegations, saying that he was just another prisoner who now had to be relocated to another prison for his safety. The judge accepted the prosecutor's argument that the attack was unprovoked and increased the defendant's sentence. During the course of the hearing, the second man was treated like a prisoner; he was in handcuffs and sat among the other prisoners. But after the hearing, I was in the hallway when he was brought out of the courtroom. Soldiers removed his handcuffs and the prosecutor handed him a set of car keys. He walked out of the building a free man.

## The Political Is Personal

When I began field research, some Israeli friends were skeptical that I would be able to obtain the kind of access to the military that this project demanded, warning that even if judges and prosecutors were willing to be interviewed, they would not be forthcoming about their experiences and opinions to a foreign academic researcher. Taking such concerns to heart, I applied to the Public Relations Office of the IDF, informing them of my project and requesting official permission to interview military judges and prosecutors. I waited for some kind of letter certifying my right to interview members of the military and feared that I would face problems if I proceeded without it.

Despite my intentions to wait, one day in the Ramallah court, an Arab Israeli lawyer, in the interest of furthering my research, introduced me to a young prosecutor, instructed me to ask him anything, and left us alone. The prosecutor turned to me and said, "So, which side are you on?" Taken aback, I stammered, "Neutral." "Impossible," he responded. "No one is neutral." If I was feeling shy or ill prepared, this little exchange did nothing to assuage my trepidation. I assumed that he was looking for a sparring partner, and the last thing I wanted to do was get into a political discussion with a prosecutor in a public area of the Ramallah military court. But my concerns, as it turned out, were completely irrelevant, as he proceeded in what was essentially a monologue for over an hour. He was quite eager to share his views.

In retrospect, after interviewing many other Israeli prosecutors and judges, I realize that his views and opinions were not as unique as they struck me at the time. But that first interview was quite a surprise because I had assumed that Israeli officers would present a clear and positive view of the court system. In contrast, the narrative he put forth combined criticisms of the system with thoughtful and elaborate explanations about why he believed things were as they were. He began by telling me that he had immigrated to Israel from the United States when he was nineteen years old because he wanted to be a "big fish in a small pond." Another reason for the move was that he believed it was important for Jews to live together, not for religious reasons (he is secular) or because of anti-Semitism (he said he did not consider anti-Semitism a major problem in the United States any longer), but because Jews had a "cultural affinity." He signed up to be a military prosecutor as a stepping stone for a career in government, stressing that it was important and necessary for an immigrant like him to demonstrate his commitment to Israel through such service.

But he made it quite clear that he opposed the occupation. He said, "I chose Israel, but I didn't choose the *intifada*." In his opinion, holding the West Bank and Gaza did not provide security for the Israeli state; rather, it was a security liability. He was fully aware that his was a minority view — and an unpopular one — among Jewish Israelis. Expanding on this issue, he said he found it hard to adjust to life in Israel because criticism of government policy on matters relating to security was far less acceptable than in the United States, especially from immigrants.

I was surprised when he said that he regularly read *Challenge,* a (now defunct) magazine published by Derech HaNitzotz, a small anti-Zionist Jewish-Palestinian organization. He said he knew that most of what *Challenge* published about the occupation was true because of his experiences in the military courts but that he read it to see "what the other side thinks." He appreciated the publication of reports and studies that were critical of the occupation because criticism could provoke public discussion, but he said he would never discuss his critical views with other soldiers because he did not want a reputation as "opinionated," which might compromise his chances for promotion and adversely affect his career. He added, "It's not wise to have your views known, especially if they are different from the mainstream."

In his work as a prosecutor, he said that he was not ideologically motivated; he just wanted to be good at his job. Some prosecutors tried to "pound" Palestinians with hard sentences, but he said that he tried to evaluate and handle each case appropriately. In his opinion, most Palestinians in the territories were manipulated and misled by a shadowy leadership from abroad (at that time, the Palestine Liberation Organization [PLO] was headquartered in Tunisia), and this leadership "drives them into the streets against their better senses." He offered up a theory about how the first *intifada* started: according to him, it was not a spontaneous rebellion against the occupation but a direct result of the Lebanon war. When the PLO was driven out of Beirut in 1983, midlevel operatives gradually infiltrated into the West Bank and masterminded the whole thing, on orders from Tunis.[32]

Before the *intifada,* he had enjoyed spending time in the Arab quarters of the Old City of Jerusalem because "Arab culture is fun!" He said that he understood Palestinians' dissatisfaction with the occupation and even sympathized with them. But he had no Palestinian friends, and the only Palestinians he knew personally were lawyers he met in the military courts. According to him, most of them lacked the legal skills needed for such work, and most of the problems in the court system were due to their incompetence. But he also considered himself smarter and more talented than most of the Israeli lawyers working in the system, including the judges. Our impromptu interview ended when he was called back into court at the end of a recess.

In the months that followed, I continued to run into him and to hear about him from others. He had a reputation among defense lawyers as a good prosecutor because he was bright and flexible. Eventually, though, a rumor began circulating that he had been chastised by his superiors for being "too easy" and, because of his ambitions, which were no secret to anyone working in the Ramallah court, had begun taking a much harder line in his handling of cases. My last encounter with him was on a day in court when he kept referring to the defendant as a "terrorist," prompting the defense lawyer to complain to the judge that such language was prejudicial and inflammatory. The judge told him to refrain. Later, I heard that he had left the military courts and gotten a job in the government.

My second interview with a prosecutor also happened spontaneously in the Ramallah court. Another lawyer introduced me to a female prosecutor (at that time, one of very few women who worked in the system other than as secretaries). She was outgoing and vivacious and obviously suffered from none of the political contradictions of the first interviewee. According to her, working as a prosecutor was a fabulous experience that every new lawyer should have. She said she appreciated the opportunity to work with some "great, really great lawyers" in a courtroom setting. For her, the military courts were a place where sharp legal minds came together to have a fair fight.

She said she found her work fascinating because it involved "some very important cases, like murder and terrorism." Enthralled and committed, she said she took work home and spent nights and weekends preparing her cases, something no other prosecutor I interviewed claimed to do. In subsequent interviews when I asked other prosecutors to comment on such overtime efforts, they said it would be unnecessary because they enjoyed so many advantages that a victory required no extra work.

She described herself as ambitious and aggressive and stressed that it was important for a woman doing this job to possess and exhibit such traits. She said, "If I don't act tough, people might try to push me around just because I am a woman." When I asked her if it was difficult for a woman to be a prosecutor in the military courts, I intended the question to refer to gender discrimination. She interpreted it differently, however, and responded, "Women make better prosecutors than men because they have a mean streak which suits the job."

Seeing her around the Ramallah court on many occasions, it was obvious to me that she consciously used very stereotypical feminine wiles in her interactions with others. One day, during a hearing, the judge issued a sentence that was lower than the one she and the Palestinian defense lawyer had agreed to in their plea bargain. Afterward, she took the lawyer aside and said that now she was mad at him and would not speak to him anymore. As he tried to explain that he had done nothing to influence the judge's decision, she crossed her arms over her chest, turned her back and started pouting. After a few minutes of ignoring his pleas for understanding, she said that if he wanted to make things right, he would have to come to her office and apologize for, in her mind, having gone behind her back to the judge and created a situation in which she had been embarrassed. The lawyer, trailing behind her on their way to her office, rolled his eyes.

She had a reputation as a tough prosecutor and took great pride in this. In a second discussion with her, we started talking about how young many of the defendants were. She said to me, "Don't let them fool you. They might look like children, but they are really adults. If they look fifteen, they are probably twenty-five. You can't trust Palestinians for anything, even their ages." When I asked if she had ever felt some compassion for those whose cases she had tried, she said that she recalled one occasion when she had "really tried to help the defendant," but in general Palestinians were guilty and it was her job to "give them what they deserve."

Aside from these two spontaneous interviews, I started getting anxious as time passed and no official letter granting permission to interview members of the military was forthcoming. In correspondence and phone calls to the IDF Public Relations Office, they were polite but unhelpful and advised me to continue waiting. As months turned into a year, I started collecting names of judges and prosecutors to approach directly for interviews. The first people I called were willing to be interviewed; from them I gathered more names, and so it went.

One middle-aged Tel Aviv lawyer I interviewed had served as a prosecutor, a full-time judge, and a legal advisor and had recently performed reserve duty as a judge. He had been the head prosecutor in Gaza in 1969–73. He began our interview by recalling how different things had been back then. During the early years, most military court cases involved serious attacks carried out by *feda'yin* (guerrillas) who were members of small, clandestine armed cells. He recounted his experience prosecuting a case against Palestinians who had thrown a grenade into an Israeli civilian car, killing three people. This was the attack that initiated the military's "pacification" campaign in Gaza to crush armed resistance and make the crowded refugee camps and towns more accessible to military vehicles and surveillance (see Chapter 2). As was common during that period, captured *feda'yin* who were charged with the grenade attack refused to plead guilty prior to their trial, but when they got to court, they announced their responsibility for the attack. He said that when the judges on the case acquitted one of the three of the charge of membership in an illegal organization, the defendant protested because, without that charge, the act would be merely "criminal" rather than "political." This man explained that Palestinians who were arrested in the early years had an "armed struggle mentality." They were proud of their actions and disdainful of Israelis, representing themselves in court as soldiers in a war of liberation.

He compared that generation of defendants to the *intifada* generation, saying that many of the latter were not politicized fighters, just "regular people." He continued, "They are not criminals in the pure legal sense, except for killers, who are definitely criminals." According to him, many of the violations that people were being charged with those days (stone throwing, membership in an illegal organization, participating in demonstrations) were not "criminal" but "political" acts. He said that Israelis should be more critically conscious about the effects of the occupation on Palestinians and should ask themselves, "Why do these people do what they do, and who are they?" In his opinion, the image of defendants as "terrorists" conflicted with the fact that most were poor people or children. He expressed acute concern and sensitivity about sending children to prison. "We have to punish them very hard because they broke the law, but what will jail do to them? I have children, and some of these Palestinians are children. I always thought about that when I was doing my work. Prosecutors *should* view sending children to jail as a moral dilemma."

He used this point as an opening to make some critical comments about prosecutors. According to him, most prosecutors were too young (early twenties) to fully understand the human issues at stake in their work, whether this meant being unable to sympathize with defendants or to work well with defense lawyers. He said that prosecutors should appreciate the advantages they had and not exploit them to always seek the highest possible sentence. He noted, "Prosecutors' work is legally easy because whenever there is a confession, the hardest part of their job is done. Any time there is a confession, which is most of the time, it is easy to get a verdict that favors the prosecution."

But when it came to the judiciary, he had no complaints. He believed that judges scrupulously adhered to rule-of-law principles and that this compensated for prosecutors' advantages, making the system "fair." In his opinion, the integrity and objectivity of judges made the military court system comparable to the domestic Israeli criminal court system. He added that he was proud of the fact that the HCJ played a role in monitoring Israeli military rule in the territories and that this served to reconcile Israeli policies with international law. As he put it, "If the High Court approves something, it proves that it is legal."

Like the first prosecutor I interviewed, he had a theory about how the first *intifada* had started. He had been the legal advisor for the West Bank in 1985 when the "Jabril exchange" took place. This was the outcome of a situation in which six Israeli soldiers, who had been captured in Lebanon and were being held by the Popular Front for the Liberation of Palestine-General Command (PFLP-GC), headed by Ahmed Jabril, were released in exchange for Israel's release of 1,150 Palestinian prisoners. Of these, about 600 were from the occupied territories, many of whom had been *feda'yin*, arrested in the early years of the occupation. He believed that such an exchange had been a huge mistake: "The legal system lost the best legal power we had — imprisonment. These people were released and two years later they brought about the *intifada*."

Although his and the first interviewee's theories about the cause of the *intifada* differed, both revealed a tendency among Jewish Israeli liberals to perceive most Palestinians as complacent and, if not necessarily happy with the occupation, at least tolerant of it. Both believed that the *intifada* was caused by militants and troublemakers who led vulnerable or naive people astray. When I asked this man if he did not see other, more structural and popular causes for resistance, namely decades of repression and political disenfranchisement, he responded that perhaps someday Palestinians might have started protesting, but it would have been delayed and never would have gathered the intensity it had were it not for the Jabril exchange.

His overall assessment of the occupation was that it was an undesirable but necessary arrangement until a total, comprehensive resolution to the Israeli-Palestinian conflict was reached. He believed that the Israeli military, including the court system, had governed the territories in a humane manner under difficult circumstances. Moreover, he believed that Palestinians had benefited from Israeli rule, as illustrated by social indicators like rising literacy and income levels since 1967. According to him, negative portrayals of Israeli rule illustrated the degree to which the media were "biased" because if they had an "inside view" they would see the humanity he had seen.

Toward the end of the interview, we turned to the question of relations in the military court system among the various categories of participants. He had a very favorable opinion about dynamics in the courts and said that he considered some of the Palestinian lawyers he came to know through his work as his friends. Curious, I asked him whom in particular he would regard as a friend, and he gave me some names. Later, when I met some of those individuals, I asked what they thought about his assessment of their relationship. Invariably, Palestinian lawyers reacted with disbelief; they said that they strove to have friendly working relations with him (and other judges and prosecutors) because this facilitated their work but that their work, which was the basis for their relationship, derived from a foreign military occupation, and it would be unimaginable to consider as friends those who exercised the repressive and discriminatory authority of the military administration.

Two of the Israelis I interviewed had become defense lawyers after they finished their service in the military court system. One had served as a prosecutor in the Nablus and Gaza courts. By the time the first *intifada* started, he had established a private practice in Petah Tikva and started representing some Palestinian clients in the Gaza court. I asked if he had found it difficult to go back to Gaza as a civilian and deal with some of the same people in a different capacity. On the contrary, he said, it was a smooth transition. He added, "Even people I sent to jail for long years greeted me on the street like an old friend."

He described himself as a "real leftist." How, I asked, did this inform his experiences as a prosecutor? He said he saw prosecuting as a job, "a game with rules." He did not feel that his opposition to the occupation contradicted his work as a prosecutor because the occupation was a political problem, but under the circumstances the military enforced the laws humanely and did the best it could. In his opinion, Palestinians deserved self-determination in a state of their own, but in the interim, the fight against terrorism was "total war." He said, "There is an unwritten law between the prosecution and the terrorist groups. It was that the trials themselves have nothing to do with politics. In other words, if a terrorist is caught, he knows that he has to be sentenced and punished. Political issues are not raised in trials by defendants or by their lawyers. No one argues 'liberation struggle' in court."

He enjoyed his work as a prosecutor very much because it gave him the opportunity to see "very interesting materials about terrorism and the secret relations between Israelis and Palestinians which are part of the daily existence of occupation." In his opinion, most of the people who were arrested were not the "real political terrorists" but just "peons in the game" who committed security violations because they were recruited by the Palestinian political leadership to do their bidding, or because they were paid off, or just because they considered it acceptable behavior. From his experience as a prosecutor, he said that many people might claim to be participating in a "war of liberation" when they were first arrested but backed down when "pushed" by interrogators and admitted that they did it for reasons of pressure or material incentive. Continuing, he said that many Palestinians who had left the territories to study in the Arab world were obligated when they returned to carry out actions because the PLO had paid for their studies. He was convinced that most Palestinians lacked real commitment to resist the occupation, as demonstrated by their willingness to confess and plead guilty. "The *real* leaders, who are politically motivated, aren't usually caught, and if they are, they don't usually confess." Hence, for him, the proportion of people who confessed indicated an underlying ambivalence about the struggle against occupation.

He was able to capitalize on his work as a prosecutor to obtain work as a defense lawyer. It was *because* he had been a prosecutor that Palestinians would hire him, believing that he might have the connections and experience that could provide them with a break in his dealing with prosecutors. He only took cases involving serious charges and no confession because these were the cases that went to trial and thus required "real legal work." People would never hire him to make a deal (i.e., plea bargain) because his fees were substantially higher than those of most other lawyers and, if there was a confession, there was little legal work to be done. In discussing his record as a defense lawyer, he said that he probably got more acquittals than most lawyers and that he was very good at getting charges dropped. Working as a defense lawyer gave him a fuller appreciation of the advantages that prosecutors enjoy. "Judges often are easier on prosecutors, but this doesn't mean that the system isn't fair."

I interviewed this man about one month after another Jewish Israeli lawyer, Ian Feinburg, had been assassinated in Gaza. Feinburg, a former prosecutor who had been capitalizing on his connections to work in the occupied territories, had been alone in the office of a British development organization when members of the PFLP had broken in and killed him, with a warning that this would be the fate of other Jewish Israelis in Gaza. The killing had scared this man, who knew Feinburg from their days as prosecutors. He had delayed all of his cases until things cooled down, and he said that this was no problem for his clients because they were facing serious charges and would be sitting in jail anyway, whether it was pre-trial detention or post-trial conviction.

The other interviewee who now took cases as a defense lawyer had been a career lawyer in the military for a decade, starting in 1977 following the Likud Party victory. During that period, he had served as a legal advisor in Gaza's Ansar II prison and in Lebanon and as a judge on various military appeals committees (which are administratively separate from the courts). He also lectured soldiers on military and international law. He retired from the army in 1987 but continued to serve as a reservist judge on administrative appeals committees.

This man, who had a private practice in Jerusalem, was a settler from Kiryat Arba. He described himself and was described by others as "very right-wing." I had gotten his name from his brother, a representative of the Israel Bar Association, who stressed that he was "moderate, not like my brother." The bar representative had suggested the interview because he believed that his brother provided a good example of the irrelevance of individuals' personal political views to their commitment to the rule of law. As I subsequently learned, this interviewee's extremist views were well known in military court circles; often when I contacted judges and prosecutors for interviews, they would ask whom else I had interviewed, and when I mentioned this man's name they would chuckle and say something like "I guess you really are covering the spectrum."

When the *intifada* started, he was among the first judges on the appeals committee at Ketziot/Ansar III, the prison camp that was opened in March 1988 in the Negev desert to accommodate the thousands of administrative detainees. He said that when he first started hearing appeals against administrative detention, he was confused because he found the evidence to be strong and thought that they should be tried and sent to prison. But because the evidence came from "Arab agents working on behalf of Israel," it could not be used in court. He acknowledged that the use of secret evidence was "a problem for Arabs' rights. Every person should have the right to confront evidence against him." However, he understood the problems of making such information public because "the IDF can't endanger the lives of others [i.e., informers] by calling them to testify."

He was quite frank about his right-wing anti-Arab political views but said that this did not affect his ability to serve impartially as a judge, as demonstrated by the fact that he released "many" prisoners. "If I can do it, surely the majority of judges can do it." I asked why he had decided to defend Palestinian clients in the military courts, and he said that it was to see that "justice is done." He had represented all kinds of clients in various Israeli courts, including Meir Kahane, founder of the ultra-right-wing Kach Party; border police accused of beating Palestinians; and Palestinians accused of shooting Israeli buses. I asked why he thought Palestinians would hire him, given his views, and he responded that the legal skills of Palestinian lawyers were "lower than low. Anyone with money would rather hire me than go to *any* Arab lawyer." He added, "Anyway, Arab lawyers are no geniuses."

He was very intent that I fully understand his political views, and he concluded our interview by explaining them in detail. He was opposed to a Palestinian state or any form of Palestinian self-government, supported the deportation of terrorists, and advocated looser open-fire regulations. He said he dreamed of a Greater Israel but would accept some limited territorial compromise if it allowed for the transfer of Arabs out of those areas where Jews lived. The important thing for him was that someday Jews would be able to live in a Jewish-only environment.

## Official Views

In the summer of 1993, the IDF Public Relations Office finally arranged three interviews with high-ranking officials. One was with David Yahav, then serving as Deputy Military Advocate General (MAG), whom I met in the military headquarters in Tel Aviv. He was the preeminent military spokesperson for handling researcher and media inquiries into matters relating to the military legal system. This meeting enabled me to check certain facts and get clarifications on some contradictory information that I had gathered from other sources.

Eventually, our discussion turned to the topic of Israeli national security and the threat posed by Islamist organizations' campaign of increasingly violent attacks on Israeli targets. In his opinion the security situation, since about 1990, had deteriorated to an all-time low. He said, "Nowadays there are more killers. The issue is the numbers. It's not a real uprising any more. It used to be popular — tens of thousands of rioters in the streets. Now it is just terror being led by a few hundred brutal and violent terrorists. Our problem is to figure out how to stop them."

Islamists affiliated with Hamas and Islamic Jihad were motivated, at least in part, by opposition to the Israeli-Palestinian negotiations that had started in 1991. But they also represented a militant antioccupation stance and were gaining popularity among a devastated Palestinian population. This situation was posing a dilemma for those in command of the military court system. For the negotiations to succeed, the Israeli government would have to offer up some immediate concessions, and to this end the MAG's office was advocating that prosecutors show flexibility in handling the cases of people suspected of membership in those Palestinian factions supporting the negotiations. The purpose of this policy was to foster support for the negotiations in order to serve the long-term interests of the Israeli government.[33] For Palestinian factions actively trying to undermine the negotiations, foremost the Islamists, the MAG office's policy was uncompromising: prosecutors should take the hardest possible line in each case, and the court system should serve not only to punish past actions but to incapacitate factions opposed to the negotiations. As Yahav described it, the dilemma was how to use the legal system to target a particular sector of Palestinian society to achieve certain political goals (support for negotiations or at least quiescence to enable them to proceed), in addition to its "regular" purpose to maintain security and punish violators. He acknowledged that harsh punitive measures aimed to crush the Islamists and other antinegotiation factions bore the threat of popularizing their political views.

During my interview with Yahav, it seemed clear that the MAG's office was floundering about how to reconcile the opposing objectives of creating conditions supportive of the negotiations while crushing sectors opposing them. As it turned out, a month later (August 1993) the dilemma was nominally resolved: secret negotiations between Israeli and Palestinian representatives in Norway had produced an agreement, which led to the signing of a Declaration of Principles in September and, half a year later, the establishment of a Palestinian Authority (PA). Thus, part of the burden of controlling the Islamists and generating Palestinian support for the negotiations was shifted onto the PA.

## Downsizing the Military Court System, Upsizing Punishments

In 1994, the military court system was "downsized" as part of the military redeployment from Palestinian towns. Although Palestinians continued to be arrested and prosecuted, the number of cases declined, as did the number of Israelis assigned to work as judges and prosecutors.

In the early 1990s, for reasons partially related to a cautious optimism about the peace process within Israel, there were moves to reduce the overall size of the IDF and to transform it from its historical role as a "people's army" into a more "professionalized" — in Stuart Cohen's term "slimmer and smarter" — institution by reducing the rate and tenure of conscription and reserve duty.[34] This reduction, coupled with Israeli feminist complaints and litigation against gender discrimination, led to more women being put into roles that previously had been given primarily or exclusively to males.[35] Consequently, more women were assigned to be judges and prosecutors in the military court system. Similarly, there was an increase in the number of Druze Israelis assigned to be prosecutors (to my knowledge, there have never been any Druze judges). Drawing more individuals from these two "marginal" groups into such roles occurred when — and perhaps because — the size and significance of the military court system were declining.

But by 1996, contrary to expectations or hopes that the negotiations might have a pacifying effect on Israeli-Palestinian relations, tensions were mounting, and violence was on the rise. For the Jewish Israeli mainstream and right, continuation of Palestinian violence was taken as evidence of the "failure" of the Oslo Accords. As in the latter years of the *intifada*, Palestinians engaging in violence against Israelis were primarily people affiliated with Islamist organizations and the "rejectionist" PLO factions. Such actions were, in no small part, manifestations of opposition to the PA and the negotiations and contributed to escalating tensions between the PA and the Israeli government (see Conclusion).

Throughout the 1990s, the military court system arguably contributed to Palestinians' frustrations and growing popular opposition to the Oslo Accords. Palestinians were still being arrested and prosecuted for "*intifada* crimes" — activities that allegedly took place prior to the signing of the Declaration of Principles. This contradicted the "forward-looking" agendas of conflict resolution. Moreover, the sentences being meted out by the court system during the interim were generally higher than during the *intifada*. For example, whereas a person previously might have been sentenced to a ten-month prison term for "membership in an illegal organization," by 1997 the same charge could bring a sentence of three to four years. The most common charge prosecuted in the military courts during the interim was "permit violation." In response to the intensive "closure" of the West Bank and Gaza that caused a dramatic economic decline in PA areas, Palestinians without permits who tried to get to Israel to work or tried to move from one Palestinian area to another (e.g., to study or seek medical treatment) and were arrested were subject to much higher penalties than in the past.

In 1997, I was in the Erez military court on a day when all the cases involved permit violations. In one case, a young Palestinian man had hidden in the trunk of a PA official's car, hoping to catch a ride from Gaza back to Birzeit University in the West Bank. He and the official had assumed — incorrectly — that the car would be able to pass through the Israeli checkpoint without being searched. By the day of his hearing, he had spent three months in prison and was in court for his sentencing. He explained to the judge that this was his last year of college and that if he could just get back to the West Bank, he could graduate, get a job, help his family, get married, et cetera. She was unmoved and sentenced him to an additional eighteen months in prison. After the hearing, she explained, "Entry [into Israel] is a security threat because everybody is a potential terrorist. It is the court's task to guard against this."

Palestinians arrested on charges of violence always had faced high sentences, and this remained true during the interim. But the use of violence by some Palestinians was used to justify punitive measures against people charged with nonviolent activities like permit violations. Two prosecutors I interviewed in 1997 readily acknowledged that they were under orders to seek high sentences for all types of cases. As one explained, "Punishment is the legal means we use to deal with the political problems caused by the peace process."

During the interim, Israel's continuing ability to prosecute and punish Palestinians took on new meanings under the changed political arrangements. Indeed, the main task of the military court system during those years, prosecuting unauthorized movement, was to enforce the enclosure and "separation" of Palestinians that the Israeli government held up to its own citizens as compensation for the territorial compromises that were being negotiated. Prosecuting people accused of violence against Israelis was not only a means of exacting retribution, a "conventional" function of the courts, but also an assertion of Israeli jurisdictional control over Israel/Palestine in its entirety. The PA was deemed to be failing its responsibility to police the separation and prevent Palestinian attacks, which diminished its jurisdictional autonomy.

The politics of punishment in the military courts begs contextualizing in relation to the negotiations. Just as, in 1993, punishment was being used instrumentally to facilitate an Israeli agenda of generating Palestinian support for the negotiations by showing leniency to people affiliated with pronegotiation factions, during the interim punishment was also used instrumentally, but for a "new" purpose. Harsher punishments for all types of crimes cannot be explained simply by the negative goal of deterrence. Rather, the punishments also served a positive political function of strengthening Israel's hand in the troubled negotiations. Palestinian prisoners were bargaining chips, and the bigger the sentence, the bigger the chip. Releasing prisoners before their sentences were over was a concession that Israel could make to the Palestinians in lieu of other types of concessions.

## Consensus, Dissent, and the Legitimacy Debate in Israel

The legitimacy of the military court system as a legal institution with a capacity to dispense justice is a subject of deep disagreement even among Jewish Israelis. When discussing the system's overall legitimacy with judges and prosecutors, I heard a variety of opinions, although people expressed high consensus on certain matters. Three main factors contributed to their appreciation of the system as generally legitimate and indicated the nature and breadth of consensus within Jewish Israeli society.[36] One was the legitimacy of the military as an institution. A second was the extent to which the military court system was (deemed) comparable to the domestic Israeli criminal legal system and the legitimacy of the latter. A third factor related to the fact that the West Bank and Gaza were not part of Israel and that therefore Palestinian residents of these areas were legitimately *unentitled* to the range of rights or the kinds of legal considerations that Israeli citizens enjoyed.

Notwithstanding this general consensus, there were discrepancies over *how much* legitimacy the court system was perceived to have. Among judges and prosecutors, there was a range of opinion, from those who regarded it as functionally legitimate (i.e., perceiving a disjuncture between the enforcement of law and the availability of justice) to those who regarded it as ideally legitimate (i.e., believing that the system dispensed justice). Even some judges and prosecutors who were harsh critics of the *occupation* perceived the *court system* as ideally legitimate, as for example the prosecutor who said that terrorists, once arrested, willingly accepted conviction as a just consequence of their actions.

Of critical importance in debates over the court system's legitimacy are people's views about the legitimacy of the Israeli state. The vast majority of Jewish Israelis share a strong consensus that the principles on which the Israeli state claims to be based — Zionism, democracy, and the rule of law — are legitimate and mutually compatible. This informs views of the military court system because judges and prosecutors, as representatives of the state, see themselves as embodying national norms. Judges' and prosecutors' willingness to regard the system as fair and just is a reflection of how they view themselves and their own politico-legal culture.

When it comes to the legitimacy of Israeli control over the occupied territories, although there are fundamental disagreements among Jewish Israelis, there is still a strong consensus that Israel took control of these areas in a defensive war, that the occupation will last until the conflict is resolved, and that legitimate security needs drive policy making. Furthermore, there is a widely shared "ideology of crime" among Jewish Israelis in which Palestinians are perceived as potentially or inherently threatening — individually and/or collectively — to Israeli security and predisposed to engage in activities that constitute crimes according to the laws in force. These factors contribute to the legitimation of the military court system as part of the apparatus of security and control.

Nevertheless, this consensus is shaded by disagreements among Jewish Israelis over how to interpret the appropriate relationship between Israeli security and Palestinians' rights. Some, especially those on the far right, regard Palestinians' very presence as illegitimate and threatening (and among those who advocate "transfer," disposable), whereas those whose views are more liberal and centrist tend to regard Palestinians as threatening only to the extent that they are willing to act out in violent and disruptive ways. For this reason, the massive arrests during the first *intifada* caused a crisis of conscience for some who were in the position to punish; sending so many "peons in the game" and "simple people" to prison was simultaneously a political and legal imperative and a moral dilemma.

There was also a range of opinion among judges and prosecutors with whom I spoke regarding the operation of the court system. Some argued that while the laws were admittedly draconian, they had been enforced "humanely" by the military. Within the system itself, they saw this humanity demonstrated by the degree to which judges and prosecutors were willing to consider factors specific to individual defendants (e.g., their age, past record, number of dependants) in the processes of plea bargaining, prosecution, and adjudication. This sense of the military's humanity was particularly strong regarding the legal domain, although some interviewees regarded the attitudes and practices of prosecutors as a weak spot in this narrative of benevolence and humanity.

All of the judges and prosecutors I spoke with identified as Zionists, but they did not concur that Israeli rule over the West Bank and Gaza was right, even as a temporary arrangement. A few believed wholeheartedly that Israeli military rule had to be maintained against the possibility of any form of Palestinian self-determination *in Israel/Palestine* (e.g., some favored the Jordan-is-Palestine option to resolve Palestinians' demands for statehood). Others were willing to entertain the prospect of Palestinian self-rule but were fearful that this would pose a perpetual threat to the Israeli state and/or resentful that it would constitute a forfeiture of Jews' right to possess and rule the "historic homeland" that spanned the Green Line. Many Jewish liberals considered protracted military rule damaging to Israeli democracy and values but necessary as long as the Israeli-Palestinian conflict remained unresolved. Those who identified as left Zionists advocated a "two-state solution" to the conflict even before the negotiations began in 1991. But despite their opposition to the occupation, judges and prosecutors who identified as liberals or left Zionists participated in the military court system willingly because it was their duty as Israeli citizens and they had no desire to estrange themselves from their own community by refusing to serve. Hence, while there is a powerful consensus among the majority of Jewish Israelis about the legitimacy of the state, the domestic legal system, and the military, there is dissent over the legitimate spatial boundaries and demographic composition of state power.

Before the establishment of the PA in 1994, when Israeli military rule over Palestinians in the West Bank and Gaza was direct and exclusive, some judges and prosecutors critical of the occupation expressed disdain or feelings of being trapped in having to work in a system in which such a vast range of Palestinian activities were criminalized, and they acknowledged that this impeded people's ability to live "normal" lives. Some even conceded that Palestinians' resistance was legitimate under the circumstance (excluding violence). To reconcile their political views with their legal roles, they needed to identify some object(s) of blame. To this end, blame was focused on the Palestinian leadership in particular and the Arab leadership in general for having failed to pursue a realistic resolution to the conflict long ago. In this way, Jewish Israeli liberals and left Zionists could rationalize their own participation in maintaining an occupation that they opposed without having to condone, let alone applaud, the massive incarceration of Palestinians.

After 1994, direct Israeli military rule over Palestinians changed into indirect rule. The Oslo Accords signaled a political victory for the liberal and left-Zionist sectors of Jewish Israeli society, to the chagrin and staunch opposition of the right. It seemed, for a brief while, that the occupation might be coming to an end and that the conflict might give way to a "two-state solution" and a "new Middle East." Jewish Israelis who vested their hope in Oslo, and who were unwilling or unable to understand why Palestinian disappointment and opposition were mounting, felt shocked and betrayed by continuing violence against Israelis.

The contradictions inherent in combining political "partnership" with Palestinians, a "separation" enforced by one side, and continuing occupation ultimately caused the collapse of the negotiations and the start of the second *intifada* in 2000 (see Conclusion). But a thread of consistency from 1967 to the present can explain the formation of a new consensus among Jewish Israeli rightists, liberals, and left Zionists: most Israelis, regardless of their stance on the occupation, have always condemned Palestinian violence against Israelis (soldiers and civilians) as terrorism. Palestinian violence during the second *intifada* (even measures that might be construed as "defensive"), and suicide bombings in particular, pushed public opinion among Jewish Israelis rightward[37] and generated strong support for the violence deployed by the state against Palestinians.

However, the consensus wrought by the crisis of the second *intifada* did not translate into consensual support for the restoration of direct military rule. As in the past, those serving as judges and prosecutors were faced with the contradictions and dilemmas of trying to utilize law to contend with a political conflict. For example, in September 2002, the Israeli daily *Ha'aretz* reported that military court judges were complaining, in ways reminiscent of the first *intifada*, that this "resembles more an 'assembly line' than a court system."[38]

There is a possibility that those Jewish Israelis who have been critical of the occupation in the past will be critical if it continues into the future. Such a development would indicate new parameters of consensus and dissent in Jewish Israeli society over the state's relationship to the West Bank and Gaza, and their Palestinian inhabitants, with the wreckage of the Oslo Accords as a new complication. Those doing military service in the courts of the West Bank and Gaza are agents of the state and have not only a vested interest as citizens in state policies and practices but a role in exercising the state's power "on the ground."

The Israeli military has always been — and indisputably remains — an important state institution in its own right, as well as an institutionalized framework for "making Israelis," with all the rights, privileges, and duties that accrue. Among the majority of Jewish Israelis, there is no debate about whether to remain committed to the military, only about what the military should commit itself to doing, and where and how. Even "refuseniks," soldiers who refuse to do military service in the West Bank and Gaza, are not rejecting "the military"; they are refusing to do a specific kind of military service in a specific area because they regard this as tantamount to maintaining what they deem to be an oppressive occupation that is deleterious *for Israel*. [39] Refuseniks emphasize their status as soldiers to legitimize their oppositional stance, risking court martial and imprisonment and thereby forcing the Jewish Israeli public to contend with the criticisms they raise about the future of Israel's relationship to the West Bank and Gaza. [40]

Most refuseniks stress that they are willing to perform duties in areas (geographical and institutional) that they accept as militarily legitimate. Perhaps one reason why no members of the military court system unit have become refuseniks is the nature of service they are asked to perform: "the law" and law enforcement enjoy a legitimacy, as I have explained in this chapter, that even opponents of the occupation can commit themselves to serving.

In this chapter, I have focused on the roles, practices, and perspectives of Jewish Israeli judges and prosecutors. In the following chapter, I focus on translators, a role filed mainly by Druze Israelis. Whereas Jews are both "citizens" and "nationals" of the Israeli state, Druze, as non-Jews, are "only" citizens. Their service in the military court system and their perspectives on the Israeli occupation of the West Bank and Gaza, therefore, raise quite different issues than those that relate to judges and prosecutors.

# CHAPTER 5

# The Politics of Language

## Translators

---

*Our community is defined by our language — our language is the set of shared expectations and common terms that enable us to think of ourselves as a "we."*

James Boyd White, *Justice as Translation*[1]

Language provides a particularly useful point of reference to analyze social relations and political identifications in multiethnic societies where different languages "coexist," like the groups of people who speak them. In many contexts, language is politicized through a discourse of rights, notably the right to self-determination; the collective "self" is often defined, at least in part, linguistically. Hence, language bears directly on contestations over the boundaries and powers of the state. In turn, governmental practices include the regulation and control (including promotion or suppression) of language usage within a state's domain. In multiethnic societies riven by conflict, language may be a marker for domination (if a politically dominant group's language has monopoly over public discourse) or a sign of a failed — or unattempted — project of assimilating differences.

In Israel/Palestine, Hebrew- and Arabic-speaking groups are both present, and in that sense they are "coexisting." But the language differences, and the barriers to communication that they reinforce, signify much more than the fact that the population of Israel/Palestine is multiethnic. Rather, the Hebrew and Arabic languages symbolize a Jewish/

Arab dichotomy within a sociopolitical order in which government is integrated *and* hierarchical.

This chapter focuses on the politics of language in the military court system, highlighting the roles, practices, and perspectives of translators, most of whom are Druze. The preference for using Druze Israelis in such a capacity is significant, given that other sectors of Israeli society (including those who serve in the military) are also bilingual in Hebrew and Arabic.[2] This preference illuminates the particular(istic) ways in which Druze Israeli identity has been politicized within the larger context of Arab-Jewish relations and the Israeli-Palestinian conflict.

## Jews and Arabs, Israelis and Palestinians

Since Israel is a Jewish state and Hebrew is the Jewish language (or at least the lingua franca), the confluence among Hebrew, the Israeli state, and Jewish identity constitutes and maintains a powerful sense of the Jewish Israeli "we." Although Arabic has the formal status as the other "official" language of Israel, it brooks no equivalence with Hebrew. The marginalization of Arabic is one sign of the marginalized status of Arab citizens of the state. The politics of inclusion and exclusion are reflected in language; to speak Arabic in Israel is to mark oneself as an "outsider" to the Jewish nation/state.

When Israel captured the West Bank and Gaza in 1967 and extended its rule over Palestinians residing in those areas, the politics of language assumed new forms. Palestinian residents of the West Bank and Gaza were clearly "othered" by their political status as an occupied population. Their own sense of "we" was reinforced in part by *not* speaking Hebrew, the language of the conqueror, although many subsequently acquired a proficiency in Hebrew.

In analyses and discussions about the conflict in Israel/Palestine, Jewish Israelis and Palestinian residents of the occupied territories garner the greatest attention. Since each "side" is identified with its own "native" language, the Jewish/Arab dichotomy is reinforced linguistically: language differences coincide with the political distinctions between occupier and occupied. The Hebrew-Arabic language barrier combines with an array of other social, political, economic, and legal barriers, including identity-based residential segregation and differentiated opportunities for employment, geographic mobility, access to resources, individual and collective rights, and so on.

The utility of the Jewish/Arab dichotomy for framing the identities and relations among people in Israel/Palestine is limited, however. Just as "native language" can be used to demarcate the central divide in the conflict, so, too, can it be used to explore the blurred and contested boundaries among communities. The explanatory power of the national dichotomy is challenged by population groups who are bilingual in Hebrew and Arabic.

Hebrew-Arabic bilingualism in Israel/Palestine is a marker for people who reside in the border zones, between a Jewish Israeli community dominated by Ashkenazim (Jews of European origins), for whom Arabic is a thoroughly foreign language, and a Palestinian community in the West Bank and Gaza, for whom Hebrew is the language of military government and an exploitative labor market. They include Mizrachim (literally "Eastern" Jews), some of whom immigrated from Arab countries and retained their Arabic after arriving in Israel, adding it to the acquired Hebrew that they were trained (and disciplined) to speak as the accepted public tongue for Jews.[3] They also include Arab citizens of Israel. Because of the dominant status of the Hebrew language in Israel and the equation of Arabic with Israel's enemies, Arabic speaking is discouraged in many quarters of the Israeli public sphere. Mizrachi Jews and Arab Israelis who speak Arabic do so "at home," within those linguistic communities inhabiting the border zones.[4]

Druze Israelis constitute one particular group of bilingual Israeli citizens.[5] For reasons elaborated below, it is difficult to provide a simple answer to the question of who the Druze "are." But this question is of critical importance in contemplating the history and status of the Druze community in Israel, which, in turn, bears directly on the preference for Druze as translators in the military courts. On one level, Druze identity is a distinctive religious/cultural designation: the Druze are a schismatic sect of Shi'i Islam. The social boundaries of the "community of believers" are relatively closed for a number of reasons related to religious doctrine, including the impossibility of conversion into the faith, the sectarian prohibition against marrying outside the faith, and a sanctified belief in the transmigration of (Druze) souls (to new generations of Druze bodies). However, the Druze are part of larger social and political communities of people whose relations are organized along different (i.e., not sectarian) axes of identity, including, foremost, along national lines.

In terms of language, culture, and history, Druze are part of the "Arab people." Druze are incorporated as citizens of Syria, Lebanon, and Israel, thereby dividing the community of believers along state lines. Those

Druze who reside in Israel have been separated (spatially and politically) from their co-religionists who reside in Arab states at war with Israel. Druze in Israel are also part of the "Palestinian people," who formed the indigenous population of historic Palestine prior to their political fragmentation and geographic dispersion in 1948. Palestinian nationalism continues to express a desire and ability to mobilize people who identify as Palestinians for the achievement of national goals, including the right to self-determination in a sovereign state of their own. Countering and repressing the appeal of Palestinian nationalism among Arabs who remained in Israel after independence have been central concerns of officials and agents of the Israeli state. The state's policies toward the Druze community provide a vivid case of social engineering to politicize and manage identity in ways that conform to and serve state interests.

## Druze Bilingualism

How Druze Israelis "became bilingual" is part of a larger history of Israeli state building and consolidation. For all Israeli citizens, acquiring fluency in modern Hebrew was part of an "Israelizing" process that involved the promotion of a common language. Hebrew fluency consolidates a multiethnic "Israeli" society. However, processes of incorporating Arab citizens into Israel, which is defined as a Jewish state, also involved the maintenance and reinforcement of a Jewish/non-Jewish distinction through geographic segregation and public and private discrimination.

The Druze occupy a particular niche in the sociopolitical order of Israel/Palestine.[6] Since independence, Israeli state policies toward the Druze community aimed at distinguishing them from all other sectors of Israeli society, especially from other Arabs. For example, they were permitted and encouraged to enlist in the military and, in 1956, became the only category of Arabs to be subject to mandatory conscription.[7] In 1957, the Ministry of Religious Affairs accorded separate status to the Druze, no longer subsuming them within the category of Muslims. In 1961, the Druze religious leadership was recognized as an independent religious council, and in 1963 the Knesset ratified the Druze Law Courts Bill, giving the council autonomy on religious and personal status matters. The consummate step in juridical separation occurred in 1962, when the state officially removed the Druze from the "Arab" nationality category and created for them a separate "national/religious" category.[8]

But this separate Druze status is ambivalent and inherently contradictory. To the extent that the Druze came to be regarded as "non-Arabs" in the eyes (and laws) of the state, conscripting them into the military would serve two purposes: reinforcing a distinction between Druze and other Arab citizens of the state and offering a means of including at least some non-Jewish Israelis in the country's most important institution. The perceived — and engineered — "non-Arabness" of the Druze was a crucial factor in selecting *them* for inclusion in the military, whereas "Arab Arabs," who were closely associated with the state's enemies, were not conscripted.

A popular truism in Israel holds that the Druze are the state's "favorite" minority and as such enjoy a "special relationship" with the Jewish majority.[9] The most readily supplied evidence is that Druze (males) serve in the Israel Defense Forces (IDF). Military service is widely regarded as a prerequisite for "true" membership and acceptance in the Israeli polity. The fact that Arab citizens (i.e., Muslims and Christians) are not conscripted frequently is invoked as a justification for official discrimination against them.[10] Conscription and a general willingness to serve have reinforced a critical difference between Druze and other Arab citizens.

When it comes to the preference for Druze as translators in the military courts, however, their lingering "Arab-ness" made them seemingly more suitable than Arabic-speaking Jewish soldiers. According to an army spokesman, "Some Jews do know the Arabic language, but translating involves more than just translating the words. It involves really understanding the people you are translating for." Furthermore, the use of Jews as translators would have run counter to state policies to de-Arabize Jewish immigrants from the Arab world. Calling upon Druze to speak Arabic in the service of the state was a logical choice because nothing was being lost or sacrificed in the process of consolidating and Hebraicizing a Jewish nation in Israel.

The Druze are preferred for the role of translators because they have both bilingual skills and a sociopolitical status as "non-Arab Arabs." In the military courts, Druze translators are called upon to navigate between the linguistic-ideological worlds of Hebrew-speaking Jewish Israelis (military judges and prosecutors and some defense lawyers) and Arabic-speaking Palestinians from the territories (defendants and nonbilingual defense lawyers). In the process, they have to negotiate their own identifications with the people whose ideas and words they are relaying. Their language skills are appropriated as instruments of communication; they are positioned as a human bridge across a barrier that is simultaneously political and linguistic. Before engaging the topic of Druze translators, however, it is necessary to consider in greater detail how Druze Israeli identity has been politicized to understand the stakes and dilemmas at issue in this form of military service.

## Particularism as Policy, or Who Is a Druze?

The state's effort to construct and promote a distinct Druze Israeli identity is one element of a broader strategy to forge alliances and foster alienation among different sectors of the population inside Israel as a means of political control.[11] There are three aspects of this process to consider: 1) the codification of differentiated legal statuses for the Druze and other "non-Jewish" citizens; 2) the effects that these institutionalized differences have had on the various communities and on intercommunal relations; and 3) the contradictions and ambiguities of Druze Israeli identity in terms of minority rights in a Jewish state.

Israeli scholarship on the Druze community has contributed to the formulation and development of state policies. According to Kais Firru, "Israeli historiography on the Druzes and the state's policy toward them are closely interrelated and mutually reinforcing. Israeli historiography has created an 'image' of the Druzes as having a 'cooperative attitude' toward the Jews throughout their history, and the policy has reinforced that attitude. The 'common destinies' of these two peoples are emphasized."[12]

Israeli scholarship has tended to emphasize a historical Druze autarky,[13] religious differences from Sunni Muslims, and the significance of *hamula* (extended family) relations within the community, which have contributed to notions about a "traditional" Druze lifestyle and "mentality."[14] It is not just that the Druze are perceived and represented as "traditional," because in the traditional/modern binary still prominent in Israeli academic and popular discourses all non-Ashkenazim are assumed to have been traditional prior to their integration into modern Westernized (i.e., Ashkenazi-dominated) Israeli society, but rather that all Druze are traditional in one common and particular way. According to Jonathan Oppenheimer, "Both the scholarly analysis and the official view are products of an ideologically distorted understanding of Druze history, by which it is transformed into a charter for the administration and political separation of the Druze from the rest of the Arab population."[15]

State policies toward the Druze devolve on a particularistic understanding about who the Druze are and how they should be governed.

This understanding attests to the durability of Israeli orientalism: Druze are represented as an ideal example of the mosaic-like nature of Middle Eastern societies. One powerful manifestation of this orientalism is a tendency to interpret and generalize about the actions and preferences of elites as an expression of the desires and views of the community as a whole.

Official and popular Israeli narratives about the Druze assume and propound that "the community" welcomed the establishment of a Jewish state because it brought a definitive end to centuries of oppressive Muslim domination and local persecution.[16] Because of a prestate Druze-Jewish alliance,[17] Israel emerged from the War of Independence (1948–49) with a duty to protect this "minority within a minority." The postindependence relationship was one of protector-client, wherein the state could expect communal loyalty and the community would be rewarded by being treated differently (that is, better) than Arabs. Officially distinguishing the Druze from all others was construed as a means of according them the kind of communal autonomy and sectarian integrity they desired, while state-directed policies of integration, the most important of which was military conscription, would help them along the road to modernization.[18] In contemporary Israel, according to this narrative, Druze enjoy legal rights and equality, and any disparities that continue to persist between the Druze and Jewish communities (as measured by standard indicators like literacy, income, and employment) are due not so much to discriminatory policies of the state (although to the extent that the state does discriminate, this is justified in terms of the legitimate prioritization of Jewish interests) as to the fact that the historical "backwardness" of the Druze community will take time to overcome. The most sensitive question is whether Druze are Arabs. Although the state no longer juridically defines them as such, they are not really "non-Arab" because they share culture and language with other Arabs. But this dilemma is resolved with a tautology: religiously and socially the Druze cannot be Arabs because they are Druze.[19] This contributes to a perception that only those Druze who are confused about their "true" identity would support Arab or Palestinian nationalism, and it is bolstered by the fact that most Druze Israelis have accepted and embraced the transformation of their status from Muslim sect to "Druze nation."[20] This transformation is framed and extolled as an historic achievement of a long-suppressed yearning, comparable to Zionism for the Jews.[21]

However, notions of Druze difference as "natural" and "historic" ignore or obscure the politicization of identity by the state. Israeli policies to *politically* distinguish the Druze from other Palestinian Arabs institutionalized Druze sectarian identity as the basis of a *civic* identity.[22] This combination of particularism and "favoritism" resonated with certain communal interests, particularly those of Druze elites whose own powers and privileges were enhanced through their ties to the state. In the 1950s and 1960s, state intervention was mediated through traditional leaders, using a complex system of patronage oriented to existing *hamula* relations.[23] By the 1970s, the singular importance of the *hamulas* was displaced somewhat by the emergence of a younger generation with their own ties to state agencies.

The process of constructing a distinctive identity for Druze Israelis is, in fact, the interplay of several processes: a tactical and calculated articulation of state imperatives and scholarly assumptions; a contestation within the Druze community over the privileging of a particular expression of Druze identity from a variety of possibilities; and the negating or silencing of alternatives. It is a governing process that *involves* the Druze, albeit in an unequal relationship to the state. As Talal Asad explains: "Political discourses do not simply 'legitimize' behavior from outside . . . or simply mobilize people with given 'interests'; they operate in diverse historical circumstances to construct motivations, to transform commitments, and to reorganize experiences — as well as to produce and codify knowledge about social behavior that is essential to all these creative functions. 'The managers of ideology' do not command silent audiences: Political discourses are collaborative processes. The collaboration may rarely be equal, but it remains nevertheless a quite different phenomenon from conditioning."[24]

The policies to separate Druze from other Arabs have been resoundingly effective overall. Although Druze and Arabs are discriminated against in comparable ways as non-Jews in a Jewish state, because the state *rhetorically* favors the Druze, they have been presented with a strategic incentive to maintain and use the sectarian divisions by lobbying for equality with Jews — the ideal they have been led to believe that they deserve because of their service to the state — rather than aligning themselves with Arabs to work for universal equality for all citizens.

The importance of military service in the construction and consolidation of a distinctive Druze Israeli identity cannot be overstated. Druze are represented and imagined as "different" from Arabs (more "Israeli") because they serve in the military; Druze deserve special treatment because they serve; discriminatory policies like land confiscation and insufficient investment in Druze villages are unjust because they serve, and so on. According to Zeidan Atash, a Druze member of Knesset, "I want all those who served in the army, including Druze, to be equals in the state of Israel, and not those who served and those who did not serve in the same classification."[25]

The consequences of particularism as policy have informed popular attitudes within the Druze community. Many Druze soldiers whom I interviewed asserted that their acceptance of Israel as a Jewish state distinguished them from most Arabs. Yet because their "de-Arabization" is a deliberately incomplete project, when questioned about whether they consider themselves Arabs, some were unsure how to answer. One replied frankly, "Because of the way Arabs are regarded in Israel, it isn't useful to emphasize a common culture. Our loyalty to the state proves that we are different." Arab Israelis also tend to accept that the Druze are "different" (although some, for political reasons, insist on considering the Druze as "confused Arabs"). Many Arabs ridicule Druze allegiance to a state that has provided them so little in return and disparage their willingness to forfeit their ties to other Arabs. This tendency was heightened during the first *intifada* because of media coverage and other representations of Druze soldiers as particularly unrestrained in their violence against Palestinians in the territories, fostering an image of Druze as vicious lackeys of the state.

## The Politics of Conscription

The utilization of Druze sectarian particularism in Israeli governing policies has "naturalized" military service as a communal obligation (exemptions are accorded only to those who are "religious").[26] But herein lies a major contradiction. The Druze are compelled to serve because they are members of a "loyal community." But they serve as individuals in what is lauded as the foremost integrating institution in Israel — the IDF — and are told in the army that their Druzeness is a nonissue because all soldiers are equal, at least where rank and unit intersect.[27]

Any individual who refuses to serve faces serious repercussions, including loss of benefits like housing loans, government subsidies, and tax breaks that veterans enjoy. Refusal also means the loss of any opportunity to work in the government or government-run institutions and even discrimination in the private sector because of the importance of an army record in a job seeker's application.[28] The authorities have dealt much more harshly with Druze than with Jews who refuse to serve, using shaming techniques like arrests in the dead of night by large army contingents in which the refuser is taken out in chains like a dangerous criminal, repeated arrests to keep the individual's refusal an issue within his family and community, and periodic psychological tests aimed at humiliating and stigmatizing him. An unwillingness to perform army service is presented as aberrant *communal* behavior, resting on the presumed homogeneity of the Druze and the mutuality of Druze and Jewish interests.

One of the translators I interviewed told the story of his short-lived refusal. He had evaded the draft for five months, not for any political reason but because he just did not want to go into the army. When he finally turned himself in, the judge who heard his case said, "You're a Druze. Aren't you ashamed of yourself?"

Members of the Druze community who oppose compulsory conscription claim that many would opt not to serve if given the choice but that communal pressure (from peers as well as authority figures) and the negative consequences of refusal are enough to ensure compliance of those who might be so inclined. The only organized opposition to compulsory conscription has been the Druze Initiative Committee (DIC), founded by a group of leftists in 1972. The DIC's mandate was to fight the state's "Druzification" process, including mandatory conscription, and to promote a sense of Arab identity in the Druze community.[29] But the DIC was never successful in gaining more than a small following for its oppositional agenda because its efforts to forge an alternative political consciousness could not compete with — or even make sense in light of — the countervailing forces organized through the state and its supporters in the community. At the beginning of the first *intifada*, a DIC-organized event like a drive to collect blood to send to Palestinian hospitals had a counterproductive effect in the Druze community. Why help the "enemy" when their brothers and sons, serving in the occupied territories, were clearly on the other side? As one DIC activist explained, "The 'blue-eyed generation' [referring to blue in the Israeli flag] is the product of a long process of alienating Druze from Arabs through the divide-and-rule strategy for minorities in Israel, and from Palestinians in the occupied territories through the process of 'Israelization.'"

Even Druze who willingly serve in the army resent the discrimination they face individually and collectively in Israeli society at large where their identity is not as clear — for them or for Jewish Israelis — as it should be, given the emphasis that is laid on their difference from Arabs.[30] A translator I interviewed told an anecdotal story that exemplifies the contradiction between rhetoric and reality. One morning he took his mother to a hospital in a Jewish town on his way to his posting in the West Bank. The woman at the reception accorded him very "warm and friendly" treatment. In the afternoon, wearing civilian clothes, he went back to get his mother. The receptionist, not recognizing him as the same young soldier she had encountered in the morning, treated him quite differently — "very badly." He said, "She thought I was just some Arab. It was a strange feeling. The next day I didn't want to put my uniform on and go to the army."

Two friends, who served together as translators in Gaza, said that they often discussed problems of discrimination in Israeli society with other Druze soldiers but that others would change the subject whenever a Jewish soldier would join them. They noted that most Druze soldiers are reluctant to discuss discrimination with Jews. These two, however, made a regular point of doing so. One of them said that Jewish soldiers would typically respond with dismay or disbelief at the thought that Druze weren't treated like "everybody else."[31]

As these two explained, the army is often the first time that Druze individuals have any sustained contact with Jews because of geographic and social segregation in Israel. Because Druze soldiers are very young — seventeen or eighteen — when they enter the army, many are insecure about displaying any tendencies or attitudes that deviate from the norm, which is defined by Jewish Israelis. As one translator stressed, "In the army, there is a lot of pressure for Israelis to stick together and not talk about their differences. You can get in trouble if you talk politics in the army."

The Israeli state recognizes the ambiguities and contradictory aspects of Druze identity and addresses this by placing inductees in Druze-only units for the first six weeks, where they undergo, among other forms of military training, ideological indoctrination to intensify or correct for any weakness in their self-image as loyal Israeli citizens who share a common destiny and obligation with Jews to preserve the security of the state against the threats posed by its enemies, namely Arabs. Following training, however, the units that Druze soldiers are assigned to and the roles they are expected to fulfill draw on the notion that they are particularly suited for positions that put them in direct contact with this enemy because of their cultural and linguistic commonalities.[32] In the documentary film *I'm Druze,* an interviewer asks a Druze soldier serving in Gaza, "Because you understand the mentality, doesn't this create problems because you are closer to Arabs than Israelis [sic]?" The soldier responds, "No. We are simply carrying out orders. . . . Because we understand the population — the relationship between orders and needs of the population — things make more sense to us."

While a number of Druze soldiers I interviewed said that they were resentful of discrimination in Israeli society, they held army experience out as an exception; military service fulfilled its promise of providing an opportunity to "integrate." Many described the social atmosphere among soldiers as the most positive aspect of their service. For those who returned to their villages after service, the army was a singular opportunity in their lives to become friends with Jews, and the only Jewish friends they had were those they had made in the army. Many also cited army service as a first opportunity to have relationships of any kind with adult women "strangers" (i.e., female soldiers), friendships as well as sexual relations. Several interviewees were quite nostalgic about the social and sexual freedoms that they enjoyed during their military service, contrasting those experiences to their pre- and postarmy lives.[33] Others who commuted daily to postings in northern parts of the West Bank said that they felt they had missed an important part of the "army experience" as described to them by friends who had spent time living on bases away from home.[34]

Gender dynamics in military settings are a contrast to social relations within the Druze community in Israel. This contrast illustrates the contradictions of Druze Israeli identity and the highly gendered nature of Druze relations to the state. Integration into "modern Westernized" Jewish Israeli society is limited to males and manifested mainly through the military.[35] Social segregation from Jewish society has been intensified through state policies, and acceptable social dynamics within the community are defined by those in positions of local communal authority. Social norms include the impermissibility of fraternizing between unmarried and unrelated males and females and pressures on women to marry early and to remain permanently within the community. The sheltered and secluded status of Druze women is held to be one of the most tangible and significant differences between Jewish and Druze societies, with the notable exception of the self-segregating ultraorthodox Jewish communities. When Druze soldiers come in contact with "liberated" Jewish women, perceptions of their own differences from Jews are reinforced. Those who enjoyed interacting with women are prone to internalize the view of their own community as traditional and "backward" and thus inferior to (secular) Jewish society.

Popular explanations that the Druze are "by nature" traditional rely on the reification of certain social dynamics rather than analysis of the ways in which those patterns are perpetuated by design. In fact, the differences are constructs of larger social and political processes. The policies that have institutionalized Druze difference and communal segregation have empowered certain elements, notably elder male leaders, to promote particular social norms and patterns as the "Druze way of life"[36] and to discourage others. Consequently, a Druze Israeli collective identity attaches meanings to Druzeness that validate conservative and inward-looking social patterns, consolidate highly gendered ties to the state, and reinforce Druze communal status and self-perceptions as a "loyal minority."

## Serving the State

Military service in the West Bank and Gaza highlights the ambiguities of Druze Israeli identity and the contradictory status of Druze citizens in a Jewish state. As Israeli soldiers, they are part of the military administration. However, as non-Jews, they serve a cause that excludes them; Druze communal interests in the occupied territories are deemed to be nonexistent. Issues like territorial sovereignty and claims to the land center around Jewish national interests and historical rights in these areas. Consequently, Druze service in the territories is paradoxical in ways that it is not for Jewish Israelis. While they are expected to serve loyally in the interests of "their" state, the occupation is a critical point of disjuncture, where there is not even a pretense of Israeli multiethnicity. The main argument that Druze put forth to explain their willingness to serve in the military is that it is an obligation that they fulfill in exchange for rights. For Druze soldiers, their obligations span the Green Line while their rights (nominal as they still are) quite clearly stop at the border.[37]

Although Druze soldiers serve alongside Jews in many units and fulfill comparable military tasks, in the military courts, translators "serve alone," so to speak. While translators are members of the same unit as judges and prosecutors, the nature of the role they perform and their identity as Druze distinguish them from other members of this unit.

The use of Arabic-Hebrew translators in this court system is essential to its functioning because of the simple fact that many Palestinians from the occupied territories cannot speak Hebrew and many Jewish Israelis cannot speak Arabic. In general, court translators work in a space where a variety of voices can and must be heard. Translation produces a comprehensibility to the proceedings that not only enables the legal process to proceed but also serves to legitimize the legal system. In this context, the role translators perform contributes to maintaining an appearance of due process and the availability of defendants' legal rights by enabling judges, prosecutors, and defense lawyers to understand one another and to communicate their points effectively.

In any courtroom, *understanding* is a charged term; even without the problem of language barriers and the mediating role of translators, there is always the question of whether the various parties are communicating and comprehending accurately in exchanges often fraught by explicitly contradictory and competing interests. In contexts where language barriers require translation, translators give voice to these contestations in the adversarial legal process. The problems are particularly acute in criminal proceedings because the stakes are so high ("innocence" vs. "guilt" and "freedom" vs. "incarceration").

When the criminal proceedings are linked explicitly to politics, as in contexts where resistance movements are active and their activities criminalized, the interests at stake assume larger significance than the issues involved in any single case. The courtrooms are staging grounds for broader struggles, and the legal process can serve as one form or forum of political engagement. In the Israeli military courts, these engagements pit the interests of the military authorities to maintain control and order against those of defendants charged with opposing the occupation or otherwise violating the military and emergency laws. Within Palestinian society, resistance has been popularized as a "national duty" and a means of struggling for the right to self-determination. There is little stigma attached to arrest, conviction, and imprisonment; on the contrary, people's statuses often are enhanced within their community as a result (see Chapter 7). This, in turn, fuels the perception on the part of many Israeli citizens that Palestinians are collectively and individually dangerous and prone to engage in or support subversive activities.

Translators who work in such an environment become the mouthpieces of authority *and* resistance. The use of translators is integral to Israel's claim that the military court system dispenses justice by operating according to the rule of law. Translators not only facilitate communication among the various parties but in doing so legitimize this system and, beyond that, the occupation as a law-driven political order. On the same grounds, critics of the system argue that translators' incompetence and/or unwillingness to translate proceedings accurately detracts from the possibility of obtaining justice.

## Translating in the Courts

In my experience in the military courts, and on the basis of discussions with members of the various categories of participants, there is little con-

cern that translation rarely if ever meets the standard of a verbatim transmission. Nor, it should be added, is there any significant expectation that
it should. The problems in the military courts are so profound that most
participants, even many of the translators themselves, consider translation
a minor issue.

Translating in the military courts can be a difficult and highly stressful
assignment for young men with no previous public speaking experience
and nominal if any grasp of the legal vocabulary. Soldiers are selected to be
translators on the basis of their competency in Arabic and Hebrew, a determination derived, first, from their scores on the *bagrut* (baccalaureate)
exams. Those with higher scores then undergo additional testing to select
the ones most competently bilingual. Such competence is relative, however, because the overall quality of education in Druze secondary schools
is generally quite poor. Once translators have been selected, they undergo
a process of training. They begin translating files and documents in the
court secretary's office in order to familiarize themselves with the legal
vocabulary. When they feel prepared to begin doing oral translations in
court, they start with easy cases and eventually move on to more difficult
cases. Translators also help, when needed, in out-of-court discussions
between lawyers and prosecutors (e.g., negotiating plea bargains).

Many of the translators I interviewed recounted that when they began,
they were very scared and nervous. The tension was exacerbated by performance anxiety relating to their high visibility in the courtroom.
However, the confidence they gained through experience enabled them
to adopt a mode of practice in which they would translate the "meaning"
of arguments rather than striving for literal translations. It was generally
held, among translators and others, that this was the normative standard
of competence. Many defense lawyers who relied on translators
confirmed that they had, relatively speaking, the highest regard for those
who could convey the meaning and tone of their arguments. While they
would complain about those who had difficulty even approximating the
arguments, no one expected a complete and exact translation. Interestingly, several judges with whom I discussed translation at first said that
they had no way of evaluating the issue, since the translators were provided for the benefit of Arabic speakers. When I reminded them that in
any interactions with Arabic speakers they would be on the other end of
the transmission process, they said that as far as they were concerned the
translations were generally adequate and that if there was a problem they
would replace the translators.

When defense lawyers speak Hebrew, the translators are supposed to translate for the defendants, but often they do not do so. When I questioned several translators about why they remained silent in such instances, I received similar responses: the lawyer will tell the defendant whatever he needs to know later. In general, translators tended to consider that the only people who needed to understand what goes on in the courtroom are the judges, prosecutors, and defense lawyers. This assumption is not entirely misplaced, since the vast majority of cases are concluded through plea bargains rather than trials, and most of what happens in court involves working out the details of a prearranged deal.

The quality of translation and attitudes of translators vary greatly. Some demonstrate great competence while others make minimal efforts and omit all but the basic outlines of arguments. I witnessed many occasions when a defense lawyer who was fluent in Hebrew would correct a translator on behalf of an Arabic-speaking colleague. I also witnessed a few instances when judges would rebuke translators for making mistakes. On one occasion, the translator, who had been doing a poor job all day, misstated the sentence in a case. Instead of saying "four years" (in prison) he said "fourteen years." An Arab Israeli lawyer present in the court then corrected the translator. But the careless error upset the judge, who immediately dismissed him. As he was leaving the courtroom, the translator pointed a finger at the defendant and said with a laugh, "Fourteen years in prison for you!"

## The Instrumentality of Translators in the Legal Process

> [I]deally, [the translator] should not exist as a distinct verbal participant in [his] own right during the course of a judicial proceeding. In effect, [he] is meant to speak solely in place of the other participants in the courtroom, those considered to legitimately hold the right to speak: the attorneys, witnesses, [prosecutors], and the judge.
>
> Susan Berk-Seligson, *The Bilingual Courtroom*[38]

Translators in the Israeli military courts, like court translators in general, play a *legally* neutral role in court proceedings. They have no legal voice of their "own" but rather give voice to others. Translators are at the service of the three parties in the legal process — the defense, the prosecution, and the judiciary. According to one man with long military court experience, "The outcome of every case is up to the translator. You are the sole communication between the three parts of the court. If the job isn't done right, an injustice will be done."

Needless to say, the ideal of an impartial and fair legal system jars with the conditions of military occupation and conflict. This general problem also applies specifically to the role of translators. The lines are blurred between translators' "neutral" role in the legal process and their role as soldiers serving in the military administration. Indeed, many of the translators I interviewed said that they saw their *role* as neutral but did not see *themselves* as neutral. Rather, they saw themselves as Israeli soldiers facing the enemy in the context to which they had been assigned — the military courts.

One translator stressed the importance of conscientiousness by saying that if someone made a mistake of even one word, "maybe the person will be found not guilty." When I asked him if the same could be said about a mistake contributing to someone erroneously being found guilty, he said that this didn't matter because in the end all Palestinians were guilty of something. According to another, the high conviction rate was understandable because courts only dealt with "*intifada* criminals." He continued, "The army arrests people because they are guilty. Everyone knows they are guilty. Even their lawyers know it. They have confessed. Therefore, translating is not so important. It is because their guilt has to be put down on the record. But it is there. They said it to us already. [He is referring here to confessions during interrogation.] . . . Palestinians are guilty. They hate us. They throw stones. If they don't throw stones today, they will throw stones tomorrow. . . . The IDF is doing exactly what it should in the territories. When you are in a war, you act like you are in a war."

Many of the translators I interviewed during the first *intifada* held similar views about the endemic guilt of Palestinians. The nature of military service in a hostile region reinforces such attitudes, which are common among Jewish soldiers as well. For translators, however, their experience with the occupation takes place under the aegis of the military court system. They are, therefore, placed in a position where they are directly subject to the two contradictory "pulls" that characterize the court system as both military and legal.

As soldiers, translators are expected to embrace the view that the military has a legitimate right to control and punish the Palestinian population. But as participants in the legal process, they also are expected to comprehend the court system's semiautonomy as a forum for dispensing justice. In practice, translators have a much harder time than judges and prosecutors in reconciling the contradictions between security and legality. No translators have prior legal experience. Additionally, as low-ranking soldiers, they have neither the right nor the capacity to question the ways in which the state exercises its authority. In contrast, judges and prosecutors, as high-ranking soldiers and well-educated legal professionals, are more actively involved in conceptualizing and enacting state policies in the legal sphere. Their roles require that they wrestle with the contradictions between the military and legal dimensions of the court system in order to understand and fulfill their own respective duties.

If translators were to grapple with the contradictions between security and legality, they might draw conclusions that would be critical of the military occupation. Indeed, some judges and prosecutors hold critical views (see Chapter 4). But for translators, the issue is affected by the fact that they are Druze and not Jews. To embrace a critical, nonconformist position would highlight their ambiguous status and vulnerability vis-à-vis the Israeli state. They know that they are more susceptible to suspicions of potential disloyalty than Jewish soldiers because they are still perceived as not completely not Arab — that is, the enemy. Most Druze soldiers accept the authority of the state and the legitimacy of its policies, a gesture that demonstrates both loyalty and subordination.

Whatever their views of the court system, most judges, prosecutors, defense lawyers, and defendants hold firm ideas about the articulation of the system's military and legal dimensions. The reason is that members of each of these categories have some vested interest in the functioning of the system and the legal outcome of cases. In contrast, translators' involvement is instrumental. They have both an institutional duty and a political incentive to remain detached from the legal contests to which they give voice.

On occasion, however, some translators do find themselves having an interest in the outcome of a case or the operation of the system. The personal dimension of their participation affects their relations with members of the other categories of participants or their attitudes about others involved in the system. One translator who worked in the Jenin court said that he had always been indifferent to the fate of defendants, accepting that harsh punishment was a just reward for "terrorism." Then one day a man who owned a store where the translator and his family used to shop was brought to court. He said that it was very upsetting to see someone he knew and liked standing in court in handcuffs. For the first time, he wanted to do something to help, but there was nothing he could do. He said, "That man did something wrong and he had to be punished. But I felt very bad — for him and for his family. I can't forget his face when the judge sent him to jail."

A translator who worked in the Gaza court said that he had very friendly relations with some of the local Palestinian defense lawyers. They would often pass the time talking politics. He was deeply affected when two of these lawyers were brought to court as defendants on charges that they were members of an illegal organization (i.e., a faction of the PLO). In describing his thoughts about their case, he said that at first he was shocked and disappointed that they "had turned out to be criminals." But then he began to think about what they had said about the situation in Gaza. He had always respected their commitment to the aspirations of their people, even if he didn't share their political views. This incident led him to start thinking differently about the court system and the occupation. Because of his respect for these lawyers as individuals, he was able to empathize with their desire to be politically active and related their situation to that of other defendants. He said, "I can't say that I wouldn't do the same thing if I lived in Gaza."

One translator told me that he had worked on the case of "the biggest murderer in the West Bank." At the end of the trial, when the man was sentenced to life in prison, his mother and sisters who were in the courtroom began wailing. The translator said he felt his heart break. "I looked at them and they reminded me of my own mother and sisters. I wondered what my family would do and how they would feel if they knew that they would never see me again. I felt very bad. Not for him, because he deserved to go to prison for what he did, but for them. . . . It made me feel very lucky that I don't live under occupation."

The common theme in these accounts is a sense of awakening to the human costs of the conflict and the humanity of "the enemy." Each one described his feelings during these incidents as dominated by a sense of confusion arising out of a personal identification with the people living under occupation. The rigid boundary between Israeli soldiers and Palestinians, which is so elemental to military service in the occupied territories, began to seem more tenuous and illusory.

## Translating Identities

Druze translators function simultaneously as Israeli soldiers involved in the maintenance of a military occupation over a hostile civilian population, neutral instruments of the legal process, and "non-Arab Arabs." Translators' experiences in the court system can be used to explore the more general contradictions and ambiguities of Druze Israeli identity.

As Israeli soldiers, Druze translators are situated on the Israeli "side" in the "us versus them" dynamics that characterize the conflict. Within the courts, the distinctions between "us" and "them" are obvious: "us" is everyone in uniform and/or armed, "them" is everyone else — Palestinian defendants, their civilian lawyers, and family members (see Chapter 3).

The "us versus them" dynamics figure prominently in translators' understandings of their duty as soldiers serving in the occupied territories. To the extent that their "side" is "Israeli" and Israel is Jewish, being perceived as indistinguishable from Jewish soldiers becomes an issue. To reinforce everyone's perceptions about which side they are on, some translators refuse to speak Arabic except in those specific instances when it is required of them in court. Druze soldiers can be sensitive that their fluency in Arabic makes them seem less "Israeli," even though Arabic is an official language of Israel. On one occasion, when I was interviewing two translators in a crowded cafeteria of a Jerusalem hotel that had been converted into housing for reservists, one refused to speak Arabic. He said, "Not here. If you come to my village, I will speak to you in Arabic. But here, the language is Hebrew." The other, however, had no such reservations, and we conducted our interview in Arabic.

Bilingual Arab lawyers frequently complain that some translators insist on conversing with them outside of court in Hebrew. In their opinion, it is because these translators are embarrassed to have Jewish soldiers see them speaking Arabic and thus demonstrating their differences from the "Israeli norm." I found it quite comical — and common — to see extended conversations between bilingual lawyers and translators when the former insisted on speaking only Arabic and the latter only Hebrew.

I witnessed a few occasions when translators declined to speak Arabic even to people who did not know Hebrew. One day in the Ramallah court a Jewish soldier was trying to get some information from people sitting in the public section. When no one understood what he was saying in Hebrew, he turned to a Druze soldier and asked for help. The latter made the exact same request — in Hebrew. Everyone in the public section burst into laughter. One Palestinian man turned to me and said, "The Israelis gave him a uniform and took away his language."

The second dimension of translators' experience in courts is the "neutral" aspect of their role in the legal process. Here, the political-national dichotomy of the conflict is displaced by the triangular equation of a defense, a prosecution, and a judiciary. Translators are not part of the equation; rather they are a mediatory element, cast in the role of linguistic tools. The politicization of their status as soldiers — in which they are clearly on one "side" — is nullified by their role in the courts. It is because they have crucial linguistic abilities rather than vested interests in the legal process that they participate at all.

The third dimension relates to the "non-Arab Arabness" of the Druze. Despite the effects of the "Israelization" of their identity as soldiers and the legal "neutrality" of their role as translators, they are put in positions that emphasize their similarities to Palestinians in the occupied territories and through which they are constantly reminded of those similarities. Druze are used as translators because of the perceived significance of a common culture, most tangibly evidenced by the fact that they speak the same language. While military service is intended to capitalize on Druze soldiers' feelings of alienation from Arabs, the daily experience of working as translators forces them to confront the humanity of the enemy. They are, in fact, required to serve as the voice of the enemy in court. For a few, this situation has presented a subversive potential to forget their "place." According to one translator, "If I forgot I was an Arab before the army, now I know I am an Arab. I am an Arab Druze Israeli. It's crazy!" But for most, the contradictions just contribute to the confusion they feel about who they are *in* and *for* Israel.

Although some Jewish soldiers who work in the military courts might sympathize with Palestinians, for the Druze such feelings carry a different meaning, given the ways in which sociocultural differences have been politicized into an essentializing Jewish/Arab dichotomy. The Druze in Israel do not fit comfortably on either side of this divide. Consequently, people develop adaptive mechanisms to deal with the contradictions of their own identity. According to one translator, "When I am in Tel Aviv I am a Jew. When I am in Rame [a mixed town in northern Israel] I am an Arab. When I am in Julis [a Druze village] I am a Druze." Under the current circumstances, the Druze do not have many options for reconciling these contradictions in their status as both "non-Jews" and "non-Arabs." The adaptive mechanism to "be" whatever the situation requires stands as a pragmatic alternative.

Through their experiences in the military courts, translators, more than other members of the Druze community, live out the contradictions of being "non-Arab Arabs" in a Jewish state engaged in an ongoing conflict with Arab enemies. Translators' speech position in the courtroom is analogous to the social location of the Druze community in the broader context: they exist in the border zones. Individuals have few options to contest the terms of their difference from all others because of the strategic value it bears for local leaders and elites and for the state. It is through translators' particular mode of service to the state, and the importance of that service in legitimizing the occupation, that these contradictions can be seen not as an oversight but as an imperative of Israeli state rule over "non-Jewish" populations on both sides of the Green Line.

Druze translators are deterred, for reasons explained in this chapter, from adopting or expressing views critical of the Israeli occupation of the West Bank and Gaza. In contrast, many defense lawyers have been motivated and guided by their criticism of the occupation to work in the military courts, as I explain in the next chapter.

CHAPTER 6

# Cause Lawyering
# and National Conflict

*Defense Lawyers*

---

*Try to realize that this vast judicial organism remains . . . in a state
of eternal equilibrium, and that if you change something on your
own where you are, you can cut the ground out from under your
own feet and fall, while the vast organism easily compensates for
the minor disturbance at some other spot — after all, everything
is interconnected — and remains unchanged, if not, which is likely,
even more resolute, more vigilant, more severe, more malicious.*

Franz Kafka, *The Trial*[1]

When rights are the stakes of a conflict, politically engaged lawyers often
play important roles. Their professional knowledge of the law, political
vision, and commitment are vital resources for articulating rights claims
and challenging rights violations. In the course of those struggles, lawyers'
skills can be put to the tasks of defending those who are fighting for rights
and formulating strategies to marshal law to their aid.

"Cause lawyering" is a concept developed by sociolegal scholars to
highlight and analyze the involvements of lawyers *as legal practitioners* on
behalf of a cause other than — or greater than — the interests of individual clients.[2] In contrast to "conventional" or "client lawyering," which is
tailored to accommodate individual clients and to maneuver within prevailing arrangements of power, cause lawyering involves the application
of professional skills and services to transform the status quo in some
goal-oriented fashion.

Working for a cause implies agency and consciousness, political identifications, social solidarity and goals. A cause also implies mobilization to achieve some kind of change and the creation or exploitation of opportunities for intervention and alliance building within a given field of hegemonic relations. The study of cause lawyering explores how legal professionals contribute to the causes with which they identify and how the politics of the cause at issue affects and is affected by lawyers' work.

Many of the Israeli and Palestinian defense lawyers who practice in the Israeli military court system in the West Bank and Gaza could be regarded as cause lawyers because their motives for doing this work are political. While they do things common to defense lawyering — providing legal counsel to people who have been arrested, defending the rights of the accused throughout the legal process, visiting clients in prison, encouraging or consoling them as they endure the travails of prosecution and incarceration, and serving as their link to the outside — the issue of cause comes to bear in understanding why individual lawyers would choose to work in this court system when other options are available to them and how they use their position as legal professionals to intervene in the Israeli-Palestinian conflict. However, while many Israeli and Palestinian lawyers have chosen to work in the military courts to serve a cause, it is not the same cause.

The situation in apartheid South Africa provides a salient contrast. There, cause lawyering exhibited a coherence of cause that included not only resistance to the racial hierarchy but also a transcendent vision of a democratic future. Cause lawyering strategies were coordinated with a larger antiapartheid movement.[3] In Israel/Palestine, there is no shared vision about the desired course of political change, nor is there a coordinated or cohesive movement uniting all those who oppose the Israeli occupation of the West Bank and Gaza. Analytically and politically, the contrast illustrates the difference between lawyers working for a cause of "national" proportions and those working in a "transnational" context (see Chapter 1). In South Africa, the politics of the state was both a focal point of organized resistance and a goal: the antiapartheid movement was seeking to transform the South African state from a racist monopoly into a nonracist democracy.

In Israel/Palestine, the Israeli state provides an enduring point of reference for struggles over rights, but there are wide variations in perceptions about the conflict and goals for change. The various causes to which military court lawyers subscribe or sympathize and their motivations for functioning as cause lawyers derive from a combination of factors. The most important are lawyers' identities, which bear on their relations to the

Israeli state and to the Palestinian population in the occupied territories who make up their clientele, and lawyers' political orientations and ideological commitments, which bear on the kinds of changes they advocate and the kinds of alliances and relations they cultivate through their work.

In this chapter, I describe and analyze cause lawyering in the military courts, highlighting two distinct but related sets of issues. One is lawyers' identities and ideologies, which are critical to understand who chooses to do this kind of work and why and to compare and contrast their motivations. The meanings of lawyers' identities vis-à-vis the state (e.g., as "nationals," "minorities," or "enemies," as "citizens" or "foreigner subjects") influence their decision to work in the military courts and bear on what they do — what they can or cannot do, what they want or refuse to do — as lawyers. Lawyers' ideological commitments are informed by the politics of the conflict and by their own experiences, both professional and personal.

The other key issue is the relationship between the military court system and the conflict. In crucial ways, cause lawyering constitutes a core history of the military court system and, by extension, a history of law and conflict in Israel/Palestine. The historical account that I provide in this chapter is particularly attentive to relations among lawyers and to changing conditions of work in the military courts since the onset of the occupation over three decades ago. In Chapter 8, I return to the issue of cause lawyering to focus on the legal process and the various factors that affect lawyers' handling of cases and their relations with others.

## Studying Cause Lawyering

Terrence Halliday offers some instructive suggestions for theorizing about cause lawyering. It should incorporate "*a motivational theory of action.*"[4] He describes this as a theory of lawyers' behavior that identifies "the interests, orientations and impulses that drive lawyers' behavior from within. Such an account should, moreover, explain where these motivations are inculcated and how they are sustained or attenuated."[5] Theorizing about professional action must also attend to the "*institutional structure of politics,* including that of the state and the structure of justice."[6] Finally, Halliday suggests the need for "*a contingent theory of professional collective action.*"[7] As he explains, "By 'contingent' I stipulate that a theory must be able to show the circumstances in which one set of outcomes . . . will occur when another will not."[8]

Pursuing a motivational theory of action should begin with an assessment of cause lawyers' conceptions about the "collective client" — the beneficiaries of cause-minded legal action. Acting in the interest of a collective client distinguishes the motives of cause lawyers from those of conventional lawyers. According to David Luban, "The politically motivated lawyer acts ethically not by evading the essentially political character of relationships but by responsibly representing the political aims of her entire client constituency, even at the price of wronging individual clients. The key point is that a responsible representative must keep one eye on the interests of future generations. The appearance of elitism arises from the fact that a responsible representative may be compelled out of concern for future generations to ignore the preferences of current constituents, but this is not really elitism — it is political courage."[9]

Motivations for cause lawyering could encompass a variety of altruistic, prosocial, or "other-regarding" impulses. For example, it could derive from sympathy or frustration over the suffering of the collective client; a desire to employ lawyerly skills as a shield against — and/or a critique of — abuse by state agents; or a willingness to empower and defend people in their struggles to build "the good society." Motivations for cause lawyering also could arise from a commitment to universalistic principles like the rule of law or human rights in contexts where they are absent or at risk.

In the early years of the Israeli occupation of the West Bank and Gaza, a small number of Israeli citizens, who were motivated by a conscious desire to traffic in the fray of the conflict, crossed the Green Line to represent Palestinian clients in the military court system. Palestinian lawyers from the occupied territories, also few in the early years, were motivated by a sense of obligation to defend members of their community who were arrested. Although these Israelis and Palestinians regarded their work — and themselves — as "political," they found few opportunities to use the legal process for any political ends of their own choosing because their practices were confined, for the most part, to plea bargaining. Thus, for the first decade, military court lawyers might have been "thinking cause," but in practice they were "acting client."

Starting in the late 1970s, cause lawyering was transformed by the founding of the first human rights organization in the occupied territories (see Chapter 2). The origins of this transformation have a rather humble, almost accidental quality but also bespeak the capacity of individuals to initiate changes with broad ramifications. Raja Shehadeh, one of the architects of this shift, recounts how this process began. In 1976, after returning to the West Bank from England where he had gone to do his legal studies, he went to work in his father's law firm in Ramallah. He was assigned to prepare a subject index of the hundreds of military orders that had been issued since the beginning of the occupation. This proved to be a pivotal moment. Shehadeh writes:

They were stacked in one corner of the office . . . loose sheets of yellowed paper typed in Hebrew with a poor translation into Arabic, headed: THE ISRAELI DEFENSE FORCES COMMAND OF JUDEA AND SAMARIA. . . . As I read, I became aware of the Israeli legal changes. . . . This went contrary to international law governing the powers of an occupying state — this much I knew. Why then was no one protesting?

I spoke to other lawyers, but they showed no interest. No one paid attention to these military orders anyway — many lawyers used the back of these sheets as scrap paper. These amendments to law were treated as though they did not exist, just as Israel itself was treated by the Arab states. But it did exist, and we were living under its domination. . . . We needed to tell the world that the Israeli claim that the occupation was the most benevolent in history was not true; that the reality of life under occupation was very different from the one portrayed to the outside world. I knew all this but I did not know how to expose the situation or how to do anything to change it.[10]

In London, Shehadeh had learned about an organization called Justice, the British affiliate of the International Commission of Jurists (ICJ). In 1979, he joined with Charles Shammas, a Lebanese American graduate of Yale Law School, and Jonathan Kuttab, a Jerusalemite lawyer with American citizenship, both of whom had moved to the West Bank to work for the Palestinian cause, and they established a West Bank ICJ affiliate, Law in the Service of Man (LSM; later renamed Al-Haq). Two years later, Raji Sourani, another military court lawyer, established an ICJ affiliate in Gaza, the Gaza Center for Rights and Law. Over the next decade, more organizations devoted to the cause of human rights were established on both sides of the Green Line.

While this process might have originated in a desire to serve Palestinian national goals, human rights provided new ways of thinking, talking about, and intervening in the conflict. The initial impetus behind this embrace of human rights was a desire to utilize international law as a counterbalance to the military and emergency laws used by the Israeli state to govern Palestinians in the occupied territories. Establishing local human rights organizations was a means to cultivate a human rights approach to the conflict and to promote a "human rights consciousness" among the populations in Israel/Palestine. These developments, in turn, enabled increasing numbers of lawyers to regard their work in the military courts as a contribution to the struggle for human rights and the rule of law. Consequently, by the mid-1980s the motives and practices of cause lawyers in the military court system began to take on a more collective, proactive, and internationalist cast. They were finding ways to "act" as well as "think cause."

In Israel/Palestine, as in many other contexts, cause lawyering became tantamount to human rights work. As Stanley Cohen notes, "Lawyers are the dominant profession to claim ownership of the human rights problem and have succeeded in establishing a virtual monopoly of knowledge (how the subject is framed) and power (what strategies of intervention are used)."[11] Palestinian and Israeli military court lawyers were among the first human rights activists in Israel/Palestine, and their efforts constituted the first manifestation of *legal* resistance to the Israeli occupation.

Human rights activism in Israel/Palestine had a heyday during the first *intifada*. But it would be inaccurate to assume that this diminished the differences among military court lawyers or mitigated the deep divisions and disparate perspectives about the conflict and goals for change. Even lawyers' perspectives on human rights were bound up with their positions in the conflict. In the following section, I provide a comparative analysis of lawyers' identities and ideologies as these issues bear on their views about themselves and their cause and on the nature of their participation as lawyers in this system.

## On Being Cause Lawyers: The Importance of Identity and Ideology

While defense lawyers working in the military court system all, generally speaking, do the same thing — represent Palestinian clients — the differences in their motivations and modes of practice illustrate the politics of identity and ideology in the broader context of Israel/Palestine. In terms of identities, lawyers who work in this system include Jewish Israelis, Arab Israelis, and Palestinian residents of Gaza and the West Bank. Among the latter, the distinction between East Jerusalemites and other Palestinians is significant because it manifests as differences in rights and, by extension, in lawyers' legal practices (e.g., people with Jerusalem identity cards are not immobilized by "closures").

The issue of political ideology is more complicated and cuts across national boundaries. Among Jewish Israeli lawyers who practice in the military courts, there are three general designations: *nonpolitical, liberal,* and *political*. These are descriptive terms used by lawyers themselves and by others to delineate differences in their political views and motivations for doing this work. *Nonpolitical* is the term used to refer to lawyers who *do not* regard themselves as proponents of Palestinians' rights (a key characteristic of "liberal" lawyers) or identify politically with the Palestinian struggle for self-determination (a characteristic of "political" lawyers). While some nonpolitical Jewish Israeli lawyers would regard themselves as conventional lawyers whose sole concerns are financial remuneration and the interests of individual clients, others regard themselves as cause lawyers whose cause is to defend their state; they choose to represent Palestinian clients as a rejoinder to criticisms that the military court system defies legality.

One relevant question, then, would be why Palestinians would hire lawyers who hold views so antithetical to their collective interests. Those who do so might believe that lawyers who identify positively with the state will have connections and influence *(wasta)* with judges and prosecutors to get better results and/or that other types of lawyers are too encumbered with negative reputations among the Israeli authorities to be effective. Also, because nonpolitical lawyers take few military court cases and charge high fees, there is reason to believe that they will give each case their undivided attention, something that cannot be assumed about busy lawyers with large military court caseloads. According to those who are critical of the hiring of nonpolitical lawyers, Palestinians who do so are not adequately "political" themselves. The assumption is that "nonpolitical" Palestinians hire "nonpolitical" Jewish Israelis and that for both the lawyer-client relationship is mutually opportunistic rather than having any basis in a shared understanding of the relevant political issues.

However, this assessment fails to take into account that nonpolitical lawyers sometimes are recommended by other types of lawyers if the issues in a case are particularly sensitive — for example, requiring the investigation of testimony by soldiers or settlers. Jewish lawyers who are not identified as "pro-Palestinian" are perceived to be uniquely suited to these tasks. Another explanation why some Palestinians, even highly politicized activists, might opt to hire nonpolitical Jewish lawyers is that they do not regard the legal terrain as a site of struggle and seek, in effect, someone who will function like a conventional lawyer. They are indifferent to lawyers' motives and care instead about their effectiveness in getting a lower sentence. The advantage that nonpolitical lawyers are perceived to have is that they "speak the same language" literally and figuratively as judges and prosecutors.

"Liberal" Jewish Israeli lawyers tend to be drawn to this work out of a concern that the state — their state — violates the rights of Palestinians in the territories. While they would describe themselves as loyal Israeli citizens — and some represent their work in the military courts as an expression of loyalty to the *ideals* of the state — they are motivated to intervene in the balance between security and legality by representing Palestinian clients against the military.

Shlomo Lecker, a Jewish Israeli who described himself as a "classic civil rights liberal," said that his decision to work in the military courts has been enigmatic for other Israelis, especially some judges and prosecutors. He serves as a reservist in an elite unit of the Israel Defense Forces (IDF) and in that regard is literally "one of them." But his decision to defend Palestinians and to make a regular habit of reporting on problems in the court system has caused other Israelis to wonder which "side" he is on and where his loyalties lie. He explained his motivations:

There is only so much that I, or any lawyer, can do in the courts. But when I see a problem, something really outrageous, I run to the media. I have good connections with journalists and they believe what I say because they know me. When I give them a story about something really outrageous, like a kid being sent to jail with some long sentence just for throwing stones, or if someone comes to court with bruises from a beating, I want people to know about it. I don't want people to say they didn't know. . . . This is my real service.

Some Jewish Israeli liberals are motivated by the negative effects that the occupation of the West Bank and Gaza has had on their own society and on Israeli legal culture. They have pursued this work out of a sense of civic duty to monitor and pressure the military to abide in practice by the legal standards the state claims to respect in principle. According to Joshua Schoffman, former legal director of the Association for Civil Rights in Israel (the flagship institution of liberal legalism in Israel), "There are problems in Israel as there are in Northern Ireland when security is an issue. Terrorists can't expect our support, but the courts have an obligation to try them fairly. . . . Everyone has a right to certain legal rights. . . . There is no formula to assess national security, and every Arab in the territories is not *necessarily* a security threat. Because of the procedural problems, lawyers have no way of knowing whether the judges and prosecutors are acting fairly in any case. . . . We have to be concerned that people get what they can from the court."

Liberal Jewish Israeli lawyers are motivated primarily by concerns about their state and tend to regard their Palestinian clients as beneficiaries of their own legal values and moral conscientiousness. But when liberals cross the Green Line to defend Palestinians, they go as critics, thereby disrupting a complacency within their own society about what the army does "over there." Liberals do not undertake such work to alienate themselves from their own society; rather, they see themselves as legal standard bearers striving to ensure that Palestinians are treated fairly under circumstances of military rule. Thus, liberals' cause could be described as a struggle to legitimize and protect Palestinian rights within Israeli state practices.

Politically, Jewish liberals tend to embrace a "centrist" view on security — accepting restrictions on Palestinians' rights but expecting those restrictions to serve a narrow purpose of security enhancement (e.g., many are critical of the flourishing of Jewish settlements). They tend to embrace a compromising position on territoriality — advocating an end to the military occupation as necessary both to resolve the conflict and to preserve or restore Israel's democratic culture. They accept the possibility and even the desirability of a Palestinian state but do not see themselves as proponents of Palestinian national ambitions.

*Political* is the term used to describe leftist Jewish Israeli lawyers who *do* identify with the Palestinian struggle for self-determination. Some describe themselves as anti-Zionist or non-Zionist, and a few of the younger ones have adopted the appellation of post-Zionist. Unlike nonpolitical and liberal Jewish lawyers, they tend to be deeply critical of the Israeli political establishment and strong opponents of the occupation and have pursued this line of work out of a motivation to act in solidarity with Palestinians in the West Bank and Gaza. As Jews, they are privileged within the sociopolitical structure of Israel/Palestine, but as anti-, non- or post-Zionists, they are politically marginalized from the Jewish Israeli mainstream. Some regard their Jewishness (with the privileges this entails) as a basis for responsibility as well as opportunity to work on behalf of Palestinians. As Andre Rosenthal described his decision to take up military court work:

When I was young, I was ideologically sympathetic to the left, but I wasn't politically active. Then I started working for Lea Tsemel [a leftist lawyer] and that opened my eyes. I saw the conditions in the territories and I saw what kind of suffering the Palestinians face. . . . I understand the political motivations of Palestinians [to resist the occupation]. It is my job to help them weather down the damage. . . . Being a Jewish Israeli makes it easier for me than for Palestinian lawyers. Palestinian lawyers have a very hard time and many of them take too much shit. I am not going to take shit from some soldier and they [sic] know it.

Leftist Jewish Israeli lawyers are actually "ultraleftists" within the politico-ideological spectrum of Jewish Israeli society. Although the ultraleft is small and politically fragmented, there is a degree of unity in their trenchant critique of the occupation and their support for Palestinians' right to self-determination.

Arab Israeli lawyers who work in the military courts often compare their motivations to those of leftist Jewish Israelis. But for Arabs, crossing the Green Line to work in the military courts means something profoundly different than it does for Jews. Many explain their motivation as emanating directly from their ethnonational ties to Palestinians living under occupation: they are "one people" in the "two-peoples" national dichotomy (see Chapter 1). According to Jawad Boulos, who emphasized national ties in describing his motivations to work in the military courts, "I am a soldier in my people's army and I use the cards I have been dealt." Others stress leftist politics over national ties. Muhammad Namneh said, "The most committed lawyers are the leftists, whether we are Jews or Arabs. When people criticize us, the first thing they point to is the fact that we are communists. But if we weren't communists, we wouldn't be here. We would be working somewhere else."

Unlike Jewish liberals, who may be critical of state practices but are motivated by a sense of loyalty to the ideals of the state, no Arab Israeli lawyer would claim loyalty to Israel as a motivating factor because Arabs are discriminated against by the state and treated as second-class citizens. And unlike Jewish leftists, who are marginalized in Israel because of their politics, Arabs are marginalized because of their identity as "non-Jews." Whereas Jewish leftists breach national boundaries to act in solidarity with Palestinians, Arab Israelis affirm national ties to do so. And while Jewish liberals and leftists who defend Palestinians may be criticized by the Jewish Israeli mainstream for supporting "the other side," Arab citizens who defend Palestinians in the occupied territories are susceptible to criticism that they are a "fifth column," acting out their political resentments and national ambitions and showing their colors as "enemies of the state."

Because Arab Israelis identify—and are identified—nationally with Palestinians in the occupied territories, this "nationalizes" the decision of those lawyers who choose to work in the military courts as an expression of cross-boundary (i.e., Green Line) solidarity. But because they are citizens of Israel, they have fundamentally different rights than their Palestinian clientele and colleagues who live under occupation, and these differences are not diminished by their decision to cross the Green Line.

On the contrary, Arab Israelis are cognizant of their relative advantages as citizens and the influence that growing up in Israel has had on them. Several stressed that they have been "Israelized," which they equated with aggressiveness and confidence. Boulos, who is renowned for his fierce and slick style and has amassed the largest practice of any military court lawyer, described himself in this way: "I am a strong man. I respect myself as a lawyer and people respect me. Knowing the language is number one, then knowing the laws and precedents, and finally being able to have good relations with judges and prosecutors. Because I work well, I have a special relationship to the courts, and clients come to me for that reason. I can get things done. I always advise other lawyers [i.e., Palestinians from the occupied territories] to respect themselves. When you show weakness, you become weaker because people take advantage."

Unlike all categories of Israeli citizens, Palestinian lawyers from the West Bank and Gaza share the political fate of their clients. Most explain their motivation for working in the military courts in terms of "national duty." Like the people they defend, Palestinian lawyers live under occupation, so solidarity with their clients derives from and reflects a common status, not a "choice," as it is for Arab and Jewish Israeli citizens who cross the Green Line. In varying ways, they see their work as a contribution to Palestinians' struggles for rights, but variations turn on perceptions about the role of law and lawyers in the politics of resistance to the occupation.

Because the military court system is part of the military administration, choosing to work in the courts raises serious questions for Palestinian lawyers themselves and for other members of their society as to whether they are helping or resisting the occupation. As Sharhabeel Al-Za'im, a lawyer from Gaza, noted, "By always plea bargaining, we just help the Israelis put Palestinians in jail faster." But others rationalize their decision to do this work as necessary and beneficial under the circumstances. Elia Theodory, who started practicing in the military courts during the first *intifada,* said,

I always ask myself if working in the military courts is what I should be doing, if I am doing anybody any good. I feel sorry for the people. Being arrested or having a family member arrested and going through the whole process is very difficult for everyone. Visiting the prisons is depressing. The detainees stink, they are cold and scared and tired. But you are not talking about strangers. These are my people. I know I am helping them, even if all I am doing is bringing them clothes and some news from their families. . . . People go to lawyers because they need them. Lawyers are part of the big picture of the struggle.

While Palestinian lawyers tend to identify personally and politically with their clients, beyond the collective stance opposing the occupation, Palestinian politics in the West Bank and Gaza is fractious, and the political scene is characterized by an array organizations, including local branches of the factions that make up the Palestine Liberation Organization (PLO): Fatah, Popular Front for the Liberation of Palestine (PFLP), Democratic Front for the Liberation of Palestine (DFLP), the Palestinian Democratic Union (FIDA), the Palestine Communist Party (renamed the Palestine People's Party in 1990); and non-PLO groups, notably the Islamist organizations Hamas and Islamic Jihad. Some Palestinian lawyers have been actively involved in the various national organizations, and others have cultivated clienteles from one faction or another, sometimes as an expression of solidarity with that faction's politics.

Living under occupation distinguishes the motives, opportunities, and rights of Palestinian lawyers from those of their Israeli colleagues, and these differences bear on comparative analysis of cause lawyering. In general, Palestinian lawyers tend to place greater emphasis on a shared identity with their clients and the extralegal aspects of their work, such as prison visits and emotional support for them and their families. According to Bahij Tammimi, a lawyer from the West Bank, "Palestinian lawyers are different from Israeli lawyers because we are Palestinians first and lawyers second. Many Israeli lawyers see their work as *work,* not as politics."

Many Palestinian lawyers see their role primarily as interlocutors between the people and the state, trying to minimize the negative repercussions of the occupation with the limited professional options at their disposal. Moreover, Palestinian lawyers are subject to the same laws as their clients and are as susceptible to harassment, arrest, land confiscations, and so on as any other Palestinians.[12] This vulnerability sets them apart from their Israeli colleagues and fortifies their identification with their clients. According to Adnan Abu Laila, a lawyer from Nablus who was arrested during the first *intifada:*

I would visit clients in prison about four days every week. When I was arrested, it wasn't in the night like other people. I was "invited" to meet with [a security officer]. That's how they arrested me. First they questioned me in Fara'a [a prison near Nablus] about being a leader of Fatah and passing information from my clients in prison to people on the outside. Then they sent me to the desert [Ansar III, the prison camp in the Negev created in 1988 to hold administrative detainees]. Even though it was totally disgusting, being there was a good experience for me. Now I could really understand how things work from the other side. . . . Just seeing a lawyer's face can be a comfort.

While all lawyers concur that political change will not come from within the military court system, most Israeli cause lawyers regard crossing the Green Line to do this work as a form of resistance (whatever motivation draws them). Similarly, some Palestinian lawyers regard working within an Israeli military institution as a form of resistance because it puts them in direct and adversarial relation with Israeli state agents. But others regard resistance as something that happens "elsewhere" — something their clients do — and regard the legal terrain as a site of *sumud* (steadfastness). For Palestinians, the tensions and contradictions are more acute between the ideology of political resistance as collective, selfless, and militant and the nature of legal practices within the military court system — especially plea bargaining, which is inherently individualizing and concessionary (see Chapter 8). Indeed, some Palestinian cause lawyers have made a conscious choice to refuse to practice in the military court system on the grounds that such work legitimizes the occupation and turns them into de facto collaborators, and others have abandoned the military courts for this reason.

As a category of participants, the only thing that unites defense lawyers is the work itself, which is difficult, depressing, and often degrading. In the remainder of this chapter, I provide a history of defense lawyering in the military courts to contextualize and elaborate on the ways in which lawyers' motivations and practices have affected and been affected by the changing conflict.


## Crossing the Line

The history of cause lawyering in the Israeli military court system begins with a bloody shirt. Felicia Langer, a leftist Jewish Israeli lawyer, starts her autobiographical book, *With My Own Eyes,*[13] with an account of a meeting in January 1968 with a Palestinian man who came to her office in West Jerusalem to solicit her services. He presented Langer with a bloody shirt belonging to his son, who had been arrested by the military several days before. The man's son became Langer's first Palestinian client from the occupied territories. This detail has a cascading significance: it set Langer's career on a new course, representing Palestinian clients in the military court system. Langer was the first — and for a brief period the only — *cause* lawyer working in the system.[14] Gradually, as other Israeli lawyers were drawn into this system, Langer served as a mentor and role model.

Before 1967, when Israel had utilized a military administration within sovereign territory to govern Arab citizens, Langer had represented many Arab clients charged with security violations. Her career decisions were guided by her affiliation with the Communist Party, and her work in the occupied territories was a geographic extension of an existing legal practice. After 1967 Langer's political views remained faithful to the Israeli Communist Party position, which advocated an end to the Israeli occupation and a two-state solution to the conflict. But in the late 1960s and early 1970s, a two-state solution was a radical and unpopular position because most Israelis rejected the idea of an independent Palestinian state and most Palestinians rejected the idea of recognizing Israel and forfeiting claims to those areas.

When Langer began working in the military courts, there were few sources interested or able to disseminate information about conditions in the newly occupied territories. Her work exposed her to the disparities between official discourse that Israeli military rule was "benign" and "enlightened" (see Chapter 2) and realities on the ground. She became a harsh and vocal critic of the occupation. As a pioneer in this "new" legal terrain, she literally invented a cause for herself: she sought to break what she referred to as a "conspiracy of silence" among Jewish Israelis by publicizing what was happening across the Green Line.

To enhance her legitimacy among her target audience — the Jewish Israeli public — and to make her critiques credible and compelling, Langer drew lines around what she considered defensible, refusing to take cases of people charged with violent crimes. The distinction she drew between "political" and "violent" resistance was similar to the mandate of Amnesty International (established in 1961), which distinguished between "prisoners of conscience," whom the organization was established to support, and those who advocated or used violence, who did not merit support (except for the right not to be tortured or executed).

Despite Langer's efforts to legitimize her criticism by being selective in the cases she took, a long career of defending Arabs already had earned her a reputation within her own society as a traitorous "self-hating Jew" and a "terrorist sympathizer." This reputation was fortified by her decision to represent Palestinians from the occupied territories; Langer crossed not only a geographic boundary but a political line that was, at that time, clearly demarcated. While defense lawyers often earn unsavory public reputations for "helping criminals," in the context of the Israeli-Palestinian conflict, Langer was positioned in an adversarial relationship not only with the military prosecutors but seemingly with the entire Jewish nation. Rather than earning praise (or even acceptance) for her legal role, her professional activities condemned her politically in the eyes of the Jewish Israeli mainstream. A Jewish Israeli friend told me that when she was a child, "Don't be a Felicia Langer!" was a typical scold directed at someone who was being bad.

Her negative reputation extended to the Israeli legal profession even though the role she was fulfilling as a defense lawyer was permitted and encouraged by the military as vital to the legitimacy of the court system. For example, Moshe Landau, when he was deputy president of the Israeli High Court of Justice (HCJ), commented on Langer's *With My Own Eyes:*

This book glorifies the views of the terrorist organizations seeking to undermine the existence of the State of Israel by various kinds of violence. It is a sort of record of the author's activities as a [defense] lawyer, especially in the military courts, and she instantly turns every allegation said by her clients to have been received from their interrogators into irrefutable truth, claiming that the rejection of these accusations by the courts would be a miscarriage of justice. The book does, indeed, contain passages [that] extol the cause of the Palestinian Arabs, but these passages grate on one's ears considering the known aim of the terrorist organizations, to which the book is, both in spirit and in its formulation, openly sympathetic.[15]

Although Langer never lacked attention and publicity, she failed in her goal of stimulating a broader Israeli critique of the occupation. However, her visibility enabled her to make a major contribution by attracting a new generation of leftist Jews and Arab Israelis to follow her into the military courts. Decades later, reflecting on Langer's contribution as a legal pioneer, a Palestinian lawyer from Gaza said, "Someday when we have a state of our own, we must put a statue of Felicia Langer in front of our Ministry of Justice. She was doing this work before anybody and she is a hero of the Palestinian people."

In 1971, Lea Tsemel became Langer's *estagiere* (apprentice). Tsemel had become radicalized after the 1967 war while studying law at Hebrew University. When she decided to practice in the military courts, Langer was the logical mentor. Tsemel soon earned a similar reputation in Israel as a "self-hating Jew" and "terrorist sympathizer."

Langer and Tsemel often are compared to one another because of the overlap in their career paths, their positioning on the far left of the Israeli political spectrum, and the international reputations they earned as Jewish Israeli defenders of Palestinians. But there are some significant differences in the nature of the cause with which they have aligned themselves. Tsemel was part of a post-1967 generation of Israeli ultraleftists, whose views of the political establishment were even more critical than those of communists. Tsemel was a member of Matzpen, a small Trotskyist group of Jews and Arabs committed to "internationalist" principles and a "denationalized" solution to the conflict (i.e., democracy and equality for everyone in Israel/Palestine rather than a two-state solution). Tsemel actively cultivated her "antinational" reputation by working out of an office in a Palestinian neighborhood of East Jerusalem and building not only professional but social connections with Palestinians throughout the West Bank and Gaza. Because Tsemel (and Matzpen more generally) regarded Israel as a colonial state on both sides of the Green Line, not only in the occupied territories (the position of the Communist Party), she positioned herself politically even farther from the mainstream Israeli pale than Langer.

The two women also differed in their understandings of their role as lawyers. Unlike Langer, who was selective in the kinds of cases she would take, Tsemel saw her role as a lawyer to provide the best possible legal services to people who were arrested and was nondiscriminating about her clientele. While Langer regarded and treated her legal work as a reflection of her own political values (i.e., supporting political resistance but opposing violence), Tsemel was doggedly committed to the interests and rights of her clients, whoever they might be and whatever charges they might face. The kind of legal ideology of defendants' rights that Tsemel embraced would eventually become popularized as a foundation of human rights, although in the early 1970s there was no public elaboration by Tsemel or anyone else of an explicit commitment to international human rights. For Tsemel, it began as "good defense lawyering."

A third difference between the two women was their regard for the utility of publicity as a catalyst for change. Langer sought the limelight, drawing attention to herself that she hoped would reflect on the problems of occupation. Tsemel did not shun publicity, but she emphasized collective action and political organization and cultivated alliances with other lawyers and activists who shared her principles and concerns. Over the years, Tsemel has had a hand in virtually every initiative that lawyers have mounted to contest Israeli policies or practices deleterious to the Palestinian population in the occupied territories.

If Langer was the grande dame of the Israeli ultraleft, Tsemel became the heavyweight champion, eventually outpacing her mentor as a tireless, defiant, and aggressive critic of the occupation, with all the fame and notoriety that entailed. The sight of her could cause soldiers to become agitated and Palestinians to exclaim with excitement, "There goes Lea!"

One Palestinian lawyer from Jerusalem, who trained under Tsemel when he started practice, recounted the first time he saw her as a young boy. He had imagined her to be a huge and intimidating figure because of her reputation and was quite surprised to find that his mythic hero was so petite. Several prosecutors told me that when they started in the military courts, they were warned by their superiors to "watch out for Lea!" And indeed, members of all categories of participants regularly used Tsemel as a point of reference in discussing their own roles in the courts and their political views vis-à-vis the conflict.

In addition to mentoring Tsemel, Langer mentored the first generation of the Arab Israeli lawyers who decided to work in the military court system. Her public persona had enlightened them to the possibilities of such work, and her membership in the Communist Party was a legitimizing factor because this was the party to which many Arab citizens belonged.

For Arab citizens, the Israeli occupation of the remainder of historic Palestine in 1967 altered the way they perceived themselves: it spurred a "rediscovery" of their identity as Palestinians that the state had actively suppressed and a growing identification with Palestinian nationalist politics.[16] Arab Israeli lawyers were attracted to the military courts as a space where they could capitalize on this identification, and Langer served as their bridge to "reconnect" with Palestinians living across the Green Line. Walid Fahum, who started his military court career in 1973 as an *estagiere* in Langer's office, described his sense of cause: "Felicia [Langer] works for other people. I work for my people. Felicia is an Israeli [i.e., Jewish]. She does this work because she is a communist and she has done great work. But when I defend a Palestinian, I am in a sense defending myself because the Palestinian struggle is my struggle."

Tsemel also mentored and trained some younger Arab and Jewish Israelis who decided to work in the military courts. Others came into the system after training with conventional lawyers in order to devote themselves to this kind of politicized legal practice. However, by the early 1980s very few new Israeli lawyers were moving into the military court system. The difficulty of the work, the scanty material rewards it provided, and the inability to contribute to substantive political change discouraged or deterred younger lawyers from following suit. As Abed Asali, an Arab lawyer who had moved from the Galilee to Jerusalem to work full time in the military court system, explained, younger lawyers "look at us and think we wasted our lives. We are poor even though we work hard . . . and the jails are still full of Palestinians."

Between 1967 and 1987, the number of Israeli citizens (Jews and

Arabs) who practiced in the military courts was small, and it proportionally decreased as the number of Palestinian lawyers grew. By the mid-1980s approximately twenty to thirty Israeli citizens worked regularly in the military courts. But until the first *intifada,* they handled 60 to 70 percent of all cases from the West Bank and a lower but still substantial portion of cases from Gaza.

## Doing National Duty

In the first years of the occupation, very few Palestinian lawyers from the occupied territories took up military court work. The entire legal profession in the West Bank went on strike in 1967 to protest the occupation.[17] The West Bank lawyers' strike capitalized on ties with Jordan, which had conquered the region in 1948 and annexed it in 1950, giving Palestinians Jordanian citizenship. Palestinian lawyers were incorporated into the Jordanian Lawyers' Union (JLU). After 1967, the Jordanian government supported the West Bank lawyers' strike by providing financial compensation for lawyers' loss of income through the JLU. Thus, lawyers could earn an income by *not* working, adding financial incentives to the political motives to maintain the strike.

In 1967, the estimated number of lawyers in the West Bank ranged from 50 to 150.[18] All lawyers initially joined the strike, but over time some grew frustrated and felt that people's need for lawyers' services was a compelling reason to break it. In 1971, ten lawyers from Ramallah, led by Aziz Shehadeh (Raja Shehadeh's father), decided to break the strike, and some of them started working in the military courts. The strikebreakers were condemned as "traitors" by the JLU and disbarred. Gradually, other lawyers joined them, leading to a split in the legal profession in the West Bank between "working" and "striking" lawyers, and every new lawyer had to decide which camp to join. By 1986, there were approximately 500 lawyers in the West Bank, of whom 280 were receiving compensation from Jordan (i.e., striking).[19]

In the Gaza Strip, there were only eight to ten lawyers in 1967, four of whom began working in the military courts at the onset of the occupation. According to Fayez Abu Rahman and Fathi Akkila, two of the four, they did so at the request of family members of people who had been arrested. Until 1971, when the Israeli "pacification" campaign had crushed armed resistance in Gaza, they were escorted to and from the courts in Israeli military vehicles.

The number of lawyers in Gaza grew gradually as young people traveled abroad to study, then returned home to practice. In 1976, eighteen Gaza lawyers formed the Gaza Bar Association (GBA), which became the corporate affiliation for all lawyers in the Strip. Although the Israeli authorities refused to register the organization, claiming that it was a front for the PLO, the GBA commanded local authority over the legal profession by providing support and cohesion for lawyers and envisioned and pursued its role as an institution functioning in solidarity with other sectors of the population.

In January 1980, working West Bank lawyers (who had been disbarred from the JLU) established the Arab Lawyers Committee (ALC). In 1984, the ALC applied for a license to function as an independent bar association.[20] However, the Israeli authorities refused to register the ALC on two grounds. First, because the ALC included East Jerusalem residents, this contradicted Israeli efforts to enforce a separation between East Jerusalem and the rest of the West Bank.[21] The second reason was "security considerations," namely suspicion that the ALC would espouse Palestinian nationalist ideology and serve as a front for the PLO.[22]

By early 1987, the total number of Palestinian lawyers working regularly in the military court system was estimated to be between eighty and one hundred.[23] Although Palestinians had the occupation in common, the situation in Gaza had always been more economically desperate and, at least until the first *intifada,* more politically volatile than in the West Bank.[24] Relatively speaking, Gaza lawyers were poorer than their West Bank colleagues, and many were unable to make a living practicing law. In acknowledgment of the poverty of the population at large, the GBA set a ceiling on lawyers' fees and censured members who overcharged. While West Bankers faced many of the same hardships and problems as Gazans, most lawyers could count themselves among the middle class. No fee ceilings were set for West Bank lawyers, although thousands of military court cases were handled on a pro bono basis or for very small fees.

Palestinian residents of East Jerusalem had a legal status as "noncitizen residents of Israel." During closures, West Bankers were unable to travel to courts and prisons in Israel or even between the northern and southern parts of the region, since roads run through Jerusalem. Jerusalemites had relative advantages in terms of mobility, a selling point for potential military court clients, fostering tensions and rivalries within the profession in the West Bank.

Tensions and rivalries also extended to Israeli lawyers (Jews and

Arabs). Because, as noted above, Israeli citizens handled a disproportionately large percentage of the total military court cases, some Palestinian lawyers criticized them as "usurpers," even those politically sympathetic or nationally aligned with the population in the territories. For example, the ALC did not accept Israeli citizens as members, even Arab Israelis who had moved to East Jerusalem. The ALC expected Israeli lawyers to abide by strikes and other collective decisions, as many did, but they resisted expanding the role that nonmembers could play in setting or influencing those policies.

## Cause Lawyering and the First *Intifada*

When the *intifada* erupted in December 1987, it taxed the military court system and all categories of participants in unprecedented ways. For defense lawyers, the flood of cases resulting from massive arrests, rising sentences even for "minor" crimes, longer delays in gaining access to detainees, and heightened security measures in the courts and prisons exacerbated their already strong frustrations and cynicism about the military court system. Contesting the deteriorating conditions and the problems they faced as legal professionals became a rallying cause for lawyers, and ad hoc collaborations among Israeli and Palestinian lawyers increased.

The escalating demand for legal services drew some two hundred additional Palestinian lawyers into the system, many with little or no prior experience. Although some came with a sense of cause — to support the *intifada* — others were motivated by a lack of alternatives and a need to earn a living. Local Palestinian courts were being boycotted, and Palestinian civil litigation declined to demonstrate collective solidarity with the *intifada*. Criminal litigation was subsumed within the military court system (which had concurrent jurisdiction with Palestinian courts), and by April 1988 most Palestinian police had resigned. Thus, most of the legal work to be found was in the military courts. The entry of so many inexperienced lawyers contributed to an overall deterioration of legal services. However, even veteran lawyers acknowledged that their own performances were deteriorating under the deluge.

Prior to the *intifada,* many defendants were well-trained activists organized along the factional lines of the PLO. Some Palestinian and Israeli lawyers had standing arrangements to represent people from particular factions. After 1987, the arrest of vast numbers of people who were nominally aligned (if at all) with factions and had no political training or previous experience with the military court system strained lawyer-client relations. For example, many lawyers were sharply critical of clients who, under interrogation, confessed to being "members" of a faction (which was a crime) when in fact they merely supported that faction's politics.

These strains worked both ways: some defendants and their families blamed their lawyers for their predicament. Even some seasoned activists who had been through the military court system many times before grew frustrated with their lawyers. Tsemel, for example, was disheartened that some longtime clients were choosing to hire different lawyers, which she interpreted as criticism of her work. She explained:

My first priority is always people in interrogation. I will do everything I can to help someone while he is in interrogation, even sacrificing work on other files. With the *intifada*, so many people were in interrogation, I didn't have time to do prison visits. It hurt me that [my clients] who are very political couldn't understand my politics. . . . I don't mind losing clients, or even feeling unappreciated. But it bothers me that people put their own interests [i.e., being visited in prison] before the bigger problems. . . . We all have our role to play, and they should understand mine.

By the end of the 1980s, Islamist activists affiliated with Hamas and Islamic Jihad were being arrested in increasing numbers. Since Islamist militancy gained prominence only during the *intifada,* there were virtually no prestanding arrangements for legal representation. Lawyers stepped in to meet the Islamist demand for their services, but secular/sectarian political differences, coupled with disagreement over the utility of violence that Islamists championed, added a new dimension to tensions in lawyer-client relations.

The conditions of work in the military courts so seriously eroded during the *intifada* that lawyers frequently went on strike to protest. Striking was a means of focusing attention on violations of lawyers' own rights as legal professionals, as well as those of their clients. In 1988, Gaza lawyers went on strike for eleven months to protest failures by the courts to provide notification of court dates, termination of translations of case materials into Arabic, increased repression by soldiers, and restrictive security measures within the courts.[25] The strike was called off — as many subsequent strikes were — in response to public pressure to continue providing legal services for those being arrested. However, Gaza lawyers collectively decided to stop charging fees for "security cases" as a demonstration of corporate solidarity with the *intifada*. Thus, working actually cost Gaza lawyers money, as they had to subsidize their own activities on behalf of their clients. Raji Sourani explained the reasoning behind this gesture of corporate solidarity: "The economic situation [in Gaza] is a big dilemma. People are so poor, and there is a relation between the lawyers and the families, a social relationship, which makes it very hard to separate personal friendships from professional relations. . . . I lose perspective on the separation between myself and my clients and their families. . . . Because lawyers are the ones who pass between the families and the prisoners, we become like members of the family. I know more about my clients' lives and their problems than I know about my cousins."

Gaza lawyers faced onerous permit requirements. In addition to their basic identification (ID) cards, they required five separate permits to work: a lawyer ID to enter courts and prisons, a "curfew permission" allowing them to move about during periods when the Gaza Strip was under complete prolonged curfew, magnetic cards to leave the Strip, a paper confirming the validity of the magnetic card, and a computerized card that was instituted in 1993 when the occupied territories were completely sealed.

The ALC also called periodic strikes throughout the *intifada*. A major strike began in January 1989 for reasons that included lack of notification of arrest; difficulty obtaining information about where prisoners were being held, coupled with deliberate misinformation by prison authorities about prisoners' whereabouts; difficulty gaining access to people in custody; mistreatment of detainees and official failure to investigate lawyers' allegations of torture; lack of privacy for lawyer-client meetings at detention centers; long delays in scheduling court dates and cumbersome procedures; mistreatment of lawyers; lack of notification about extension-of-detention hearings; denial of bail; arbitrary sentencing by judges; and judicial refusal to give serious consideration to testimony of defense witnesses.[26]

Israeli lawyers, most of whom honored the strikes called by the Palestinian lawyers' organizations, occasionally sought to press the Israel Bar Association (IBA) to lend its support to their demands on the military authorities.[27] During the 1989 ALC strike, a group of Israeli military court lawyers met with the Criminal Committee of the IBA to discuss the problems at issue in the strike, but Yaacov Rubin, then president of the IBA, refused to discuss lawyers' demands while they were striking.[28]

Israeli closures of the occupied territories became more frequent after 1989 in response to escalating armed attacks on soldiers and settlers. Closures, coupled with a waning number of arrests (since so many people were already in prison), intensified competition among lawyers for clients. Mary Rock, a lawyer from Bethlehem, complained, "Because of the closure I have had to delay all my files for Ramallah and the north. Jerusalem lawyers are starting to get a monopoly on new cases. Now when people come into my office, the first thing they ask is if I can do prison visits, which I can't because I can't cross the Green Line. This is enough for many to decide not to hire me. I think we should all go on strike. This would solve at least part of the problem."

Human rights activism and organizing during the first *intifada* was the one bright spot sustaining and encouraging lawyers about the virtue and value of their work. Local human rights organizations were propelled into the international limelight because of their ability to provide information and explanations about the unrest and escalating violence. This provided cause lawyers with more and better ways to convey information about their work through press conferences and meetings with representatives of international organizations and foreign governments. The more prominent military court lawyers were in heavy demand as "expert" informants, but even lawyers who had no direct involvement with human rights organizations were inclined to speak about their work in human rights terms.

The *intifada* contributed to the burgeoning global visibility of local Palestinian and Israeli human rights organizations and added resonance to criticisms framed in terms of international law. Israeli lawyers representing Palestinian clients made more extensive use of petitions to the HCJ to challenge state practices that constituted human rights violations (e.g., brutal interrogation tactics, inhumane conditions of detention, detention without trial, and protracted incommunicado detention). Although these initiatives rarely achieved clear legal victories for petitioners, and lawyers had no illusions that they would, they used petitions to embroil the HCJ more deeply in the conflict and to expose the state's legal rationales for its policies. HCJ decisions — even ones disadvantageous to Palestinians — had an "educative" effect by drawing attention to conditions in the West Bank and Gaza.

Some lawyers devoted themselves full time to human rights work. For example, four lawyers from Khan Yunis quit the military court system to establish a new organization that would serve, primarily, the southern part of the Gaza Strip. Ahmed Sayyad, a lawyer from Ramallah, established the Mandela Institute for Political Prisoners with a mandate to investigate and address the needs of prisoners that overburdened lawyers were not able to handle. In 1990, Tsemel and other leftist Israeli lawyers and activists formed the Public Committee against Torture in Israel

(PCATI) to wage a concerted legal campaign against torture, focusing especially on the HCJ. Allegra Pacheco, a member of PCATI, described the campaign as a "Sisyphus-like struggle in the highest court in Israel to permanently abolish torture in Israel."[29]

During the first *intifada*, cause lawyers could derive some solace from the international attention and criticism being directed at the Israeli occupation, including the military court system, by foreign governments, media, and international human rights organizations. According to Boulos: "[I]t took the efforts of many lawyers to bring international attention to what is going on. A few years ago, no [international] organization dared to challenge or criticize Israel. . . . But by exposing the facts about the occupation, now organizations and people not only can criticize Israel but must do so because the evidence is growing. Even the U.S. State Department criticizes Israel for its policies in the territories. This is an achievement for Palestinians."

But on the ground, criticism and negative publicity proved unable to redress the grievances and problems in the military court system. Many lawyers were burning out and becoming politically demoralized. In the summer of 1990, Felicia Langer decided to emigrate to Germany. She had become disgusted by the idea that she was lending legitimacy to oppression by continuing to work in the military courts, and she felt unmoored by the demise of communism as an international political force.[30] The grande dame's departure marked the end of an era.[31]

I met Langer a few days before she left the country. Like many lawyers, she was deeply ambivalent about whether her career had been a positive contribution in the greater scheme of things. But one thing she was rightly proud of was the publicity she had drawn to the military court system. Toward the end of our interview, she said her life was a story of heroic struggle in the face of enormous adversity and would make a great Hollywood movie. She asked who should play her, and I responded, "Shirley MacLaine," since there was a physical similarity. She retorted with a smile, "No. Kim Basinger!"

## Things Fall Apart

The Israeli-Palestinian negotiations, which started in 1991, took their toll on cause lawyering in complex ways. The negotiations were premised on the notion that conflict resolution hinged on geopolitical separation. The political aspirations and diplomatic steps to achieve separation affected the military court system because this was a setting where Israelis and Palestinians had, for better and worse, been coming together for decades.

For Arab Israeli lawyers who had taken up work in the military courts to support "their people," the negotiations redivided them; the fate and status of Arab citizens would not be part of the discussions, and the PLO, as a condition of the negotiations, renounced any claim to represent them. Many Arab Israeli lawyers decided to quit military court work and relocate their practices back inside the Green Line. Some said that their services were no longer needed because the number of arrests was declining, and many Palestinian lawyers had acquired legal and language skills that had at one time been their main advantage and contribution. Others cited sheer exhaustion and felt that they had "paid their dues." Namneh, for example, said that he had accumulated a 33,000 shekel debt in unpaid taxes for his years of military court work. He added, "Israelis do three years of national service. I did eleven."

While some Arab Israelis who left the military courts opted to become conventional lawyers, others redirected their cause-lawyering energies to struggles for equality and rights for their own community inside the Green Line. Indeed, civil rights and human rights activism and organizing among Arab Israelis picked up markedly after 1991. As Mohammed Zaydan explained, "The peace process had a major effect because it forced Palestinian citizens of Israel to see that they are not part of [it] and won't get anything from the U.S. They were not represented in the peace process, and this realization pushed us to create new NGOs. Lots of lawyers and activists who spent years working for Palestinians in the West Bank and Gaza now know that they need to start representing themselves. We have nobody else to help us fight for our rights."

When the Palestinian Authority (PA) was established in 1994, many Israeli and Palestinian lawyers saw this as an opportunity or reason to quit military court work. Some quit on the belief that the cause that had brought them into the courts was emerging victorious, and others quit out of frustration at the inexorably flawed nature of the negotiations.

Jewish liberals, whose sense of cause was animated primarily by concern about the legal behavior of their own state, left the military courts when the Israeli military redeployed from Palestinian population centers. Some Palestinian lawyers quit in order to seek new careers in the Palestinian legal system or in the new institutions of the PA. Even those Palestinians who would have continued working in the Israeli military courts found it nearly impossible to do so after 1994 because of the intensification of closures and permit restrictions.

The Oslo Accords transformed the political geography of Israel/ Palestine but failed to resolve the conflict. But the politics of separation divided many former allies. A poignant illustration of this occurred in the immediate aftermath of the Hebron massacre in February 1994. A delegation of Palestinian lawyers met in Jerusalem to go to Hebron to pay their respects to the families of the twenty-nine people slain by Baruch Goldstein, an American-Israeli settler from Kiryat Arba. When Tsemel heard of the visit, she sought to go along, but Palestinian lawyers refused. In response, she published in *Al-Quds* "An Open Letter to My Friends in the Arab Lawyers Committee." She wrote:

I arrived at the [meeting place] . . . and inquired as to why I had not been notified earlier of the visit. I was then confronted by the evil that I have been battling all my life — racism — and from people from whom I least expected it, namely, my colleagues in the daily legal struggle against the occupation. . . .

"You can't come with us," they told me. "We are the Committee of Arab Lawyers and you belong to the [Israel Bar Association]. True, you have fought with us all the way, obeyed all of our strike days, were with us through the great storms of our struggle, traveled with us any time negotiations with the authorities were needed, wrote our leaflets with us, founded in our name the Committee for the Defense of Administrative Detainees, served as a member of the Lawyers Committee to Appear in Military Courts, and helped us to organize countless campaigns. But don't forget, you are not one of us."

. . .

I have done no favors and deserve no thanks. I am simply trying to make the place where I live free of occupation, oppression, exploitation and racism. When I find such racism amongst my friends, I will not rest until it, too, is defeated.

The politics of separation wrought by the Oslo Accords not only reconfigured the relations among lawyers by impeding contacts and undermining a sense of collaborative solidarity that had arisen out of working together in the military courts but also affected lawyers' professional and political motives and goals. While human rights violations did not diminish during the interim, the concern they commanded internationally dissipated. In 1997, Tsemel said, "During the 1980s, I was very optimistic about all these international human rights people who were coming to join the struggle. But I became cynical about them too, because after they did their reports, they moved on, and I never heard from many of them again. Human rights is just an industry, not a political cause."

Sourani, who was unable to practice in the Israeli military courts after 1994 because of permit restrictions and was confined by closures to

Gaza, focused his cause-lawyering energies on monitoring and protesting PA human rights violations. He saw this as a continuation of the struggle for Palestinians' rights and building the rule of law and was cognizant and critical that the terms of the Oslo Accords, which prioritized Israeli security, fostered an atmosphere of authoritarianism, lawlessness, and political violence. The PA dealt harshly with Sourani, arresting him and orchestrating a takeover of his organization. But he formed a new organization, the Palestine Center for Rights and Law. Commenting on the difficulties of human rights work during the interim, Sourani said, "We are in a position that no one envies. We are needed more than ever, but we are in a cross fire, exposed as though we are against peace. We need international support more than ever. But the only thing people want is a briefing 'off the record.' . . . We will harvest our results someday, but we don't know when."

Ibrahim Abu Dakka, a Gaza lawyer who had worked in the military courts since the late 1960s, was given a sort of ombudsman position to advise the PA about human rights issues. He acknowledged that this put him in a compromising position: "How can we control and protect human rights? We must respect and protect the agreement, which means that some of our people who are against Oslo are in prison. I oppose this, but Arafat was obliged to prioritize the protection of the agreement over the protection of human rights. . . . We are sitting on a bomb waiting for the explosion."

Referring to the negative effects of the Oslo Accords, Asali said, "The most horrible thing is that patriotic Palestinians, including lawyers, are afraid to criticize the PA. . . . Morally, you cannot make separate standards for Palestinians and Israelis." In a similar vein, Iyad Alami, a lawyer from Gaza who worked with Sourani, said, "People used to talk and complain about human rights and Israeli violations because there were no personal relations between society and the Israeli military. But now with the PA, things are more personal. Any policeman can go to someone's house and beat him for talking or complaining about the PA."

Sayyad, head of the Mandela Institute, felt caught between a desire to support Palestinian national goals and concern about PA human rights violations. He said,

[H]uman rights organizations were an important part of the political struggle against the occupation. But for human rights organizations after Oslo, and especially after redeployment, our big fault is that we didn't change our tactics. The PA must be dealt with differently than the occupation authorities. They are part of our own people. Most human rights organizations deal with the PA like they dealt with the Israelis — like they are the enemy. This makes our work harder and more dangerous. We should get close to the PA and help them learn what it means to respect the rule of law. Human rights shouldn't be used to undermine PA legitimacy. Our goal should be to end PA violations, not destroy the PA.

Israeli and Palestinian lawyers who remained committed to human rights work were critical of their former military court colleagues who, during the interim, were turning a blind eye to human rights violations out of indifference or political opportunism. Two lawyers who attracted particularly strong criticism as cause-lawyering "turncoats" were Freih Abu Middain and Joshua Schoffman. Abu Middain was appointed the PA's minister of justice and, from his position of power, became one of the staunchest and most vocal critics of Palestinian human rights organizations that monitored and protested PA violations.[32] He oversaw the PA's introduction and use of the death penalty. Schoffman left ACRI to join the Israeli Attorney General's Office in 1994, assuming a position of defending the practices he had once protested. Several lawyers also angrily pointed out that he was the main author of Israeli legislation, passed in 2002 in the heat of the second *intifada* but retroactive to 1994, that would prevent Palestinians from seeking financial compensation in Israeli courts for injuries, destruction, or confiscation of property.[33]

During the interim, cause lawyering in the military courts became a truncated enterprise. The only lawyers able or willing to continue doing it were a small number of leftist Jews, Arab Israelis who decided to remain in Jerusalem, East Jerusalem residents, and the few Palestinians who could obtain the necessary permits.

## Back to the Trenches

The collapse of the negotiations and the start of a second *intifada* in 2000 illustrated, among other things, that unrequited demands for rights fuel political anger and frustration and inevitably perpetuate the conflict. Israeli and Palestinian lawyers who had been critical of Oslo because it failed to adequately address those demands — and who had been chastised by Oslo supporters as "enemies of peace" — could take cold comfort in having been correct. As Sourani observed, "Human rights was the victim of the interim. That brought about feelings of defeat and disbelief. By ignoring international law, you invite the most radical elements to take over."

The resurgence of Palestinian arrests by the Israeli military reinvigorated the military court system and created a pressing demand for lawyers. In certain ways, the second *intifada* resembled the first: many lawyers were drawn into the military courts out of a sense of cause, but returning veterans, who had quit the system in the early 1990s, were rusty, and new lawyers had no military court experience. To redress these problems and improve the services lawyers could provide to their clients, Israeli lawyers affiliated with PCATI produced an Arabic-language *Lawyers' Guide* detailing the current laws and procedures and convened training seminars in Jerusalem for lawyers from the occupied territories who could manage to get permits.[34]

The strong networks among Israeli and Palestinian lawyers that had built up during the 1980s had broken down during the interim and were exceedingly difficult to rebuild. The ALC and the GBA had stopped functioning effectively and thus were unable to provide any cohesion or direction for lawyers after 2000. But other institutions, including many human rights organizations, provided support for lawyers, including, for example, HaMoked, an Israeli organization that took the lead in tracking down prisoners.

The violence and vastly heightened security measures of the second *intifada* severely hampered lawyers' abilities to do their work and impeded professional and political collaborations. No longer could Israelis move freely in the West Bank and Gaza; instead, they had to hire taxis to get to court and back. Palestinian lawyers could appear in courts only in areas near where they lived, assuming they could get the necessary permits to enter the military compounds. Accessing prisons became exceedingly difficult for everyone, and so did face-to-face meetings between lawyers and the families of clients; most contacts were made and sustained by phone and fax.

One significant development after 2000 was the entry of a new generation of Arab Israeli lawyers, young activists who, like their elder colleagues two decades ago, were choosing to cross the Green Line to make a political stand in support of Palestinians in the occupied territories. Dan Rabinowitz and Khawla Abu-Baker coined a term — the "stand-tall generation"[35] — that captured the sense of cause among lawyers who came to work in the military court system. Azim Bishara, from the Galilee village of Tarshiha, who worked with the Palestinian organization LAW (the Palestinian Society for the Protection of Human Rights and the Environment), said, "I oppose the occupation as a political principle. I am a Palestinian. I am part of this people. Whatever happens in the occupied territories also affects Palestinians in Israel, so the solution will affect all of us. My generation is fed up, and we are more courageous, more knowledgeable about our rights. We don't take inequality for granted like the older generation. We come to the West Bank to use our skills and our energy for the sake of our people."

Labib Habib, a young lawyer from Nazareth, who joined Lea Tsemel's office, explained: "After Oslo proved a failure, when this dream crashed, some [Arab Israeli] lawyers found a need to do their part. This is why I [came]. For a Palestinian and an Israeli citizen especially, I felt that I should do what I can to help as a lawyer. The work is frustrating and very hard, but it is important work. The most important thing we can do is give detainees encouragement. . . . You can't work [with Tsemel] without believing in justice and people's right to be free and independent."

The abiding reality of cause lawyering is that it is needed most when things are bad. If cause lawyering in Israel/Palestine dissipated and diluted during the 1990s when some people believed that the conflict was on its way to resolution, the political crisis of the second *intifada* provided a renewed appreciation and need for cause lawyers. Indeed, it is this need that motivates lawyers and sustains their commitment to the work. Many Israeli and Palestinian lawyers I interviewed in 2002, although devastated by the violence and frustrated by the problems they were (again) facing as legal professionals, also expressed a resolute sense of purpose. Gabi Lasky, who works with PCATI, explained well the sentiments and sense of cause that many lawyers share:

What gives us strength to continue is knowing that the real test for democracy is passing through difficult times. Can you continue to keep human rights alive during these periods? . . . It has become harder to raise the flag of human rights in this period. Now we are on the defensive. It's not even a matter of moving forward. We put all our energy into not making it worse. That's very frustrating. Since 9/11, even countries like the U.S. that used to at least talk about human rights are questioning the relevance of human rights in the war on terror. . . . Tomorrow the nation will wake up and find that they lost their moral standards. I don't want to be the one to tell them, "I told you so."

Tsemel, who never slowed down her work in the military courts or tempered her criticism of the occupation, has retained her title as the heavyweight champion — the cause lawyer par excellence. In September 2002, a Haifa weekly published an article about Tsemel entitled, "I Would Represent Bin Laden."[36] While aiming to be inflammatory, the title captured a commitment she has maintained for over thirty years to defend the rights of people who are arrested. Haggai Finegold writes, "She fights her war daily, knowing she has no chance of winning. A woman like Lea Tsemel won't give up." Tsemel explains, "I am proud of my professional work. . . . The benefit is to be there. This is better than to give up. It's even good for the victims and for the suicide bombers [that I don't give up]. If there are legal tools, we have to use them and to see the results. . . . Of course it makes you upset to lose many cases, but I always think about the Palestinians as a collective, not about specific individuals."

Finegold asks, "You aren't tired of all these struggles?" She replies, "I am a little tired, but what keeps me going is anger against injustice. . . . We have to live together, Arabs and Jews." Finegold: "Where is there justice in the world?" Tsemel: "In my heart."

In this chapter, I have highlighted the ways in which politics shape the identities and ideologies of lawyers and animate and orient their sense of cause. In the next chapter, I turn to Palestinians who are prosecuted and defended in the military court system.

CHAPTER 7

# Political Subjects, Legal Objects

*Defendants*

---

*The military court system is a part of our lives as Palestinians. The Israelis have been successful in shifting our struggle from the political arena to the courts.*

A former prisoner

*Prison will bring us together.*

Raymonda Tawil, *Women Prisoners in the Prison Country*[1]

In the Israeli military court system, the "defendant" category includes Palestinians from all walks of life. All Palestinian residents of the West Bank and Gaza are potential defendants, since all are subject to the jurisdiction of this court system. And hundreds of thousands have been actual defendants, among a population that now numbers 3.6 million.[2]

There are no firm figures of the number of people who have been prosecuted in the military courts since 1967.[3] But according to a widely acknowledged rule of thumb, approximately 50 percent of Palestinians who are arrested are released or administratively detained without charges, and the other 50 percent are charged with crimes and prosecuted. Approximately 813,000 Palestinians were arrested between 1967 and 1993.[4] Within that period, during the first *intifada* (1987–93), at least 20,000 to 25,000 were arrested every year, the highest per capita incarceration rate in the world at that time.[5] In 1994 and 1995, the start of the Oslo Accords, arrest rates declined to approximately 6,000 per year. Between 1996 and September 2000, the annual average varied from 1,200 to 3,600.[6] Between September 29, 2000 (the start of the second *intifada*) and September 2002, approximately 15,000 were arrested.[7] Hence, applying the rule of thumb, the estimated number of prosecutions since 1967 would be in the neighborhood of half a million.

The magnitude of these numbers in relation to the size of the population illuminates the carceral nature of Israeli military rule in the West Bank and Gaza. The kinds of activities that have been criminalized by the military and emergency laws used to govern Palestinians include not only violence but anything the authorities deem menacing to security or disruptive of order. Even the most basic aspirations and "normal" activities — education, marriage, work, health care, movement — have been regulated by punitive laws that impose criminal sanctions for breaches and violations. As Uri Savir, a leading Israeli political figure, observes: "In the course of the . . . occupation almost every third Palestinian in the territories had at some time or another been imprisoned or detained, and the population as a whole had suffered great humiliation at our hands."[8]

*Carceralism* is the term I use to describe Israeli rule over Palestinians in the West Bank and Gaza because it captures the fact that they are treated collectively as suspect and punishable and are imprisoned, literally in that thousands or tens of thousands are in prison at any given time, and equally literally in that, like prisoners, they are "unfree."[9] The military court system is an institutional centerpiece of this carceralism, part of a broader array of governing institutions and practices in which Palestinians are enmeshed and tracked in grids of surveillance, subjected to restrictive codes of conduct and interaction, physically immobilized through the use of permits, closures, curfews, checkpoints, and walls, and incarcerated in huge numbers.[10]

This chapter addresses the carceral nature of government in the West Bank and Gaza as it affects and is perceived by Palestinians who are prosecuted in the military court system. However, it is impossible to understand Palestinian defendants' perspectives on the court system without extending the scope of analysis to consider the impact of military occupation on Palestinian society at large and resistance against it. Palestinian resistance has a history and takes many forms, but it has been and remains a valorized as well as dangerous endeavor to contest protracted military occupation and statelessness.

## The Structural Violence of Occupation

The concept of structural violence connotes the institutionalization of conditions in which deprivations, injuries, restrictions, and losses are sustained, routinized, and pervasive. Structural violence has different and uneven impacts on individuals (e.g., by gender, age, class, locale, and so on) but nevertheless generates common and collective experiences that can be described as "social suffering." Arthur Kleinman explains, "Suffering, in this anthropological perspective, is the effect of the *social violence* that social orders — local, national, global — bring to bear on people."[11] For Palestinians living under military occupation, like other communities subjected to repressive and discriminatory rule, both structural violence and its effect, social suffering, are constitutive of the social life of the community and the subjectivity of its members.

The Israeli-Palestinian conflict is at the root of structural violence and social suffering in the West Bank and Gaza. However, the conflict is not the explanation but rather that which needs to be explained by analyzing the nature and contours of relations and practices that sustain and alter it. Relations that are constitutive of conflicts are unequal and often violent. But in these relations, everyone "has power" — to act and interact. Michel Foucault writes, "[P]ower is not an institution, and not a structure; neither is it a certain strength we are endowed with; it is the name that one attributes to a complex strategical situation in a particular society."[12] This relational conception of power is useful to the study of conflicts because it makes apparent that even people subjected to degrading and dehumanizing treatment are the subjects of their own lives and in that sense are empowered social actors.

Acknowledging that Palestinian residents of the West Bank and Gaza are empowered social actors is crucial for understanding their experiences and perspectives on the military court system. This acknowledgment also serves as a rejoinder to accounts and analyses that would flatten people into two-dimensional figures, whether as irrational hate-driven terrorists or helpless victims.

Virtually all Palestinians have had some experience with the military court system, whether personally or through the arrest and prosecution of relatives, friends, neighbors, and/or colleagues. For defendants, "participation" encompasses arrest, interrogation, prosecution, and incarceration. I contextualize their experiences and perspectives as defendants within the broader context of conflict in Israel/Palestine and consider how the functioning of the military court system affects not only those who are prosecuted but also their families and Palestinian society as a whole.

## Defendants' Perspectives on the Military Court System

In Palestinian national discourse, "the prison" occupies a prominent position in analyses and narratives of the Israeli occupation of the West Bank and Gaza. Prisons have been the subject of numerous studies, political tracts, and petitions and the settings of countless plays, poems, and novels. Prisons also feature centrally in personal and collective narratives of resistance, steadfastness, and suffering. Indeed, for many Palestinians, especially males, going to prison is a rite of passage and imprisonment is a critically important autobiographical episode.[13] In contrast, the military court system — through which some half a million have passed — is a silence in this discourse.

When I began research, I knew that very little had been written about the military court system from defendants' perspective. But I assumed that this was merely a lacuna. I did not realize and was confronted with the fact that this was a *meaningful silence*. Initially, I was perplexed and frustrated by the refusal or reluctance of defendants I interviewed to recount and describe their experiences in the courts. People were forthcoming, even effusive, in talking about their political activism and their prison experiences. But they fell silent, or changed the subject, or seemed confused by my questions about the courts. No one voluntarily mentioned the courts, and when I questioned people directly about their experiences and recollections, most had little to say. Eventually, my frustration yielded an insight about defendants' participation in the military court system and, more generally, about the silence regarding the system in the Palestinian popular imagination and national discourse: in the system, Palestinian defendants are transformed from political subjects into objects of the legal process, handled, discussed, and treated as "cases" or "files."

Through the process of interviewing individuals, I became aware of the distinctive perspective that defendants brought to this study. The key was to grasp the centrality of interrogation, and this realization forced me to recognize that "the military court system" extends to those processes and sites. While members of the other categories recognized the importance of interrogation, many considered interrogation itself to be a separate domain. But for many defendants, the interrogation wings of prisons and jails were extensions of the courts. Or, as one defendant explained, "The interrogation is the real trial. What goes on in the courts is just theater." Defendants emphasized or even privileged interrogation in discussing their experiences in the military court system because this was where they defended themselves.

People tended to narrate their experiences of interrogation as subjects, albeit subjugated subjects. Although Israeli interrogation tactics entailed routine and pervasive torture and ill-treatment, people described and recalled their experiences in terms of resistance and endurance. Even admissions of submission and defeat at the hands of interrogators were recounted in the language of action and consciousness. Such narratives contradict analyses of the interrogation experience as objectifying. For example, in *The Body in Pain,* Elaine Scarry argues that people who are subjected to torture during interrogation lose all agency as the pain "unmakes" their world.[14] She argues that the person becomes an object both of the interrogator who is causing the pain and of the pain itself, expressed poignantly with the phrase "my body hurts *me.*" In *Formations of Violence,* an ethnography of political violence in Northern Ireland, Allen Feldman contextualizes interrogation and torture within the broader context of the conflict in which it occurs.[15] While he concurs with Scarry about the painful effects of torture on its victims, he argues that captured Irish republicans who were subjected to torture and ill-treatment by British interrogators retained their agency because they comprehended their suffering as part of the national struggle in which they were actively engaged. Like Feldman's informants, some of the Palestinians I interviewed discussed interrogation as a "shared political arena" in which both interrogators and interrogees were participants rather than actors and objects.

In contrast to their descriptions of interrogation, Palestinian defendants tended to narrate their experiences in the court system in a language of exclusion, helplessness, ignorance, and passivity. They became, in that institutional setting, objects. The objectification of defendants in the legal process is concomitant with the politics and procedures of the criminal trial because judges, prosecutors, and defense lawyers determine what happens in the courtroom. Defendants sit silently, called upon to speak only at the discretion of one or another of the legal professionals. The ambivalence and indifference that many defendants express about the goings-on in court reflect their institutionalized passivity: they lack the capacity and are denied the opportunity to act in their own behalf in this context.

The institutionally passive role of the defendant begins to take shape from the point after the interrogation is finished. That is when the prosecutor draws up a charge sheet and the defense lawyer steps in to handle the defendant's case. According to one man who had been arrested for being a leader of the first *intifada,* "The only control a prisoner has is during interrogation. After that, the control starts diminishing and the lawyer takes over." In his case, he said that after the interrogation he felt strong because he hadn't confessed. But charges were brought against him based on secret evidence and the confessions of others. His feelings of strength diminished as the process of arranging a deal wore on. He became more and more dependent on his lawyer and found that there was little he could contribute to the handling of his case. Like others, he could recount his interrogation experience in detail but had scant recollection of what went on in the courtroom and only secondhand knowledge of the plea-bargaining process through which his deal was arranged.

Because many Palestinian defendants consider interrogation to be their "real" trial, their perspectives on the military court system are filtered through their experiences in interrogation. Moreover, interrogation is a decisive element of the legal process, since confessions constitute the main source of evidence against defendants in most cases.

## Arrest and Interrogation

Arrest and interrogation are two complementary and coordinated means for a state to exercise its law enforcement powers. The process of arrest "removes" the suspected lawbreaker from society and puts that person in state custody. The process of interrogation aims to ascertain the validity of the suspicion in the form of a confession. The processes of arrest and interrogation often entail violence against suspects.[16] In Israel/Palestine, violence in the processes of law enforcement is pervasive and routine. According to James Ron, who has conducted extensive research on the arrest and interrogation of Palestinians by Israeli state agents, the use of violence in these processes is not incidental but deliberate and calibrated to induce and exacerbate suffering.[17]

In the West Bank and Gaza, every Israeli soldier has the authority to arrest any Palestinian if he or she suspects that the person has committed, planned, or conspired to commit an offense. "Initiated" arrests generally are ordered by the General Security Services (GSS) and are carried out by the military, often in the middle of the night. Those sought and detained in initiated arrests tend to be people suspected of more serious offenses.

Upon arrest, they are turned over to the GSS for interrogation. "Roundups" sometimes involve mass arrests at demonstrations or public events or in the course of military operations. In roundups, GSS agents do a brief check on each person (termed "sorting"), keeping people they want to interrogate and turning over those suspected of minor offenses to the Israel Defense Forces (IDF) or Israeli police for interrogation.

Arrested Palestinians from the West Bank and Gaza can be held for eighteen days before being brought before a judge. During this period, they tend to be held incommunicado, unable to meet with a lawyer. Representatives of the International Committee of the Red Cross (ICRC) are authorized to meet with detainees on the fourteenth day to take stock of who is in custody but are barred (by the terms of the agreement between the Israeli government and the ICRC) from relaying information about detainees' conditions or whereabouts to others, including lawyers and family members. Tens of thousands of people have been arrested and then released on or before the eighteenth day.

The "universe" of arrestable Palestinians includes children.[18] The age of "criminal responsibility" in the occupied territories is twelve. Children younger than twelve can be arrested but not interrogated. In the West Bank and Gaza, an idealized notion of the "innocence of youth" finds no resonance in carceral government, and youthfulness provides neither sanctuary nor protection from the grip of law enforcement.[19] According to Anton Shammas, "The state of Israel hasn't only confiscated the land from under the feet of the Palestinians in the occupied territories; it has also taken away their childhood. [Since 1967,] officially there has been no childhood in the West Bank and the Gaza Strip. The word 'child' is never used in military announcements: they refer to either an infant or a youth, but never a child. So a ten-year-old boy shot by the military forces is reported to be a 'young man of ten.'"[20]

In 1988, in response to the first *intifada,* military orders were promulgated for the West Bank and Gaza making stone throwing a felony offense and allowing the arrest of children, including very young children.[21] Parents could post bail for their child's release, but the money (usually U.S.$400–500) would be forfeited if the child was arrested again within a specific period. If parents could not pay this bail, children could be administratively detained for up to one year. In cases when charges were actually brought (typically on the basis of testimony by arresting soldiers), children often were prosecuted in "quick trials," which took place within a few days of arrest, usually in prisons or detention facilities rather than courts.

Palestinians twelve and older are classified legally as "minors"; those aged twelve to thirteen are "juveniles" and those aged fourteen to sixteen are "youths." The maximum sentence for juveniles is six months and for youths one year for those who are convicted of "simple" crimes (see Appendix). However, if they are convicted of "hard" crimes, these maximum-sentence restrictions do not apply. Palestinians sixteen and younger have received sentences of up to four years in prison for throwing stones. In principle, minors legally are distinguished from adults and are supposed to be afforded certain special protections. In practice, the legal status distinction has little effect, especially among those fourteen or older who are treated as adults, including in interrogation.[22]

Arrest does not always entail interrogation, and interrogation does not always involve torture or ill-treatment. But these would be exceptions. Approximately 85 percent of arrestees are interrogated, and interrogation places Palestinians "in a universe of discomfort, pain, humiliation and threats, from which there is no exit until the interrogation ends or the detainee provides information to the interrogators' satisfaction."[23]

Although interrogation is a covert enterprise, details about GSS interrogation practices have been made public through investigations by human rights organizations and litigation in the Israeli High Court of Justice (HCJ). For example, following the publication of the Landau Commission report in 1987 (see Chapter 2), B'Tselem documented extensive use of various abusive methods,[24] which were affirmed by other investigations over the next few years. These methods included wide use of

Insults, verbal abuse, and threats

Sleep and food deprivation

Protracted hooding and blindfolding

Solitary confinement, sometimes in refrigerated or overheated closets (zinzana)

Protracted position abuse (shabeh), specifically forcing detainees to stand or tying them in painful positions to hooks on walls or to child-sized chairs with uneven legs

Confinement in cells with collaborators ('asafir) who have license to treat detainees violently

Forced physical exercise

Blows to the body and forms of shaking that produce a whiplash effect with the head and neck

Subjection to excessively filthy conditions, including forcing detainees to eat meals in the toilet and denying them the right to shower

Deliberate subjection to loud and continuous noise[25]

The Israeli government authorized and justified the use of such tactics, euphemistically termed "moderate physical pressure," as necessary in the interrogation of "hardened terrorists." However, such tactics have characterized interrogation even of people suspected of minor and nonviolent crimes. In 1993, the Gaza Community Mental Health Programme published findings of a survey study based on a sample of 477 ex-prisoners who had spent between six months and ten years in prison. Of this total, 91.7 percent had spent five years or less in prison, meaning that they were convicted of "simple" crimes. The findings revealed the incidence of specific interrogation methods on the following percentages of the sample: beatings (95.8); exposure to extreme cold (92.9); exposure to extreme heat (76.7); prolonged standing (91.6); applied pressure on the neck (68.1); food deprivation (77.4); solitary confinement (86); sleep deprivation (71.5); intense noise (81.6); verbal humiliation (94.8); threats against personal safety (90.6); forced witnessing of torture of other detainees (70.2); applied pressure on testicles (66); electric shock (5.9); tear gas (13.4); pushing instruments into the penis or rectum (11.1); witnessing torture of family members (28.1); threats of torture or rape of female family members (27.9).[26] Other studies and investigations of interrogation tactics have generated similar findings.[27]

GSS interrogations are characterized by three "states of being" for detainees: interrogation, "waiting," and "rest." Until 1999, waiting entailed physical discomfort (often extreme) and sleep deprivation to "soften up" the detainee for the interrogation. Most detainees were held in waiting twenty-four hours a day for five-and-a-half-day intervals, the only interruptions being active interrogation and three daily five-minute breaks when the detainee was placed in a toilet in order to relieve himself while at the same time being given his meal. Detainees were placed in the "rest" position during the Sabbath, when the GSS interrogators went home, at which time they were unhooded and unshackled in cells where they could sleep.

IDF and police interrogations are less orchestrated and less sophisticated than those by the GSS. In the past, they tended to entail beating confessions out of detainees. In 1991, in response to the international controversy surrounding the official sanctioning of moderate physical pressure, the IDF established its own commission of inquiry, which recommended that the IDF reduce its involvement in interrogation and, to the extent possible, transfer these responsibilities to the GSS. It also clarified IDF interrogation guidelines, and as a result there was a decline in beatings and a move toward the adoption of methods used by the GSS, namely prolonged position abuse and sleep deprivation.

In 1991, a police interrogation unit operating in the West Bank, composed of five policemen, became the focus of a public scandal following the publication of a report by the Palestine Human Rights Information Center (PHRIC), which claimed that this unit used electric shock and other forms of torture in its interrogation of people suspected of minor offenses such as throwing stones and hanging Palestinian flags.[28] Israeli journalist Doron Meiri conducted his own investigation into the PHRIC allegations and found confirming evidence of a police "torture unit." His sources included Palestinians, as well as members of the police, military, and security agencies. Meiri reported that their "success rate" in extracting confessions was remarkable, increasing by "several hundred percentages." The unit's self-proclaimed motto was "confession at any price."[29] Meiri's article included an account by an Israeli police officer: "Several times, I arrived early in the morning to the office where [the 'torture unit'] interrogated the prisoners; it looked like a battlefield. Broken wooden clubs, ropes, blood, an abnormal mess. They used to smash the prisoners; finish them. Make them like meatloaf. . . . People [Israeli soldiers and police] heard the screaming of the prisoners during many nights, and some of them even cried with them. But they were afraid to talk. After all, this unit is the baby of the [police] Commander, and since it was established it had tremendous success."[30]

In response to these revelations, a police official confirmed the existence of a unit that interrogated stone throwers but denied that it engaged in "torture." He also confirmed that in certain cases, detainees had confessed to tens of stone-throwing incidents. He was responding to the fact that some people interrogated by this unit had confessed to as many as 150 to 200 separate incidents. He stated, "But the unit checks every confession to see if it coincides with an actual event. They do all this in order not to have false confessions."[31]

In 1993, another interrogation-related scandal broke, this one emanating from the discovery of a "medical fitness form" to be filled out by a prison doctor before a detainee was interrogated by the GSS.[32] Tamar Peleg, a Jewish Israeli lawyer, found a copy of this form, which had been left by mistake in the file of a client. The form asked for an assessment of the detainee's health and included the following questions: "Are there any restrictions on putting the prisoner in an isolation cell?" "Are there any restrictions on tying up the prisoner?" "Are there any restrictions on putting a head/eye cover on him?" "Are there any restrictions on standing for extended periods?"[33] The revelation of this form was scandalous because it clearly implicated doctors in torture and ill-treatment, thus constituting a violation of both the Hippocratic oath and the 1975 Tokyo Convention against Torture, to which the Israeli Medical Association is a signatory.

Torture and ill-treatment have remained enduring characteristics of Israeli interrogation of Palestinians. In 1999, a HCJ ruling (discussed in Chapter 2) limited the routine use of moderate physical pressure. However the decision did not prohibit the use of sleep deprivation and shackling *during* interrogation. Hence, since 1999, tactics that once characterized waiting have been shifted to interrogation, and detainees now can be kept in "protracted interrogation," painfully shackled and deprived of sleep for up to twenty hours a day for many days in a row.[34]

## Gendered Carceralism

Although the number of Palestinian women and girls who have been arrested is miniscule in comparison to the number of men and boys, it is in the thousands.[35] Palestinian females who are arrested are subjected to many of the same interrogation methods as males. They also can be subjected to special methods that capitalize on their gender, such as sexual harassment and abuse and techniques and threats that manipulate notions of "female honor" and women's feelings for their family members, especially their children.[36]

The threat of interrogation as a "dishonoring" experience was, in the past, exploited to inhibit Palestinian women's participation in national politics. But the costs of the conflict and the increasingly collective mobilization to resist the occupation eroded the effectiveness of this gendered form of control.[37] According to Nada Muzzafar, "[T]he women prisoners respond in the face of their interrogators, 'our honor is in removing you from our land, honor is when the nation has become free, honor is the end of occupation.'"[38]

Many incidents have been reported of women and girls being detained and brought to interrogation where they are threatened or abused to pressure male family members to confess. Women prisoners also have been used instrumentally in the interrogation of male prisoners. Torturing women in front of men is a means of pressuring men to confess to "save" women from further abuse. Fadl Yunis, in his prison memoir, *Cell Number 7*, describes an experience of a Palestinian woman commando, stripped naked, being interrogated in front of him. He writes, "Tears came to my eyes, but she said, addressing me in a collected voice: 'Don't worry brother. It doesn't matter that you see me naked. After all, you're my brother . . . and I'm your sister.' "[39]

Gendered violence and gendered resistance are aspects of the conflict in Israel/Palestine and articulate with national violence and resistance in complex ways.[40] In addition to those who are arrested, interrogated, prosecuted, and incarcerated, women and girls experience carceralism as members of Palestinian society. For example, females often try to impede the law enforcement process by putting themselves in the path of soldiers who are attempting to arrest or beat others. Describing this form of resistance, Julie Peteet writes, "They tug at the soldiers, exhorting and pleading with them to stop. Armed only with determination and their voices, they hurl insults that challenge the humanity of the occupier: 'Has God abandoned you?' 'Have you no compassion and pity?' 'Aren't we human beings, too?' 'Don't you have mothers and sons — how would your mother feel if you were treated this way — would you like to see your sons beaten like this?' 'What kind of people takes the land of another and then beats them when they protest?' "[41]

Hundreds of thousands of women and girls — wives and mothers, sisters and daughters — "experience" the military court system through their relations with men and boys who are taken into custody. They function as interlocutors, assuming the tasks of trying to track down arrested family members, hiring lawyers, attending court hearings, and visiting prisons. Although men also experience the system through these activities, because women are regarded by the Israeli authorities as *relatively* less dangerous, they have more mobility to travel to these sites. Indeed, to walk past the walls of a prison on visiting day, one can appreciate the gendered nature of carceral government, with men on the inside and mostly women gathered on the outside.

## Routines of Abuse

A number of defendants I interviewed offered detailed accounts of their own interrogation experiences, including the changing nature of tactics, which reflected the impact of negative publicity and litigation to prohibit torture. One defendant, "Khalid," said that when he was arrested in 1989, interrogators used physical methods like strangulation, hair pulling, and *falaqa* (beatings on the bare soles of feet). He recounted the words of one of his interrogators, "If you don't speak with your mouth, we'll make you speak from your ass."

When Khalid was arrested again in 1991, while physical methods were still used, the main emphasis was psychological. He said that he found this to be more insidious than physical abuse. Due to prolonged sleep deprivation, he was disoriented and consequently more vulnerable to psychological manipulation. Each round of interrogation would last six or seven hours. The interrogator would enter the room, introduce himself by a pseudonym, and state that there was nothing personal but that they had security information about Khalid's activities. In addition to straightforward questioning, the interrogator would try to draw Khalid into conversation by provoking him. Sometimes he would talk about how strong Israel was and how weak the Palestinians were, or how unfair it was that public personalities like Hanan Ashrawi and Faisal Husseini were getting all the attention and credit for Palestinians' struggle.[42] The interrogator would tell Khalid that he would be charged, tried, sentenced, and sent to prison, that he would spend his time, get released, and go back to the movement, and that nothing would change. This strategy succeeded to a degree: even though Khalid didn't confess, such talk added to his depression and vulnerability. He said, "At least when someone is getting beaten, his body becomes numb to the pain, but being deprived of sleep, being forced to sit on small chairs in painful positions in the cold, being reminded of the political problems, the mind begins to break."

"Riyad" recounted a similar experience of being subjected to hours of "story/lectures." The interrogator would say things like "All Arabs are Bedouin, and Bedouin are Saudis, so Palestinians should go back to Saudi Arabia where they came from. You don't belong here." According to Riyad, "It might seem more humane on one level because they aren't suffering physically the way they do during a beating, but it is a strategy to make Palestinians defeat themselves — both in interrogation itself and in the long term by manipulating their political views." He said that the combined effects of sleep deprivation and subjection to such lectures "broke" him. He added, "While the body can take a lot and can use the mind to shut out the pain, when the mind is the target, there is no defense."

In addition to the use of various physical and psychological "pressure" tactics, interrogators routinely use trickery and collaborators (*'asafir*) to get people to confess.[43] Trickery is standard practice in interrogations and takes many forms. Sometimes interrogators lie to detainees about having confessions of others or secret evidence implicating them in serious crimes in order to get people to confess to lesser crimes. Sometimes they threaten the safety of the detainee's family members. One man said that he and his wife, both political activists, were arrested at the same time. After about a week, interrogators showed him a confession written in handwriting that looked like his wife's. While he wasn't sure whether she had written it, he refused to confess and after forty days of interrogation was released. When he got home, he found out that the confession had not, in fact, been written by his wife.

Interrogators have used *'asafir* since at least 1979 (see Chapter 2), but their use increased during the first *intifada*.[44] *'Asafir* sometimes are special agents planted in prisons and detention centers. But many are actually prisoners themselves, who were recruited while undergoing interrogation or serving a sentence. The two main tactics in the *'asafir* repertoire, deception and violence, often are used in sequence. First a detainee is placed in a cell with several *'asafir*, who try to win his confidence by presenting themselves as members of the same faction. They ask the detainee to give them information about activities, arms caches, other members of the faction, and so on under the pretext that they will pass the information on to the leadership outside. If that doesn't work, they then resort to violence and intimidation. Anything the detainee says to *'asafir* is relayed to the interrogators and becomes evidence in his file.

One West Bank lawyer who was arrested in 1988 described the calibrated use of various tactics. For the first few days, he was tied in the *shabeh* position with a dirty sack over his head. His interrogation sessions would last eight to ten hours. The questioning was aimed at getting him to confess to being a member of Fatah. When he didn't confess, the interrogators told him that they had secret evidence and didn't need a confession to try him. He was then taken to the Ramallah prison and placed in a cell with other prisoners, who told him that they, too, were awaiting trial. They started asking him questions about his interrogation. Because he had never been arrested before, he had no experience with *'asafir*. But he suspected that something was strange about these cellmates because they were so intent upon getting him to talk. When he told them he had nothing to say, they beat him up.

The next day he was taken back to interrogation, where he realized that his move to the Ramallah prison had been part of the overall interrogation. He continued to be interrogated for another five days, during which he was held for hours in a toilet filled with sewage, put in a *zinzana,* and beaten. In the end, he was released because he didn't confess and there was no other evidence against him. In remarking on his experience with the *'asafir,* he said, "When you finally come out of interrogation and see other prisoners, your first feeling is relief, especially when they act like your friends who want to help you. If I had anything to confess, I would have been fooled."

## Narrating Violence

> *The interrogator "Cohen" and another interrogator called "Dori" showed me a photo album: a picture of a cripple and a picture of a naked man dancing like a madman, and other photographs of the same kind, of people with defects, or crazy people. The interrogators told me that I would come out . . . like them.*
>
> From affidavit of Hani Saleh Muzheir,
> a Palestinian detainee[45]

Threats are an integral part of interrogation to produce or exacerbate fear in order to induce a detainee to confess. Threatening to do serious damage to a detainee is both common and "real" in the sense of heightening fear, but such threats are often also rhetorical because most people who have been interrogated do not come out crippled or crazy.[46] But some do. "Salah," who lives in Kalandia refugee camp, became paralyzed as a result of interrogation. This physical incapacitation destroyed life as he once knew it.

Salah, one of the founders of the "karate movement" in the West Bank, was a local celebrity for his athletic prowess.[47] On the day of his arrest in 1991, he had given a black belt demonstration in Ramallah. Because he has Jerusalem residency, the authorities took advantage of his presence "in the West Bank" to arrest him there, thus affording themselves greater leeway for interrogation; Jerusalem residents arrested in Jerusalem can be held incommunicado for only forty-eight hours, as compared to eighteen days for West Bankers or people arrested in the West Bank. Salah recounted that when he arrived at interrogation, the interrogator said, "See how we can get around the laws to get you where we want you?"

Salah's questioning was aimed at getting him to confess to a number of crimes, but he staunchly denied all the interrogators' allegations. On the first day, he was suffocated and beaten on the genitals. On the second day, while handcuffed, he jumped up and karate-kicked a picture of Theodore Herzl that was hanging on the wall of the interrogation room. The interrogators got angry and smashed his head against the wall. He fell unconscious. When he was revived with an injection and water, he found himself semiparalyzed as a result of the head injury. He also found that his wrists had been cut and bandaged to provide the interrogators with a "suicide option" should he not regain consciousness. After he came to, his wrists were stitched without the use of anesthesia. He was then shackled with barbed cuffs to produce scars to obscure the traces of the incisions. When I met him, both sets of scars — straight lines from a razor and jagged lines from barbs — were visible on his wrists.

Despite his injuries, Salah was interrogated for fifty-seven days. During this entire period, he never saw a doctor, only a prison paramedic. His lawyer, who saw Salah for the first time at the extension-of-detention hearing on the eighteenth day of his incarceration, pressed to have him taken to a hospital, but GSS agents in charge of his interrogation opposed any interruptions, and the judge concurred.

Salah never gave a confession, but charges were brought against him based on secret evidence. Once charged, his case took several months to conclude. Hearings were moved from the military court in Ramallah to Hebron to avoid public protests and media coverage of the "paralyzed karate star." In court, too weak to stand, he fell down. He told the judge that he felt like he was dying. The judge responded, "Everyone feels that way." Initially, the prosecutor offered a deal of five years of "voluntary exile," meaning that he would have to agree to his own deportation. When Salah refused, the prosecutor sought a sentence of five years in prison. But his lawyer eventually was able to work out a deal in which most of the charges were dropped. In the end, he was found guilty of "aiding an illegal organization." The basis for the charge was that he had given a bag of flour to someone who, according to secret evidence, was a member of Fatah. Salah admitted having given the flour but denied that this was a politically motivated act. Rather, he had been helping out a neighbor. He was sentenced to one-and-a-half years in prison.

When he got to prison, he saw a doctor, who took head x-rays and decided that he was "okay" even though he was still suffering bouts of unconsciousness and occasionally vomiting blood. When his sentence was up and he was released, he went to Maqqasad, the Arab hospital in Jerusalem. There, doctors discovered that he had a concussion, blood clots, water on the brain, and calcification on the spine. The prognosis:

permanent paralysis. In summarizing his experience, Salah said, "They tried me in that interrogation room and gave me a life sentence for nothing."

But Salah was not the only one to suffer the effects of his interrogation. His physical incapacitation deprived him of his livelihood. As a consequence, his plans to send his son abroad to study medicine had to be aborted. In his opinion his son, too, is a victim of that interrogation. During Salah's incarceration, his brother and nephew also were arrested. His brother fell gravely ill in prison, and when he was taken to a hospital it was discovered that he had serious blockage of the heart arteries. This, coupled with Salah's paralysis, was too much for his father, who got so upset that he had a stroke and died.

During my interview with Salah, he challenged me in a way that few other interviewees did. After recounting these details, he angrily asked, "And what will you do with this information? Will you help anyone? Will you prevent these things from happening to others?" We concluded the interview with a discussion about the role and responsibility of researchers, especially those who work in conflict zones, to *do something* with the information that their informants share with them. As I was leaving Salah's home, he took a framed picture of the Dome of the Rock off his wall and gave it to me, saying, "Keep this as a memory of what you heard here today. Use that memory."

Salah, who had shared his story of pain and frustration, had enjoined me to use my memory of his narrative of violence and suffering. Ethnographers of violence often confront and are confronted with an expectation that they — privileged researchers who "take the time" — theirs and their informants' time — to "get the story" — will tell it to "the world" and that the "told story" will have some consequences. Salah was not asking me simply if I would tell his story, for he had no reason to doubt that I would. Rather, he was asking me whether I was capable of telling of his story in some way that would have some positive effect someday on *his world*. In this vein, E. Valentine Daniel writes:

On so many occasions, after giving me accounts of their trials, victims of violence would say, in despair, "What do they in America care about what happens to us!" or wonder, "Would they understand what is being done?" Questions or rhetorical assertions such as these are the performatives of those whose participation in the ongoing process of being human has been stifled by the . . . inescapable presence of violence, and who want to be free again. Such performatives are uttered as a means to move the world, even if only by a sort of magical hope, to incorporate their particular condition into the care-structure of a larger humanity.[48]

The researcher's responsibility to "do something" about violence born (and borne) in an ethnographic encounter extends outward to "the world" through writing. And through reading.

## Confession from the Defendants' Perspective

Interrogation is a process aimed and calibrated to get general information about the political situation in the West Bank and Gaza in order to facilitate Israeli control and thwart resistance and specific information that can be used to incriminate and prosecute individuals. Palestinians have no interest in giving information to their interrogators because the purposes served by that information are harmful to them individually and collectively. Violence and "pressure" are the means of taking from them what they are unwilling to give away.

From the perspective of defendants, confessions have multiple, contradictory, and weighty meanings. Confessing means not only giving up information but also giving up the struggle to endure the interrogation. People often confess to save themselves from further abuse and deprivation. In that sense, confessing is a survival strategy. As one defendant said, "By the time I was ready to confess, I was broken. I didn't care what happened to me. I just wanted to be left alone." According to another who had been arrested and interrogated numerous times, "During interrogation you feel like you are outside the legal system. What they do to you is illegal, but no one can help you. You are all alone with people who hate you and are hurting you. When you finally confess, you can't even read what you sign because it is written in Hebrew. Then you go to prison."

If *not* confessing is the goal of the prisoner, then to confess is to admit defeat at the hands of interrogators. For some, being "beaten" in this way carries a stigma of shame and weakness. The confession, which is put to use against the one who gave it (and anyone else implicated in it), takes on life-altering meanings of disgrace and dejection or revenge. According to Khalid Batrawi, a researcher for al-Haq, "The effects of arrest on people, especially young people, can be very damaging. If a person confesses, he has two choices. He can either accept that he confessed, which is a psychological burden and requires a lot of support and consolation from other prisoners. If he can't face the fact that he confessed, this has its own consequences. Some become collaborators out of guilt, to make others confess so that he can convince himself that he is no worse than others. Others who can't face the fact that they confessed just withdraw into themselves."

During the first *intifada,* the arrest of a much wider segment of the Palestinian population altered the political meanings and consequences of confessions. Many people who had no previous interrogation experience, no training that would have prepared them to withstand the process, and no knowledge of the legal implications of confession found out, after the fact, as it were, what they had "done to themselves" by confessing.

One longtime activist in the Democratic Front for the Liberation of Palestine (DFLP) described how his attitudes about confession had changed. When he was young, and before he had ever been arrested, he was very dogmatic in his belief that no one should confess. But when he was arrested for the first time and brutally interrogated, he confessed. "Life experience taught me that different people can withstand different kinds of pressure. I realized that a person who confesses isn't necessarily weak or a traitor." He and other local leaders learned from experience the importance of training cadres to withstand interrogation. He became a trainer for his faction, holding mock interrogations replicating the tactics used by the GSS.

When he was arrested again in 1989, he didn't confess, but evidence against him came from the confession of a close friend. He said that at first he was mad because his friend's confession was the only solid evidence against him and it became the basis for his conviction. Eventually he realized that his anger at his friend was misdirected and that forgiving his friend was a process of maturing politically. He is particularly sympathetic to young people who confess. But he still retains a strong animosity toward people who confess about others just to end their own interrogation or to work out a better deal for themselves.

Confession has factored into representations of Palestinian politics, feeding rumors and inflecting stereotypes about which factions are "tough" and "committed" enough to withstand the pressures and abuses of interrogation and which are not. Thus, ideas about confessing take on collective and competitive meanings. I often heard people proclaim (conflicting) factionalized ideas about confession: "Hamas are strong. They never confess." "Islamic Jihad act tough, but put them in an interrogation room and they cry like girls." "Fatah always confess." "Fatah never confess." "PFLP [Popular Front for the Liberation of Palestine] break their interrogators."

Confessing has a history, or rather it is an element of the history of the conflict. This history is marked by changes in why people confess, what they confess to, and what their confessions mean to them and others. For example, when the Israeli-Palestinian negotiations started, some people who were affiliated with factions supportive of the negotiations found an interest in confessing. Referred to as "Madrid fever" (Madrid was the city where the "peace process" was launched), it sprang from the belief that Palestinians in Israeli prisons would be released as one of the terms of an agreement. Therefore, getting out of interrogation (by confessing) and into prison was a way to get onto that list, which, they believed, was a step toward "Palestine," the independent state that would be the outcome of the negotiations. For people with "Madrid fever," confessing was an expression of political faith in their leaders to get them out of prison and into a state of freedom in a free state.

Recently, there has been a change in confessions that reflects the political ramifications of the collapse of the Oslo Accords, the outbreak of a second *intifada* in 2000, and the increase in armed violence by the Israeli military and Palestinian factions. These changes are being narrated in the form of confessions. Lawyers who have spent their professional lives representing Palestinian defendants have expressed amazement — and, as their legal representatives, consternation — at the unprecedented willingness of Palestinians to confess and at the volume, detail, and contents of confessions since the start of the second *intifada*.

In September 2002, I interviewed 'Ala'a Jaradat, who works for Addammeer, a Palestinian organization that provides support for prisoners. He offered a variety of reasons why "everybody is confessing — huge confessions!" According to him, "Some are imaginary heroes, but they get sentenced for their imaginations." As an example, he told of a case of two Palestinians from Jalazoun refugee camp who were charged for planning to assassinate Israeli Prime Minister Ariel Sharon. Their "plan" entailed talking about what a good idea it would be to eliminate Sharon, but they confessed to an assassination attempt and were sentenced accordingly. Others confess just to end their interrogation and get into prison, where they will be able to sleep and eat more. Some persuade themselves that there is no reason *not* to confess to because their interrogators seem to know about their activities, and struggling against admission seems futile. Some assume that the negotiations will eventually resume and that they will be released in a prisoner exchange, and others deliberately confess because they believe they are actually better off in prison than outside, given the death tolls of military campaigns and the collapse of the Palestinian economy.

Jaradat offered two more explanations that, together, reflect the poles of Palestinian politics: Some detainees offer voluminous confessions as autobiographies of their participation in a resurgent armed struggle. These types regard themselves as "prisoners of war," and their confessions are reminiscent of *feda'yin* (guerrilla) confessions in the first years of occupation. Others offer voluminous confessions as a gesture of personal defeat that is consonant with the devastation of the second *intifada* and a sense of collective defeat.

## The Legal Process

Once the interrogation is finished, if there is evidence to charge the detainee, the prosecutor prepares the charge sheet and the legal process begins. From that point onward, defendants become "files" to be handled and resolved by defense lawyers and prosecutors.

If a confession is the main evidence, the prosecutor needs an additional scintilla *(dvar ma* in Hebrew). In this court system, the scintilla could be the protocol of the extension-of-detention hearing; if a detainee did not tell the presiding judge that he was "innocent," the prosecutor could use this as an admission of guilt. Given that detainees often are not represented by counsel at extension hearings, many are unaware that declaring their innocence is even an option. Corroborating evidence also can include the testimony of arresting soldiers, general information that a particular event for which the defendant is being charged actually occurred, or secret evidence.

Despite all of the factors weighing against Palestinians in this court system, many defendants and their family members cling to the belief that in their case, acquittal or at least leniency is possible. "Procedural justice" is a sociolegal concept that refers to people's belief that the legal process is one of rational deliberation. It signals people's faith that "the law" will vindicate them and translates as a desire to have their day in court. According to one lawyer, "Palestinians arrested for the first time during the [first] *intifada* exhibited a remarkably high level of expectations about the military courts at a personal level — that is, believing that the individual person they know will get a fair trial." And for those who harbor hope of acquittal, when they are convicted — as almost all who face charges are — they often blame their lawyer.

I witnessed a scene in the Ramallah court that illustrates the prevalence of a faith in procedural justice. Late in the morning, a lawyer complained to the judge that the prosecutor's witness against his client had not shown up and that this was the third hearing he had missed. On these grounds, the lawyer asked the judge to dismiss the case and release his client, a thirteen-year-old boy accused of stone throwing. At that point, one of the soldiers in the courtroom announced that the soldier/witness had just arrived. The lawyer went out of the courtroom to check, and when he came back in, he pled his client guilty. The judge sentenced the boy to two more months in prison.

Later, the lawyer explained to me that when a soldier is ready to testify, there is no chance that the court will find in favor of the defendant. Therefore, it is better to plead guilty and get a lower sentence. He said, "The 'court' took place outside the courtroom when I questioned the soldier and found out what he would be saying to the judge." With his case finished, the lawyer left. But during the midafternoon break, Palestinians in the courtroom got into a discussion about the incident. People were upset that the lawyer had deprived that poor boy of justice by pleading him guilty and not allowing the judge to decide. As people's anger mounted, they took it out on two other Palestinian lawyers who happened into the courtroom. The discussion then turned into a debate.

The lawyers started lecturing about how the system worked and the disproportionate weight of prosecution witnesses' testimony. One Palestinian man responded that if lawyers were better at their job, this wouldn't be the case. One of the lawyers retorted that the problem was not the fault of lawyers but of the people: they engaged in illegal activities and then expected miracles in the courtroom. He reminded them that judges were part of the same army that arrested, shot, and beat them. Afterwards, the lawyers complained to me that they had to deal with this kind of naïveté all the time. And the Palestinian man who had most vociferously protested the handling of the boy's case complained to me about the pervasive cynicism, corruption, and incompetence of lawyers.

By the time most defendants get to court, they already have been in custody for weeks or months, and many know that they will be returning to prison after their court session. They tend to see the legal process not as a *process* but as a bureaucratic affirmation of their incarceration. Their experience in court conforms to their perceptions of the carceralism of occupation.

Late one afternoon in February 1993, after a long day of hearings in the Ramallah military court involving youthful offenders, three young boys between the ages of thirteen and fourteen were brought in. They had been arrested for throwing stones and had been held for the last five days in the Ramallah military detention center. The section of the prison where they were held was composed of tents, and because the weather was unseasonably cold, when they came into the courtroom they were blue and shivering from exposure. They didn't have a lawyer. But a Palestinian lawyer in the courtroom noticed that one of the boys had two black eyes. He demanded that the judge take note of that fact and add it to the protocol of the boy's file. The lawyer asked the boy who had hurt him. Scared and sullen, the boy was reluctant to say anything. At the lawyer's prodding, he finally said that when he hadn't confessed to throwing stones, soldiers had put him in a tent with other prisoners who beat him up.

The lawyer complained to the judge about holding these boys without bail. The judge said that he was ready to consider releasing them if someone was willing to put up bail, but no one from their families was present. Consequently, the judge remanded them in custody until the prosecution's case was ready and a hearing could be scheduled. After the judge made his decision, the lawyer sat with the boys and learned that two of the three were brothers (including the one with the black eyes) and that they had another four brothers in jail in Bethlehem. Their mother was a widow who could never afford bail or a lawyer. They assumed that she couldn't leave her younger children alone, or couldn't afford the trip to Ramallah, or perhaps didn't even know about the hearing. After the boys were taken back to prison, the lawyer said, "Yesterday it was stones. Tomorrow it will be Molotovs and who knows what next. When all you know is suffering and hardship, you have nothing to lose."

## A Society within a Society

> *Political prison is critical to the life histories and personal itineraries of partisans involved in organized resistance movements. The prison experience, as necessitated by circumstance, figures in crucially structural ways in the written autobiographical or testimonial narrations of those lives.*
>
> Barbara Harlow, *Barred*[49]

In prison, having passed through the court system as objects, people reemerge as political subjects. Because hundreds of thousands of Palestinians have been imprisoned over the decades of Israeli occupation, the prison system is an extremely important institution for Palestinian society. One man who spent a combined total of fifteen years in prison said, "The society inside a prison is a society within a society."

In addition to their "conventional" purpose as sites of incarceration, prisons have served certain functions, the most important being education. According to one former prisoner, expressing a widely popular view, "Education in prisons is very important. Many people come out better educated than they were when they went in." Another man, who spent seven years in prison when he was very young, talked about how the experience had changed his entire outlook; not only did he have the opportunity to learn "dialectical thinking," but he "unlearned" the lessons of his upbringing and shed his preincarceration ideas about gender relations, religion, and politics. He said, "Before I went into prison, I was a typical boy. I believed that women were inferior, put on earth to serve men. In prison, we spent a lot of time talking about the role of women in society. Other prisoners talked about how women play an important role and are equal to men. I became ashamed of my childish views, and the education I got in prison helped me change."

Prisons occupy a place in the popular imagination as sites of personal and collective learning and growth, often referred to as "Palestinian universities." Indeed, while schools and universities in the West Bank and Gaza often are closed down, the prisons are always in business. In prison, many Palestinians sharpen and refine their political awareness and their resolve to resist and combat the occupation. According to Israeli commentators Ze'ev Schiff and Ehud Ya'ari:

Rather than serving as a deterrent and a punitive framework for breaking the PLO's [Palestine Liberation Organization's] strongest cadres, Israel's prisons were transformed into higher "academies," as the inmates called them, for reflection and education, ideological and spiritual rehabilitation, and experiments with new political constructs. . . . Many prisoners studied Hebrew "to get to know the enemy better." . . . Prisoners who had attended officers' courses in one of the Arab states gave lessons in topography and field craft, military tactics and history. The prisoners pored over the works of Marx, Mao, and Franz Fanon, developing a new lexicon of strategy and learning the value of consensus over ideological purity.[50]

Several Palestinians I interviewed together, who had been arrested in the early years of the occupation for engaging in armed struggle, were among the prisoners released in the 1985 "Jabril exchange."[51] During their incarceration, these men had become prison leaders and had helped to erect highly organized structures within prisons, orchestrating various resistance activities, primarily hunger strikes, to struggle for and eventually win some accommodations in the treatment of prisoners.[52] Since most of them had life sentences, they were, of course, relieved to be released in the exchange. But they said that the release of political prisoners like themselves created a vacuum in prison leadership and an erosion of the gains from their prison struggles.

When these men were arrested during the first *intifada,* they were shocked by how badly the situation in prisons had deteriorated. With so many people passing in and out of prisons, jails, and detention centers, and the expanded use of *'asafir,* prisoners had a harder time knowing whom to trust. This made it more difficult — although not impossible — for prisoners to organize themselves and mount periodic strikes to protest inhumane prison conditions.

Although prisoners tended to divide up along factional lines, many expressed the idea that political factionalism is less pronounced within prisons than on the outside. Prisoners constantly are exposed to one another, and these circumstances provide opportunities for debate and discussion. According to a former prisoner, "People have time — nothing but time — to think and talk about their differences. The atmosphere in prisons encourages people to listen to others' ideas."

The most debilitating prison experience is prolonged solitary confinement, which is used in both interrogation and postconviction incarceration; some people spend years in solitary. Raji Sourani, a lawyer and human rights activist from Gaza, said that contesting the use of solitary confinement is extremely difficult because those on the outside can do little to influence how people are treated in prison. Punishments like solitary confinement are the prerogative of prison authorities, whose discretion is not subject to judicial oversight.

The experiences of imprisonment that so many individual Palestinians have endured are part of the sociocultural bonds that unite Palestinians in the occupied territories as a community. The prevalence of these experiences informs constructions of national and personal identities. People's personal histories are fragmented between time spent inside (prisons) and out, and they emphasize accounts of these travails. Family histories are marked by arrest-related absences and reunions, both of which require various forms of coping.

Arrest and imprisonment on such a massive scale among Palestinians has a contradictory significance to the population as a whole. On the one hand, arrest has a positive symbolic meaning as a sign of the ongoing struggle against the occupation and a refusal to submit to foreign military rule and statelessness. Since the beginning of the occupation, arrest has been regarded as a respectable and admirable sacrifice for the national cause. On the other hand, being arrested is difficult and often has tragic consequences for individuals and families.

The social meanings and significance of arrest and imprisonment combine coming-of-age experiences, opportunities for personal development and education, and solidarity building with the degradations of interrogation and the privations of incarceration. Likewise, feelings of guilt coexist with feelings of resolve about the legitimacy of the struggle. Some feel guilty about actions they carried out, others about having confessed against friends or relatives, and others about the suffering that their arrest caused their families. The images of collective solidarity in which the political prisoner is a respected and revered national figure belie the social traumas that inevitably result from the arrest of so many.

## Those Left Behind

When a person is arrested, the entire family is affected. Arrests that occur in homes often involve brutality against the entire household. Then follows a period of days or even weeks during which the family doesn't know what has become of those arrested, since they are held incommunicado. Shardia Sarraj, a psychologist with the Gaza Mental Health Programme, said that when wives and children witness the "patriarchal figure" of the household being abused and unable to protect them from the soldiers, their own feelings of vulnerability are exacerbated.

In 1993, Sarraj conducted a sociopsychological study involving one hundred Gazan families whose primary breadwinners were sentenced to twenty-five years or more. The wives had to assume full responsibility for parenting, but none of those in her study worked outside the home or had any independent financial resources, and all of them moved in with their in-laws (as is customary in Arab societies). Whatever independence from the extended family they and their husbands had been able to achieve when they were together was negated by the arrest. Almost all of the women Sarraj interviewed expressed feelings of guilt for the burden their presence added to their in-laws' household, and this was exacerbated by the knowledge that they would be there for an extended period — possibly forever. At the same time, however, many resented the restrictions and added duties that relatives imposed on them.

Some of the women in Sarraj's study showed signs of clinical depression, such as talk of suicide, refusal to eat, and insomnia. Some said that the stress had caused them to begin beating their children. Because many of the women were consumed by worry and depression, the children suffered a lack of attention, and some took to acting out at home. Older male children were expected to take on some of the responsibilities of the male head of household, including, in some cases, going into the job market, which meant dropping out of school. One fourteen-year-old boy with thirteen younger siblings was so burdened with responsibilities that he attempted to kill his mother. A three-year-old girl who was burned with hot tea by soldiers during her father's arrest became violent and mute.[53]

Women whose husbands are in prison are subject to a variety of problems and pressures. They are expected to immerse themselves in their husband's legal affairs and, if possible, to make visits to prison. Many Palestinian women lack their own financial resources, which compounds their feelings of vulnerability and dependence on others. Collaborators sometimes preyed on wives of prisoners with offers of help and money or misled them with false information about their husbands.

Many women in Palestinian society are politicized and educated. But in comparison to men and boys, women and girls have fewer educational opportunities and less exposure to organizational politics. During the first *intifada,* closures, curfews, and violent confrontations made it increasingly difficult or impossible to work or go to school. For women and girls, these declining or disrupted opportunities contributed to a declining age of marriage. Consequently, many wives of prisoners were young, undereducated, and unprepared emotionally or politically for their husband's arrest. To the extent that some women imagined that their husband's release from prison would resolve their problems, they were unprepared for the problems and difficulties of the husband's release and reintegration into the family and society. Indeed, many found that their husband's release brought on a new set of problems. But because release from prison is regarded and lauded as a resolution to a family's problems, it was difficult and embarrassing for people to talk about or seek help adjusting to their reunions.

Women who are highly politicized are, in some ways, better prepared to contend with their husband's incarceration. However, during the first *intifada,* several Gaza women activists described a contradiction that women in their circles faced when their husband was arrested. They were able to maintain or even increase their independence, financially and socially, experiencing a greater sense of personal autonomy. Some said that they felt conflicted about their husband's release from prison, anticipating the event while resenting the inevitable loss of freedom and independence once the men returned to the household.

One of these activists, "Leila," had married her husband in 1986, within months of his release after having served a twelve-year sentence. She said, "Our match was politics, not passion. He was a member of [my faction], and people told me he was a good man who needed a wife." But they developed a very supportive relationship, and he encouraged her activism and praised her accomplishments. In 1988, he was arrested and put in administrative detention. At that time there were no family visits to Ketziot/Ansar III, where he was being held, so the only way that she could get information about him was from people who had been released. One man told her that her husband had joined Islamic Jihad. Although she found it hard to believe, she had no reason to doubt this man and no way to find out whether this was true. The fear that her husband might have become an Islamist caused her to think about divorcing him. A month later, she met another released prisoner and learned that the conversion story was a lie.

In 1990, Leila's husband was arrested again. Soldiers came to take him in the middle of the night. After they left, none of her neighbors came to comfort her because they were afraid that collaborators would be watching and reporting on her. This time, her husband went through three months of very intense interrogation during which he was held incommunicado, not even allowed to see his lawyer. That was the same period when Khalid Sheikh 'Ali, another Gazan, was killed in interrogation, which intensified Leila's fears for her husband's safety. Ironically, it was Sheikh 'Ali's death that brought an end to her husband's interrogation.

Because there were several confessions against Leila's husband, he finally confessed in order to enable his lawyer to begin working out a deal. The prosecutor wanted six years. Since he had spent twelve years in prison already, the prospect was extremely depressing. Leila and her husband agreed with the lawyer that the best strategy would be to delay the case in the hope that this would wear down the prosecutor and force him to reduce the sentence he was seeking.

Leila said that she found going to court to be the most difficult and degrading aspect of her husband's incarceration, as far as it affected her. The soldiers were rude and abusive, and they prevented people from communicating with one another in the courtroom. She said that being in court made her feel helpless and angry because all she could do was look at her husband being led in and out in chains. After he was sentenced, when she went to visit him in prison, he tried to avoid worrying her. He refused to talk about himself. While she appreciated his intentions, she felt like she was losing touch with him.

But for Leila's husband, her visits were a relief from the monotony of prison. He constantly expressed happiness that she was self-reliant and independent and gratitude that he did not have to worry about her. He maintained an active interest in her and their children's well-being and used her visits to offer suggestions about how she should redecorate their apartment. Through these decorating tips, he was projecting all of his hopes onto his release and reunion with his family. She, too, said that she was looking forward to his release, but she felt some conflicts about the prospect. While she was confident that he would continue to support her work and activities, she had become even more independent since his imprisonment. She was concerned that he might start to resent her or that she might start to resent him. And to compound this, she said she felt guilty for having any negative thoughts about his release. In fact, the reunion proved too difficult, and eventually they divorced.

In general, prison release poses another set of problems as ex-prisoners reintegrate with their families and society. One man who was arrested when his youngest daughter was an infant was released when she was four. I interviewed him at home and saw how she refused to speak to him, treating him like an unwanted stranger in the house. Embarrassed and upset, he said that this exacerbated his own already strong feelings of alienation and loss. Imprisonment both constitutes a condition — a particular kind of "unfreedom" for those who are actually in prison — and imposes itself on relations among all Palestinians.

## Resistance Politics

A unifying dimension of Palestinian politics is the collective rejection of military occupation and statelessness. But resistance in the West Bank and Gaza has never been exclusively focused on Israel; rather, resistance has had dynamic and constitutive effects on relations within Palestinian society. This includes political factionalism — the agendas, activities, rivalries, and alliances of distinct factions and the influence of factional politics on national struggles. It also includes the embrace or rejection of violence as a strategy of resistance to serve collective goals.[54]

In the early years, few Palestinians living in the occupied territories engaged in resistance activities, the exceptions being *feda'yin*. But the negative effects of massive land confiscations, punitive administrative measures, taxation to subsidize the military administration, and increasing use of collective punishments fostered the appeal and necessity of resistance, which became, by the mid-1970s, a more collective enterprise. Even steadfastness (*summud*) and the building of national institutions were construed as forms of resistance.

The *intifada,* which literally means "shaking off," began spontaneously in 1987 as a mass mobilization to shatter the status quo of stalemate. Hundreds of thousands of Palestinians engaged in demonstrations, strikes, boycotts of Israeli products, stone throwing, political graffiti writing, and barricade building to try to block the Israeli military from incursions into towns, villages, and refugee camps. A Unified National Leadership (UNL), composed of members from the various factions affiliated with the PLO as well as political independents, provided grassroots leadership and guidance, distributing mimeographed *bayan*s (directives) that provided instructions and information to the population. Local communities formed popular committees to organize demonstrations, to distribute food and medical supplies, and to coordinate underground schools to compensate for protracted closure of regular schools. All of these activities were outlawed, and anyone participating in or responsible for them could be arrested.[55]

By 1989, the political vacuum caused by the arrest of leaders and disciplined cadres was filled by youths (*shabab*) with little or no political training. Many Palestinians came to fear not only the violence of Israeli soldiers and security agents but also that of masked *shabab,* who imposed their own local authority with impunity, injuring or killing people suspected of collaborating with the Israeli authorities or waging personal and "nonpolitical" vendettas. Masking also provided the Israeli security agents with opportunities to move about in Palestinian areas to hunt down and execute "wanted" Palestinians. According to Graham Usher, "The upshot [of the arrest of leaders and the increase in Israeli covert operations] was a security offensive that succeeded in divesting the uprising of its mass character, turning it instead into the private property of rival bands of armed 'strike forces.'"[56]

The rise of the Islamist movement during the first *intifada* transformed the politics of resistance previously dominated by the secular nationalist factions. Hamas (Arabic acronym for Islamic Resistance Movement; *hamas* also means "zeal" in Arabic), formed in Gaza in 1987 as the "*intifada* wing" of the Muslim Brothers in Palestine,[57] was able to garner a growing following through its provision of social services and its strong sectarian message.[58] Islamic Jihad is smaller and more clandestine than Hamas. The Islamists' rise was attributable in part to the militancy of their message and to the weakening of the PLO factions caused by mass arrests. Hamas and Islamic Jihad were successful in redefining resistance, first in the form of armed attacks against Israelis and Palestinians known or suspected to collaborate with the Israeli military administration and later against Palestinian members of rival factions.

By the start of direct Israeli-Palestinian negotiations in 1991, Palestinian resistance had fragmented along a variety of fault lines, dividing Islamists and secularists, militants and supporters of a negotiated settlement, and indeed Palestinian society as a whole.[59] This was the political climate in which the Israeli-Palestinian Declaration of Principles was signed in 1993 and the Palestinian Authority (PA) was created in 1994. However, the Oslo Accords institutionalized not national separation but a differently configured segregation. The Israeli military redeployed from Palestinian population centers, and the PA assumed direct control over the "civic" aspects of Palestinians' lives. But Israel retained effective control over all of Israel/Palestine, evidenced by and exercised through the regulation and restriction of Palestinians' movement by means of permits and closures; an exclusive monopoly of control over air space, external borders, and water resources; a determining role in the movement of goods, food, and aid into PA areas; and veto power over any legislation that might be passed by the Palestinian Legislative Council.

The continuing use of the military court system during the interim to arrest, prosecute, and convict Palestinians contributed to the maintenance of the Israeli state's political hegemony and signaled that while the occupation changed, it did not end. The Oslo Accords failed to satisfy even minimum Palestinian expectations and aspirations. Standards of living fell precipitously (i.e., no "peace dividend"); Israeli land confiscation and house demolitions continued unabated, and the number of Jewish Israeli settlers increased at a faster rate than any previous period since 1967 (i.e., no end to occupation); Palestinian statehood remained deferred (i.e., no self-determination); and the repatriation of Palestinian refugees was identified as a "red line" that Israel would never cross (i.e., no right of return). Intensive closures barred Palestinians not only from Israel (less than 5 percent were able to get work permits) but from each other: Palestinians in the West Bank and Gaza were confined in enclaves that many critics compared to apartheid South African "bantustans."

During the interim, the PA's relationship to the Israeli state was that of a subordinate proxy, filling in for the redeployed military to provide for Israeli security and to maintain order.[60] The PA was permitted to obtain small arms for the purpose of law enforcement, and PA and Israeli security forces partook in joint security operations.

Palestinian factions that opposed the negotiations (foremost the

Islamist organizations) also opposed the PA, and one means of expressing this opposition was to continue striking Israeli targets throughout the interim. This had complex consequences: The continuation of Palestinian violence eroded the legitimacy of the PA as a "partner" among Jewish Israelis who supported the negotiations (even though the use of violence was not a one-sided phenomenon). In that the PA's very survival was contingent on its capacity to function effectively as a proxy for the redeployed Israeli military, political pressure by Israel (and the United States) to prioritize Israeli security fostered brutal measures and contributed to PA authoritarianism, which deepened tensions and fissures within Palestinian society.[61] Thus, the PA had to contend with a legitimacy problem among its own constituency, exacerbated by the continuation of the occupation and by its perceived ineffectiveness in the negotiations to defend, let alone advance, Palestinian national goals.[62]

Fatah *tanzim* (organizations), founded at the start of the interim to absorb cadres who had been mobilized during the first *intifada,* including people released from prison as part of the terms of the Oslo Accords, initially provided a popular base of support for the negotiations and the PA. They helped fulfill the PA's control mandate by contending (sometimes violently) with Islamists and other opposition factions. However, by 1998, responding to popular disaffection with the Oslo Accords, the *tanzim* became a quasi-oppositional force in their own right, criticizing PA authoritarianism and corruption and mobilizing protests against increasing settlement building. The card the *tanzim* held, and were ready to play when the negotiations broke down in July 2000,[63] was "the street"—namely, mobilizing Palestinians in the hope of achieving through popular protests what the leadership had failed to get at "the table." As with the start of the first *intifada,* one goal was to make the occupation a liability for Israel. Other goals included the recuperation of Palestinian "national unity" that had eroded during the interim and the "internationalization" of the conflict to counter the U.S. monopoly over the "peace process." Fatah *tanzim* also had a domestic agenda to sustain a non-Islamist character to Palestinian national politics, putting them in competition for populist credentials with Hamas. This had been a factor in interfactional violence during the first *intifada* and the interim and would become a deadly and disastrous competition during the second *intifada* (see Conclusion).[64]

The durability of Palestinian resistance should be — indeed, must be — comprehended in light of protracted military occupation in which their rights are routinely, rampantly, and pervasively restricted and violated.

Consequently, resistance has been a source of national pride and cohesion. But the obstacles and difficulties to achieving national goals through resistance have also had deleterious effects on relations within Palestinian society. Frustrated aspirations and social fragmentation from the first *intifada* through the Oslo years have complicated prospects for future political stability. Indeed, the second *intifada* is inexplicable without taking account of the effects of decades of carceralism on Palestinian society.

The history and the future of conflict in Israel/Palestine are informed by the experiences of hundreds of thousands of people who have been arrested, tortured, and imprisoned and the costs and losses wrought by these experiences. In this chapter, I have provided an account of carceralism as it affects defendants in the Israeli military court system, their families, and society as a whole. Carceralism is premised on presumptions of Palestinian criminality and guilt. This presumption affects the legal process and is one of the reasons why plea bargaining is so pervasive, as I address in the following chapter.

CHAPTER 8

# A *Suq* of Deals

*Plea Bargaining*

---

> [P]lea bargaining conjure[s] up images of a Middle Eastern bazaar,
> in which each transaction . . . involves haggling and haggling anew,
> in an effort to obtain the best possible deal.
>
> Malcolm Feeley, *The Process Is the Punishment*[1]

Is this really a *legal* system? This is a recurring reaction I encountered when
describing my research on the Israeli military court system. What people
were asking, in essence, was what possibly could be learned that wasn't
already obvious: that the Israeli state has the power to punish Palestinians
and that punishment is what they get. Such skepticism is understandable
and, in many ways, is an accurate assessment of the problems and limits of
law in the context of conflict and military occupation.

But, I would reply, we must think about "law" neither as some pristine
ideal nor as a blunt instrument of power. Law *is* utilized instrumentally in
the service of the state, but it is not a monopoly of the state or its agents,
as I have elaborated in previous chapters. "Law" also should be apprehended as a *terrain* on which people act and interact. Responding to skep-
tics, I would add that despite innumerable problems the Israeli military
court system is an institutional setting where some people have spent
months, years, or even their entire professional lives; they are not cogs in
some machine but professionals engaging in legal work. Certainly, the
range of possible outcomes that result from this work is constrained by the
politics of the conflict, and the outcomes are predictable — some 90 to 95

percent of Palestinians who are charged with crimes are convicted. But within the broad patterns there are specificities and differences, produced through actions and interactions among individuals.

Overwhelmingly, the legal work that goes on in the military court system involves plea bargaining. Over 97 percent of all cases in which charges are brought are concluded in this way. In general, plea bargaining demands a concession on the part of the defendant to plead guilty in exchange for a concession from the prosecutor to reduce the charges and/or the sentence being sought. Although the percentage of cases plea-bargained in this court system compares to criminal court systems elsewhere, the nature of the laws (military and emergency) and the relationship between the state and the defendants (occupier and occupied) make plea bargaining a comparatively more "rational" choice for Palestinian defendants and their lawyers. Moreover, the sheer number of cases that have been processed through this system since 1967 in relation to the size of the Palestinian population casts plea bargaining in a light of carceral frenzy. It should be unsurprising that many defense lawyers describe the system disparagingly as a "*suq* (market) of deals" and themselves as "deal merchants."

But analyzing why people opt to plea-bargain and how plea bargaining occurs draws attention to nuances, strategies, and variations in the practices of various participants. Despite the patterned regularities and institutional constraints that serve to impel and rationalize plea bargaining, it is a *process* that is neither mechanical nor homogeneous. In this chapter, I analyze the factors that affect plea bargaining, compare how outcomes are achieved, and describe how legal work and the legal process are perceived by those directly involved in this court system.

## The Rationalities of Plea Bargaining

Plea bargaining is a negotiating process, and the main stakes are "time" and "punishment." Defense lawyers and prosecutors negotiate over the charges and the merits of evidence in a case in an effort to come to an arrangement — to "strike a deal" — on the sentence. For the defense, the incentive to plea-bargain is negative: it assumes the likelihood of defeat at trial with the consequence of a higher sentence. For the prosecution, the incentive is positive, albeit also a compromise: it provides a quick, easy, and assured conviction of the accused, saving the time, effort, and resources that a trial would entail.

In many criminal court systems, plea bargaining is the routine and predominant way to resolve most cases. Proponents laud its expediency, while detractors deride the "presumption of guilt" that pressures defense lawyers to abandon claims of innocence to come to the table where their task is to negotiate over how much guilt and at what cost to the defendant.

In the military court system, the official Israeli position holds that plea bargaining is a just and efficient resolution to cases in which the defendant has already confessed to the crime(s) and/or there is substantiating evidence that would ensure a conviction at trial.[2] Many military court judges regard any attempt to have a trial when the prosecution has a prima facie case to be political grandstanding and actively discourage it as a waste of the court's time. For defense lawyers, staking a Palestinian defendant's fate on the hope of acquittal is widely regarded as risky or cavalier because of the myriad difficulties of actually winning. While many defense lawyers disparage plea bargaining, whether because they regard it as a "low" form of legal work or as politically defeatist, or both, they do it for almost all cases, and they rationalize doing it because of a lack of alternatives. Hence, dealing is a rational choice for all parties, but for differing reasons.

The factors that contribute to the rationality of plea bargaining include the high rates and evidentiary weight of confessions, the use of "secret evidence," and judicial preference for the testimony of prosecution witnesses. In Chapter 4, I address these factors as they affect the work of judges and prosecutors and inform their perceptions of the legitimacy of the military court system. Here, I focus on how these factors bear upon the legal process and constitute pressures on defense lawyers to plea-bargain.

Judges, prosecutors, and defense lawyers alike generally concur that a confession virtually ensures a conviction. For most judges and prosecutors, a confession is "proof" of guilt, and for defense lawyers, the evidentiary weight of confessions curtails their options. According to Lea Tsemel, a Jewish Israeli defense lawyer, "I would go to the ends of the earth for a client who doesn't confess. But when there is a confession, I have no choice but to make a deal."

Because most Palestinians who are arrested are held incommunicado for the first several weeks, and sometimes throughout the duration of their interrogation, defense lawyers have no opportunity to advise or assist their clients during this period. The first time that many lawyers get to meet with their clients is after the interrogation process ends, so they "inherit" whatever comes out of it. Consequently, lawyers' legal options are circumscribed by events that ensue prior to their actual involvement in the case.

Although a defense lawyer can challenge a confession on the grounds that it was coerced by calling for a special hearing *(zuta),* judges virtually never rule that a confession is inadmissible, and losing a *zuta* can add to the defendant's punishment as reprisal for wasting the court's time. However, in the plea-bargaining process, lawyers can challenge or chip away at the contents or the significance of confessions by bringing in other information or exculpatory evidence to try to persuade a prosecutor to knock out or reduce certain charges. Whether or not a prosecutor finds such evidence persuasive, the time this process takes can itself be a reason to make concessions on charges based on a confession.

Like confessions, secret evidence is extremely difficult to challenge because defense lawyers and defendants are barred from knowing its contents. As Andre Rosenthal, a Jewish Israeli lawyer, explained, "Trying a case based on secret evidence is like working with your hands tied behind your back." Most lawyers concur that a case in which charges are based on secret evidence is virtually impossible to try. But in the plea-bargaining process, defense lawyers can maneuver around secret evidence by arguing that the defendant is not a "real threat" to Israeli security — and can marshal information to support such claims, such as the client's youthfulness, or lack of a previous arrest record, or the many family members who depend on this person's income.

Defendants who are innocent of the charges leveled against them are actually more disadvantaged by secret evidence because they have no way of surmising its nature or contents. For political activists and militants, the charges themselves can be revealing of security sources and secret information. One defendant I interviewed, who was a political leader of the Popular Front for the Liberation of Palestine (PFLP), said that he realized that the secret evidence against him was weak because many of his activities did not appear as charges. He instructed his lawyer to accept the deal the prosecutor was offering without hesitation and felt that he had "won" his case.

Judicial preference for prosecution evidence strengthens the significance of confessions and secret evidence, thereby deterring defense lawyers from trying cases with either or both. However, perceptions about judicial bias have a more general deterring effect on defense lawyers' willingness to take cases to trial. Some of the lawyers I interviewed expressed regret for trying cases because their clients suffered in the end, not only being convicted but facing added punishment for wasting the court's time. Furthermore, because release on bail is rarely granted, defendants are held in pretrial detention until their case is resolved. Attempting to pursue an acquittal through trial in cases involving allegations of minor crimes could keep the person in prison longer than the sentence negotiated in a deal. Thus, a lack of faith in the impartiality of the judiciary contributes to the prevalence of plea bargaining.

The issue of judicial bias is a prominent theme in many defense lawyers' narratives about their own constricted legal options. A Gaza lawyer told me of a case in which he brought eleven defense witnesses to challenge the testimony of one soldier, but the judge still found his client guilty. After the hearing, when the lawyer asked the judge how he could ignore "the facts" like that, the judge responded that he was unwilling to challenge the "dignity" of the soldier because to do otherwise would send the wrong message and might diminish the weight of soldiers' testimony in other cases.

However, judges are not uniformly biased toward the prosecution, and herein, paradoxically, lies another deterrent for defense lawyers: even if a defense lawyer were to win a trial, the prosecutor could submit the case to the military court of appeals for reconsideration. The military appeals court, which was established in 1989, has a record of favoring the prosecution, and this constitutes an added disincentive for defense lawyers to try rather than plea-bargain cases.

The few cases that defense lawyers have taken to trial and won are recounted like battle victories, with tactical intrigues or lucky breaks. One Gaza lawyer described a case in which his client had been charged with stone throwing on the basis of the arresting soldier's affidavit. At the hearing, the lawyer questioned the soldier if his client had thrown the stones with his feet. The soldier responded that he had thrown them with his hands. The lawyer then called his client to show his hands to the judge, revealing that he was physically disabled. The judge dismissed the case and released the client. A Ramallah lawyer told of posing as the defendant and approaching the prosecution's witness, a Jewish settler, at the start of the trial. The settler fell into the lawyer's trap by shouting to the judge that this was the man who had thrown stones at his car. This case, too, was dismissed.

For defense lawyers, if winning is understood as getting a client acquitted through trial, their victory rate is negligible. Sharhabeel al-Za'im said that he had the "best record" of any Gazan lawyer; of the thousand cases he had handled over the years, he had gotten eleven acquittals. Fayez Abu Rahman, who started practicing in the military courts in 1968, said that in fifteen years he had gotten three acquittals. Tsemel, who has represented thousands of clients since she started practicing in the military courts in 1971, said that for every hundred cases she is lucky if she can win one. Most lawyers say that they have never gotten a client acquitted, and many have never brought a single case to trial.

Because trials are so rare, some lawyers, especially Palestinians whose only professional experience is in the military courts, are unfamiliar with procedures. One trial I observed in the Ramallah court unfolded like a comedy of errors. The stakes were relatively minor because the case involved not a crime but a road accident involving a car driven by a Palestinian and an Israeli military vehicle. The soldier who had been driving the jeep testified first. He said that everything happened quickly, and both parties shared responsibility for the accident. The prosecutor was ready to drop his demand that the Palestinian driver be fined. But the Palestinian defense lawyer seized the opportunity of a low-stakes case to give his client his day in court and called the driver, an elderly man, to the stand. Rather than directing his testimony with questions, the lawyer just let his client talk. The man gave such an elaborate description — the speed of the vehicles, weather conditions, potholes and curves in the road, the number of trees — that he began to contradict himself. The judge, a Mizrahi Jew who spoke Arabic, finally interrupted to ask the man whether he had been in a *sayara* (car) or a *tayara* (airplane). In the end, the judge used the conflicts in the Palestinian man's own testimony against him, ruling that he was at fault and would have to pay a fine. The lawyer, realizing he had let his client run the case into the ground, slumped in his seat with embarrassment over a defeat that he had not anticipated. Other lawyers in the courtroom smirked and chided him for bungling his case.

## Time and Money

Time and money bear heavily on the prevalence of plea bargaining. Most defense lawyers (Israelis and Palestinians) are "solo practitioners," which means that they have no partners with whom to share the burdens of their caseload. Under these circumstances, many lawyers find it difficult to devote the time that would be needed to prepare and take a case to trial. Even if a lawyer thinks that a case warrants a trial — that is, believes that the trial could be won because of weaknesses in the prosecution's evidence and/or the innocence of the client — to pursue such a course would compromise the handling of the cases of other clients. Thus, time is a factor that relates to the overall demands of a lawyer's caseload.

The time commitment involved in taking a case to trial can be enormous. The lawyer would have to make repeated prison visits to meet with the client to discuss the evidence and plan defense strategies. Prison visits are extremely onerous and time consuming; lawyers have to make arrangements ahead of time and, assuming permission to meet the client is granted, are often kept waiting for long periods before the person is brought from his or her cell. Many lawyers refuse to try cases because of the obstacles and harassment they face in obtaining access to their clients in prison.

In preparing a case for trial, the lawyer would have to investigate the evidence to challenge prosecution witnesses and to search for witnesses whose testimony would support the defendant's case. Because most prosecution witnesses are Israeli soldiers, it is difficult, if not impossible, for most lawyers to question them prior to a court hearing. And because many Palestinians refuse to testify on behalf of others for fear of retribution by Israeli soldiers and security agents, seeking out Palestinian witnesses can be a waste of time. Even in those rare instances when lawyers do opt to take a case to trial, time remains a factor because trials often drag on for months and sometimes years. Every hearing requires a lawyer to put off other work, and for busy lawyers this becomes a difficult choice about priorities.

Since plea bargaining is generally the faster way to resolve a case, and the sentence (time in prison) can be shortened with a deal, many clients and their families pressure lawyers to deal — and deal quickly. As one West Bank lawyer explained, "The uncertainty is stressful, and many people just want to get things over with as fast as possible. They pressure us to make a deal, even if the prosecutor's offer isn't very good." Palestinian lawyers are relatively more susceptible to such pressures than Israeli lawyers because of their proximity (geographical and social) to the families of their clients.

Money is another important factor and in some ways is related to time. The expenses involved in having a trial are financially prohibitive for many lawyers and clients. Lawyers often say that they are not paid enough to make it worth their while to spend months or even years on a single file. It is not simply that lawyers want full restitution for their work, because many are not adequately compensated, at least in their opinions, even for work they put into making deals.[3] Rather, they do not have the resources to handle the task.

The expenses involved in preparing and taking a case to trial include those related to investigating the evidence, making numerous visits to prisons to consult with the client, and appearing many times in court during the course of the trial. Palestinian lawyers who cannot read Hebrew face an added expense because they must hire someone to translate materials in a file into Arabic.

## Professional Skills and Training

Israeli citizens (Jews and Arabs) and Palestinian residents of the occupied territories who work as defense lawyers in the military courts bring different kinds of professional skills and training. With the exception of a few of the oldest Jewish and Palestinian lawyers who were educated together in British-run law classes during the mandate in Palestine, Israeli and Palestinian lawyers are educated in different law faculties. Most Israeli citizens attained their law degrees in Israeli universities, and most Palestinians attained theirs from universities in the Arab world.[4]

Israelis have the advantage of education about the Israeli legal system when they begin working in the military courts. Although the military courts are separate and different from domestic Israeli courts, there are certain similarities, including rules of procedure and evidence and the adversarial system modeled on the British common-law system. Most Palestinian lawyers have no prior training in Israeli law, and most legal systems in the Arab world are modeled on the continental civil law system. These educational differences mean that Palestinian lawyers have higher hurdles and steeper learning curves for military court work than their Israeli colleagues. However, Israeli lawyers' educational advantages are limited because Israeli law faculties do not offer courses that prepare lawyers specifically to practice in the military court system.

Fluency or proficiency in Hebrew is a relevant skill for working in the military court system. Reading Hebrew facilitates lawyers' ability to understand the laws, confessions, affidavits, and decisions. But all defense lawyers regularly face problems in obtaining copies of new laws (i.e., military orders), and there is limited value in researching past court decisions because no decisions (including those of the military court of appeals) have the power of legally binding precedent. Hebrew fluency is most relevant and advantageous in facilitating interactions with judges and prosecutors. This advantage is heightened by the generally poor quality of court translations. Most Israeli lawyers have "native fluency" in Hebrew. However, over the years many Palestinian lawyers have acquired proficiency in Hebrew, and some are nearly as fluent as their Israeli colleagues.

Hence, while education and language skills differ between Israelis and Palestinians, the differences are neither categorical nor static. Some lawyers certainly lack the professional skills needed to handle the pressures of a trial, so they "need" to plea-bargain. But in this court system, plea bargaining is the norm, not the exception.

## Knowledge Fetishes

Despite commonalities in practices, the issue of professional knowledge has disputed currency among lawyers. Although most lawyers acknowledge the importance of legal education and language, there are sharp disagreements over how relevant they are in a system where the odds are so heavily stacked against the defense. Other types of knowledge are also held up and debated as qualifications to defend Palestinians in the military courts. Differences — real and imagined — are expressed in terms of competing "insider-outsider" discourses and manifest as "knowledge fetishes." For example, during the first *intifada,* when hundreds of Palestinian lawyers with no previous experience moved into the military court system, some Jewish and Arab Israeli lawyers offered to give free seminars on Israeli laws and procedures. But to the extent that such offers, well intentioned though they might have been, were premised on the assumption that Israeli citizens were more knowledgeable, many Palestinians resented the implications. Ali Ghuzlan, head of the Arab Lawyers Committee, explained why there was no interest in taking up these offers for training: "Israeli lawyers who emphasize how important knowing the system is are just promoting themselves. We considered the idea of seminars, but learning Israeli law isn't important because the military courts don't apply the laws. And we don't need help learning the procedures because none exist. Whenever we try to raise the issue of procedure or law, judges say, 'This isn't Israel.'"

Many Israeli lawyers (Jews and Arabs) claim superior "technical knowledge" of the court system because of their legal training in Israeli law schools, fluency in Hebrew, and familiarity with the Israeli state and society. They tend to regard themselves as more "professional" than Palestinian lawyers. These claims have some merit: historically, Israeli lawyers were relatively more confident and capable of working in the military court system than Palestinians and enjoyed reputations as better suited to investigate prosecution evidence and challenge prosecution witnesses. But all lawyers who practice regularly in the military courts plea-bargain the vast majority of their cases, and no one can claim more than a handful of real victories. Even more rarely are those scattered victories unquestionably attributable to superior knowledge of language, laws, or procedures. One feature of this court system is the insurmountable difficulty in obtaining and using technical knowledge, a difficulty that is certainly not limited to Palestinian lawyers.

In this court system, technical knowledge has limited (and dubious) value. For example, during an interview in 1993 with the president of the military court of appeals, he told me that sometime in the last six months the permitted duration of incommunicado detention had been reduced from eighteen to eight days, although he did not know exactly when this new order had gone into effect. The head prosecutor of the West Bank said that he was unaware of any change, as did the president of the Tulkaram court. A reservist judge working in Ramallah said that he had a vague recollection that there had been such a change. Tsemel said that there was such a change but that it applied only to people suspected of minor crimes and was never actually implemented. Tamar Peleg, another Jewish Israeli lawyer, agreed that there had been a change but added that the whole issue should be moot because there was no legally prescribed period of incommunicado detention unless there was a written order. This example illustrates that confusion and misinformation about the law is pervasive, even among military officials.

Palestinian lawyers also tend to lay claim to a form of knowledge that equips them for this work, namely the knowledge that derives from the experience of living under occupation. Such claims also have some merit, in that being Palestinian and living under occupation subjects people to a particular kind of shared experience (overwhelmingly negative) from which Israeli citizens are spared. But this does not in and of itself constitute a legal-professional endowment that can be utilized for the benefit of clients. In fact, acquiring and using knowledge about local events and circumstances and cultivating networks of relations in the occupied territories are not the exclusive prerogatives of Palestinian lawyers. Although Israeli lawyers don't live under occupation, many have become intimately aware of the situation affecting Palestinians in the West Bank and Gaza through their work.

"Occupation politics" plays out among lawyers in another way: some Palestinian lawyers portray themselves as victims in order to excuse or explain their limitations as lawyers — including, in some cases, gross incompetence. Some see no need and make no effort to develop their legal skills, to familiarize themselves with the laws used to charge their clients, or to use tactical strategies in their negotiations with prosecutors, and they justify this by arguing that the entire system is totally biased against all Palestinians, including lawyers. For such lawyers, the "knowledge" they claim is that all is futile. For them, legal practice amounts to commiseration with their clients. But other Palestinian lawyers expend great energy to develop and use their professional skills.

How lawyers debate ideas about knowledge — who knows what, what can be known, how legal knowledge can and should be used — reflects and articulates with the politics of the conflict. The fetishization of knowledge that (re)produces an Israeli-Palestinian dichotomy of competing claims does not hold up well under critical scrutiny, as I have argued. In a different sense, though, debates about knowledge among lawyers manifest as disagreements about the possibilities and limits of law.

In June 1993, I spent a day in Gaza with Tamar Peleg and Raji Sourani. They are both renowned human rights lawyers and are good friends. Peleg had represented Sourani several times when he had been administratively detained by Israel. Our discussion began with the two of them taking turns discussing the problems facing lawyers and defendants in the military court system in that period. But it soon took an unexpected turn: Peleg began arguing that lawyers do a disservice to their clients by not exploiting the legal options available to them. She was referring implicitly to Palestinian lawyers and was frustrated in particular by their willingness to accept or tolerate the denial of access to their clients for prolonged periods.

Sourani chided Peleg for not giving adequate consideration to the fact that Palestinian lawyers, *as Palestinians,* were more vulnerable and disadvantaged than Israeli lawyers and therefore were unable to capitalize on their legal professional rights in the same way. Moreover, he added, the only legal recourse for dealing with the problem of denied access to a client was to petition the HCJ, and only members of the Israel Bar Association could do so. Peleg countered that most Palestinian lawyers didn't exercise their rights because they had not bothered to find out what their options were. Many contributed to their own victimization (and that of their clients) through ignorance or inertia. How, Sourani asked, could lawyers know their options or act differently under circumstances of military occupation? He added, "You talk about our rights as if Israel actually respected our rights, as if they were there for the asking. The basic rights we deserve are part of international law, and what is the Israeli position on that? Forget it! We have lived without any rights since 1967, and no lawyer is going to change that."

Their disagreement was being expressed in comradely terms and stemmed from shared concerns and common experiences of working in the military court system. Indeed, on other occasions I had heard Sourani express criticisms identical to those that Peleg was expressing that day. And Peleg was just as willing, in a different context, to express the very points Sourani was making, and with just as much sincerity. In a published interview, Peleg said, "A lawyer in Gaza knows that he will not be allowed to meet with the prisoner until after his interrogation, even though this is illegal, and he also knows that he has no tools with which to deal with this. . . . The options of the lawyer from Gaza are limited. For him, even to go to Tel Aviv is a problem. The smallest task demands tremendous effort."[5]

One insight I drew from that meeting with Peleg and Sourani was that disputes about legal knowledge are the very substance of struggles over rights. The "naming," "claiming," and "blaming" that narrate and guide these struggles are all about the interpretation, mobilization, and utilization of knowledge to achieve certain kinds of goals. If the goal, as the example that Peleg used, is to gain access to a prisoner in order to protect his or her right to due process, she was correct in asserting that there are legal options available to lawyers and that knowledge about those options is one crucial step to utilizing them. However, Sourani was also correct in asserting that the ability to know and to use the law is informed — and constricted — by politics. In Israel/Palestine, the politics of occupation and the conflict situates, empowers, and privileges people differently, depending on "who they are" in relation to the ruling state.

In the military court system, the "knowledge" that matters most cannot be fetishized because it cannot be monopolized. It includes technical knowledge of the law, acquired through experience (not endowed on the basis of identity) and deployed with reason and calculus. It also includes practical knowledge of the political environment (also not endowed on the basis of identity or social location). And it includes a knowledgeable (i.e., informed) appreciation for the limits of the law and the ways those limits affect people differently, depending on their position within the broader context of Israel/Palestine.

Most military court lawyers have a "common knowledge" that plea bargaining is usually the most viable option if their goal is to minimize the punishment of their clients. How lawyers plea-bargain and how effective they are raises another set of questions about knowledge, namely how they knowingly use tactics and strategies to maneuver for advantage within a politically constricted environment.

## Weapons of the Weak

One lawyer expressed a common sentiment when he described lawyers' role as being limited in most cases to "begging for mercy in a merciless environment." But in the plea-bargaining process, lawyers can pursue various strategies to strengthen their hand in their dealings with prosecutors in order to get charges dropped and sentences lowered.

Many lawyers use time strategically to their advantage. Delaying a case by stalling, "forgetting" to bring the file, and avoiding meetings are means of putting pressure on prosecutors who are under orders to finish cases as quickly as possible. Lawyers refer to this as "hiding the file" and do it on the assumption that after a while the prosecutor will be more willing to make concessions in order to finish. It requires the agreement of the client and is generally done only in cases involving serious charges in which the person would invariably be spending a long time in prison anyway. In addition, lawyers often delay cases during periods of political unrest to avoid having cases conclude when prosecutors are under pressure to seek maximum sentences.

A similar strategy, called "switching the file," entails delaying until a prosecutor is replaced or rotated off the case. The aim is to have the file transferred to a different prosecutor who will be more amenable to making concessions. But prosecutors also use this switching tactic, delaying files to avoid having them go before "easy" judges.

Knowing when and how to "hide" or "switch" files requires a certain level of acumen, which derives foremost from practical experience. Indeed, this type of "insider knowledge" is at least as important as professional skills, if not more so, for being a "good" or "successful" plea bargainer. This type of acumen is contingent on a high level of familiarity with the various personalities who work in the court system as judges and prosecutors. It makes sense for lawyers to hide or switch files only if they are aware of the alternatives.

The size of a lawyer's caseload also can bear upon plea-bargaining strategies. Lawyers with small caseloads do not have the problem of having to balance their attention to any one case against the demands of others, and this can be an advantage: lawyers with few cases can devote more time to each file, wearing down a prosecutor by insisting on multiple meetings to haggle over an offer. But a large caseload also can provide an advantage because there is more to deal with when negotiating with a prosecutor. As Jawad Boulos, an Arab Israeli lawyer with the largest caseload of any lawyer working in the military court system, explained,

"Dealing with cases is like a card game. Whoever has the most cards is in the best position." Some lawyers, particularly those with very large clienteles, have a tendency to "deal across files," meaning that they will give in to a prosecutor's demands on one file in order to gain concessions on another.

Another strategy that some lawyers use to get a better deal is to threaten go to trial or to have a *zuta*. Just calling for a full-blown legal proceeding may be enough to force a busy prosecutor to make concessions in order to avoid the hassles of going through the added process. If this doesn't work, lawyers sometimes start a trial or a *zuta* and then try to renegotiate a better deal while it is underway. Even lawyers who intend to resolve a case through a plea bargain sometimes call hearings with witnesses to challenge specific elements of the charge sheet.

In September 2002, I went with Tsemel to the Beit El court, where she had a hearing in a case that had been dragging on for years. Two of her clients, along with two other Palestinians, had been arrested in 1998 for stoning an Israeli car near the West Bank village of Betunya. The driver of the car suffered a head injury and went into a coma. Four years later (in 2002) he died. Another lawyer, who represented the other two Palestinians, had taken their cases to trial because he refused to accept the prosecutor's offer of nineteen years in prison. The clients were found guilty of murder, and the judges had issued a sentence of eleven years, but the prosecutor was now intending to appeal that decision to get the nineteen years he was seeking. Tsemel said that her defense strategies were motivated by the actions of the prosecutor. She refused to plea-bargain because he was insisting on what she regarded as an excessively high sentence, and she also refused to let the case end because he refused to agree not to appeal the judges' decision, whatever it might be.

That day in the Beit El court, Tsemel spent hours questioning the doctor who had treated the man before he died. She was seeking to put the dead man's full medical record into evidence in order to undermine the charge of "murder" and replace it with "injury" as originally caused by the stoning. At the end of the hearing, she gave a long list of additional witnesses she intended to call for future hearings. As she explained, her aim was not to "win" the case but rather to force the prosecutor back to the table with a better offer or to agree not to appeal the judges' decision if she agreed to end the case. If neither option worked, she said, she would let the case drag on until another prosecutor took it over.

Even the most common practices employed by defense lawyers in this system, which effectively amount to begging for mercy, illustrate the ways in which information can be used tactically. Lawyers use information about their clients — their age, past records, personal circumstances — to argue for leniency. While begging for mercy can be a sign of a lawyer's incompetence, it also can be pursued as a shrewd and calculated strategy by playing into Israeli narratives and stereotypes about Palestinians. For example, playing on the idea that Israeli rule has been good — or at least not that bad — for most Palestinians, a lawyer may argue that this particular client was "led astray" by troublemakers or coerced to engage in illegal activities. In this way, the lawyer uses to his or her advantage judges' and prosecutors' ideas about Palestinian society as fragmented and individual Palestinians as cooptable. Thus, "good" plea bargainers are able to play up the "innocence" of their clients, representing them as naifs for whom minimal punishment should satisfy the prosecutor. In plea bargaining, the mark of a successful lawyer is the ability and willingness to do or say whatever it takes to get charges dropped and sentences lowered, whether this entails wearing down prosecutors, waiting for more lenient judges, or begging for mercy.

## The Atomization of Legal Practice

Plea bargaining "atomizes" the legal process because each lawyer negotiates separately and individually with the prosecutor. Plea bargaining both reflects and reinforces the fragmentation of lawyers as a corporate group and impedes the mounting of a collective stance to press for better treatment of their clients or themselves. Although many defense lawyers choose to work in the military courts because they are motivated by a sense of "cause" (see Chapter 6), plea bargaining, which is inherently concessionary, undermines possibilities of challenging the legality of the laws and procedures, let alone the occupation, within the legal process.

Since 1967, very little *political* attention has been devoted to the legal processes that occur within the military court system. Neither Palestinian political factions nor antioccupation groups within Israel have made the legal process part of their agendas or articulated resistance strategies for the military court system, aside from statements of solidarity and support for political prisoners. During the first *intifada,* one exception was *bayan* (directive) no. 31, which called for an end to plea bargaining. But lawyers rejected this unilateral decree because, among other reasons, it was not accompanied by a demand that prisoners refuse to confess.

The lack of political direction has left legal strategies to the discretion of lawyers. Israeli and Palestinian lawyers periodically have mobilized collectively in an ad hoc fashion to go on strike to protest and contest conditions in the military courts that adversely affect them and/or their clients. Many lawyers I interviewed claim that they would like to politicize their legal practice by instituting a collective ban on plea bargaining. However, as long as any lawyer is willing to plea-bargain to get lower sentences for his or her clients, there is pressure on all lawyers to do the same or risk losing clients.

The political consequences of a collective ban on plea bargaining would be dramatic. If lawyers mounted a work-stop strike, it would bring the court system to a halt, since people charged with serious crimes cannot be convicted without legal counsel. Alternatively, if lawyers took a collective decision to bring every case to trial, the system would be crippled by the demands of trying hundreds or thousands of cases. This not only would slow down the work of the courts through bureaucratic backlogging but would force countless soldiers to spend days in court testifying and would disrupt the work of interrogators and other security agents. Given this potential, the question must be asked why such a collective stance has never been adopted. In raising this issue with lawyers, I heard a variety of explanations. One commonly cited reason is that lawyers cannot mount or sustain any collective stance because they lack a unified institutional base to enforce such a decision. Another commonly cited reason is more individualistic: many lawyers say that *they* favor such a strategy, but other lawyers — for reasons such as selfishness, incompetence, or lack of commitment — sabotage collective strategies.

A third commonly cited reason is that prisoners lack the political commitment to sustain any ban on plea bargaining. If any prisoner insists on dealing to get a lower sentence, it makes it all the more difficult — unappealing and "unfair" — for others to face the prospect of harsher punishment. But on this count, lawyers acknowledge that it is prisoners who would pay the real price for a collective decision to refuse to deal and that the human costs would be great not only for prisoners but for their families as well.

For many defendants, their only interest is getting out of prison in the shortest possible time, and therefore they insist that their lawyers cut deals; they are uninterested in sacrificing themselves to put pressure on the military court system. But some of the defendants I interviewed offered a different explanation; they insist on dealing for *political* reasons. For them, the concession entailed in a plea bargain is categorically different from conceding to have a trial. With a plea bargain, they concede that the laws and the system are stacked against them and take what they can get, whereas going to trial would concede the idea that the system was capable of dispensing "justice," and they refuse on the grounds that they would be collaborating in a legal farce. For them, plea bargaining is an appropriately "dirty" reflection of the military court system and the military occupation.

However, during the second *intifada*, some Palestinian prisoners adopted a stance of refusing to "participate" in the military court system. The first to articulate this strategy was Marwan Barghouti, a popular and prominent West Bank leader of Fatah and an elected member of the Palestinian Legislative Council, who was arrested in April 2002 during the Israeli military's "Operation Defensive Shield." Because of his political stature as the highest-ranking Palestinian Authority (PA) official to be captured and arrested, the Israeli authorities decided to prosecute Barghouti in an Israeli civilian court in Tel Aviv rather than a military court in the occupied territories as a means of putting the PA on trial for terrorism.[6] Barghouti refused to allow his lawyers to plea-bargain or even to represent him in court, other than the initial (unsuccessful) challenge to Israel's jurisdiction to try him. Barghouti's stance inspired some other Palestinian prisoners to follow his example by refusing to appear in court or to authorize lawyers to make deals on their behalf.[7] According to lawyers who represent some of these "refusing" prisoners, the logic of this strategy combines a repudiation of the Israeli military court system with an assumption that the fate of prisoners will be resolved politically in future Israeli-Palestinian negotiations.

Legally and politically, the prevalence of plea bargaining in the military court system is a rational response to the carceral nature of military occupation and the constricted options available to Palestinian defendants and their lawyers. But plea bargaining also reveals that people can and do maneuver for advantages, even under such conditions. In the Conclusion, I address the second *intifada* and insights that can be gleaned about the power and the limits of law in the context of this enduring conflict.

# Conclusion

## *The Second* Intifada *and the Global "War on Terror"*

---

*No nation at war with another shall permit such acts of war as shall make mutual trust impossible during some future time of peace.*
Immanuel Kant, *Perpetual Peace and Other Essays*[1]

The second *intifada,* which began on September 29, 2000, has been the most intensely deadly and destructive period in Israel/Palestine since 1967.[2] It terminated the interim, shattering any prospects that diplomacy might have held for an end to Israel's occupation of the West Bank and Gaza and a two-state solution.[3] Palestinian towns, villages, and refugee camps have been laid waste, and Israeli buses and cafes have been blown apart in paroxysms of violence that Richard Falk aptly termed a "death dance."[4] The dance metaphor is so fitting because it cuts through the nationalist polemics and polarizations that have been generated by all the suffering, loss, and fear to capture the fact that the conflict in Israel/Palestine grips everyone, albeit in markedly different ways. Whether a political resolution is possible in the future remains an open question. But the answer has been complicated inexorably by the violence and destruction of the last years.

The history and analysis of the Israeli military court system presented in this book provide a basis for understanding the effects of the conflict on the lives and relations among people in Israel/Palestine. The roots of the second *intifada* are entwined in the military court system, which has been a central setting for the conflict. However, the second *intifada* does mark a change in Israel's occupation of the West Bank and Gaza, notably the expansion from a predominantly "law enforcement model" to a "war model."

During the second *intifada,* the Israeli military court system has continued to function in its conventional capacity as an institutional setting where the Israeli military enforces military and emergency laws by arresting, interrogating, prosecuting, convicting, and imprisoning Palestinians. But to some extent the system has been marginalized as extrajudicial executions (i.e., assassinations) have come to vie with prosecutions as means of punishment and deterrence for suicide bombings by Palestinian militants.[5] Both suicide bombings and assassinations have a history that predates the second *intifada,*[6] and both emanate from rights claims — dystopian in the extreme — to kill to survive. The increased use of both and the cyclical relationship between them attest to political failures to accommodate the interests that people would kill for. As Ghassan Hage writes, "It is only because of the failure of the political that such . . . violence emerges as a matter-of-fact possibility."[7]

Suicide bombings and assassinations can by no means be considered equivalent except in their effects (death).[8] Nor are these the only forms of violence that characterize the death dance. But together they illustrate with brutal clarity the human costs of unbearable injustice and intractable conflict. The violence of the second *intifada* has been compounded and political recourse complicated by the fateful overlap of the terrorist attacks of September 11, 2001, and the U.S. government's launching of a global "war on terror." Consequently, Israel/Palestine has the ignominious distinction of providing a testing ground to debate the interpretations, applicability, and enforceability of international humanitarian law (i.e., the laws of war) in the twenty-first century.[9]

Contrary to the claim that in war law is silent (*inter armes silent leges*), in Israel/Palestine, law speaks volumes, in a cacophony. In this conclusion, I continue my inquiry into law and conflict during the second *intifada,* highlighting connections between events and developments in this context and the U.S. government's global "war on terror."

## Law Enforcement and War

The continuing operation of the Israeli military court system during the interim (1994–2000) and its enduring jurisdiction over the entire West Bank and Gaza are clear evidence of the continuation of the occupation.

The Palestinian Authority (PA), established by negotiated agreement in 1994, created its own security courts with jurisdiction over Palestinians in Areas A and B. Politically, this overlapping jurisdiction manifested itself as a proxy role for the PA to control Palestinians and punish those who threatened Israel. While Israel had relinquished administrative control over some aspects of Palestinians' lives, the state retained effective control over Israel/Palestine in its entirety because of its continuing capacity to regulate the movement of people and goods and access to resources, and because the PA was a subordinate rather than an independent entity.

The Israeli military had been preparing for the possibility of a second *intifada* since the mid-1990s as relations between the Israeli state and the PA deteriorated and Palestinian frustration and unrest increased. These preparations were informed by several factors, including a retrospective conclusion that it had been a strategic mistake not to take more decisive military action in 1987 when the first *intifada* started. Related to this was a perception that the duration of the first *intifada* had forced the Israeli government to make concessions to Palestinians and that these concessions, namely the redeployment from Palestinian population centers, had weakened the military's ability to provide for Israeli security, creating a reliance on the PA that was ineffective in preventing suicide bombings and other types of attacks on Israelis. According to Yoram Peri, Israel Defense Forces (IDF) strategists realized they "could not win . . . low-intensity conflicts. [The IDF] was restrained by political pressures and its scope of action was restricted by the international media."[10] What this meant to Israeli strategists was that if there was a second *intifada,* it would have to be treated — and fought — as a "war."

The triggering event was the visit on September 28, 2000, by Ariel Sharon, then Israel's minister of defense, to the complex in the Old City of Jerusalem where al-Aqsa mosque is located, accompanied by one thousand armed guards. Sharon's visit was an openly declared political gesture to assert Jewish Israeli access and sovereignty over this site.[11] The following day, thousands of Palestinians took to the streets in protest, and four were killed in clashes with soldiers and police.

While the Israeli military had assumed, according to Peri, that a "real show of strength immediately following an outbreak of violence would make the rioters understand the heavy price they would have to pay . . . and that would cool their ardor at once," to the contrary these "hard blows . . . led to an escalation of violence as the Palestinians became increasingly angry at the strikes directed against them."[12] The immediate militarization of the second *intifada,* including Israel's use of tanks and helicopter gunships against demonstrating Palestinian crowds, was rationalized by officials on the grounds that the Israeli military was "out" of Palestinian areas, so that policing and riot control tactics were not an option, and that there were now about forty thousand Palestinian police and security forces with small arms, some of whom joined in demonstrations.

Hence, although "Palestine" was by no stretch of the imagination an independent state, Israeli officials claimed that the belligerent occupation had ended with the redeployment of forces, that Palestinians now constituted a foreign "armed adversary," and that they had started a "war."[13] Initially, the Israeli military was fighting Palestinian demonstrators who were confined in enclaves. Most clashes in the first few months were concentrated at military checkpoints, and most Palestinian fatalities were from Israeli sharpshooters firing on demonstrating crowds.[14]

In retaliation for military targeting of Palestinian civilians, in November 2000 Palestinian militant organizations (*tanzim*) launched a campaign to attack Israeli bases and settlements in the occupied territories. This reciprocal militarization, combined with the *tanzim*'s affiliation with Fatah (the dominant faction in the PA), transformed the second *intifada* into "asymmetrical warfare."[15] For Palestinians, the rising civilian death toll and the destruction of properties and political infrastructure popularized support for "armed struggle."

On November 9, 2000, Fatah leader Hussein Abayat was assassinated by fire from a helicopter, along with two women who were walking nearby. The killing initiated a new Israeli policy of *publicly* acknowledging assassinations — officially termed "targeted killings," "liquidations," and "preemptive strikes." This policy was premised on a set of interconnected justifications: (1) that Palestinians were to blame for the hostilities, which constituted a war of terror against Israel; (2) that the laws of war permit states to kill their enemies; (3) that targeted individuals were "ticking bombs" who had to be killed because they could not be arrested by Israeli soldiers; and (4) that killing terrorists by means of assassination was a lawful form of national defense.[16] "Bystander" deaths were termed, in accordance with the discourse of war, "collateral damage."[17]

On January 1, 2001, Hamas and Islamic Jihad launched a suicide bombing campaign inside Israel. Given that Palestinians had no military weaponry with which to combat Israeli planes, helicopters, and tanks, some extolled suicide bombs as an "equalizer" in this war.[18] Other Palestinians publicly condemned suicide bombings as deplorable and illegal, and as inciting military violence against them, but they also resented and condemned the idea that suicide bombs were categorically worse than — and unconnected to — the violence to which they were collectively subjected by the Israeli military. Among Israelis, the carnage, vulnerability, and anger wrought by suicide bombings contributed to public support for military strikes and assassinations, even though, as numerous opinion polls revealed, there was little faith that such measures would enhance security or stop the violence.

In 2001, Ariel Sharon was elected prime minister of Israel. Neither he nor U.S. President George W. Bush felt bound by the political commitments of his predecessor (Ehud Barak, Bill Clinton), effectively cementing the demise of the Oslo Accords. By March 2001, many Palestinian areas were under military siege, *tanzim* were escalating attacks in the occupied territories, Islamists were escalating suicide bombings inside the Green Line, and the Israeli military was escalating its campaign to systematically destroy the infrastructure of the PA.

On September 11, 2001, the multiple, synchronized suicide bombing attacks on the United States further intensified and complicated the war in Israel/Palestine.[19] Some Israeli and American officials perceived that they were joined in a common "war on terror," and the Sharon government sought to portray the PA as "Israel's al-Qaeda." In the wake of 9/11, Alex Fishman, a military commentator for *Yediot Aharonot,* wrote: "The [Israeli] government's understanding is that the Western world will be more open to buy the elimination of the Palestinian Authority when it is packaged with current images and comparisons [to the U.S. war in Afghanistan]. . . . Sharon hopes that the elimination of the Taliban and the elimination of the [PA] will be conceived as two parallel goals."[20]

However, the conflation of the second *intifada* and the United States' war on terror was unpersuasive because the PA, unlike al-Qaeda, has international status as a national representative with legitimate aspirations to Palestinian statehood, and because Israel remains the de facto sovereign over the West Bank and Gaza. Moreover, the cycle of retaliatory violence in Israel/Palestine contributed to regional instability, stimulating international concern and criticism about the spiraling death toll. This weighed on the Bush administration, which sought to build support for its war in Afghanistan and to pursue its geostrategic interests in the Middle East. U.S. officials issued confused signals, combining political support for Israel's characterization of the *intifada* as a terror war and its use of military force (since the Bush administration also had opted for a military response to 9/11) with periodic condemnations of Israeli "excesses" and calls for some kind of renewed political process.[21]

The Israeli assassinations of Fatah political leader Thabet Thabet on

December 31, 2001, and *tanzim* leader Ra'ed Karmi on January 14, 2002, were retaliated against with a suicide bombing on January 27, 2002, by the Al-Aqsa Martyrs Brigade, a clandestine group associated with Fatah. This was the first suicide bombing by a non-Islamist organization, thus upping the retaliatory ante with highly destructive consequences on both sides of the Green Line.

At the end of March 2002, Israel launched Operation Defensive Shield, a full-scale military invasion of the West Bank triggered by a horrific Hamas suicide bombing in Netanya on Passover in which thirty people were killed and 140 injured. Military operations in Jenin in April 2002 initially aimed to capture or kill militants deemed responsible for the Netanya and other suicide bombings, but the town and neighboring refugee camp became a battle zone after four Israeli soldiers were killed.

During the battle, reports coming from Jenin relayed that Israeli soldiers were using Palestinian civilians as "human shields" as they moved from house to house and that armor-plated bulldozers were destroying hundreds of homes — some with people still inside.[22] On April 10, 2002, in the midst of the battle, the Association for Civil Rights in Israel (ACRI) published a document in *Ha'aretz* under the headline "Operation to Liquidate Human Rights." It read: "According to the information that has reached us, for the past week the Jenin refugee camp has been subjected to indiscriminate mass house demolitions. . . . Dozens of bodies are piled in houses and in the streets. The army is not permitting the evacuation of wounded — they are bleeding to death. With deep pain [ACRI] warns that war crimes are being perpetrated by the forces of the IDF in the territories."[23]

The battle of Jenin riveted international media attention and generated much criticism,[24] including criticism by the U.S. government.[25] After it ended, on April 19, 2002, the UN Security Council voted unanimously to send a fact-finding mission and assembled a delegation to investigate what had happened in Jenin (i.e., how many people had died and how). This mission inevitably would have raised questions of contemporary global significance about legal options and constraints on the use of force by armies and militants. However, Israel refused to accept the UN delegation, and on May 1, under threat of a U.S. veto, it was disbanded.[26] In exchange, Israel eased the siege of PA leader Yasir Arafat, who had been pinned down for months in his Ramallah headquarters (formerly the site of the Israeli military court). A new joint Israeli-U.S. stance insisted on a total reform of the PA, including the ouster of Arafat as head. Israeli officials began publicly debating the possibility and efficacy of deporting or assassinating him.

In May, there was another spate of suicide bombings, claimed as retaliation for Operation Defensive Shield, and in June Israel mounted a second massive military assault in the West Bank, named Operation Determined Path. Together these events turned the entire country into a front and every person into a potential target; the overwhelming majority of casualties from military assaults and suicide bombings were civilians. In this regard, the second *intifada* was not unique but illustrative of the humanitarian crises characteristic of modern war.[27]

By July 2002, the Israeli military was present in every Palestinian town in the West Bank, and the ratio of arrests to assassinations became between ten and fifteen to one.[28] That month, the military began building a massive wall in the West Bank, starting in the Jenin area, to enclose Palestinians and fortify their separation from Israelis (and one another).[29] Since then, the rising wall has been a site of demonstrations, clashes, and deaths, and the subject of litigation and international criticism.

The Israeli government's stated aim in building a fortified physical barrier in the West Bank was to prevent suicide bombers from entering Israel.[30] But its geographical course, which cuts deeply into the West Bank and encircles Palestinian areas,[31] adds to checkpoints, curfews, and permit-regulated closures to collectively incarcerate Palestinians.[32] Critics have condemned it as a new dimension of an apartheid-like segregation relegating Palestinians to ghettos policed from the outside and periodically invaded by the Israeli military.

Israeli strategies in the West Bank and Gaza since September 2000 have combined war and law enforcement tactics: killing the enemy; negating the jurisdiction of the PA; arresting thousands of Palestinians, including leaders who were "wanted" but not assassinated; and intensifying the carceral infrastructure of the occupation. Although the PA's capacity (not to mention willingness) to fulfill the proxy role has been largely eviscerated, it continues to be held accountable by Israeli officials for failing to stop suicide bombings and to arrest militants.

This paradoxical failure is most clearly symbolized by Arafat, trapped in his Ramallah headquarters, who is blamed (and threatened) by Israel for sustaining the war. According to David Rieff,

Since late September 2002, when the Israel Defense Forces systematically destroyed most of the complex, Arafat has been unable to leave the [compound]. He has stayed holed up there knowing that were he to venture out, even just to Ramallah's main mosque, the Israeli military would probably seize and expel him . . . and finish the destruction that Prime Minister Ariel Sharon of Israel is generally believed to have halted only under intense pressure from the Bush administration. For most ordinary Palestinians, Arafat's imprisonment in the [compound] mirrors what they view as their own: since the start of the second *intifada* in 2000, and in particular since 2002, the Israeli occupation has made most Palestinians prisoners in their own towns and villages on the West Bank and in the Gaza Strip.[33]

These events and developments have significantly altered the nature of rule in the West Bank and Gaza: until 1994, the Israeli military directly governed Palestinians residing in these areas. During the interim, government was hierarchically divided between the military, which retained overarching powers and authority, and the PA, which exercised limited "self-government" over Palestinians. In the current period, while the Israeli military has reasserted its capacity to control Palestinians through the combination of military force, law enforcement, and geographic segregation, it neither claims the responsibilities of a belligerent occupant over foreign civilians nor provides for their needs, claiming those are the responsibility of the PA. But the PA's incapacitation has left Palestinians bereft of resources, and this has contributed to a humanitarian crisis (including mass unemployment, impoverishment, and malnutrition) that exacerbates social suffering and stokes the conflict.[34]

## International Law in an Age of Global War

The conflict in Israel/Palestine connects to and influences the U.S. government's "war on terror."[35] Although these conflicts differ substantially, they raise some common concerns about the utility and applicability of international humanitarian law to conflicts and asymmetrical warfare pitting stateless peoples and nonstate organizations against states with powerful militaries, with fighting targeting and amidst civilian populations.[36] While war and conflict might be cast in popular or political terms as "lawless," the use of violence under any circumstances is always a legal matter. Therefore, these conflicts are waged, in part, on the terrain of international humanitarian law.

Israel provides a salient model for the U.S. "war on terror" because it has been in a continuous state of war since 1948, has engaged in military preemption on numerous occasions, and has a long track record of military administration and security operations in occupied territories. Israel also serves as a model for its elaborate system of emergency laws and legal rationales to legitimize the engagement and handling of enemies in battle and in custody. And having faced decades of sustained international criticism for violations of international law, Israeli officials have expended great effort to articulate legal rebuttals. U.S. officials have looked to the Israeli example for military and other security tactics and for rationales to justify those tactics as legal.

What distinguishes the Israeli model from many other states embroiled in protracted conflict is that Israel does not repudiate or ignore international law; rather, it "domesticates" international law by forging interpretations of its rights and duties in the West Bank and Gaza to accommodate state practices and domestic agendas. For example, claiming that there was no belligerent occupation in September 2000 served to justify the use of military force as a necessary and legal option to contend with Palestinian demonstrations. Likewise, the definitions and categories of conflict in international law have been selectively interpreted to characterize the second *intifada* as a "war of terror" in order to deny that Palestinians had any right to use force to end the occupation or even to defend themselves.

Since 9/11, the U.S. government has pursued a similar strategy to domesticate international law by advancing legal reasoning to authorize and justify preemptive war in Iraq, to promulgate emergency legislation, and to reject or subjectively apply the Geneva Conventions to prisoners captured in the "war on terror."

But such domestication of international law, when the interpretations contradict international opinion and the outcomes contravene established legal principles, bodes ill for global peace and security.[37] Kenneth Anderson writes: "Even while there is agreement on the need for fundamental rules governing the conduct of war, there is profound disagreement over who has the authority to declare, interpret, and enforce those rules, as well as who — and what developments in the so-called art of war — will shape them now and into the future."[38] He offers an answer to who *should* "own" the laws of war that comports with the domesticating impulses of U.S. (and Israeli) officials:

For the past 20 years, the center of gravity in establishing, interpreting and shaping the law of war has gradually shifted away from the military establishments of leading states and their "state practice." It has even shifted away from the International [Committee of] the Red Cross (invested by the Geneva Conventions with special authority) and toward more activist and publicly aggressive N.G.O.'s [nongovernmental organizations]. . . . These N.G.O.'s are indispensable in advancing the cause of humanitarianism in war. But the pendulum shift toward them has gone further than is useful and the ownership of the laws of war needs to give much greater weight to the state practices of leading countries. . . . N.G.O.'s are also wedded far too much to a procedural preference for the international over the national.

But that agenda increasingly amounts to internationalism for its own sake, and its specific purpose is to constrain American sovereignty.[39]

Many states engage in practices that deviate from and thus challenge prevailing interpretations of international law. However, when powerful and dominant states like the U.S. and Israel do so, this cannot simply be written off or criticized as "violations" because it produces an alternative legality. Contrary to the claims of both critics who take prevailing interpretations of international law as their point of reference and political realists who disparage the relevance of law, neither state ignores the law. Rather, both use laws and legal discourse to authorize and defend the legality of policies such as military preemption, indefinite incommunicado detention, abusive interrogation tactics, assassinations, and targeting of areas dense with civilians. However, this domestication of international law, especially by a "superpower," poses the risk of eroding the normative foundations of international law that have built up since the end of World War II. Indeed, it is the global strength and stature of the United States as the lone superpower that make the models drawn from Israel/Palestine globally significant. Likewise, American policies and practices bolster Israel's.

For over a decade Israel incarcerated people captured in Lebanon, neither trying them nor permitting them access to lawyers. Some Israeli lawyers challenged this indefinite extralegal detention in the High Court of Justice (HCJ), which ruled in April 2000 that the state could not hold people "hostage," thus rejecting the state's stance that they were "bargaining chips" for the return of Israeli soldiers missing in Lebanon. Subsequently, thirteen were released. But the state refused to release Sheikh 'Abd al-Karim 'Obeid, captured in 1989, and Mustafa al-Dirani, captured in 1994. In June 2000, the government submitted a new draft law in the Knesset to legally authorize indefinite detention. At the time (i.e., prior to the start of the second *intifada*), the draft law came under intense domestic and international criticism and was withdrawn. However, after 9/11 and the passage in the United States of an "unlawful combatants" law permitting indefinite incommunicado detention and denying prisoner-of-war status to captives from the war on terror, in March 2002 the Israeli Knesset passed a new "illegal combatants law" that allows for indefinite detention of anyone suspected of engaging in "hostile activity against Israel, directly or indirectly" or belonging "to a force engaged in hostile activity against the State of Israel."[40]

Both governments have used the concept of "unlawful combatants" to encode the idea (and derivative state practices) that in "war(s) on terror," international humanitarian law does not apply to the treatment of their enemies.[41] Thus detainees at the American prison camp at Guantanamo Bay,[42] and some detainees in Israeli prisons and detention centers[43] have been excluded from the recognized categories of international law (i.e., "civilian" or "combatant"), and their status as such has been authorized by domestic law.

Another strategic convergence can be found in the practices of inter-rogation and torture. In a December 2002 investigative report by two *Washington Post* journalists, U.S. security agents working in Afghanistan acknowledged the use of "stress and duress" tactics in the interrogation of people taken into custody.[44] The tactics they described bear a striking resemblance to the tactics Israel has used and characterized as "moderate physical pressure" (various forms of physical abuse and sleep deprivation). Responding to criticisms of these revelations, U.S. officials affirmed that torture was illegal while denying that the interrogation tactics used by their agents constituted "torture."

In April 2004, photos of torture of Iraqi detainees by U.S. soldiers working in interrogation wings run by military intelligence and private security contractors at Abu Ghraib prison outside of Baghdad were first revealed to the public on CBS *60 Minutes II,* and immediately became headline news around the world. Investigative journalist Seymour Hersh, writing in the *New Yorker,* published details about a report from a U.S. army general, Antonio Taguba, who investigated prisons and interrogation centers in Iraq between October and December 2003, and found "sadis-tic, wanton and criminal abuses" that were systematic and rampant.[45] The crisis caused by these revelations for the Bush administration was com-pounded by other reports by military investigators and the International Committee of the Red Cross, and leaked "torture memos" by government lawyers, which led to Congressional hearings to try to determine how far up the chain of command responsibility for the debacle went.

Another state practice that impicates the U.S. in torture is the "ren-dering" of some detainees for interrogation to countries with well-documented records of torture (including Syria, Jordan, Morocco, and Egypt). The purpose of this policy of rendering is to derive the intelli-gence "benefits" without involving U.S. interrogators in more brutal tac-tics. Christopher H. Pyle writes, "Our intelligence agencies have a name for this torture-by-proxy. They call it 'extraordinary rendition.' As one intelligence official explained: 'We don't kick the s—— out of them. We send them to other countries so they can kick the s—— out of them.' This secret program for torturing suspects has been authorized, if that is the right word for it, by a secret presidential finding. Where the president gets the authority to have anyone tortured has never been explained."[46]

In 2002, the U.S. government adopted the tactic of assassination, which had been prohibited by executive orders since 1977.[47] U.S. officials studied Israeli legal arguments to justify the assassination of 'Ali Qaed Sinan al-Harithi and five others (including a U.S. citizen) in Yemen by a pilotless drone.[48] The U.S. government proclaimed that because it was at war with al-Qaeda (of which al-Harithi was allegedly a member) and because arrest was impossible, assassination was a legitimate tactic, even against a person located in a country not at war with the United States (i.e., Yemen).

The U.S. military has received briefings and training from members of the Israeli military for fighting and quelling resistance in urban areas. In Afghanistan and Iraq, the U.S. military has utilized practices long used by Israeli forces in occupied territories, including house demolitions and collective confinement, that have been roundly condemned as violations of the Geneva Conventions. These practices have been defended by U.S. officials as legitimate and necessary to deter resistance and punish attacks against U.S.-led coalition forces occupying the two countries.[49]

The U.S. government established a new class of military commissions (i.e., tribunals) to prosecute some detainees held in Guantanamo. The Bush administration's military order of November 13, 2001, establishing these commissions[50] instituted many features characteristic of the Israeli military court system in the West Bank and Gaza, including protracted incommunicado detention, extreme difficulties for lawyers to meet with defendants, no presumption of innocence, and use of "secret evidence" unavailable to defendants or their lawyers. Although the order was modified in 2002 in response to criticism,[51] the U.S. military commissions appear likely to impose even greater barriers to due process of law than the Israeli military court system, such as a gag on defense lawyers that prohibits them from discussing issues or evidence associated with cases.

Of preeminent importance — and great dispute — at this juncture is whether states (especially powerful states) can be governed by international law in the conduct of war and the treatment of enemies.[52] But law is a double-edged sword, and it is also important to acknowledge that legalistic resistance has been mounted to contest the violations of international law. In this way, too, Israel/Palestine is a model for law and conflict on a global scale.

Some Israeli and Palestinian lawyers (including veterans of the military court system) have sought to challenge the legality of military practice by bringing cases to the Israeli HCJ. Such litigation during the second *intifada* is not new, except in the details of petitions and circumstances to which they pertain. Rather, it is a continuation of a long history of legal activism in Israel/Palestine in which the HCJ is both a setting for and a party to the conflict.

Lawyers have brought petitions challenging the Israeli military's use of Palestinians as "human shields" during military operations,[53] torture,[54] arbitrary arrests and inhumane conditions of detention,[55] and the policy of assassination.[56] The objective of petitioners is to elicit the HCJ's intervention to order the state to stop engaging in practices that are illegal under international and/or domestic law. But petitioning is not premised on idealism. Rather, it constitutes a kind of legal activism to illuminate and publicize problems and violations. The submission of petitions to the HCJ often is preceded or followed by press conferences, and the outcomes are reported by the media and human rights organizations. Hence, one motivation for litigation is the "educative" effects it might have among various publics and constituencies, both in Israel/Palestine and beyond.

Litigating the tactics and costs of war in court may not change warmaking, but it is a means of drawing public attention to human suffering and unlawful policies. Israeli officials' responses to petitions and petitioners' responses to those serve to articulate and clarify arguments about the uses of force. Litigation impels the court to render judgments that a state claiming commitment to the rule of law cannot ignore. Even dismissals of petitions on grounds that they raise issues that are nonjusticiable or rulings that go against the petitioners are important to clarify and to wage struggles over the uses and interpretations of law.

Courts may not be — indeed, rarely are — the source of solutions to problems that sustain conflicts. But courts are important settings where those conflicts play out on the terrain of law. The rights of a state and its citizens, the rights of an occupied population, the right to use violence and the limits of that right, the right to be "free" and "secure" — struggles over these rights *are* the conflict in Israel/Palestine, and all of these rights are, in hotly contested ways, *legal matters.*

· · ·

Law is a constitutive force of life everywhere, including contexts embroiled in conflict. In Israel/Palestine, the many "layers" of law have affected the course of the conflict, including the military and emergency laws made and used by the Israeli state to govern and punish Palestinians residing in the West Bank and Gaza and the various bodies of international law that have been deployed and referenced by state officials, lawyers, human rights activists, and others to legitimize, contest, and redress violence. In Israel/Palestine, there is no consensus on "what is legal," but this does not diminish the relevance of law. On the contrary, the contradictions and contestations over law are an inextricable part of the conflict itself.

Any effort to understand and assess the relationship between law and conflict necessarily engages questions about "law in action." This includes not only the ways in which laws are made, used, enforced, and violated but also the ways in which ideas and discourses of legality and justice inform people's consciousness and activities in the pursuit of their rights, however those rights are construed. The complexities and contradictions of laws in Israel/Palestine generate ideas about rights that are contradictory and, some might argue, irreconcilable. For this reason, I have sought to illustrate and explain the conflict as, ultimately, a struggle over rights. There is no law or legal mechanism that will resolve this conflict, nor is there much basis for hope that a consensus on legality and justice will emerge in the near future to ameliorate the strife, suffering, and violence in Israel/Palestine. Law will not solve the conflict, but it matters to understand the conflict as a force and feature of life.

I promised at the start of this book that I would not provide a "solution" to the conflict. What I have striven to provide instead is a sociological analysis of the role and limits of law in the context of this conflict, the ways in which law in its complexity has affected the lives of people, and the impacts of these effects on changes and developments in the conflict. The advantage or benefit of sustained and critical inquiry of the relationship between law and conflict is that it illuminates avenues of struggle for rights, elicits concern beyond those directly affected by this conflict, and hopefully contributes to an understanding about why this particular conflict is so difficult to resolve that does justice to the humanity of those whose lives are directly affected by it.

# Epilogue

On September 19, 2002, I spent my last day in an Israeli military court. I went with Andre Rosenthal, a leftist Jewish Israeli lawyer, to Erez, the court located in a base at the edge of the Gaza Strip. On the drive from Jerusalem to Gaza, we talked about changes in the military court system over the last few years, the political situation in Israel/Palestine, and the trials and tribulation of defense lawyering. Rosenthal wondered aloud whether all the work he and others have done in the military courts made any difference in the larger scheme of things and whether the situation would ever improve.

Rosenthal recounted what it had been like — and what *he* had been like — back in the 1980s when he had started working in the military courts; he had been so energized and idealistic. Now, he said, he was tired and cynical. Several days earlier, I had gone to the Beit El military court with Lea Tsemel, and during that ride, we had a very similar conversation. She described herself, back in the 1970s when she began working, as a tomboyish firebrand and mentioned how she used to tease her mentor, Felicia Langer, for primping before going to court. As we approached Beit El, she pulled out a mirror and lipstick, turned to me and said, "Look at me. I've become Felicia."

When Rosenthal and I arrived at Erez, he left me in the outdoor waiting area surrounded by walls of barbed wire, while he went to get someone who could clear my entry. I joined five Gaza women, also waiting to enter. Soldiers on the other side of the barbed wire called to me, asking why I was there. I said I had come with Rosenthal to watch the day's hearings. They responded that I was wasting my time because nothing happened here, nothing except sending Palestinian terrorists to prison.

When the six of us were finally granted permission to enter, we wound our way through a maze of barbed wire and were taken, one at a time, into a wooden cubicle — an outhouselike structure — to undergo a full-body check by female soldiers. When I was alone in the airless cubicle with two young Israeli soldiers, they took the opportunity to ask me questions: "Do you hate Israel?" "Do you love Palestinians?" I responded that I was an academic researcher and that "love" and "hate" had little bearing on what I did and why I did it. It was an odd moment; clearly, they were disconcerted to have to run their hands over an American and seemed to want either some vindication that I needed to be frisked or some recognition that I understood that they were just doing their job. I was disconcerted, too; I prefer a silent frisking.

In the courtroom, waiting for the hearings to get underway, soldiers on guard duty kept instructing the five Gaza women and me not to talk or lean on the benches in front of us, and they periodically ordered one or another of us to move to a different spot. One of the Gaza women, very late into a pregnancy, began to sweat and shake. But she could not go to the public bathroom, which was located on the other side of the barbed wire entrance, because if she did, she would not be permitted to return and would miss the opportunity to see her husband. When she tried to lie down on the bench, soldiers shouted that she had to sit up or leave.

Rosenthal's first case was the high-profile and widely publicized "Palestinian from al-Qaeda." His client, Nabil Okal, had gone to Pakistan and Afghanistan in 1998, where he underwent training in camps run by al-Qaeda. When he returned to Gaza, according to the indictment, he allegedly set up "sleeper cells" to plan and launch attacks against Israeli targets.

Okal had been arrested in the summer of 2000 — before the start of the second *intifada* and before the 9/11 attacks on the United States. At the time, Rosenthal had wanted to make a deal, but Okal had resisted, hoping that a delay would wear down the prosecutor and reduce the sentence he was asking. After 9/11, plea bargaining became virtually impossible because of the symbolic significance of this particular case to the global "war on terror." That day in court, the military prosecutor repeatedly invoked the name of Bin Laden to drive home this defendant's dangerous and despicable character. However, there in the courtroom, there was no excitement or agitation; the reading of charges was a formality, and the defendant, securely shackled and confined in the dock, looked bored, like everyone else.

The hearing was not a trial because there were no witnesses. Rather, it was part of an ongoing plea bargaining process in which evidence was being presented and debated in front of the judges. Rosenthal pointed out a gap in logic between the charges and the confession. Okal had been arrested crossing to Jordan with dozens of cell phones and had confessed to planning to build cell phone bombs. Why, Rosenthal asked, would he be smuggling phones *out* of Israel/Palestine if he planned to use the bombs inside? If he had been trained as a bomb maker in Afghanistan, why did he need to go to Jordan? The judges were uninterested in engaging these issues and felt no need to do so, since the confession itself would ensure conviction. Half a year later, in February 2003, the case against Okal finally concluded with a negotiated sentence of twenty-seven years in prison, to much media fanfare.

Rosenthal's other case that day in Erez involved a Palestinian truck driver from Issawiya (a village near Jerusalem) who had been caught transporting bullets in the spare tire holder of his truck. This case turned on a dispute over the defendant's motives. After the reading of charges, Rosenthal insisted that his client was a poor man who had been motivated to transport the bullets for money, not for "ideological" reasons. To support Rosenthal's appeal for leniency in sentencing, he had asked the man's wife to come to court to testify about the family's desperate economic situation. She came with a newborn baby in tow and was hours late, as she explained to a furious Rosenthal, due to all the checkpoints along the way that had slowed her travel; she had left at dawn but had not arrived in Erez (thirty miles from Jerusalem) until 2:30 in the afternoon. Called to the stand, she testified that they and their ten children lived in a two-room house, that she did not work, and that because her husband was the sole source of support for the family, if he went to jail for a long time they would fall to utter ruin.

The defendant was then called to the stand. He explained that the bullets were for use at weddings; Palestinians often shoot guns in the air during celebrations. The judge, however, was not persuaded by this claim. He responded, "We can only imagine what these bullets could be used for . . . or have been used for!" The prosecutor was asking for a four-year prison sentence, Rosenthal was asking for one year, and the judge decided to sentence the man to three-and-a-half years.

When the hearing was over, the wife wanted to go to the dock to say goodbye to her husband, but soldiers guarding the court refused.

Rosenthal argued with them, and in the end they reached a compromise: the defendant's mother, who had come along, could take the newborn baby, who had been born after the man had been arrested, to the dock so that he could hug and kiss his son for a few moments before going to prison.

That was it. The end of another day in an Israeli military court. I went outside to wait for Rosenthal, who had to finalize the paperwork for the incarceration of his last client. I sat down on the dusty curb next to his car, lit a cigarette, and stared back across the barbed wire at the military compound in that corner of the Gaza Strip. I was overwhelmed by two simultaneous and utterly contradictory emotions. One was a sense of being filled to the brim with sadness. I was saddened by the knowledge that this court system would continue to function as a setting in the conflict that seemed farther than ever from resolution. The other emotion was a heady relief that I could leave it all behind.

I may never spend another day in an Israeli military court, but I cannot leave behind the searing memories and lessons I have learned. In fact, I do not want to leave behind or turn away from the suffering and the struggles for rights and justice. I share with many of my informants, Israeli citizens and Palestinian residents of the West Bank and Gaza, the hope that someday this court system and the occupation that sustains it really will become "history."

# The Institutional Structure and Administrative Features of the Military Court System

## Military Structure and Personnel

The Israeli military court system is part of the military administration, which is headed by the military commander of each region (West Bank and Gaza). The military commander has "supreme" legislative authority to issue, amend, and repeal military orders (MOs). All military legislation, such as orders of the various military administration departments, draw their validity from the area commander's orders, which are equivalent to "supreme legislation."

Administratively, the court system is under the direct authority of the Military Advocate General (MAG), who occupies the highest position within the legal substructure of the Israel Defense Forces (IDF). The MAG recommends people as judges to the military commander of the region and assigns judges to specific courts. For the judiciary, the administrative hierarchy is:

Military Advocate General

President of the Military Court of Appeals
(established in 1989)

Presidents of Military Courts

Other Judges

Direct supervision of the courts falls to the president of the military court of appeals. Presidents of the military courts must have the rank of lieutenant colonel or higher. Other judges have the rank of major or higher. Permanent judges (i.e., nonreservists) always are appointed from the ranks of the IDF's legal staff by a selection committee headed by the MAG. Reservist judges always have had some prior military legal experience (e.g., as prosecutors or legal advisors). They are appointed by a selection committee headed by the Deputy MAG, which includes the president of the military court of appeals and his deputy, another senior member of the unit, and the president of the Israel Bar Association. At any given time, there are approximately ten to fifteen permanent judges and fifty to sixty available reservists.

The prosecution is administratively distinct from the judiciary, although judges and prosecutors are members of the same IDF unit. The administrative hierarchy for the prosecution is:

Military Advocate General

Legal Advisor (West Bank/Gaza)          Head Prosecutor (West Bank/Gaza)

Head Prosecutors of Military Courts

Other Prosecutors

Israelis who defer their compulsory military service to attend university to pursue a law degree are then conscripted and usually perform their service as lawyers for the IDF. They enter with the rank of lieutenant, and those assigned to serve in the military courts become prosecutors. Reservists appointed to be prosecutors are civilian lawyers.

The MAG, who is advised on an ongoing basis by the military chief of staff and military commanders in the field, convenes regular meetings at the military headquarters in Tel Aviv with the legal advisor and head prosecutor of each region to discuss the situation on the ground and trends in the military courts (number of arrests, convictions, sentences, etc.). At these meetings, policy directives are formulated about how particular kinds of cases should be prosecuted, and this information is passed on to prosecutors working in the courts.

Full-time prosecutors have the right to use their own discretion to make plea bargains with defense lawyers on "simple cases" (see below), whereas reservists often are instructed on how to handle all their cases. All plea bargains for "hard cases" must be done in consultation with the court's head prosecutor. Prosecutors have legal immunity for their work (i.e., they cannot be court-martialed for "mistakes").

# Courts

Military courts of the first instance are distinguished by the number of judges (one or three) and the maximum sentencing power. One-judge courts handle simple cases involving charges with lesser maximum sentences. Until July 1991, the maximum sentence that could be issued by a one-judge court was five years in prison, but this was raised to a maximum of ten years. Three-judge courts handle hard cases and are empowered to pass sentences up to the maximum of life in prison or the death penalty. Although several death sentences have been handed down by military courts, they subsequently were commuted to life sentences.

All judges serving in one-judge courts must be legal professionals. In three-judge courts only one *must* be a legal professional, and the other two can be officers with a rank of major or higher. In capital cases, all three judges usually are legal professionals. The military court of appeals is composed of a three-judge panel, although there is a provision for a five-judge panel. In three-judge panels at least two must be legal professionals, and in five-judge panels at least three must be.

Decisions of one-judge courts can be appealed by prosecutors and/or defense lawyers if permission is set out in the original decision or if permission is granted by the president or acting president of the appeals court. There are no restrictions on appealing decisions of three-judge courts. But the decision to accept any appeal application is at the discretion of the appeals court. The military commander has the authority to reduce or commute a sentence of any military court.

# Jurisdiction

In 1967, the military court system was accorded concurrent jurisdiction with local (Palestinian) courts. Over the years, the Israeli authorities expanded the use of the military courts to try Palestinians for all kinds of crimes, even those unrelated to security (e.g., driving violations, petty crimes, tax evasion, price fixing). In principle, Jewish Israelis can be charged and tried in the military courts, but rarely are offenses committed by Jews considered "security violations," and even those that are tend to be prosecuted in domestic courts.

The military courts have jurisdiction to try Palestinian residents of the territories for crimes committed anywhere (i.e., personal jurisdiction); any crimes committed in the territories (i.e., territorial jurisdiction); or crimes committed anywhere that might have an impact on the security situation in the territories (i.e., extraterritorial jurisdiction).

# Laws

Three bodies of legislation are enforced through the military courts: original Israeli military legislation, the British Defense (Emergency) Regulations (1945), and local criminal laws (Jordanian in the West Bank and Egyptian in Gaza). The

Israeli military laws override local laws when there is a contradiction and supersede local laws when there is an overlap. The HCJ, in response to petitions challenging the legality of certain military laws, decided that it does not have the competence to review legislative acts of military commanders.

Israeli military orders constitute the main body of law regulating the operation of the military courts. The orders pertaining to the legal process often are based on Israeli domestic and military laws. Military orders also designate specific offenses, including violations of security (e.g., sabotage or attacks on military installations, carrying and possessing firearms, attacks on roads, contacts with the enemy, spying); criminal offenses with security implications (e.g., not preventing attacks or reporting planned attacks, distributing literature that incites disorder); offenses relating to the operation of the military courts (e.g., escaping from custody, perjury, disobeying a summons to appear in court); and criminal offenses not related to security (e.g., failure to pay taxes, bribery, trade violations). The criminal provisions of the British Defense Regulations outlaw membership in an "illegal organization," aiding and abetting members of illegal organizations, and threats to public order and safety.

In the early years of the occupation, there was confusion and debate about the applicability of the Fourth Geneva Convention vis-à-vis the functioning of the military courts (see Chapter 2). One position held that the convention had to constitute the basis for legislation because it was binding on all Israeli soldiers. A second position held that military courts had to follow military orders because the military commander's authority was "supreme" over residents of the territories. A third position held that the military commander's legislative authority did not originate in international law but rather stemmed from IDF rule in these areas. Within a few years, military courts came to accept that the Fourth Geneva Convention could not be utilized to challenge or force a military judicial review of the legality of Israeli military legislation.

## Charges and Sentences

There are three general classes of cases: Hard cases involve charges of security violations with serious implications, including murder and attempted murder, attacks and weapons possession, and membership in an illegal organization. Simple cases involve security violations with incidental or minor implications, such as demonstrating, displaying the Palestinian flag or national colors, writing graffiti, throwing stones (if no injury resulted), and building or manning barricades. The third type of cases, also simple, involves violations of public order such as driving violations, inter-Palestinian conflicts, tax evasion, and permit violations.

No decision of a military court (including the court of appeals) has status as a legally binding precedent. Consequently, there is a great deal of disparity in the sentences issued for similar charges.

Most cases are concluded through a plea bargain (see Chapter 8). The agreements worked out between prosecutors and defense lawyers depend on factors specific to the case (i.e., evidence, prior record of the accused), as well as current military sentencing policies. In general, sentencing patterns in Gaza have been higher than those in the West Bank.

## Rules of Evidence, Procedure, and Detention

Military court trials generally follow common-law adversarial procedures and approximate those used in the Israeli domestic criminal court system. Military courts use the rules of evidence set out in the Military Justice Law (1955) (which applies to court-martials) and the various laws of evidence in the Israeli domestic criminal court system. Rules of procedure are more flexible: the courts have the discretion to use any "just procedure" if there is a gap between existing rules and the needs of a case. Rules of procedure are derived from the Military Justice Law and the (domestic) Law of Criminal Procedure.

There is no requirement that an arrest be preceded by a detention order or that a person be informed of the reason for arrest at the time he or she is taken into custody. In principle, there is a provision for habeas corpus (challenging the lawfulness of an arrest and the necessity of detention), but in practice this is treated as a request for release on bail, and bail is very rarely granted. In most cases, people are detained throughout the entire duration of proceedings until their case is concluded.

A detained person can be held in custody for up to eighteen days without charges before being brought before a judge. This eighteen days breaks down as follows: ninety-six hours of detention on the order of any soldier and two seven-day extensions of detention on the order of police officers (usually at the request of members of the General Security Services). Following the initial eighteen days, detention can be extended by order of a judge. This is done when the interrogation has not been completed (i.e., the person has not confessed) or when the authorities have not had time to act on the confession (e.g., arresting people implicated in the detainee's statement). A judge can grant an extension of detention without charges for up to six months. In 1992, a new policy was issued reducing the maximum time before an extension hearing from eighteen to eight days for minors and people suspected of simple crimes. But there was no institutionalized oversight of this shortened detention, and its implementation was irregular.

Although in principle detained Palestinians have the right to meet with a lawyer, lawyer-client meetings tend to be prohibited as long as the person is undergoing interrogation. Provisions in military legislation can prohibit detainees access to lawyers for up to ninety days for reasons of security. Interrogators have the authority to prevent a lawyer-client meeting for up to thirty days (two fifteen-day periods, the second on the order of someone of higher rank than the person who ordered the first period). Following that, a military judge can issue another thirty-day order barring the meeting, and a third thirty-day order can be issued by the president or acting president of a military court. Lawyers can petition the

HCJ on matters pertaining to denial of the right to meet their clients, bail, writ of habeas corpus, and other administrative decisions that relate to arrest, interrogation, and pretrial detention.

In April 2002, the IDF issued MO 1500 reaffirming the policy to allow for eighteen days of incommunicado detention. This order instituted a blanket prohibition of lawyers' right to meet clients for eighteen days. In response to a petition submitted to the HCJ, the order was amended in July 2002. Under MO 1505, prisoners could be held for twelve days incommunicado, but lawyers would have to petition the courts on a case-by-case basis to meet their clients after that period.

# Notes

## Introduction

1. In the 1967 war, Israel also captured and occupied the Sinai Peninsula and the Golan Heights.

2. See David Garland, *Punishment and Modern Society: A Study in Social Theory* (Chicago: University of Chicago Press, 1993).

3. I use the noun *Israeli* to refer to all those who are citizens of Israel and modify that noun with the adjectives denoting the ethnonational identities that the state uses to distinguish among the citizenry (*Jewish, Arab,* and *Druze*). These terms are admittedly problematic because they divide and define people in ways that some regard as artificial or inaccurate. I use them because they reflect the legal and political distinctions that the state imposes and uses to govern its citizens.

4. See Al-Haq, *Punishing a Nation* (Ramallah: Al-Haq, 1988), and *Nation under Siege* (Ramallah: al-Haq, 1989).

5. Dan Horowitz, "Israel and the Occupation," *Jerusalem Quarterly* 43 (1987): 21.

6. Liisa Malkki, "News and Culture: Transitory Phenomena and the Fieldwork Tradition," in *Anthropological Locations: Boundaries and Grounds of a Field Science,* ed. Akhil Gupta and James Ferguson (Berkeley: University of California Press, 1997), p. 92.

7. Ibid. As Malkki notes, it is the "communities" rather than the activities occurring within them that are "accidental."

8. Three events are particularly important to understand the political deterioration. On February 25, 1994, an American-Israeli settler massacred twenty-nine Palestinian worshipers at a mosque in Hebron before killing himself, sparking massive protests throughout the occupied territories. The first Hamas suicide bus bombing inside Israel, on April 4, 1994, was claimed as a reprisal for

the Hebron massacre. On November 4, 1995, Rabin was assassinated by a right-wing ultrareligious Jew who accused Rabin of being a "traitor" for negotiating away "Jewish land" to the enemy.

9.  A clear distillation of this debate can be found in a pair of articles: Benny Morris, "Camp David and After: An Exchange (1. An Interview with Ehud Barak)," and Hussein Agha and Robert Malley, "Camp David and After: An Exchange (2. A Reply to Ehud Barak)," both in *New York Review of Books,* June 13, 2002.

10.  There are also military courts attached to prisons and detention centers to handle hearings for extension of detention and appeals against administrative detention.

11.  Kristin Bumiller, *The Civil Rights Society: The Social Construction of Victims* (Baltimore: Johns Hopkins University Press, 1988), pp. 33–34.

# Chapter 1: A Political Geography of Law and Conflict

1  Alan Hunt, "Foucault's Expulsion of Law: Toward a Retrieval," Law and Social Inquiry 17/1 (1992), p. 1026.

2.  Zachary Lockman, *Comrades and Enemies: Arab and Jewish Workers in Palestine, 1906–1948* (Berkeley: University of California Press, 1996), p. 4. See also Baruch Kimmerling, "Sociology, Ideology, and Nation-Building: The Palestinians and Their Meaning in Israeli Sociology," *American Sociological Review* 57 (1992): 446–60.

3.  Patricia Ewick and Susan Silbey provide a useful definition of *legality* for sociolegal research: "[T]he term 'legality' [refers] to the meanings, sources of authority, and cultural practices that are commonly recognized as legal, regardless of who employs them or for what ends. In this rendering, people may invoke and enact legality in ways neither approved nor acknowledged by the law." Patricia Ewick and Susan Silbey, *The Common Place of Law: Stories from Everyday Life* (Chicago: University of Chicago Press, 1998), p. 22.

4.  James Ron, "Savage Restraint: Israel, Palestine and the Dialectics of Legal Repression," *Social Problems* 47/4 (2000): 445–72.

5.  Colin Gordon, "Governmental Rationality: An Introduction," in *The Foucault Effect: Studies in Governmentality,* ed. Graham Burchell, Colin Gordon, and Peter Miller (Chicago: University of Chicago Press, 1991), p. 3.

6.  Oren Yiftachel, "Israeli Society and Jewish-Palestinian Reconciliation: 'Ethnocracy' and Its Territorial Contradictions," *Middle East Journal* 51 (Autumn 1997): 507.

7.  According to this law, it is also illegal for a party to deny the democratic character of the state or to incite racism. See David Kretzmer, *The Legal Status of the Arabs in Israel* (Boulder, CO: Westview, 1990); Nadim Rouhana, *Palestinians in an Ethnic Jewish State: Identities in Conflict* (New Haven, CT: Yale University Press, 1997); Gershon Shafir and Yoav Peled, "Citizenship and Stratification in an Ethnic Democracy," *Ethnic and Racial Studies* 21 (May 1998): 408–27.

8.  See Asher Arian, Ilan Talmud, and Tamar Hermann, *National Security and*

*Public Opinion in Israel* (Boulder, CO: Westview Press, 1988); Menachem Hofnung, *Democracy, Law and National Security in Israel* (Hanover, NH: Dartmouth Publishing, 1996); Itzhak Zamir, "Rule of Law and Control of Terrorism," *Tel Aviv University Studies in Law* 8 (1988): 81–156.

9. Itzhak Zamir, "Human Rights and National Security," *Israel Law Review* 23/2–3 (1989): 376–77.

10. Under the military administration instituted to govern Arabs in Israel from 1948 to 1966, the country was divided into three districts, each under a separate military command. Arab citizens' mobility and rights were restricted, and those suspected of engaging in activities that violated Israeli security, including expressions of Palestinian or Arab nationalism, were tried in a special military court for civilians in Lydda-cum-Lod. See Sabri Jiryis, *The Arabs in Israel* (New York: Monthly Review Press, 1976); Ian Lustick, *Arabs in the Jewish State: Israel's Control of a National Minority* (Austin: University of Texas Press, 1980); Shira Robinson, "Occupied Citizens in a Liberal State: Palestinians under Military Rule and the Colonial Formation of Israeli Society, 1948–1966" (Ph.D. diss., Stanford University, in progress); Elia Zureik, *The Palestinians in Israel: A Study in Internal Colonialism* (Boston: KPI, 1979).

11. See Fouzi el-Asmar, *To Be an Arab in Israel* (Washington, DC: Institute of Palestine Studies, 1978); Alouph Haraven, ed., *Every Sixth Israeli: Relations between the Jewish Majority and the Arab Minority in Israel* (Jerusalem: Van Leer Jerusalem Foundation, 1983); Adalah, *Institutionalized Discrimination against Palestinian Citizens of Israel: Adalah's Report to the World Conference against Racism, Racial Discrimination, Xenophobia and Related Intolerance, Durban, South Africa, 2001* (Shafaʿamr, Israel: Adalah, 2001).

12. Terrence Halliday, "Politics and Civic Professionalism: Legal Elites and Cause Lawyers," *Law and Social Inquiry* 24/4 (1994): 1026.

13. See Pierre Bourdieu, "The Force of Law: Toward a Sociology of the Juridical Field," *Hastings Law Journal* 38 (1987): 805–53.

14. See Isaac Balbus, *The Dialectics of Legal Repression: Black Rebels before the American Criminal Courts* (New York: Russell Sage Foundation, 1973); Robert Cover, "Violence and the Word," in *Narrative, Violence and the Law: The Essays of Robert Cover,* ed. Martha Minow, Michael Ryan, and Austin Sarat (Ann Arbor: University of Michigan Press, 1992); Austin Sarat and Thomas R. Kearns, eds., *Law's Violence* (Ann Arbor: University of Michigan Press, 1993).

15. See Mindie Lazarus-Black and Susan Hirsch, eds., *Contested States: Law, Hegemony and Resistance* (New York: Routledge, 1994); June Starr and Jane Collier, eds., *History and Power in the Study of Law: New Directions in Legal Anthropology* (Ithaca, NY: Cornell University Press, 1989); J. L. Comaroff and S. A. Roberts, *Rules and Processes: The Cultural Logic of Dispute in an African Context* (Chicago: University of Chicago Press, 1981); Ernesto Laclau and Chantal Mouffe, *Hegemony and Socialist Strategy* (London: Verso, 1985).

16. Sally Engle Merry, *Getting Justice and Getting Even: Legal Consciousness among Working Class Americans* (Chicago: University of Chicago Press, 1990), p. 7.

17. See Kimberle Crenshaw, "Race, Reform and Retrenchment: Transforma-

tion and Legitimation in Anti-discrimination Law," in *Critical Race Theory,* ed. Kimberle Crenshaw et al. (New York: New Press, 1995).

18. Martha Minow, "Partial Justice: Law and Minorities," in *The Fate of Law,* ed. Austin Sarat and Thomas Kearns (Ann Arbor: University of Michigan Press, 1997), p. 74.

19. According to Lisa Wedeen, "The term 'hegemony' does not have the precision to specify the dominance-producing aspects of claims that are themselves transparently unconvincing." Lisa Wedeen, *Ambiguities of Domination: Politics, Rhetoric and Symbols in Contemporary Syria* (Chicago: University of Chicago Press, 1999), p. 12.

20. The rights of Jews (both individual and collective/national) are coterminous with the territorial reach of Israeli state power, as evident in the "right" of Jews (and only Jews) to take up residency (i.e., become settlers) in territories occupied in 1967 without any forfeiting or alteration of their status as Israeli citizens.

21. According to the English-language summary of a 2003 report by the Israel Democracy Institute (IDI), a nonpartisan Israeli research institution, "[M]ore than half (53%) of the Jews in Israel state out loud that they are against full equality for the Arabs [i.e., citizens]; 77% say there should be a Jewish majority on crucial political decisions; less than a third (31%) support having Arab political parties in the government; and the majority (57%) think that the Arabs should be encouraged to emigrate." Israel Democracy Institute, *The Democracy Index: Major Findings 2003* (Tel Aviv: Israel Democracy Institute, 2003).

22. James Scott makes a useful distinction between "ideal legitimacy" and "functional legitimacy." The former is an ideological acceptance of the way things are, while the latter would describe a form of resignation to what seems inevitable. James Scott, *Weapons of the Weak: Everyday Forms of Peasant Resistance* (New Haven, CT: Yale University Press, 1985), pp. 324–30.

23. For example, on March 30, 1976, Arab Israelis declared a "national strike" to protest continuing confiscation of their land. The strike was put down violently and six Arabs were killed. Since then, "Land Day" has been commemorated annually with demonstrations and strikes.

24. Rouhana, *Palestinian Citizens,* p. 152.

25. The nexus of the Israeli-Palestinian conflict has come to turn on the fate of the West Bank and Gaza, namely whether this will become the site of an independent, sovereign Palestinian state, "autonomous self-government," or perpetual occupation by Israel. One consequence of focusing the struggle for Palestinian national rights on the fate of West Bank and Gaza is that Palestinians in these areas have come to represent "the nation," to the exclusion of all those who reside elsewhere, whether inside Israel or in the diaspora.

26. Baruch Kimmerling uses the concept "control system" to discuss the political and ideological dimensions of Israeli rule throughout Israel/Palestine. According to Kimmerling, a "control system" comprises

several sub-collectivities, held together by purely military and police forces and their civil extensions (e.g., bureaucracies and settlers). . . . The central component . . . [of]

the control system is the ruling sector's virtually total lack of interest and ability in creating a common identity or basic value system to legitimize the use of violence to maintain the system. . . . Orientation toward the "controlled" population is purely instrumental. Thus, in exchange for . . . minimal obedience to the authorities, the rulers grant these collectivities minimal human rights and guarantee "law and order," so long as these privileges are not perceived as contradicting the interests of the system's ruling sector. In the control system's frame of reference, the system's *raison d'e- tre* and legitimacy are only created "internally," as formulated by the ruling sector. (Baruch Kimmerling, "Boundaries and Frontiers of the Israeli Control System," in *The Israeli State and Society: Boundaries and Frontiers,* ed. Baruch Kimmerling [Albany: SUNY Press, 1989], pp. 266–67.)

My conception of hegemony differs from Kimmerling's "control system." While I agree with the nature and scope of authority and the "internal" frame of reference for legitimacy, I take issue with his notion of ruling relations as "purely instrumental." His discussion of the subjugation of different communities of non-Jews (his "controlled collectivities") by Jews (his "ruling sector") elides the distinction between domination and hegemony. Hegemony entails consent by those who are not in the ruling group. As I show in this study, people are conscious agents whose actions cannot be reduced to coping strategies.

27. Wendy Brown describes rights as "protean and irresolute signifiers" that "necessarily operate in and as an ahistorical, acultural, acontextual idiom: they claim distance from specific political context and historical vicissitudes, and they necessarily participate in a discourse of enduring universality rather than provisionality or partiality." Wendy Brown, "Rights and Identity in Late Modernity: Revisiting the 'Jewish Question,'" in *Identities, Politics, and Rights,* ed. Austin Sarat and Thomas R. Kearns (Ann Arbor: University of Michigan Press, 1995), pp. 86–87.

28. Austin Sarat and Thomas R. Kearns, "Editorial Introduction," in Sarat and Kearns, *Identities, Politics, and Rights,* p. 8.

29. Louis Henkin, *The Age of Rights* (New York: Columbia University Press, 1990).

30. See David Cole and James Dempsey, *Terrorism and the Constitution: Sacrificing Civil Liberties in the Name of National Security* (New York: New Press, 2002).

31. See United Nations, "Report of the Policy Working Group on the United Nations and Terrorism," A/57/273, S/2002/875, August 2002, retrieved March 1, 2004, from www.un.org/terrorism/.

32. Richard Falk, *The Great Terror War* (New York: Olive Branch Press, 2002), p. xix.

33. Dana Briskman, "National Security versus Human Rights: An Analysis of the Approach of the Israeli Supreme Court" (M.A. thesis, Harvard University Law School, 1987), p. 57.

34. In the early 1990s, this criminalization of Palestinian nationalism was tempered by the imperatives of a negotiating process that began in 1991. Palestinian factions supportive of the negotiations were "decriminalized" to some extent, as were some of the nonviolent expressions and manifestations of Pales-

tinian nationalism. Arguably, Palestinian nationalism has been "recriminalized" since the start of the second *intifada* in 2000.

35. *Jerusalem Post,* February 20, 1987, quoted in Penny Johnson, "The Routine of Repression," *Middle East Report,* no. 150 (January-February 1988): 6.

36. See Henry J. Steiner and Philip Alston, *International Human Rights in Context: Law, Politics, Morals* (Oxford: Clarendon Press, 1996).

37. See Abdullahi An-Na'im, "State Responsibility under International Human Rights Law to Change Religious and Customary Laws," in *Human Rights of Women: National and International Perspectives,* ed. Rebecca Cook (Philadelphia: University of Pennsylvania Press, 1994).

38. See Margaret Keck and Kathryn Sikkink, *Activists beyond Borders: Advocacy Networks in International Politics* (Ithaca, NY: Cornell University Press, 1998).

39. See Stanley Cohen, *Denial and Acknowledgement: The Impact of Information about Human Rights Violations* (Jerusalem: Center for Human Rights, Hebrew University, 1995).

40. Debates about the enforceability of international law encompass everything from states' use of the death penalty and corporal punishment, to the deleterious social and economic consequences of unbridled economic privatization, to religious or cultural practices that sanction certain harms.

# Chapter 2: Legal Discourses and the Conflict in Israel/Palestine

1. Sally Engle Merry, *Getting Justice and Getting Even: Legal Consciousness among Working-Class Americans* (Chicago: University of Chicago Press, 1990), pp. 8–9.

2. See Yoram Dinstein, "Terrorism and Wars of Liberation Applied to the Arab-Israeli Conflict: An Israeli Perspective," *Israel Yearbook on Human Rights* 3 (1973): 78–92. Dinstein writes: "The war is, and was, not between Israel and the Palestinian Arabs, but between Israel, on the one hand, and Egypt, Jordan and Syria on the other. It is, and was, an international war, and these three Arab states are the ones responsible for its breaking out in violation of international law" (p. 84).

3. These preparations included Egypt's closure of the Straits of Tiran and demands that UN peacekeeping forces evacuate the Sinai Peninsula and Syrian responses to Soviet misinformation about Israeli troop mobilization in the north.

4. The military court system was established by Proclamation No. 3 in the West Bank and an unnumbered order in Gaza. These orders were amended several times and in 1970 were replaced by (Israeli) Military Order (MO) 378 for the West Bank and MO 300 for Gaza. See Zvi Hadar, "The Military Courts," in *Military Government in the Territories Administered by Israel, 1967–1980: The Legal Aspects,* ed. Meir Shamgar (Jerusalem: Harry Sacher Institute for Legislative Research and Comparative Law, 1982).

5. According to Shabtai Teveth, "It seemed that if [the Israel Defense Forces] did enter the West Bank, it would have to put into effect the lessons the military government had learnt in the Gaza Strip in 1956." Shabtai Teveth, *The Cursed Blessing: The Story of Israel's Occupation of the West Bank* (London: Weidenfeld and Nicolson, 1970), p. 10.

6. These plans included the creation of an administrative command for the West Bank and the appointment of Reserve General Chaim Herzog as its head. Thus, a military administration was ready in waiting years before any territory was actually conquered and occupied.

7. Meir Shamgar, "Legal Concepts and Problems of the Israeli Military Government: The Initial Stage," in Shamgar, *Military Government*, p. 25n.

8. Ibid. (emphasis added).

9. Ibid., p. 27.

10. Quoted in ibid., p. 27n (emphasis in the original). The term *peacetime* appears in the text preceding this excerpt.

11. See "What Happened to the Dream? A Roundtable Discussion with Longtime Ex-Prisoners," *News from Within* 11/2 (1995): 3–13.

12. After 1948, Palestinian nationalist politics tended to be subsumed within the pan-Arab national movement, especially after the coming to power of regimes proclaiming their commitment to liberate Palestine. After 1967, Palestinian nationalism (re)emerged as a distinct ideology rooted in an increasingly independent political base. See William Quandt, Fuad Jabber, and Ann Mosely Lesch, *The Politics of Palestinian Nationalism* (Berkeley: University of California Press, 1973).

13. See Rashid Khalidi, "The PLO as the Representative of the Palestinian People," in *The International Relations of the PLO,* ed. Augustus Richard Norton and Martin Greenberg (Carbondale: Southern Illinois University Press, 1989).

14. See Yehoshafat Harkabi, *The Palestinian Covenant and Its Meaning* (London: Vallentine Mitchell, 1979).

15. See Dan Horowitz, *Israel's Concept of Defensible Borders* (Jerusalem: Leonard Davis Institute, Hebrew University, 1975).

16. See Meir Shamgar, "The Observance of International Law in the Administered Territories," *Israel Yearbook on Human Rights* 1 (1971): 262–77.

17. See Shamgar, "Legal Concepts," p. 43.

18. According to William O'Brien, "Presumably what Israel applies is considered 'humanitarian' and what she rejects is not." William O'Brien, *Law and Morality in Israel's War with the PLO* (New York: Routledge, 1991), p. 229.

19. See Jean Pictet, *Development and Principles of International Humanitarian Law* (Dordrecht: Martinus Nijhoff, 1985).

20. Shamgar, "Legal Concepts," pp. 32–33.

21. See Shamgar, "Observance of International Law."

22. See International Committee of the Red Cross, "Treaties and Customary International Law," 2004, retrieved March 1, 2004, from www.icrc.org/web/eng/siteengo.nsf/iwpList2/Humanitarian_law:treaties_and_customary_law.

23. See Yoram Dinstein, "The Expulsion of the Mayors from Judea" (in Hebrew), *Iyunei Mishpat* 8 (1981): 157–71.

24. Yehuda Blum, "The Missing Reversioner: Reflections on the Status of Judea and Samaria," *Israel Law Review* 3 (1968): 279–88.

25. Renato Jarach, "Judicial Review of the Military Government by the High Court of Justice," in *Israel, the "Intifada" and the Rule of Law*, ed. David Yahav (Tel Aviv: Israel Ministry of Defense Publications, 1993).

26. See Nissim Bar-Yaacov, "The Applicability of the Laws of War to Judea and Samaria (the West Bank) and to Gaza," *Israel Law Review* 24/3–4 (1990): 486–505; Moshe Drori, "The Israeli Settlements in Judea and Samaria: Legal Aspects," in *Judea, Samaria and Gaza: Views on the Present and Future*, ed. Daniel Elazar (Washington, DC: American Enterprise Institute, 1982).

27. See Dov Shefi, "The Protection of Human Rights in the Areas Administered by Israel: United Nations Findings and Reality," *Israel Yearbook on Human Rights* 3 (1973), and "The Reports of the UN Special Committees on Israeli Practices in the Territories: A Survey and Evaluation," in Shamgar, *Military Government*.

28. Shamgar, "Legal Concepts," p. 43n.

29. Ibid., pp. 57–58.

30. The HCJ has two distinct functions: it is the highest appellate court in the domestic legal system (i.e., a "Supreme Court"), and it sits as a High Court of Justice for petitions against administrative measures taken by state agencies.

31. See Ronen Shamir, "'Landmark Cases' and the Reproduction of Legitimacy: The Case of Israel's High Court of Justice," *Law and Society Review* 24/3 (1990): 781–805. For an alternative interpretation, see Yoav Dotan, "Judicial Rhetoric, Government Lawyers, and Human Rights: The Case of the Israeli High Court of Justice during the Intifada," *Law and Society Review* 33/2 (1999): 401–25.

32. High Court [hereafter HC] 302/72, *Piskei Din* [hereafter *PD*] 27(2), p. 169. See also *Amira et al. v. Minister of Defense*, in which the decision stated: "When a professional military controversy arises, in which the court does not have sufficient knowledge, he who speaks in the name of those responsible for security of the administered territories . . . will be considered to hold innocent considerations. Very strong evidence will be needed to contradict this presumption." HC 258/79, *PD* 34(1), p. 90, quoted in Shamir, "'Landmark Cases,'" p. 788.

33. According to Jonathan Kuttab, the three areas where the HCJ does provide potential relief for Palestinian petitioners are instances in which the Israeli authorities violate their own procedures, as in the case of *Qawasmeh et al. v. Minister of Defense*, HC 320/80, *PD* 35(1), p. 617; in obtaining temporary injunctions against actions in the form of orders nisi; and in functioning as a useful threat in that an application to the HCJ is sometimes sufficient to prevent an action from being carried out. Jonathan Kuttab, "Avenues Open for Defence of Human Rights in the Israeli-Occupied Territories," in *International Law and the Administration of Occupied Territories: Two Decades of Israeli Occupation of the West Bank and the Gaza Strip*, ed. Emma Playfair (New York: Oxford University Press, 1995).

34. David Kretzmer, *The Occupation of Justice: The Supreme Court of Israel and the Occupied Territories* (Albany: SUNY Press, 2002), p. 163.

35. See Baruch Kimmerling, *Zionism and Territory: The Socioterritorial Dimension of Zionist Politics* (Berkeley: University of California Press, 1983).

36. Emergency Resolution (Offenses Committed in the Israel-Held Areas — Jurisdiction and Legal Assistance) Law.

37. See Lea Tsemel, "Double Standard Justice in Israel: The Case of the Jewish Terror Organization," *Palestine Yearbook of International Law* 2 (1985): 37–68; Association for Civil Rights in Israel, *The Legal and Administrative System* (Jerusalem: Association for Civil Rights in Israel, 1985).

38. See Eyal Benvenisti, *Legal Dualism: The Absorption of the Occupied Territories into Israel* (Boulder, CO: Westview Press, 1990); George Bisharat, "Land, Law and Legitimacy in Israel and the Occupied Territories," *American University Law Review* 43/2 (1994): 467–561; Amnon Rubenstein, "The Changing Status of the 'Territories' (West Bank and Gaza): From Escrow to Legal Mongrel," *Tel Aviv University Studies in Law* 8 (1988): 59–80; Raja Shehadeh, *The Law of the Land: Settlements and Land Issues under Israeli Military Occupation* (Jerusalem: Palestinian Academic Society for the Study of International Affairs, 1993).

39. The original proclamation establishing a military court system in June 1967 declared that the military courts would be run in accordance with the Fourth Geneva Convention, and soldiers were instructed to abide by this convention in any instance where there was a contradiction between it and original military legislation. This provision was abolished in September 1967 because it contradicted the legal doctrine that the Fourth Geneva Convention was not applicable to Israeli rule in the West Bank and Gaza on a de jure basis. However, this complicated the operation of the military court system. First, because all members of the Israel Defense Forces (IDF) were bound by the Geneva Conventions on the basis of General Staff Order Number 33.0133, it became unclear when the Fourth Geneva Convention would *not* apply to IDF activities in the territories. Second, because the state claimed to abide by the "humanitarian provisions" of the convention but never explicitly established what it considered those to be, it was unclear whether or to what extent original military legislation had to adhere to the convention's provisions. Third, when military laws contradicted the convention, there was a question as to whether a defendant whose case was affected by this contradiction could draw upon the convention to challenge military legislation.

40. 'Abd al-Jawad Salih produced a four-volume collection of available military orders (in Arabic), *Israeli Military Orders* (n.p., 1986), and Jamil Rabah and Natasha Fairweather authored a summary of military orders in the West Bank (in English), *Israeli Military Orders in the Occupied Palestinian West Bank, 1967–92* (Jerusalem: Jerusalem Media and Communication Centre, 1993).

41. Only a small number of military court decisions have been published in volumes entitled *Select Judgments of the Military Courts in the Administered Territories* (Tel Aviv: Israel Ministry of Defense).

42. *HaPraklit* 2/46, quoted in Sabri Jiryis, *The Arabs in Israel* (New York: Monthly Review Press, 1976), pp. 11–12.

43. See Alina Korn, "Political Control and Crime: The Use of Defense

(Emergency) Regulations during the Military Government," *Adalah's Review* 4 (2004): 23-32.

44. Since the late 1970s, the British Defense Regulations inside Israel have been largely replaced by domestic legislation (i.e., various "Prevention of Terrorism" laws).

45. This was promulgated as the Palestine (Revocation) Order in Council. See Martha Roadstrum Moffett, *Perpetual Emergency: A Legal Analysis of Israel's Use of the British Defense (Emergency) Regulations, 1945, in the Occupied Territories* (Ramallah, West Bank: Al-Haq/Law in the Service of Man, 1989).

46. *Abu Awad v. Regional Commander of Judea and Samaria,* HC 97/79, *PD* 33(3), p. 309. See also *Nazal et al. v. Military Commander of the Judea and Samaria Region,* HC 256/85, *PD* 39(3), p. 645.

47. See Baruch Bracha, "Restriction of Personal Freedom without Due Process of Law According to the Defense (Emergency) Regulations, 1945," *Israel Yearbook on Human Rights* 8 (1978), and "Addendum: Some Remarks on Israeli Law Regarding Security," *Israel Yearbook on Human Rights* 10 (1980): 286-90; Uzi Amit-Kohn, "The Defense (Emergency) Regulations, 1945," in Yahav, *Israel, the "Intifada."*

48. According to Zvi Hadar, Israel "continued to rely on the local legal systems, including the [British] Defense Regulations, whenever possible, as *additional* security provisions supplementary to [its] own [military legislation]." Hadar, "The Military Courts," p. 176 (emphasis in the original).

49. For example, Yoram Dinstein writes that the Israeli government's position that the territories are not occupied "is based on dubious legal grounds, considering that the Fourth Geneva Convention does not make its applicability conditional on recognition of titles." Yoram Dinstein, "The International Law of Belligerent Occupation and Human Rights," *Israel Yearbook on Human Rights* 8 (1978): 107. See also Yoram Dinstein, "Legislative Authority in the Administered Territories" (in Hebrew), *Iyunei Mishpat* 3 (1972): 505-12; Thomas Kuttner, "Israel and the West Bank: Aspects of the Law of Belligerent Occupation," *Israel Yearbook on Human Rights* 7 (1977): 166-221; Theodore Meron, "West Bank and Gaza: Human Rights and Humanitarian Law in the Period of Transition," *Israel Yearbook on Human Rights* 9 (1979): 106-20.

50. The latter took the form of a "Know Your Rights" series. See Joost Hiltermann, "Al-Haq: The First Twenty Years," *Middle East Report* 214 (Fall 2000): 43.

51. Mouin Rabbani, "Palestinian Human Rights Activism under Israeli Occupation: The Case of Al-Haq," *Arab Studies Quarterly* 16/2 (1994): 29.

52. This credibility was crucial to securing financial and other support from foreign organizations. It also served to attract a number of foreign lawyers and human rights activists who came to the West Bank to work with LSM.

53. Raja Shehadeh and Jonathan Kuttab, *The West Bank and the Rule of Law* (Ramallah: Law in the Service of Man, 1980).

54. Israel National Section of the International Commission of Jurists, *The Rule of Law in the Areas Administered by Israel* (Tel Aviv: Israel National

Section of the International Commission of Jurists, 1981). Although this book bears the name of the ICJ, that organization played no part in its authorship or publication.

55. Haim Cohen, foreword to Israel National Section, *Rule of Law,* p. xii.

56. Ibid., pp. viii–ix.

57. Raja Shehadeh, *Occupier's Law: Israel and the West Bank,* rev. ed. (Washington, DC: Institute for Palestine Studies, 1988), pp. 3–4.

58. See Meron Benvenisti, *Israeli Rule in the West Bank: Legal and Administrative Aspects* (Jerusalem: West Bank Data Base Project, 1983); David Kretzmer, *Israel and the West Bank: Legal Issues* (Jerusalem: West Bank Database Project, 1984); Hillel Somer, "The Application of the Fourth Geneva Convention in Israeli Law" (in Hebrew), *Iyunei Mishpat* 11 (1986): 263–80; Leah Tsemel, "Applicability of Geneva Conventions," *Palestine Yearbook of International Law* 1 (1984).

59. Penny Johnson, "The Routine of Repression," *MERIP Middle East Report* 150 (January–February 1988): 10.

60. ACRI has nurtured its reputation as a "mainstream" Israel organization by not appearing to side with Palestinians, even when taking positions critical of the Israeli state. For example, the stated purpose of a monograph published by the organization in Jerusalem in 1985, *The Legal and Administrative System,* was to "explain" rather than "criticize" (p. 5). It offered no independent assessment of the legality of the British Defense Regulations, other than to note that they were regarded as applicable by the military courts and the HCJ. Moreover, the monograph referred to the West Bank (the focus of the study) as "the Areas" to avoid taking a position on the debate over whether it was "occupied" or "administered."

61. Nabeel Abraham et al., "International Human Rights Organizations and the Palestine Question," *Middle East Report,* no. 150 (1988): 13.

62. See ibid, p. 14.

63. Quoted in Hiltermann, "Al-Haq," p. 44.

64. See Amnesty International, *The Military Justice System in the Occupied Territories: Detention, Interrogation and Trial Procedures* (New York: Amnesty International, 1991); Lawyers Committee for Human Rights, *Lawyers and the Military Justice System* (New York: Lawyers Committee for Human Rights, 1992); Jordan Paust, Gerhard von Glahn, and Gunter Woratsch, *Inquiry into the Israeli Military Court System in the Occupied West Bank and Gaza* (Geneva: International Commission of Jurists, 1989); Daphna Golan, *The Military Judicial System in the West Bank* (Jerusalem: B'Tselem, 1989).

65. While many of the texts tackling the subject of the military courts (and related themes) offer complex legal arguments, the literature demonstrates very little use of critical social theory — or theory of any kind, for that matter. Exceptions include George Bisharat, *Palestinian Lawyers and Israeli Rule: Law and Disorder in the West Bank* (Austin: University of Texas Press, 1989); and Stanley Cohen, *The Human Rights Movement in Israel and South Africa: Some Paradoxical Comparisons* (Jerusalem: Truman Institute of Hebrew University, 1991).

66. "Summary," in Amnesty International, *Military Justice System*.

67. Tamar Gaulan, letter dated April 8, 1992 (file no. 164.1–717), published in Office of the Military Advocate General, *Response of the IDF Military Advocate General's Unit to the Amnesty International Report on the Military Justice System in the Administered Areas* (Tel Aviv: Office of the Military Advocate General, 1992).

68. Lawyers Committee for Human Rights, *Lawyers,* p. ii.

69. Appendix I to Lawyers Committee for Human Rights, *A Continuing Cause for Concern: The Military Justice System of the Israeli-Occupied Territories* (New York: Lawyers Committee for Human Rights, 1993), p. App. I 1.

70. Lawyers Committee for Human Rights, *Continuing Cause for Concern,* pp. 2–3.

71. Yahav, *Israel, the "Intifada."*

72. Ibid., pp. 238–39 (emphasis in original).

73. Amnon Straschnov, *Justice under Fire: The Legal System during the Intifada* (in Hebrew) (Tel Aviv: Yediot Aharonot, 1994).

74. Ibid., pp. 42–43.

75. See Playfair, *International Law*; Carol Bisharat, "Palestine and Humanitarian Law: Israeli Practices in the West Bank and Gaza," *Hastings International and Comparative Law Review* 12 (1989): 325–42.

76. Paul Hunt, *Justice? The Military Court System in the Israeli-Occupied Territories* (Ramallah: Al-Haq/ Law in the Service of Man, 1987).

77. Quoted in Adnan Amad, ed., *Israeli League for Human and Civil Rights (The Shahak Papers)* (Beirut: Palestine Research Center, 1973), p. 19.

78. Stanley Cohen, "Talking about Torture in Israel," *Tikkun* 6 (1991): 24.

79. "Israel Tortures Arab Prisoners: Special Investigation by Insight," *Sunday Times* (London), June 19, 1977.

80. *Times* (London), July 3, 1977, Letters section.

81. To compensate for restrictions on this means of gathering information and evidence, beginning around 1979 the GSS developed a new technique: the procurement and use of Palestinian informers in prisons. See Yizhar Be'er and Saleh 'Abdel-Jawad, *Collaborators in the Occupied Territories: Human Rights Abuses and Violations* (Jerusalem: B'Tselem, 1994), p. 63.

82. An important legal development relating to interrogation was instituted in 1981; henceforth, a person could be convicted on the basis of a third-party confession, whereas previously a conviction was contingent on a first-party confession or material evidence. See Lea Tsemel, "Personal Status and Rights," in *Occupation: Israel over Palestine,* 2nd ed., ed. Naseer Aruri (Belmont, MA: Association of Arab-American University Graduates, 1989), p. 130. This change expanded the "benefits" accruing from interrogation: each conviction that resulted from an interrogation was recorded as a credit in the personnel file of the GSS agents who conducted the interrogation. See Gideon Levy, "The Best Years of Their Lives," *Ha'aretz Magazine,* January 5, 1990.

83. Moshe Landau et al., *Commission of Inquiry into the Methods of Investigation of the General Security Services Regarding Hostile Terrorist Activity* (Jerusalem: Government Press Office, 1987).

84. See Pnina Lahav, "A Barrel without Hoops: The Impact of Counterterrorism on Israel's Legal Culture," *Cardoza Law Review* 10 (1988): 529-60.

85. In Israeli courts, rules of evidence require that a confession be given of the detainee's free will in order to be legally admissible. Nevertheless, even if coercive methods are used, the confession can be admissible if it was *signed* without coercion. See Human Rights Watch/Middle East, *Torture and Ill-Treatment: Israel's Interrogation of Palestinians from the Occupied Territories* (New York: Human Rights Watch, 1994), pp. 243-44.

86. See Landau et al., *Commission of Inquiry*, pp. 31-39.

87. Ibid., p. 4.

88. The tendentiousness of this logic is evident in the fact that at least 50 percent of Palestinians who are arrested are eventually released without charge, as noted elsewhere in the report.

89. The law at issue is Section 277 of Israel's penal code, which prohibits the use of physical force during interrogation. According to this law, a public servant is liable to imprisonment for three years if he or she uses or directs the use of force against a person or threatens or directs a person to be threatened for the purpose of extorting a confession or information relating to an offense. The Landau Commission suggested that this prohibition could be legally circumvented by using a broader interpretation of the "necessity defense," as contained in Section 22 (Article 34[11]) of Penal Law, 1977.

90. Alan Dershowitz writes, "It is ironic . . . that in an effort to incorporate the interrogation methods of the GSS into 'the law itself,' the Commission has selected the most lawless of legal doctrines — that of necessity — as the prime candidate for coverage." Alan Dershowitz, "Is It Necessary to Apply 'Physical Pressure' to Terrorists — and to Lie about It?" *Israel Law Review* 23/2-3 (1989): 196.

91. The Landau Commission report suggested that the necessity defense could be interpreted to include not only its originally intended exception for cases of "imminent danger" but also "the concept of lesser evil," by which "the harm done by violating a provision of the law during an interrogation must be weighed against the harm to the life or person of others which could occur sooner or LATER." Landau et al., *Commission of Inquiry*, p. 57 (emphasis in original).

92. See Lisa Hajjar, "Sovereign Bodies, Sovereign States and the Problem of Torture," *Studies in Law, Politics and Society* 21 (2000): 101-34.

93. For example, the Office of the Military Advocate General stated, in *Response of the IDF*, "While, in dealing with hardened terrorists involved in the commission of grave security offenses, the use of a certain degree of force is often necessary to obtain information, the disproportionate exertion of pressure on subjects (i.e., by torture or maltreatment) is strictly forbidden. Israel has repeatedly condemned all use of torture" (p. 10).

94. A double issue of *Israel Law Review* (1989, vol. 23, nos. 2-3) was devoted to critical assessments of the Landau Commission report.

95. See Public Committee against Torture in Israel, *Moderate Physical Pressure: Interrogation Methods in Israel* (Jerusalem: Public Committee against Torture in Israel, 1990).

96. In 1995, the Israeli cabinet approved "shaking" in "exceptional circumstances." Following the death of a Palestinian detainee, 'Abd a-Samad Harizat, as a direct result of shaking, Prime Minister Yitzhak Rabin said, "There was a malfunction in the interrogation method. It had been used against 8,000 interrogees and there was no problem." Interview on Kol Israel, July 29, 1995, quoted in Yuval Ginbar, "The Face and the Mirror: Israel's View of Its Interrogation Techniques Examined" (L.L.M. diss., University of Essex, United Kingdom, 1996), p. 58.

97. See Stanley Cohen and Daphna Golan, *The Interrogation of Palestinians during the Intifada: Ill-Treatment, "Moderate Physical Pressure" or Torture?* (Jerusalem: B'Tselem, 1991); Human Rights Watch/Middle East, *Torture and Ill-Treatment.*

98. This exception takes no account of the fact that some of the interrogation facilities are within the territory of Israel (i.e., inside the 1949 armistice line).

99. Human Rights Watch/Middle East, *Israeli Interrogation Methods under Fire after Death of Detained Palestinian* (New York: Human Rights Watch, 1992).

100. Quoted in Public Committee against Torture in Israel, *Report on Third Year's Activities, January 1992–December 1992* (Jerusalem: Public Committee against Torture in Israel, 1992), p. 3.

101. Public Committee against Torture in Israel, *Flawed Defense: Torture and Ill-Treatment in GSS Interrogations following the Supreme Court Ruling, 6 September 1999–6 September 2001* (Jerusalem: Public Committee against Torture in Israel, 2001), p. 24.

102. According to official sources, the "new procedures" limited the combined use of various "pressure" tactics and the circumstances under which certain tactics could be used; restricted particular methods to the extraction of "vital information" that interrogators believe a detainee is concealing; and prohibitions against food, drink, and lavatory deprivation and against "abandoning" a detainee to heat or cold. Yuval Ginbar, *The "New Procedure" in GSS Interrogation: The Case of 'Abd A-Nasser 'Ubeid* (Jerusalem: B'Tselem, 1993).

103. Stanley Cohen and Daphna Golan, *The Interrogation of Palestinians during the Intifada: Follow-up to March 1991 B'Tselem Report* (Jerusalem: B'Tselem, 1992).

104. Allegra Pacheco, ed., *The Case against Torture in Israel: A Compilation of Petitions, Briefs and Other Documents Submitted to the Israeli High Court of Justice* (Jerusalem: Public Committee against Torture in Israel, 1999), p. 16.

105. Ibid., pp. 13, 25–27.

106. See Yuval Ginbar, *Legitimizing Torture: The High Court of Justice Rulings in the Bilbeisi, Hamdan and Mubarak Cases: An Annotated Sourcebook* (Jerusalem: B'Tselem, 1997).

107. Eitan Felner, "Legally Sanctioned Human Rights Violations," *B'Tselem Human Rights Report* 6 (1998): 1, 15.

108. Quoted in Daphna Baram, "President of ACRI: Torture Is Not Necessarily a Civil Rights Offense," *Kol Ha'Ir,* January 30, 1998. Retrieved June 1999 from *Ha'aretz* Web site: www.haaretzdaily.com.

109. See Gideon Levy, "What We Owe the Radical Left," *Ha'aretz*, September 13, 1999.

110. The day before the scheduled HCJ hearing, B'Tselem released a new report, *Routine Torture*, at a press conference during which actors demonstrated common forms of position abuse while hooded. Pictures of these reenactments were published in all the major Israeli media.

111. *Public Committee against Torture in Israel v. State of Israel*, HCJ 5100/94, Sept 6, 1999.

112. See Public Committee against Torture in Israel, *Flawed Defense;* Joseph Algazy, "Fear and Trembling," *Ha'aretz*, January 6, 2003.


# Chapter 3: Going to Court

1. Michel Foucault, *Discipline and Punish: The Birth of the Prison* (New York: Vintage Books, 1979), p. 10.

2. Allen Feldman, *Formations of Violence: The Narrative of the Body and Political Terror in Northern Ireland* (Chicago: University of Chicago Press, 1991), p. 22.

3. Ibid., p. 2.

4. Here I put quotation marks around "Israel" and "Israeli-administered areas" to indicate a boundary that is less a matter of geography than a politico-legal demarcation. Parts of the territories conquered in 1967 have become extensions of domestic Israeli space through the processes of land confiscation, settlement, and the extension of domestic Israeli laws and jurisdictions. Indeed, some of the soldiers who come to court never have to cross the geographic boundary of the Green Line to get there, since they are settlers.

5. Pierre Bourdieu, *The Logic of Practice,* trans. Richard Nice (Stanford, CA: Stanford University Press, 1990), p. 54.

6. Usually I sat in the public section with Palestinians, but sometimes I sat with the defense lawyers if invited to do so and if soldiers on guard duty did not object. On several occasions, soldiers insisted that I sit with them.

7. Until 1994, the courts were in military bases located in Palestinian towns. In Hebron, the compound was on a hill some distance from any residential or commercial area, whereas in Nablus and Gaza the compounds were centrally located. In all three, the compounds also housed prisons. In Ramallah, Jenin, and Tulkaram, the compounds were in residential neighborhoods, within walking distance of the center. After 1994, the courts were relocated to bases remote from Palestinian towns and difficult for Palestinians to reach or enter.

8. Michel Warshawski, "Beyond My Wildest Dreams: A Few Hours in the Gaza Military Court," *News from Within* 7/7 (July 3, 1991): 14.

9. According to several lawyers, the impetus for creating physical barriers in all the courtrooms swelled from an incident in the Gaza court when a woman armed with a knife rushed to the front of the courtroom, although they disagreed whether she was aiming for a soldier or her husband's lawyer.

10. Israel has one of the world's highest per capita ratios of members of the armed forces (including reservists) to total population. See Dan Horowitz and Moshe Lissak, "Democracy and National Security in a Protracted Conflict," *Jerusalem Quarterly* 51 (Summer 1989): 2–40; Baruch Kimmerling, "Making Conflict a Routine: Cumulative Effects of the Arab-Jewish Conflict upon Israeli Society," in *Israeli Society and Its Defense Establishment: The Social and Political Impact of a Protracted Violent Conflict,* ed. Moshe Lissak (London: Frank Cass, 1984); Amia Leblich and Meir Perlow, "Transition to Adulthood during Military Service," *Jerusalem Quarterly* 47 (Summer 1988): 40–76; Moshe Lissak, "The IDF as an Agent of Socialization and Education: A Study of Role Expansion in a Democratic Society," in *The Perceived Role of the Military,* ed. M. R. Gills (Rotterdam: Rotterdam University Press, 1971); Edward Luttwak and Dan Horowitz, *The Israeli Army* (New York: Harper and Row, 1975); Maurice Roumani, *From Immigrant to Citizen: The Contribution of Army to National Integration in Israel* (The Hague: Foundation for the Study of Plural Societies, 1979).

11. Sara Helman, "Militarism and the Construction of the Life-World of Israeli Males," in *The Military and Militarism in Israeli Society,* ed. Edna Lomsky-Feder and Eyal Ben-Ari (Albany: SUNY Press, 1999), p. 204.

12. See Lomsky-Feder and Ben-Ari, *The Military and Militarism;* Yoram Peri, "Civil-Military Relations in Israel in Crisis," in *Military, State and Society in Israel,* ed. Daniel Maman, Eyal Ben-Ari, and Zeev Rosenhek (New Brunswick, NJ: Transaction Publishers, 2001).

13. See Dafna Izraeli, "Paradoxes of Women's Service in the Israel Defense Forces," in Maman, Ben-Ari, and Rosenhek, *Military, State and Society;* Simona Sharoni, "To Be a Man in the Jewish State: The Sociopolitical Context of Violence and Oppression," *Challenge* 2/5 (September–October 1991): 26–28.

14. Eyal Ben-Ari, "Masks and Soldiering: The Israeli Army and the Palestinian Uprising," *Cultural Anthropology* 44 (1989): 377–78.

15. Ibid, pp. 378–79 (emphasis in original).

16. According to survey research and polling in Israel, such views are not uncommon. For example, findings from a 1988 survey revealed that some 38 percent of Jewish Israelis believed that Arabs were "primitive," 40 percent believed that Arabs would never reach "Jewish levels of development," and some 70 percent supported a military "liquidation" of the Palestine Liberation Organization. Sammy Smooha, *Arabs and Jews in Israel: Changes and Continuity in Mutual Intolerance* (Boulder, CO: Westview Press, 1992). See Asher Arian, Ilan Talmud, and Tamar Hermann, *National Security and Public Opinion in Israel* (Boulder, CO: Westview Press, 1990); Asher Arian, *Security Threatened: Surveying Israeli Opinion on Peace and War* (New York: Cambridge University Press, 1995); Mark Tessler, "The Intifada and Political Discourse in Israel," *Journal of Palestine Studies* 19/2 (1990): 43–61.

17. Robin Wagner-Pacifici, *Theorizing the Standoff: Contingency in Action* (New York: Cambridge University Press, 2000), pp. 6, 8.

18. According to Wagner-Pacifici, there are "three ideal-typical modes of ending for standoffs: deals, surrenders and violence." Ibid., p. 214.

## Chapter 4: The Face and Arms of Military Justice

1. See James Ron, "Savage Restraint: Israel, Palestine, and the Dialectics of Legal Repression," *Social Problems* 47/4 (2000): 445–72.

2. In general, the officer class in the Israeli military has been dominated by people whose views tend to be to the center or left Zionist on the Jewish Israeli ideologico-political spectrum. See Yoram Peri, *The Israeli Military and Israel's Palestinian Policy: From Oslo to the Al Aqsa Intifada* (Washington, DC: U.S. Institute of Peace, 2002), p. 45.

3. The role(s) of the Israeli military and the relationship between the military and Israeli society have featured prominently in Israeli sociology. However, in this literature, strikingly little, if any, attention has been focused specifically on the military court system. See Uri Ben-Eliezer, *The Making of Israeli Militarism* (Bloomington: Indiana University Press, 1998); Sarit Helman, "Militarism and the Construction of Community," *Journal of Political and Military Sociology* 25 (1997): 305–32; Baruch Kimmerling, *The Interrupted System: Israeli Civilians in War and Routine Times* (New Brunswick, NJ: Transaction Books, 1985); Moshe Lissak, *Israeli Society and Its Defense Establishment: The Social and Political Impact of a Protracted Violent Conflict* (London: Frank Cass, 1984); Edna Lomsky-Feder and Eyal Ben-Ari, eds., *The Military and Militarism in Israeli Society* (Albany: SUNY Press, 1999); Daniel Maman, Eyal Ben-Ari, and Zeev Rosenhek, eds., *Military, State, and Society in Israel* (New Brunswick, NJ: Transaction Publishers, 2001).

4. Allen Feldman, *Formations of Violence: The Narrative of the Body and Political Terror in Northern Ireland* (Chicago: University of Chicago Press, 1991), p. 2.

5. John Meyer and Brian Rowan, "Institutionalized Organizations: Formal Structure as Myth and Ceremony," in *The New Institutionalism in Organizational Analysis,* ed. Walter Powell and Paul DiMaggio (Chicago: University of Chicago Press, 1991), p. 58.

6. A West Bank military order concerning the judiciary states: "In matters of adjudication, a person possessing judicial jurisdiction is subject to no authority save the authority of the law and the security legislation." According to Uzi Amit-Kohn, "It seems unlikely that—even without that provision—anyone would attempt to influence a Judge's decision, or that an Israeli-trained jurist schooled in Western legal thinking would be open to such influence. Such an attempt would be antithetical to the basic principles of Israeli society and jurisprudence and is thus unlikely to occur." Uzi Amit-Kohn, "The Criminal Justice System," in *Israel, the "Intifada" and the Rule of Law,* ed. David Yahav (Tel Aviv: Israeli Ministry of Defense Publications, 1993), p. 86.

7. Until 1990, the IDF appointed judges from the domestic legal system to serve as judges in the military courts (as reservists). Meir Shamgar, then president of the HCJ, decided that it would be improper to use civilian judges in such a capacity because their "civil impartiality and independence could be compromised or questioned." Consequently, the IDF stopped appointing professional judges and restricted the pool to lawyers. David Yahav, deputy Military

Advocate General, interview, June 1993. Amit-Kohn writes, in "The Criminal Justice System," that "[a] derivative benefit of the massive use of reserve officers for these positions [as judges] has been to maintain a healthy connection to the civilian legal world. . . . This has an overall effect of reinforcing judicial independence and maintaining high standards of judicial integrity" (p. 94).

8. Patricia Ewick and Sustan Silbey, *The Common Place of Law: Stories from Everyday Life* (Chicago: University of Chicago Press, 1998), p. 29.

9. Sara Leibovitz-Dar, "No Justice in the Territories," *Hadashot* (suppl.), October 11, 1991.

10. Revisionist Zionism, a movement that emerged during the British Mandate, sought to "revise" the territorial borders available for Jewish settlement to include the East Bank of the Jordan River. The political heirs of this "Greater Israel" position eventually consolidated to form the Likud Party.

11. See Myron Aronoff, "Wars as Catalysts of Political and Cultural Change," in Lomsky-Feder and Ben-Ari, *The Military and Militarism.*

12. This is an allusion to the slogan "Beat 'em and weep," used to refer to liberal angst about the violent and repressive dimensions of military service in the territories.

13. Many Israelis criticized the Lebanon invasion because they construed it as Israel's first "war of choice" rather than a "war of defense" or "necessity."

14. See Ephraim Inbar, "Israel's Small War: The Military Reaction to the Intifada," *Armed Forces and Society* 18 (1991): 29–50; Ze'ev Schiff and Ehud Ya'ari, *Intifada: The Palestinian Uprising: Israel's Third Front* (New York: Simon and Schuster, 1989).

15. See Gad Barzilai and Efraim Inbar, "The Use of Force: Israeli Public Opinion on Military Options," *Armed Forces and Society* 23 (1996): 49–80; Yaron Ezrahi, *Rubber Bullets: Power and Conscience in Modern Israel* (Berkeley: University of California Press, 1998); Hanna Levinsohn and Elihu Katz, "The *Intifada* Is Not a War: Jewish Public Opinion on the Arab-Israeli Conflict," in *Framing the Intifada: People and the Media,* ed. Akiba Cohen and Gadi Wolfsfeld (Norwood, NJ: Ablex, 1994).

16. Aryeh Shalev, *The Intifada: Causes and Effects* (Tel Aviv and Boulder, CO: Jaffee Center for Strategic Studies and Westview Press, 1991), p. 1.

17. Yoram Peri, "Getting the Territories out of the IDF," *New Outlook,* April 1990, p. 8.

18. Ibid., p. 10.

19. Emmanual Sivan, "Upon the Dawning of the Intifada's Third Year," *Ha'aretz,* December 8, 1989.

20. Ibid.

21. See Sara Helman, "Negotiating Obligations, Creating Rights: Conscientious Objection and the Redefinition of Citizenship in Israel," *Citizenship Studies* 3/1 (1999): 45–70; Ruth Linn, "When the Individual Soldier Says 'No' to War: A Look at Selective Refusal during the Intifada," *Journal of Peace Research* 33 (1996): 421–32.

22. Rela Mezali, "Military Service as Initiation Rite," *Challenge* 4/4 (July–August 1993): 36.

23. Ibid.

24. Stanley Cohen, "Criminology and the Uprising," *Tikkun* 3/5 (1988): 95.

25. Moshe Landau et al., *Commission of Inquiry into the Methods of Investigation of the General Security Service Regarding Hostile Terrorist Activity* (Jerusalem: Government Press Office, 1987).

26. Ibid., p. 29.

27. Public Committee against Torture in Israel, *Moderate Physical Pressure: Interrogation Methods in Israel* (Jerusalem: Public Committee against Torture in Israel, 1990), pp. 26–27.

28. Yizhar Be'er and Saleh 'Abdel-Jawad, *Collaborators in the Occupied Territories: Human Rights Abuses and Violations* (Jerusalem: B'Tselem, 1994), p. 10.

29. The first *intifada* caused a near-total collapse of the collaborator network. But this information gap was compensated by a reorganization of the military and security apparatus, including the recruitment of a new network of informants within prisons (*'asafir,* literally "birds"), using strategies of entrapment, promises of shorter sentences or vital services (e.g., medical treatment), or better prison conditions. See Salim Tamari, "Eyeless in Judea: Israel's Strategy of Collaborators and Forgeries," *Middle East Report* 164–65 (May-August 1990): 39–45; Michal Karpa, "Dangerous Relations," *Ma'ariv,* January 8, 1992.

30. Prima facie evidence can include material evidence, affidavits from witnesses (including arresting soldiers), secret evidence, and first- or third-party confessions.

31. See Zvi Hadar, "The Military Courts," in *Military Government in the Territories Administered by Israel, 1967–1980: The Legal Aspects,* ed. Meir Shamgar (Jerusalem: Harry Sacher Institute for Legislative and Comparative Law of Hebrew University, 1982), p. 212.

32. In his 1989 report to the Israeli cabinet, the head of the IDF's intelligence division "stated explicitly that the Intifada was directed and led by the PLO." Peri, *Israeli Military,* p. 15. However, this interviewee's theory differs — or "expands" — on the (disputed) claim that the PLO masterminded and ran the *intifada* by claiming the infiltration of PLO operatives.

33. According to Peri: "The IDF's support of the peace process in the early 1990s was perceived as one of expression of the 'nonmilitaristic' character of the military and of the instrumentalist principle that guides it: When the politicians decided on a historic compromise, the military cooperated and fulfilled its role in the process." Peri, *Israeli Military,* p. 12.

34. Stuart Cohen, "The Peace Process and Its Impact on the Development of a 'Slimmer and Smarter' Israel Defense Forces," *Israel Affairs* 1 (1995): 1–21.

35. See Dafna Izraeli, "Paradoxes of Women's Service in the Israel Defense Forces," in Maman, Ben-Ari, and Rosenhek, *Military, State and Society.*

36. See Dan Horowitz and Moshe Lissak, *Trouble in Utopia: The Overburdened Polity of Israel* (Albany: SUNY Press, 1989).

37. See Robert Blecher, "Living on the Edge: The Threat of 'Transfer' in Israel and Palestine," *Middle East Report,* no. 225 (Winter 2002): 22–29.

38. Amos Harel, "IDF Mulls Change in Military Court System in the Territories," *Ha'aretz English,* September 19, 2002.

39. For the text of refuseniks' public statement, see "Combatants' Letter," 2002, retrieved March 2, 2004, from www.seruv.org.il/english/combatants_letter.asp.

40. See Dan Leon, "Refusal to Serve: An Israeli Phenomenon and Its Implications," *Palestine-Israel Journal of Politics, Economics and Culture* 9/3 (2002): 83–89.

# Chapter 5: The Politics of Language

1. James Boyd White, *Justice as Translation: An Essay in Cultural and Legal Criticism* (Chicago: University of Chicago Press, 1990), p. 23.

2. See Alon Peled, "The Politics of Language in Multiethnic Militaries: The Case of Oriental Jews in the Israel Defense Forces, 1950–59," *Armed Forces and Society* 26/4 (2000): 587–606.

3. See Ella Shohat, "Sephardim in Israel: Zionism from the Standpoint of Its Jewish Victims," in *Dangerous Liaisons: Gender, Nation, and Postcolonial Perspectives,* ed. Anne McClintock, Aamir Mufti, and Ella Shohat (Minneapolis: University of Minnesota Press, 1997).

4. There are a variety of linguistic communities in Israel, including native speakers of Russian, Amharic, Yiddish, and English. Only Arabic, though, bears the negative association of being the "enemy" language.

5. Druze Israelis' bilingualism symbolizes their ties to various, sometimes overlapping, linguistic communities. Fluency in Hebrew (which is not universal within the Druze community) places them within the multiethnic "Israeli" community. Fluency in Arabic links them to other Arabic-speaking Israelis (including Jews from the Arab world). And their Palestinian dialect is shared by all other Arabs indigenous to Palestine, including other citizens, residents of the occupied territories, and those in the diaspora.

6. See Kais Firru, *The Druzes in the Jewish State: A Brief History* (Leiden: E. J. Brill, 1999).

7. According to Gabriel Ben-Dor, the state complied with "Druze requests" for military conscription as a reward for the service of Druze soldiers as scouts in the southern region against guerrilla activities in the 1954–56 period (a period that culminated in the Israeli, British, and French invasion of Egypt). Gabriel Ben-Dor, "The Military in the Politics of Integration and Innovation: The Case of the Druze Minority in Israel," *African and Asian Studies* 9 (1973): 348. Because of the importance of the military in Israeli society, early on some Druze leaders advocated military service to enhance their own position vis-à-vis the state and to ensure state support for communal needs.

8. In 1976, the Ministry of Education and Culture created a Druze committee with a mandate to solve lingering "identity problems" among Druze Israelis. The committee created a new Druze curriculum for primary and secondary schools. According to Salman Falah, one of the key architects of this curriculum,

Druze education is not oriented to preparing students for the university; rather, it contains "more important things related to Druze identity," namely preparation for army service and a feeling of communal loyalty to the state. Quoted in *Jerusalem Post*, April 4, 1986 (weekly supplement), p. 14.

9. For example, Walter Schwarz writes: "The Druzes are the most warlike of the Arab communities in Israel, yet they are the most trusted. They are the most primitive, yet they are the favourites." Walter Schwarz, *The Arabs in Israel* (London: Faber and Faber, 1959), p. 148.

10. Since the early 1990s (when the Israeli-Palestinian negotiations began), an estimated five thousand Arab Israelis have enlisted in the IDF. See Rhoda Kanaaneh, "Embattled Identities: Palestinian Soldiers in the Israeli Military," *Journal of Palestine Studies* 32/3 (2003): 5–20.

11. See Ian Lustick, *Arabs in the Jewish State: Israel's Control of a National Minority* (Austin: University of Texas Press, 1980).

12. Kais Firru, "Reshaping Druze Particularism in Israel," *Journal of Palestine Studies* 30/3 (2001): 46.

13. This autarky is interpreted as a historical animosity between Druze and Muslims in Palestine, as evident in residential patterns: Druze have tended to live in geographically remote villages or in mixed villages (Christian and/or Muslim) but not among a majority of Muslims. See Kais Firru, "Druze Identity: The Historical Dimension," in *The Druze in Israel* (in Hebrew) (Haifa: University of Haifa, Occasional Papers on the Middle East, 1982).

14. Israeli scholars, beginning in the 1950s with Haim Blanc, fixated on *taqiyya* (usually translated as "dissimulation") to understand and explain Druze relations with others and their communal "behavior." According to Kais Firru, "*taqiyya* became for Israeli scholars and politicians the 'essence' of Druze existence." Firru, "Reshaping Druze Particularism," p. 47.

15. Jonathan Oppenheimer, "The Druze in Israel as Arabs and Non-Arabs: Manipulation of Categories of Identity in a Non-Civil State," in *Studies in Israeli Ethnicity: After the Ingathering,* ed. Alex Weingrod (New York: Gordon and Breach Science Publishers, 1985), p. 264.

16. The decision to ally with the Zionists came primarily from Sheikh Labib Abu Rukn of 'Usfiya and Sheikh Salih Kneifes of Shafa'amr, both of whom later became members of the Israeli Knesset.

17. See Laila Parsons, *The Druze between Palestine and Israel, 1947–49* (New York: Oxford University Press, 2000); Yoav Gelber, "Antecedents of the Jewish-Druze Alliance in Palestine," *Middle Eastern Studies* 31 (1995): 352–73, and "Druze and Jews in the War of 1948," *Middle Eastern Studies* 31 (1992): 229–52.

18. See Ben-Dor, "The Military," p. 347; Gabriel Ben-Dor, *The Druzes in Israel: A Political Study* (Jerusalem: Magnes University Press, 1979); Yehuda Oliva, "Political Involvement of the Druse in Israel," in *The Druse: A Religious Community in Transition,* ed. Nissim Dana (Jerusalem: Israel Economist, 1980), p. 128; Hillel Frisch, "The Druze Minority in the Israeli Military: Traditionalizing an Ethnic Policing Role," *Armed Forces and Society* 20 (1993): 52.

19. Such reasoning is based on a conflation of Islam with Arabness and an emphasis on the distinction between the Druze sect and Sunni Islam (the religious identity of Palestinian Muslims). For example, according to Hillel Frisch, "The greatest barrier between Druze and Muslim Arabs, of course, is religion. Their highly secretive religion is a fusion of Platonism, pagan elements, Christianity, and Islam, a fusion that has aroused the ire of Islamic puritans in the past." Frisch, "The Druze Minority," p. 55. See also Martin Edelman, "The Druze Courts in the Political System of Israel," *Middle East Review* 19 (1987): 54–61.

20. In the early years of Israeli statehood, a similar approach was tried unsuccessfully on Christian Palestinians. See Usama Halaby, *The Druze in Israel: From Sect to Nation* (in Arabic) (Majdal Shams, Golan Heights: Golan Academic Association, 1989).

21. According to Jonathan Oppenheimer, the ways in which Druze communal boundaries (endogamous) were politicized harmonized better with Jewish than Arab nationalism. This became the cornerstone of manipulation of Druze identity by the Israeli state. Oppenheimer, "The Druze in Israel," pp. 266–67.

22. *All* Israeli citizens are incorporated on the basis of some collective classification (i.e., Jews, Arabs, Bedouin, Circassians).

23. See Ori Stendel, *The Minorities in Israel: Trends in the Development of the Arab and Druze Communities* (Jerusalem: Israel Economist, 1973), p. 103; Oppenheimer, "The Druze in Israel," p. 261.

24. Talal Asad, "Are There Histories of Peoples without Europe? A Review Article," *Comparative Studies in Society and History* 29 (1987): 606–7.

25. Zeidan Atash, "Testimony of a Druze Member of Knesset," in *Every Sixth Israeli: Relations between the Jewish Majority and the Arab Minority in Israel,* ed. Alouph Haraven (Jerusalem: Van Leer Jerusalem Foundation, 1983), pp. 65–66. See also Hillel Frisch, "State Ethnicization and the Crisis of Leadership Succession among Israel's Druze," *Ethnic and Racial Studies* 20 (1997): 588.

26. According to Gabriel Ben-Dor, Druze service in the military "[fits] their self-image." He claims that they are especially suited to the Border Police *(Mishmar Gvul)* because of their "special skills," which he describes as "courage, resourcefulness, physical fitness, familiarity with effectiveness in small infantry formations, and knowledge of Arabic." Ben-Dor, "The Military," p. 353.

27. According to Hillel Frisch, "The IDF does not deliberately ethnicize the Druze. In fact, the opposite is true. The IDF is committed to integration and to the promotion of Druze on the basis of merit." Frisch, "The Druze Minority," p. 62.

28. Because of institutionalized discrimination against non-Jews in the Israeli economy and generally low educational achievement within the Druze community, approximately 30 to 40 percent of the Druze workforce is employed in security-related jobs, compared to approximately 15 percent of the Jewish majority. Frisch, "State Ethnicization," p. 587. In a study by Hassan Zarka of Haifa University, 38.9 percent of Druze youngsters (i.e., males) want to remain in the army after their compulsory service, as compared to 7.4 percent of Jewish youngsters. The security services are one area of the labor market where

Druze do not have to compete with Arabs for jobs, since the latter are excluded because they do not serve in the army. Cited in Steve Rodan and Jacob Dallal, "Secret of Success," *Jerusalem Post Magazine,* August 11, 1995.

29. The goals of the DIC also include an end to land confiscation and return of confiscated land, termination of all state intervention in Druze religious affairs, cancellation of "Druze Heritage" courses (because of their false and chauvinistic presentations of Druze history and relations with Arabs and Jews), and total equality for all citizens of Israel.

30. One of the main themes in the documentary film *I'm Druze* is the state's failure to treat the Druze fairly in light of their strong and ongoing demonstrations of loyalty. In an interview with the late Sheikh Amin Tarif, spiritual head of the community, he says, "Druze treat Israel better than Israel treats the Druze. They are loyal, respectful and work according to the law. But Israel doesn't. In the past, Israel turned to the Druze and said to them, 'You live separately and you are separate from the Arabs.' And the Druze accepted this. But they treated us exactly like they treated the Arabs. . . . We sacrificed our blood and our children because the Arabs were their enemies. In the hearts of the Druze, a burden has been created and this is the government's fault."

31. One of these two, who went on to study at Technion University, told of the constant discrimination he faced in Haifa. Jewish students would often tell him that he did not "seem" Druze, intending this as a compliment. In his year-long quest to find an apartment, whenever he would call to inquire about an advertisement, speaking perfect Hebrew on the phone, landlords would welcome him to come and see their places. However, when he gave his name, they would invariably "remember" that they had already promised it to someone else. He began resorting to deceptions, such as lying about his name and where he was from.

32. See Frisch, "The Druze Minority," p. 93.

33. This issue of social and sexual relations illustrates a contrast between Druze and Jewish experiences in the military. According to a study of Jewish male soldiers, "None of the participants saw the army as a good opportunity to meet women, in spite of the fact that women do serve on bases with men and [Jewish] Israelis believe that the army is the country's greatest matchmaker. On the contrary, several men described their service away from home as causing an interruption of their former heterosexual relationships." Amia Lieblich and Meir Perlow, "Transition to Adulthood during Military Service," *Jerusalem Quarterly* 47 (1988): 50.

34. Those who raised the issue of sexual relations typically put forth two common stereotypes: that Jewish female soldiers were sexually uninhibited and available and that Jewish women wanted to have sex with Druze men because they were "curious." Not surprisingly, the issue of homosexual relations never came up in interviews.

35. In the negotiations in the mid-1950s between Druze leaders and Israeli officials, it was agreed that Druze women would be excluded from conscription.

36. The spuriousness of treating sectarian particularism as the *explanation* for

social roles and relations is evident in the significantly different norms that prevail in the Syrian Druze community in the occupied Golan Heights. There, male-female relations are comparatively much less restricted and women have relatively greater liberties and opportunities. Syrian Druze women in the Golan tend to marry older, and among the younger generations male/female literacy is nearly identical. Furthermore, hundreds of women have chosen — and been permitted and encouraged — to pursue university educations, including dozens who have studied abroad. See Hassan Abu Libdeh et al., *A Survey of the Syrian Population in the Occupied Golan Heights: Demography and Health* (Majdal Shams, Golan Heights: Arab Association for Development, 1994); Lisa Hajjar, ed., *Twenty-Five Years of Israeli Occupation of the Syrian Golan Heights* (Jerusalem: Arab Association for Development, 1993), and "Making Identity Policy: Israel's Interventions among the Druze," *Middle East Report* 200 (1996): 2–6; Bashar Tarabieh, "Education, Control and Resistance in the Golan Heights," *Middle East Report* 194–95 (1995): 43–47.

37. The Druze Zionist Organization, a group established to express and capitalize on support for state policies, requested permission to establish a Druze settlement in the territories, but the request was refused because only Jews are granted the "right" to settle.

38. Susan Berk-Seligson, *The Bilingual Courtroom: Court Interpreters in the Judicial Process* (Chicago: University of Chicago Press, 1990), p. 54.


# Chapter 6: Cause Lawyering and National Conflict

1. Franz Kafka, *The Trial,* trans. Breon Mitchell (New York: Schocken Books, 1998), pp. 119–20.

2. See Austin Sarat and Stuart Scheingold, eds., *Cause Lawyering: Political Commitments and Professional Responsibilities* (New York: Oxford University Press, 1998), and *Cause Lawyering and the State in a Global Era* (New York: Oxford University Press, 2001).

3. See Richard Abel, *Politics by Other Means: Law in the Struggle against Apartheid, 1980–1984* (New York: Routledge, 1995); Stephen Ellman, *In a Time of Trouble: Law and Liberty in South Africa's State of Emergency* (New York: Oxford University Press, 1992).

4. Terrence Halliday, "Politics and Civic Professionalism: Legal Elites and Cause Lawyers," *Law and Social Inquiry* 24/4 (1999): 1016 (emphasis in original).

5. Ibid.

6. Ibid., p. 1017 (emphasis in original).

7. Ibid. (emphasis in original).

8. Ibid.

9. David Luban, *Lawyers and Justice: An Ethical Study* (Princeton, NJ: Princeton University Press, 1988), p. xxv.

10. Raja Shehadeh, *Strangers in the House: Coming of Age in Occupied Palestine* (South Royalton, VT: Steerforth Press, 2002), pp. 135–36.

11. Stanley Cohen, *Denial and Acknowledgement: The Impact of Information about Human Rights Violations* (Jerusalem: Center for Human Rights, Hebrew University, 1995), p. 5.

12. See Lawyers Committee for Human Rights, *An Examination of Human Rights Workers and Lawyers from the West Bank and Gaza and Conditions of Detention at Ketziot* (New York: Lawyers Committee for Human Rights, 1988), and *Lawyers and the Military Justice System of the Israeli-Occupied Territories* (New York: Lawyers Committee for Human Rights, 1992).

13. Felicia Langer, *With My Own Eyes: Israel and the Occupied Territories, 1967–73* (London: Ithaca Press, 1975). Langer published two other autobiographical accounts of her work: *These Are My Brothers: Israel and the Occupied Territories, Part II* (London: Ithaca Press, 1979); and *An Age of Stone* (New York: Quartet, 1988).

14. Israeli civilian lawyers were granted permission to represent Palestinian clients in the military courts on the basis of Military Order 145, which was promulgated in reaction to the West Bank lawyers' strike (see below).

15. Quoted in Dov Shefi, "The Reports of the U.N. Special Committees on Israeli Practices in the Territories: A Survey and Evaluation," in *Military Government in the Territories Administered by Israel, 1967–1980: The Legal Aspects,* ed. Meir Shamgar (Jerusalem: Harry Sacher Institute for Legislative Research and Comparative Law, Hebrew University, 1982). To appreciate the irony and credulity of this quote, see the discussion of the Landau Commission in Chapter 2.

16. See Nadim Rouhana, *Palestinian Citizens in an Ethnic Jewish State: Identities in Conflict* (New Haven, CT: Yale University Press, 1997).

17. See George Bisharat, *Palestinian Lawyers and Israeli Rule: Law and Disorder in the West Bank* (Austin: University of Texas Press, 1989).

18. Bisharat, in *Palestinian Lawyers,* estimated the number at about 50 (p. 70). Bahij Tammimi, former head of the Arab Lawyers' Committee, estimated the number at 120, as recorded in the notes of a meeting on June 25, 1991, between Palestinian lawyers and Jordan Paust, a representative of the ICJ (on file with Al-Haq). The Centre for the Independence of Judges and Lawyers put the number at 150, as reported in *CIJL Bulletin,* no. 21 (April 1988): 5.

19. "Jordan to Resume Paying Striking West Bank Lawyers," *Jerusalem Post,* January 10, 1986.

20. The application was based on Jordanian Law 11 of 1966. According to international humanitarian law, as an occupying force, Israel is obligated to preserve local laws, which served as the legal basis for the ALC's application.

21. East Jerusalem residents can join the Israel Bar Association, but few have chosen to do so.

22. In 1985, the ALC petitioned the HCJ to force the military authorities to license an independent professional organization. Before the HCJ had reached a decision, the military authorities in the West Bank promulgated Military Order (MO) 1164, which created a Lawyers Council Bar Association. According to this order, the chair and council members would be appointed by the military administration. The ALC protested that appointment rather than elections

would compromise the independence of lawyers and would serve the interests of military authorities rather than the needs or interests of legal professionals and the Palestinian community. The HCJ subsequently held that the proposed Lawyers Council was not sufficiently independent, but it did not object to the military authorities' opposition to the inclusion of East Jerusalem residents. Consequently, the military authorities never implemented MO 1164, but neither did they permit the registration of the ALC. For an English translation of MO 1164 and commentary by Jonathan Kuttab, see *Palestine Yearbook of International Law* 2 (1985): 156–61; see also "Military Order 1164 Threatens the Independence of the Bar Association," *CIJL Bulletin*, no. 17 (April 1986): 17–22.

23. This figure is based on combined estimates from Freih Abu Middain, then head of the GBA, and Ali Ghuzlan, head of the ALC.

24. See Marianne Heiberg and Geir Øvensen, *Palestinian Society in Gaza, West Bank and Arab Jerusalem: A Survey of Living Conditions* (Oslo: Fafo, 1993).

25. See Mona Rishmawi, "The Lawyers' Strike in Gaza," *CIJL Bulletin*, no. 21 (April 1988): 23–25.

26. See Lawyers Committee for Human Rights, *Boycott of the Military Courts by West Bank and Israeli Lawyers*, Background Memorandum (New York: Lawyers Committee for Human Rights, 1989).

27. The IBA has provided little institutional support for those who work in the military courts. According to two IBA representatives, Matti Atzmon and Yaacov Rubin, issues arising from military court work are more "political" than "legal professional" and therefore are deemed to fall beyond the scope of the organization's mandate. However, an IBA representative does advise the military on the appointment of judges for the military courts.

28. Lawyers Committee for Human Rights, *Boycott of the Military Courts*, pp. 14–15.

29. Allegra Pacheco, introduction to *The Case against Torture in Israel: A Compilation of Petitions, Briefs and Other Documents Submitted to the Israeli High Court of Justice*, ed. Allegra Pacheco (Jerusalem: Public Committee against Torture in Israel, 1999), p. 9.

30. See George Moffett, "A Judicial System Where Even Kafka Would Be Lost: An Interview with Felicia Langer," *Journal of Palestine Studies* 20/1 (1990): 24–36.

31. Some lawyers implored Langer to turn over her files because they were an incomparable part of the historic record of the occupation, but she decided to destroy them before leaving the country.

32. See Lisa Hajjar, "Law against Order: Human Rights Organizations and (versus?) the Palestinian Authority," *University of Miami Law Review* 56 (October 2001): 59–76; Rema Hammami, Jamil Hilal, and Salim Tamari, "Civil Society in Palestine," unpublished paper, 1999.

33. "Torts Law, Amendment 'Law for Handling Claims Related to IDF Activity in Judea and Samaria,'" was passed by the Israeli Knesset on July 24, 2002.

34. Public Committee against Torture in Israel, *Lawyers Guide: Defending*

*Detainees' Rights during Interrogation by the GSS* (in Arabic) (Jerusalem: Public Committee against Torture in Israel, 2001).

35. Dan Rabinowitz and Khawla Abu-Baker, *The Stand-Tall Generation* (in Hebrew) (Jerusalem: Keter, 2002).

36. Haggai Finegold, "I Would Represent Bin Laden," *Kolbo,* September 13, 2002.

# Chapter 7: Political Subjects, Legal Objects

1. Raymonda Tawil, *Women Prisoners in the Prison Country* (Akka: Dar Al-Aswar, 1988; Arabic), p. 184.

2. Palestine Central Bureau of Statistics, *Palestinians at the End of Year 2002* (Ramallah, West Bank: Palestine Central Bureau of Statistics, 2002).

3. The Israel Defense Forces (IDF) Public Relations Office does not keep records of totals. Human rights organizations obtain and report figures from the IDF on a year-by-year or month-by-month basis.

4. Khaled Al-Hindi, *The Democratic Practice of the Palestinian Prisoners Movement* (in Arabic) (Ramallah, West Bank: Muwatin, 2000). Al-Hindi calculated these figures from Amnesty International annual reports.

5. During the first *intifada,* the rate of incarceration in the West Bank and Gaza was "by far the highest known anywhere in the world: close to 1,000 prisoners per 100,000 population, or one prisoner for every 100 persons." Middle East Watch, *Prison Conditions in Israel and the Occupied Territories* (New York: Human Rights Watch, 1991), p. 16.

6. These figures are drawn from reports by Amnesty International, B'Tselem, the International Committee of the Red Cross, and Al-Haq.

7. "July 28, 2002: Latest Statistics for Palestinian Prisoners in Israeli Jails, Detention Centers and Interrogation Centers," retrieved March 3, 2004, from www.addameer.org/index2.html.

8. Uri Savir, *The Process* (in Hebrew) (Tel Aviv: Miskal-Yediot Aharonot Books, 1998), p. 237, quoted in Yoram Peri, *The Israeli Military and Israel's Palestinian Policy* (Washington, DC: U.S. Institute of Peace, 2002), p. 49.

9. Frantz Fanon, among others, has used the concept of carceralism to analyze and criticize colonialism. See *The Wretched of the Earth,* trans. Constance Farrington (Harmondsworth: Penguin Books, 1982), pp. 50–53. While conditions of life for Palestinians in the West Bank and Gaza have many attributes of "colonialism" (e.g., foreign rule; expropriation of land and resources), military occupation differs from more "conventional" forms of colonial rule (i.e., conquest originating from international war and internationally regarded as temporary). Michel Foucault, among others, has described modern society as carceral, analogizing the surveillance and discipline of prisons to other social spheres. See Michel Foucault, *Discipline and Punish: The Birth of the Prison* (New York: Vintage Books, 1979).

10. According to Gadi Algazy, Palestinians "will be prisoners in their own

country, entirely dependent on the goodwill of the occupying forces and penned in their enclaves by barbed wire, unable to go anywhere without a pass. This is the Middle Eastern version of apartheid. . . . Yet there is a major difference between South Africa and Palestine: Israel no longer needs the local workforce, which has been made redundant by fencing the occupied territories and by bringing in non-Jewish immigrant labor. The Palestinians will be joining those millions of men and women who, thanks to globalization, are not even worth exploiting." Gadi Algazy, "Israel: A Contemporary Ghetto," *Le Monde Diplomatique,* July 2003, p. 5.

11. Arthur Kleinman, "The Violences of Everyday Life: The Multiple Forms and Dynamics of Social Violence," in *Violence and Subjectivity,* ed. Veena Das, Arthur Kleinman, Mamphela Ramphele, and Pamela Reynolds (Berkeley: University of California Press, 2000), p. 226.

12. Michel Foucault, *The History of Sexuality: An Introduction,* vol. 1 (New York: Vintage Books, 1990), p. 93; see generally pp. 92–102.

13. See Esmail Nashif, "Identity, Community, and Text: The Production of Meaning among Palestinian Political Captives" (Ph.D. diss., University of Texas-Austin, 2004); Julie Peteet, "Male Gender and Rituals of Resistance in the Palestinian *Intifada:* A Cultural Politics of Violence," *American Ethnologist* 21/1 (1994): 31–49.

14. Elaine Scarry, *The Body in Pain: The Making and Unmaking of the World* (New York: Oxford University Press, 1985), pp. 56–58.

15. Allen Feldman, *Formations of Violence: The Narrative of the Body and Political Terror in Northern Ireland* (Chicago: University of Chicago Press, 1991), pp. 138–46.

16. Approximately 180 Palestinians have died in interrogation since 1967. Palestinian Prisoner Society, "Palestinian Prisoners in Israeli Jails," Press Release No. 02, June 10, 2002.

17. James Ron was the principal investigator for Human Rights Watch, *Torture and Ill-Treatment: Israel's Interrogation of Palestinians from the Occupied Territories* (New York: Human Rights Watch, 1994). See also James Ron, "Savage Restraint: Israel, Palestine and the Dialectics of Legal Repression," *Social Problems* 47/4 (2000): 445–72, and *Frontiers and Ghettos: State Violence in Israel and Serbia* (Berkeley: University of California Press, 2003).

18. See Catherine Cook, Adam Hanieh, and Adah Kay, *Stolen Youth: The Politics of Israel's Detention of Palestinian Children* (London: Pluto Press, 2003).

19. Although Israel ratified the UN Convention on the Rights of the Child in 1991, it refuses to regard this as binding vis-à-vis the treatment of Palestinian children for reasons related to the unresolved status of the West Bank and Gaza (see Chapter 2).

20. Anton Shammas, "A Stone's Throw," *New York Review of Books,* March 31, 1988.

21. More than 2 percent of Palestinian children (between the ages of nine and seventeen) were arrested during the first *intifada.* James Graff, *Palestinian Children and Israeli State Violence* (Toronto: Near East Cultural and Educational Foundation of Canada, 1991), p. 110.

22. See Adam Hanieh, Adah Kay, and Catherine Cook, "Paying the Price of Injustice: Palestinian Child Prisoners and the UN Human Rights System," *Middle East Report* 229 (Winter 2003): 26–31.

23. Human Rights Watch, *Torture and Ill-Treatment,* p. 15.

24. Stanley Cohen and Daphna Golan, *The Interrogation of Palestinians during the Intifada: Ill-Treatment, "Moderate Physical Pressure," or Torture?* (Jerusalem: B'Tselem, 1991).

25. Human Rights Watch, *Torture and Ill-Treatment,* pp. 27–29, 61; Yuval Ginbar and Yael Stein, *Torture during Interrogations: Testimony of Palestinian Detainees, Testimony of Interrogators* (Jerusalem: B'Tselem, 1994), p. 4. The last method, subjection to loud and continuous noise, was added to the repertoire of interrogation tactics in 1992.

26. Eyad Sarraj and Sohail Salmi, *Torture and Mental Health: The Experience of Palestinians in Israeli Prisons* (Gaza: Gaza Community Mental Health Programme, 1993), p. 2.

27. See Al-Haq, *Palestinian Victims of Torture Speak Out: Thirteen Accounts of Torture during Interrogation in Israeli Prisons* (Ramallah: Al-Haq, 1993), and *Torture and Intimidation in the West Bank: The Case of al-Fara'a Prison* (Ramallah: Al-Haq, 1985); Yuval Ginbar, "The Face and the Mirror: Israel's View of Its Interrogation Techniques Examined" (L.L.M. diss., University of Essex, 1996); Neve Gordon and Rela Mazali, *"The Slaughter House": The General Security Service Interrogation at Gaza Central Prison* (Tel Aviv: Israeli-Palestinian Physicians for Human Rights, 1993); Mohammad Jaradat, Tikva Honig-Parnass, and Ingrid Gassner-Jaradat, *Hebron Prison: A View from Inside* (Jerusalem: Alternative Information Center, 1992); Allegra Pacheco, *Torture by the Israeli Security Services* (Jerusalem: Public Committee against Torture in Israel, 1996).

28. Jeffrey Dillman and Musa Bakri, *Israel's Use of Electric Shock Torture in the Interrogation of Palestinian Detainees,* 2nd ed. (Jerusalem: Palestine Human Rights Information Center, 1992), p. 2. At the press conference when this PHRIC report was released, advocate Na'ila Attiyah said that when she complained to a military court judge during an extension-of-detention hearing that one of her clients had been tortured with electricity in Hebron, he had responded that this method was "permitted under the guidelines of the Landau Commission's report as it was a form of 'moderate physical pressure' and would not kill" the detainee. Ibid, p. 62.

29. Doron Meiri, "Torture Unit," *Hadashot,* February 24, 1992.

30. Ibid.

31. Ibid.

32. See Michal Sela, "Is It Permitted to Tie up, to Beat, to Cover?" *Davar,* May 16, 1993; Tom Segev, "Our Man in Amnesty," *Ha'aretz,* June 18, 1993.

33. The medical fitness form is reproduced in Ruhama Marton, "The White Coat Passes Like a Shadow," *Challenge* 4/4 (July–August 1993): 33.

34. Yuval Ginbar, *Flawed Defense: Torture and Ill-Treatment in GSS Interrogations following the Supreme Court Ruling, 6 September 1999–6 September 2001* (Jerusalem: Public Committee against Torture in Israel, 2001).

35. See Soraya Antonius, "Prisoners for Palestine: A List of Women Political Prisoners," *Journal of Palestine Studies* 9/3 (1980): 29–80; Walid Fahum, *Birds of Neve Tirza* (in Arabic) (Nazareth: Maktaba Al-Fahum, 1984); Hunaida Ghanem, "Palestinian Women Political Prisoners," *Palestine-Israel Journal* 2/3 (1995): 32–36.

36. See Teresa Thornhill, *Making Women Talk: The Interrogation of Palestinian Women Detainees* (London: Lawyers for Palestinian Human Rights, 1992).

37. Nadira Shalhoub-Kevorkian, "Fear of Sexual Harassment: Palestinian Adolescent Girls in the Intifada," in *Palestinian Women: Identity and Experience,* ed. Ebba Augustin (London: Zed Books, 1993); Simona Sharoni, "Homefront as Battlefield: Gender, Military Occupation and Violence against Women," in *Women and the Israeli Occupation: The Politics of Change,* ed. Tamar Mayer (New York: Routledge, 1994).

38. Nada Muzzafar, "Women Defeat the Zionist Concentration Camps," *Sawt al-mara'a* 7 (1987), quoted in Barbara Harlow, *Barred: Women, Writing, and Political Detention* (Hanover, NH: Wesleyan University Press, 1992), p. 18.

39. Fadl Yunis, *Cell Number 7* (Amman: Dar Al-Jalil, 1983), pp. 76–77, quoted in Harlow, *Barred,* p. 36.

40. See Nahla Abdo, "Women and the Intifada: Gender, Class and National Liberation," *Race and Class* 32/4 (1991): 19–34; Islah Abdul-Jawwad, "The Evolution of the Political Role of the Palestinian Women's Movement in the Uprising," in *The Palestinians: New Directions,* ed. Michael Hudson (Washington, DC: Georgetown University, Center for Contemporary Arab Studies, 1990); Simona Sharoni, "Every Woman Is an Occupied Territory: The Politics of Militarism and Sexism and the Israeli-Palestinian Conflict," *Journal of Gender Studies* 1/4 (1992): 447–62, and *Gender and the Israeli-Palestinian Conflict: The Politics of Women's Resistance* (Syracuse, NY: Syracuse University Press, 1995).

41. Julie Peteet, "Icons and Militants: Mothering in the Danger Zone," *Signs* 23/1 (1997): 122.

42. At the time, Ashrawi and Husseini were the spokespeople for the Palestinian delegation in the negotiations with Israel.

43. See Ehud Ya'ari, "The Line of Questioning," *Jerusalem Report,* July 15, 1993, p. 27.

44. Yizhar Be'er and Saleh 'Abdel-Jawad, *Collaborators in the Occupied Territories: Human Rights Abuses and Violations* (Jerusalem: B'Tselem, 1994).

45. Quoted in Ginbar and Stein, *Torture during Interrogations,* p. 9.

46. However, injuries resulting from interrogation are not unusual. In the 1991 B'Tselem study, eleven of the forty-one people in the sample were treated in hospitals as a result of their interrogation. Cohen and Golan, *Interrogation of Palestinians.*

47. The karate movement, composed of athletic clubs and competitions, was established to provide a creative outlet and to teach Palestinians self-defense.

48. E. Valentine Daniel, "Mood, Moment, and Mind," in Das, Kleinman, Ramphele, and Reynolds, *Violence and Subjectivity,* p. 352.

49. Harlow, *Barred,* p. 46.

50. Ze'ev Schiff and Ehud Ya'ari, "Israel's Prison Academies," *Atlantic,* October 1989, pp. 26–27.

51. The "Jabril exchange" was a negotiated arrangement in which 1,150 Palestinian prisoners in Israeli custody, 600 of whom were from the occupied territories, were released in exchange for six Israeli soldiers who had been captured in Lebanon by the Palestinian Front for the Liberation of Palestine-General Command, headed by Ahmed Jabril.

52. For a history of hunger strikes among Palestinian prisoners, see Sick Prisoners Care Society, *Intifada inside the Bars: Palestinian Prisoners on Hunger Strike, September 27 — October 11, 1992* (Jerusalem: Sick Prisoners Care Society, 1993).

53. A mental health survey–based study in 2003 to investigate the prevalence of post-traumatic stress disorder (PTSD) on Palestinian children in Gaza found the following rates of trauma: 94.6 percent had witnessed funerals; 83.2 percent had witnessed shootings; 66.9 percent had seen injured or dead who were not relatives, and 61.6 percent had seen family members injured or killed. The researchers concluded that 32.7 percent of the 944 surveyed children suffered from acute levels of PTSD symptoms and were in need of psychological intervention; 49.2 percent suffered from moderate levels, 15.6 percent suffered from low levels, and 2.5 percent had no symptoms. Samir Qouta, "Prevalence of PTSD among Palestinian Children," press release, Gaza Community Mental Health Programme, April 2003.

54. See Yezid Sayigh, *Armed Struggle and the Search for a State: The Palestinian National Movement, 1949–1993* (New York: Oxford University Press, 1997).

55. See Jamal Nassar and Roger Heacock, *Intifada: Palestine at the Crossroads* (New York: Praeger Publishers, 1990); Zachary Lockman and Joel Beinin, eds., *Intifada: The Palestinian Uprising against Israeli Occupation* (Boston: South End Press, 1989); Shaul Mishal and Reuben Aharoni, *Speaking Stones: Communiques from the Intifada Underground* (Syracuse, NY: Syracuse University Press, 1994).

56. Graham Usher, *Palestine in Crisis: The Struggle for Peace and Political Independence after Oslo,* 2nd ed. (London: Pluto Press, 1997), p. 5.

57. Prior to the *intifada,* Israel encouraged and facilitated the rise of Islamist organizations on the assumption that this would foster divisions within Palestinian society and weaken the PLO. See Schiff and Ya'ari, *Intifada,* pp. 222–28.

58. See Ziad Abu-Amr, *Islamic Fundamentalism in the West Bank and Gaza: Muslim Brotherhood and Islamic Jihad* (Bloomington: Indiana University Press, 1994); Muhammad Muslih, *The Foreign Policy of Hamas* (New York: Council on Foreign Relations, 1999).

59. See Sara Roy, "Gaza: New Dynamics of Civic Disintegration," *Journal of Palestine Studies* 22/4 (1993): 20–31; Usher, *Palestine in Crisis.*

60. PA obligations to maintain security and public order were set out in Articles XII–XV and Annex I of the 1995 Interim Agreement on the West Bank and Gaza, signed in Washington, D.C., on September 28, 1995.

61. See Lisa Hajjar, "Law against Order: Human Rights Organizations and (versus?) the Palestinian Authority," *University of Miami Law Review* 56/1 (October 2001): 59–76.

62. See Usher, *Palestine in Crisis.*

63. Although negotiations actually continued and even produced an agreement in January 2001, they were hobbled by the events and outcomes of the summit at Camp David in July, the start of the second *intifada* in September, and electoral politics in Israel and the United States (an election year in both countries).

64. See Graham Usher, "Facing Defeat: The Intifada Two Years On," *Journal of Palestine Studies* 32/2 (2003): 41–62.

## Chapter 8: A *Suq* of Deals

1. Malcolm Feeley, *The Process Is the Punishment: Handling Cases in a Lower Criminal Court* (New York: Russell Sage Foundation), p. 187.

2. See Uzi Amit-Kohn, "The Criminal Justice System," in *Israel, the "Intifada" and the Rule of Law,* ed. David Yahav (Tel Aviv: Israel Ministry of Defense Publications, 1993); Office of the Military Advocate General, *Response of the IDF Military Advocate General's Unit to the Amnesty International Report on the Military Justice System in the Administered Areas* (Tel Aviv: Office of the Military Advocate General, 1992).

3. The payment of lawyers has a history that varies by region and over time. In 1978, a "Steadfastness Fund" was established at the Baghdad Conference of Arab States to support Palestinians in the occupied territories, including money for political prisoners that could be used to pay lawyers' fees. These funds were disbursed through a Jordan-based Joint Committee run by the Palestine Liberation Organization (PLO) and the Jordanian government. Palestinian and Israeli lawyers representing defendants from the West Bank have had access to this funding, which was unavailable or unequally available to Gazans because the latter were not permitted to travel to Jordan. Similarly, West Bankers had easier access to funding from PLO factions with offices in Jordan. While some PLO funding also reached lawyers in Gaza, this dried up after the Gulf War in 1991. Some funding for Gazan lawyers was provided by the Libyan government, but Libya stopped making contributions in 1993 to protest the Israeli-Palestinian negotiations. There were also a variety of legal aid programs in the West Bank that did not have counterparts in Gaza. In 1974, the American Friends Service Committee established a Quakers' Legal Aid Center in East Jerusalem, which served the West Bank. This program was expanded during the first *intifada* but was canceled in 1994 due to a reorientation of priorities. In 1990, the United Nations Relief and Works Agency established a fund to pay lawyers representing West Bankers classified as refugees, but no similar fund was established for refugees in Gaza. In the early 1990s, groups of ex-prisoners established organizations to provide legal aid and other assistance to prisoners, including Addameer and Nadi al-Asir. In 1994, Nadi al-Asir was taken over by the Palestinian Authority (PA) and funded lawyers' fees for people arrested by Israel but not the PA. After 2000, when PA funding dried up, LAW (the Palestinian Society for the Protection of Human

Rights and the Environment), a Palestinian human rights organization head-quartered in East Jerusalem, began providing legal aid for families of West Bank prisoners, but following a financial scandal involving LAW's executive director in 2003, this service dwindled. In 1999, the Israeli Public Defenders Office (estab-lished inside Israel in 1995) began providing funds for military court lawyers to represent people who could not pay for their own counsel, but this funding was scaled back (on both sides of the Green Line) in 2002.

4. Since 1967, there have been two means for Palestinians from the occupied territories to obtain law degrees. Some travel abroad to study, and others attain their degree through correspondence-type programs *(intisab)*, studying course materials at home and going once a year to sit for exams. The main university for *intisab* is Beirut Arab University, an affiliate of Alexandria University in Egypt. See George Bisharat, *Palestinian Lawyers and Israeli Rule: Law and Dis-order in the West Bank* (Austin: University of Texas Press, 1989).

5. Maya Rosenfeld, "I Now Have a New Identity: Interview with Tamar Peleg," *Challenge* 3/3 (June 1992): 9.

6. See Lisa Hajjar, "The Making of a Political Trial: The Marwan Barghouti Case," *Middle East Report* 225 (Winter 2002): 30–37.

7. See Amira Hass, "Incarcerated Palestinians Push for Boycott of Proceedings in Israeli Courts," *Ha'aretz,* October 3, 2002; Arjan El Fassed, "Israel Resumes Trial against Barghouti," April 6, 2003, retrieved from www.electronicintifada .net.

## Conclusion: The Second *Intifada* and the Global "War on Terror"

1. Immanuel Kant, *Perpetual Peace and Other Essays* (Indianapolis, IN: Hack-ett Publishing, 1983), p. 110.

2. According to the Palestine Human Rights Monitoring Group, between September 29, 2000, and March 31, 2004, 2,780 Palestinian residents of the West Bank and Gaza were killed by Israelis ("Summary of Palestinian Fatalities from September 29, 2000 to March 31, 2004," and "Summary of Israeli Fatalities from September 29, 2000 to March 10, 2004," retrieved April 28, 2004, from www.phrmg.org). Of this total, 167 were targeted for assassination and 73 were "bystanders" killed during assassinations; 264 were children fifteen or younger; 236 were children between fifteen and seventeen; 25 were killed by Israeli set-tlers; and 81 died at checkpoints. Other Palestinian fatalities in this period included 152 suicide bombers, six people who died in PA custody, and 137 who were killed in unclear circumstances. During this same period, 962 Israeli citi-zens were killed by Palestinians. Of this total, 198 adult civilians and 30 children were killed in the occupied territories, and 395 adults and 74 children were killed inside Israel; 184 Israeli soldiers and security agents were killed in the occupied territories, and 81 were killed inside Israel.

3. See Charles Enderlin, *Shattered Dreams: The Failure of the Peace Process in*

*the Middle East, 1995–2002,* trans. Susan Fairfield (New York: Other Press, 2003); Ari Shavit, "Cry the Beloved Two-State Solution," *Ha'aretz,* August 7, 2003; Avraham Burg, "A Failed Israeli Society Collapses While Its Leaders Remain Silent," *Forward,* August 29, 2003.

4. Richard Falk, "Ending the Death Dance," *Nation,* April 7, 2002.

5. In 1987 (coinciding with the start of the first *intifada*), the "ticking bomb" scenario was invoked by Israeli officials to justify and authorize "moderate physical pressure" in interrogation (to which tens of thousands of Palestinians have been subjected). The ticking bomb scenario included Palestinian nationalist activities and resistance to the Israeli occupation, which were characterized as "hostile terrorist activity" by the Landau Commission, the General Security Services (GSS), and other sectors of the Israeli government (see Chapter 2). By the start of the second *intifada,* the "ticking bomb" had acquired a more literal meaning and was invoked to authorize the policy of assassinations and other military operations in the West Bank and Gaza.

6. Between 1993 and September 2000, there were fourteen Palestinian suicide bombings against Israeli civilians, all claimed by either Hamas or Islamic Jihad. The first bus bombing by Hamas inside Israel took place on April 4, 1994, declared as retaliation for the massacre in February 1994 of twenty-nine Palestinian worshipers at a mosque in Hebron by an American Israeli settler. Hamas launched a campaign of bus bombings in 1996 following the Israeli assassination of Yahya Ayash, nicknamed "the Engineer" for his bomb-making skills. Islamic Jihad claimed responsibility for several suicide bombings in 1994 and 1995 in retaliation for the assassinations of militant Hani Abed in Gaza and leader Fathi Shiqaqi in Malta. In addition to retaliations for assassinations, suicide bombings were mounted in response to deadly clashes in 1995 that occurred when Israeli Prime Minister Yitzhak Rabin refused to release over six thousand prisoners as part of the Oslo II agreement, and in 1997 following land confiscation and the construction of a massive new settlement complex near Bethlehem. There were two suicide bombings between 1998 and 2000. See Steve Niva, "Bombings, Provocations and the Cycle of Violence," *Peace Review* 15/1 (2003): 33–38; Human Rights Watch, *Erased in a Moment: Suicide Bombing Attacks against Israeli Civilians* (New York: Human Rights Watch, 2002).

Israel has engaged in assassinations since the 1970s. Following the 1972 killings of members of the Israeli Olympic team in Munich, Prime Minister Golda Meir ordered the Mossad (Israel's external security service) to hunt and assassinate the Palestinians who perpetrated these assaults. The "Meir doctrine" authorized the killing of people outside Israel/Palestine deemed to be responsible for terrorist attacks on Israelis. During the first *intifada,* assassinations of Palestinians in the West Bank and Gaza became undeclared policy, pursued by undercover units of the GSS. The rationale for "extrajudicial executions" was that people whom the army was unable to arrest could be killed. Assassinations continued throughout the interim. See James Ron, *License to Kill: Israeli Undercover Operations against "Wanted" and Masked Palestinians* (New York: Human Rights Watch/Middle East, 1993); David Margolick, "Israel's Payback Principle," *Vanity Fair* 509 (January 2003): 40–47.

7. Ghassan Hage, "'Comes a Time We Are All Enthusiasm': Understanding Palestinian Suicide Bombers in Times of Exighophobia," *Public Culture* 15/1 (2003): 75.

8. Suicide bombings constitute systematic and/or large-scale attacks against civilians and thus qualify as "crimes against humanity." They may also be "war crimes" if perpetrated by armed organizations in the context of conflict. See Human Rights Watch, *Erased in a Moment.* Assassinations constitute the targeted killing of individuals by government forces and/or by order of a government. If, at the time when the targeted individuals are killed, they are neither engaged in hostilities nor pose an "imminent threat," assassinations could qualify as "war crimes." See Amnesty International, *Israel and the Occupied Territories: State Assassinations and Other Unlawful Killings* (London: Amnesty International, 2001); Moshe Reinfeld, "IDF Assassinations Could Be Considered War Crimes, Says UN Rights Expert," *Ha'aretz,* June 18, 2003.

9. The Four Geneva Conventions (1949) are the main body of international humanitarian law governing the use of force and the treatment of combatants and civilians. The Additional Protocols I and II (1977) expanded international humanitarian law; Additional Protocol I addresses (among other issues) conflicts involving nonstate groups fighting against "colonial domination," "alien occupation," and "racist regimes," thereby extending the protections of international humanitarian law to these types of conflicts and imposing legal obligations and restrictions upon nonstate groups. See Dieter Fleck, ed., *The Handbook of Humanitarian Law in Armed Conflict* (Oxford: Oxford University Press, 1995); Jakob Kellenberger, "International Humanitarian Law at the Beginning of the 21st Century," May 9, 2002, retrieved March 3, 2004, from www.icrc.org/Web/eng/siteengo.nsf/html/5E2C8V?Opendocument.

10. Yoram Peri, *The Israeli Military and Israel's Palestinian Policy: From Oslo to the Al Aqsa Intifada* (Washington, DC: U.S. Institute of Peace, 2002), p. 31.

11. At the time, Sharon was preparing for the upcoming Israeli election in which he would run for prime minister.

12. Peri, *Israeli Military,* pp. 30–31.

13. Israel is not a signatory to Additional Protocol I and has refused to accept either of the two existing categories of conflict in international humanitarian law (i.e., "international" and "internal" war) as relevant to the second *intifada,* terming it instead a "war against terror."

14. See Rema Hammami and Salim Tamari, "Anatomy of Another Rebellion," *Middle East Report,* no. 217 (Winter 2000): 2–15.

15. According to Michael Quinion,

Much of western military thinking has traditionally assumed that conflicts will involve conventional warfare against an opponent of comparable might, using similar weapons on a known battlefield. However, military experts have been pointing out for years that resistance forces in places like Chechnya have been conducting a very different kind of war, in which defenders fight on their own terms, not those of the enemy — petrol bombs against tanks, for example. This has been given the name of *asymmetrical warfare* by counter-terrorism experts, a term that appears to date from the early 1990s. In it, a relatively small and lightly equipped force attacks points of weakness in an otherwise stronger opponent by unorthodox means. All guerrilla activity, especially urban terrorism, falls within this definition. (Michael Quinion, "Asymmetrical Warfare," *World Wide Words*, retrieved April 26, 2004, from www.quinion.com/words/turnsofphrase/tp-asy2.htm)

16. In 2002, the Public Committee against Torture in Israel (PCATI) and LAW (The Palestinian Society for the Protection of Human Rights and the Environment) brought a petition before the Israeli High Court of Justice challenging the legality of assassinations: *PCATI and LAW v. Government of Israel et al.*, HCJ 769/02. English translation of the briefs by the petitioners retrieved March 17, 2004, from www.stoptorture.org.il. For the government's response, see "Supplemental Response on Behalf of the State Attorney's Office," 2004, unpublished document (English translation obtained through PCATI, on file with author).

17. Neve Gordon analyzed media coverage of Israeli assassinations in three major Israeli newspapers (*Ha'aretz, Yediot Aharnot,* and *Ma'ariv*) and found a striking and consistent pattern of reporting.

[I]t is almost as if the newspapers were staging a trial. The subject on trial, however, is not the executed person, but rather the state of Israel and its policy of extra-judicial executions. The objective is to acquit the state of what might appear to be an unlawful act through the production and dissemination of the rationality and morality of executions. . . . [T]he narratives' objective is . . . to vindicate Israel by creating a sense that, given the situation, the assassination was both inevitable and was carried out in a principled manner. . . . [The assassinated person's] guilt is established after the punishment [by reporting past actions and insinuating evidence of plans for future crimes] and the person is transformed into a "ticking bomb" after (and because?) he is already dead.

Neve Gordon, "Rationalizing Extra-Judicial Executions: The Israeli Press and the Legitimization of Abuse," *International Journal of Human Rights* 8 (2004).

18. For example, Hamas spokesman 'Abd al-'Aziz Rantisi said, "We don't have F-16s, Apache helicopters and missiles. . . .They are attacking us with weapons against which we can't defend ourselves. And now we have a weapon they can't defend themselves against. . . . We believe this weapon creates a kind of balance, because this weapon is like an F-16." Molly Moore and John Ward Anderson, "Suicide Bombers Change Mideast's Military Balance," *Washington Post,* August 17, 2002, p. A1. Rantisi was assassinated on April 16, 2004.

19. On September 7, 2001, Israel assassinated Abu 'Ali Mustafa, General Secretary of the Popular Front for the Liberation of Palestine (PFLP), and on October 17, the PFLP assassinated Israeli cabinet minister Rehavam Ze'evi in retaliation. Ze'evi's status as a member of the government and the timing of his killing (i.e., after 9/11) spurred major military assaults in a number of West Bank towns.

20. Alex Fishman, *Yediot Aharonot,* October 19, 2001, quoted in Tanya Rein-

hart, *Israel/Palestine: How to End the War of 1948* (New York: Seven Stories Press, 2002), p. 105.

21. For example, President Bush and Secretary of State Colin Powell both pronounced that a "viable Palestinian state" was necessary and inevitable and should be created through negotiations. But this outcome was held to be contingent on the PA leadership unequivocally renouncing and stopping "violence and terror directed against Israel."

22. Armored Israeli bulldozers flattened the entire Hawashin district, demolishing more than one hundred multistory homes in this area of the Jenin refugee camp. The destruction left some four thousand people homeless, more than a quarter of the population of the camp.

23. Aviv Lavie, "Uncivil Society," *Ha'aretz,* January 17, 2003. Lavie's article focuses on debates among ACRI staff and board of directors over the language and objectives of criticism: whether to use the term *terrorism* in public statements as a means of showing support for the government, whether to characterize the occupation as a fundamental violation of human rights, and whether the organization's position should be to call for a UN commission of inquiry.

24. Gush Shalom, an Israeli peace group, launched an initiative to gather information about possible Israeli war crimes and made public statements that this information would be passed to international tribunals if Israeli soldiers and officers responsible for grave breaches of the Geneva Conventions were not prosecuted in Israeli courts. The organization issued a "Soldiers' Pocket Guide on War Crimes" that warned: "IDF Soldier: Do not commit war crimes! War crimes will haunt you all your life, anywhere on earth. There is no statute of limitations for war crimes." In response, the Israeli government threatened to prosecute members of Gush Shalom, and the Israeli Knesset passed legislation making it a crime for any Israeli citizen to disseminate information about alleged Israeli war crimes to any foreign sources or international legal bodies.

25. Although at the time of the Jenin assault the U.S. government criticized the "excessive use of force," in preparing for the war on Iraq, American military officials studied Israeli tactics in Jenin as a model of successful "urban warfare" and bought from Israel nine of the armor-plated bulldozers. See Justin Huggler, "Israelis Trained US Troops in Jenin-Style Urban Warfare," *Independent,* March 29, 2003.

26. See Human Rights Watch, *Jenin: IDF Military Operations* (New York: Human Rights Watch, 2002).

27. Richard Goldstone writes, "[I]n World War I some 95 percent of all deaths were suffered by soldiers. . . . In World War II the figure dropped to 50 percent. . . . In the Korean War, 84 percent of those killed were civilians and in the Vietnam War it rose to 90 percent. In more than 100 civil wars since 1945, civilians were also the targets of war and the overwhelming number of deaths [was] suffered by civilians." Richard Goldstone, "International Law and Justice and America's War on Terrorism," *Social Research* 69 (2002): 1045.

28. Margolick, "Israel's Payback Principle," p. 51.

29. One difference between the wall being built in the West Bank and the

Gaza wall (erected in 1994) is that the latter follows the Green Line (the 1949 armistice) and does not divide Palestinian areas within the Gaza Strip.

30. According to the Israel Defense Forces (IDF), "The 'Security Fence' is a manifestation of Israel's basic commitment to defend its citizens, and once completed, it will improve the ability of the IDF to prevent the infiltration of terrorists and criminal elements into Israel for the purpose of carrying out terrorist attacks or the smuggling of arms and explosives." "Israel's Security Fence," 2004, retrieved April 14, 2004, from www.israelnewsagency.com/israelsecurityfence.html.

31. See "Maps," March 21, 2004, retrieved May 11, 2004, from http://stopthewall.org/news/maps.shtml.

32. In July 2004, the International Court of Justice, at the request of the UN General Assembly, issued an advisory opinion on the legal issues and consequences, concluding that the wall violates international law.

33. David Rieff, "Arafat among the Ruins," *New York Times Magazine,* April 25, 2004, pp. 52, 54. Rieff notes that "[t]he likelihood that only policy disagreements within the Israeli government, and American opposition to [Arafat's] assassination, were keeping him alive illustrated Palestinian powerlessness to Palestinians in a way that people on the West Bank described to me, over and over again, as unbearable" (p. 55).

34. According to a 2002 World Bank report, 70 percent of Palestinians in the West Bank and Gaza are living in poverty (officially set at under US$2 a day). According to a report prepared by the U.S. Agency for International Development and John Hopkins University, 30 percent of children under five suffer from chronic malnutrition and 21 percent from acute malnutrition, a huge increase since the survey was last carried out in 2000, when the figures were 7.5 percent and 2.5 percent respectively. More than 30 percent of Palestinians now rely on food aid to feed themselves and their families. "Humanitarian Crisis in the West Bank/Gaza Strip," *Palestine Monitor,* July 29, 2002, retrieved April 25, 2004, from www.palestinemonitor.org/updates/humanitarian_crisis_in_the_wbga_28july.htm

35. In 2001, the United States launched a war in Afghanistan in retaliation for 9/11 to try to destroy al-Qaeda, which was based there, and its patron regime, the Taliban. That war garnered international support because it was construed as an act of "self-defense" given al-Qaeda's declared commitment to continue attacking the United States. In 2003, the United States expanded its war on terror to attack Iraq and topple the regime of Saddam Hussein. The latter was condemned by governments and people around the world as an aggressive and unlawful war, and the subsequent U.S. occupation of Iraq was roiled by controversy.

36. See Michael Ignatieff, "Human Rights, the Laws of War, and Terrorism," *Social Research* 69 (Winter 2002): 1138–58.

37. See the special issue entitled "International Justice, War Crimes, and Terrorism: The U.S. Record," *Social Research* 69, no. 4 (Winter 2002); Daphne Eviatar, "Civilian Toll: A Moral and Legal Bog," *New York Times,* March 22, 2003;

Anthony Dworkin, "Revising the Laws of War to Account for Terrorism: The Case against Updating the Geneva Conventions, on the Ground That Changes Are Likely Only to Damage Human Rights," *Findlaw's Legal Commentary,* February 4, 2003; Steven Ratner, "Codifying the Unconventional," Crimes of War Project, January 30, 2003.

38. Kenneth Anderson, "Who Owns the Rules of War?" *New York Times Magazine,* April 13, 2003, p. 39.

39. Ibid., p. 43.

40. Human Rights Watch, "Israel: Opportunistic Law Condemned," press release, March 7, 2002.

41. See Knut Dormann, "The Legal Situation of 'Unlawful/Unprivileged Combatants,'" *International Review of the Red Cross* 85 (2003): 461–86.

42. A prison camp at the U.S. military base in Guantanamo on the island of Cuba was designated to house prisoners characterized by the U.S. government as "unlawful combatants" in the war on terror.

43. See Jonathan Cook, "Facility 1391: Israel's Guantanamo," *Le Monde Diplomatique,* November 2003.

44. Dana Priest and Barton Gellman, "US Decries Abuse but Defends Interrogations: 'Stress and Duress' Tactics Used on Terrorism Suspects Held in Secret Overseas Facilities," *Washington Post,* December 26, 2002.

45. Seymour Hersch, "Torture at Abu Graib," *New Yorker,* May 10, 2004. See also Lisa Hajjar, "Torture and the Future," *Middle East Report Online,* available at http://www.merip.org/mero/interventions/hajjar_interv.html.

46. Christopher H. Pyle, "Torture by Proxy," *San Francisco Chronicle,* January 4, 2004.

47. In 1977, in response to revelations of U.S. plots to kill several foreign leaders, President Gerald Ford promulgated Executive Order (EO) 11905, which prohibited any employee of the U.S. government "to engage in, or conspire to engage in, political assassination." That order was expanded by Jimmy Carter to include all types of assassinations. Ronald Reagan reissued the prohibition in EO 12333, which was maintained by George H. W. Bush and Bill Clinton.

48. See Seymour Hersch, "Manhunt: The Bush Administration's New Strategy in the War against Terror," *New Yorker,* December 23 & 30, 2002.

49. See Esther Schrader and Josh Mayer, "US Seeks Advice from Israel on Iraq," *Los Angeles Times,* November 22, 2003; Dexter Filkins, "Tough New Tactics by US Tighten Grip on Iraqi Towns," *New York Times,* December 7, 2003.

50. Military Order of November 13, 2001, "Detention, Treatment, and Trial of Certain Non-Citizens in the War Against Terrorism," retrieved April 26, 2004, from www.whitehouse.gov/news/releases/2001/11/20011113-27.html

51. See Aryeh Neier, "The Military Tribunals on Trial," *New York Review of Books,* February 14, 2002, pp. 11–15; "ACLU Comments on Draft Military Commission Instruction, 'Crimes and Elements for Trials by Military Commissions,' released on February 28, 2003," letter from the American Civil Liberties Union to William J. Haynes II, General Counsel, [U.S.] Department of Defense, March 19, 2003; Human Rights Watch, "Human Rights Watch Briefing Paper on US

Military Commissions," June 25, 2003; Edward Alden, "National Security versus Due Process," *Financial Times,* July 15, 2003.

52. See Lisa Hajjar, "From Nuremberg to Guantanamo: International Law and American Power Politics," *Middle East Report* 229 (Winter 2003): 8–15; Oren Gross, "Chaos and Rules: Should Responses to Violent Crises Always Be Constitutional?" *Yale Law Journal* 112 (March 2003): 1011–1134.

53. In April 2002, in the aftermath of the battle of Jenin, Human Rights Watch published *In a Dark Hour: The Use of Civilians during IDF Operations* (New York, 2002). Following this, seven Israeli and Palestinian human rights organizations (Adalah, LAW, Israeli and Palestinian Physicians for Human Rights, HaMoked, PCATI, B'Tselem, and ACRI) petitioned the HCJ to prohibit the practice that the military termed the "neighbor procedure" (HCJ 3799/02 *Adalah et al v. Yitzhak, OC Central Command et al.,* filed May 5, 2002). Following the killing of a Palestinian who was used as a human shield, the organizations went back to the HCJ on August 18, 2002, and obtained a temporary injunction. However, the HCJ, essentially conceding to the state's "clarifying guidelines" for the practice (prohibiting "human shields" but permitting the "neighbor procedure"), rendered a decision permitting the military to use Palestinian civilians to "help" in operations as long as the military commander was of the opinion that this would not put the civilian in danger and the civilian "agreed." The petitioners went back to the HCJ on January 1, 2003, presenting a case (including expert testimony by Israeli law professor Eyal Benvenisti) that international humanitarian law categorically prohibits the use of civilians in military operations and that doing so constitutes a grave breach of the Geneva Conventions. The HCJ again granted a temporary injunction, but following reports of continued use of human shields (i.e., the "neighbor procedure"), the petitioners filled a contempt of court petition against the military. See Adalah, *The Use of Palestinian Civilians as Human Shields by the Israeli Army: Briefing Paper* (Shfaram, Israel: Adalah, 2003); "The 'Neighbor Procedure,'" retrieved March 3, 2004, from www.btselem.org/English/Human_Shield/Neighbor_Procedure .asp; Gideon Levy, "Some Lives Are Cheaper Than Others," *Ha'aretz,* September 12, 2003.

54. According to PCATI, "[S]ince the beginning of 2003 there has been a sharp rise in the torture, ill treatment, humiliation and incarceration in inhuman conditions of Palestinian detainees by the GSS. The Public Committee against Torture in Israel therefore estimates that during first half of 2003, hundreds of Palestinians were subjected to one degree or another of torture or other cruel, inhuman or degrading treatment at the hands of the GSS. By way of comparison, in September 2001 PCATI estimated that the total number of detainees being subjected to torture and other forms of ill treatment reached 'only' dozens." Public Committee against Torture in Israel, *Back to a Routine of Torture: Torture and Ill-Treatment of Palestinian Detainees during Arrest, Detention and Interrogation, September 2001–April 2003* (Jerusalem: Public Committee against Torture in Israel, 2003).

55. See *Comments on Issues Relating to Palestinian Detainees in the Third Peri-*

*odic Report of the State of Israel Concerning the Implementation of the International Covenant on Civil and Political Rights* (Jerusalem: LAW, PCATI, and the World Organization against Torture [OMCT], 2002).

56. See *Siham Thabet v. Prime Minister of Israel Ariel Sharon et al.* HJC 192/01; PCATI, *The Assassination Policy of the State of Israel, November 2000– January 2002* (Jerusalem: Public Committee against Torture in Israel, 2002). Although the Human Rights Committee of the Israel Bar Association (IBA) declared assassinations illegal, the IBA refused to adopt this as their position.

# Index

Abayat, Hussein, 238
Abed, Hani, 292n6
Abu Dakka, Ibrahim, 180
*Abu Hilu et al. v. Government of Israel,* 57
Abu Laila, Adnan, 165
Abu Middain, Freih, 181. *See also* Gaza Bar Association
Abu Rahman, Fayez, 171, 222
Abu Rukn, Sheikh Labib, 279n16
acquittal, chances of, 205–6, 221–23
Addameer, 204, 290n3
administered areas. *See* occupied territories
administrative detention, 64, 110, 122–23, 191, 212
Adoreim military court, 16
adversarial legal system, 111–13, 225
Afghanistan, war in, 239, 244, 245, 296n35
Akar, Mamduh, xxii–xxiii
Akawi, Mustafa, xviii–xxiii
Akkila, Fathi, 171
Alami, Iyad, 180
American Friends Service Committee, 290n3
Amin, Amin, xxi–xxii
*Amira et al. v. Minister of Defense,* 266n32
Amit-Kohn, Uzi, 275n6, 276n7
Amnesty International (AI): founding of, 46; and nonstate movements, 64–65; and political vs. violent resistance, 167; report on military courts, 66–67; and torture, 69
anti-Semitism, 56

anti-Zionist politics, 115, 162, 169. *See also* Zionism/Zionist politics
Al-Aqsa Martyrs Brigade, 240
Arabic language, and Jewish/Arab dichotomy, 132–34, 278n4
Arab Israelis: as defense lawyers, 163–64, 170, 178, 182–83, 226–27; definition of, 5; Jewish Israeli views of, 274n16; military service, 279n10; and political vs. ideological hegemony, 38–39; rights of, 33–34
Arab Lawyers Committee (ALC), 226; establishment of, 172, 182; international law and, 283n20; and Israeli-Palestinian networks, 179, 182; strikes called by, 175
Arafat, Yasir, 13, 53, 240, 241–42
Area A, 13, 34, 237. *See also* negotiations, Israeli-Palestinian; Palestinian Authority
Area B, 13, 34, 237. *See also* negotiations, Israeli-Palestinian; Palestinian Authority
Area C, 13–14. *See also* negotiations, Israeli-Palestinian
armed struggle. See *feda'yin;* militancy
arrests: of children, 191–92, 286n21; initiated, 190–91; and interrogation, 66–67, 191–95; as Israeli strategy, 66; numbers of, 3, 44, 66, 72, 106–7, 185–86; political impact of, 128; roundups, 191; social impact of, 208–9
Asad, Talal, 139
*'asafir.* See collaborators, Palestinian
Asali, Abed, 170

301

| Compositor: | BookMatters, Berkeley |
| Indexer: | Kevin Millham |
| Cartographer: | Bill Nelson |
| Text: | 10/13 Galliard |
| Display: | Galliard |
| Printer and binder: | IBT Global |